Understanding
Fabrics

Language of Fashion Series

Understanding Fabrics:
From Fiber to Finished Cloth

Debbie Ann Gioello

Adjunct Associate Professor: Fashion Design Department
Fashion Institute of Technology

Fairchild Publications
New York

Janet Solgaard, book designer

Barbara Scholey, cover illustration

Unless otherwise noted photography by author

Standard Book Number: 87005-377-9

Library of Congress Catalog Card Number: 82-071553

Printed in the United States of America

Contents

Preface

The development and expansion of the textile industry is reflected in the development of raw materials into natural and man-made fibers, advances in processing and engineering technology, new machinery and methods of manufacturing, changes in apparel production, and consumer's needs.

The advances and changes in the textile industry have resulted in the production of a variety of fabrics with different and complex characteristics and properties. This complexity necessitates clarification of existing terms, identification of newly emerging textile products, and clarification of product information.

Understanding Fabrics: from Fiber to Finished Cloth covers product facts including:

- Language and terms of textiles
- Usage of current technology
- Functional and technical aspects of fabrics
- Materials and methods of textile production
- Interrelationship of fiber, yarn, fabric structure, and finish
- Performance expectations and behavior of fabric
- Relationship of fiber properties to fabric behavior

This text is arranged and presented in an order that relates the definite parts of a textile fabric and the usual evolution in the manufacturing process from fiber to structure. Definite parts and components of a textile fabric include:

- Fiber content—fiber used
- Yarn construction—arrangement of fibers
- Fabric structure—arrangement of fibers or yarns
- Finishes—type, durability and method of application
- Color and/or surface design—type, durability and method of application

Arrangement of the definite parts and components affect, alter or modify the fabric's:

- Appearance
- Texture
- Hand
- Weight
- Drapability qualities
- Performance expectations/behavior

These interrelated factors influence the fabric's and garment's:

- End use
- Selection
- Durability
- Comfort
- Care factors

Understanding Fabrics, fourth in a series entitled *Language of Fashion*, is intended to be used by the textile designer, manufacturer, converter; in the textile showroom by management, sales force, purchasing agent; by the fashion designer, stylist, showroom staff, production room technician; by the retail merchandiser of textiles, textile products, and apparel; by the educator and student involved with textiles and textile-related fields; by the consumer and layperson who wish more knowledge and understanding of fabrics.

Information has been compiled from my personal experience as a designer and educator; through research of trade journals and publications; by communication with textile designers, manufacturers, converters and textile-related personnel; through personal contact with technicians, individuals and educators knowledgeable in the various fields of textiles. Accuracy has been of great importance, but new works are rarely free from error. I hope that the reader will call attention to errors of commission or omission.

Due to lack of space, some judgment regarding information to be included was required. For detailed information regarding the relationship of fibers, yarns, fabric structure, finishing processes, color and surface design application, performance expectation, width, weight, hand, texture, opacity, drapability qualities, and care factors of specific fabrics, refer to the third text in this series, *Profiling Fabrics: Properties, Performance & Construction Techniques*. Individual fabrics are analyzed, discussed and photographed. It is hoped that the presentation of these combined texts dealing with individual fabrics and related terms will supply background knowledge of fabric terms and an understanding of fabric usage.

Other books in the *Language of Fashion* series include *Fashion Production Terms* and *Figure Types and Size Ranges*. The next volume will cover *Working with Fabrics*. Another future work in this continuing series will give extensive coverage to *silhouettes*, including parts of the garment and design details.

1982

Debbie Ann Gioello
New York

Acknowledgments

A pictorial encyclopedia as inclusive as *Understanding Fabrics: from Fiber to Finished Cloth* required the assistance of many people. Without their continued cooperation, generosity and encouragement, the monumental task of compiling all the information relating to the understanding of fabrics would have been impossible.

The author wishes to acknowledge the following people and companies for technical information and photographs regarding fiber and yarn specifications and fabric structure procedures: James Adshead Jr., E.I. du Pont de Nemours & Company; James P. Allen, Celanese Corporation; Walter J. Bartlett, American Cyanamid Company; Walter C. Caudle, Allied Chemical Corporation; Libby Clark, Cotton Inc.; Donald R. Clark and Harold W. Young, American Enka Company; Wanda H. Coffen, Badische Corporation; R.D. Colman, Eastman Chemical Products, Inc.; Elizabeth Dagget, Avtex Fibers Inc.; James Donovan, American Textiles Manufacturing Institute (ATMI); F.C. Flint, Monsanto Textiles Company; Dee Graper, American Hoechst Corporation; Thomas C. Haas, The Wool Bureau, Inc.; International Silk Association; Francesca Joelion, Mohair Council of America; Frank McNeirney, International Nonwoven & Disposables Association (INDA); Linda Muller, U.S. Department of Agriculture; National Knitted Outerwear Association; Julie Rlymes, Man-made Fiber Producers Association, Inc.; Lynn Sanders, Belgian Linen Association; Maria Sciandra, Courtaulds North America, Inc.

The following people and companies supplied technical information, specifications and photographs related to coloring, printing and finishing processes of fabrics and information related to care of specific fabrics; David W. Adams, Pellerin Milnor Corp; Jeffrey R. Allen, Com-Tex Corp.; L.B. Arnold Jr., Vikon Chemical Co. Inc.; Vincent Baldassari, Lembo Corp.; Martha Barker, Wise Industries Inc.; Richard Bennett, Bruckner Machinery Corp.; Dieter H. Bailek, American Artos Corp.; Broad Street Machine Company; H.S. Bultman Jr., Custom Scientific Instruments Inc.; H.L. Cauffman, Simco Co. Inc.; A.C. Chapman, Albright & Wilson Ltd.; T.F. Devlin Jr., James Hunter Machine Co. Inc.; Robyn Dowling, C.S.I.R.O. Division of Textile Industries, Wool Research Lab.; Joseph D. Dyer, Tubular Textile Machinery; Glenn Fabbri, Temac Inc.; Murry Firman and William Nathan, Hartford Corp.; Vlastimil Filous, Elitex Concern Research Industries; G.R. Goettelman, Proctor and Schwartz Inc.; Alan Goldburg, Krantz American Inc.; Leonard E. Herrmann, Precision Screen Machines Inc.; Robert C. Honour, Bently Machinery Inc.; Leon E. Hotz, Saurer Corporation Textile Machinery; Robert M. Humphreys, Tuftco Corp.; Maureen Jacolucci, Frank G.W. McKittrick Co.; Craig Jensen, Proctor and Gamble Co.; Joyce L. Johnson, Cobble Tufting Equipment; Paul Kelso, Chomolox Instruments & Control; Jan Laundau and Janice Liverance, Embroidery Council of America; Penny Lempenau and Mario Putzrath, Springs Mills Inc.; Joil Levitt, Custom Fabrics Finishing Mills; Reiner Liebscher, Zangs Corporation; W.R. Litzler, C.A. Litzler Co. Inc.; A.S. Mafilios, Surplice Chemical Co. Inc; Yves Mahe, Sublistatic Corporation of America; Honora Maresco, Spellman High Voltage Electronics Corp.; Kathleen A. Marshall, Hollingsworth Vose Co.; Eugene R. Massey, David Gessner Co.; I. May, American Hoechst Corporation; Karl Mayer, Karl Mayer Textilmaschinen Fabric GMBH; McCoy-Ellison Inc.; Joel T. Merritt, Ahiba-Mathis Inc.; Erik B. Nagel, Edda Textile Machine Inc.; John A. Pasquale III, Liberty Machine Co. Inc.; Siegfried W. Posner, Greenville Machinery Corp.; Nance Presson, Keiltex Corp.; William Quinn, Bouligny Co.; Jean T. Rednick, Thies Corporation.; Joseph B. Resch Jr., Melton Corporation; James S. Robinson, C.G. Sargent's Sons Corp.; Helmut Ruef, Fleissner Corp.; Saueressig Gmbh Intra Inc.; Albert A. Scala, ABC Industries Inc.; Joachim Schreiba, BASF Wyandotte Corp.; Joanne Shaw and Laura Skolar, Orphalese Designs; D.B. Stafford, Rice Barton Corp.; Richard Steele, Consolidated Engravers Corp.; H.B. Sturtevant Jr. E.I. du Pont de Nemours & Co. Inc.; Tekmatex Inc.; Mike Thompson and Steve Little, Gaston Country Sales & Service Corp.; Charles L. Tighe, Mega Marketing Inc.; H.W. Todd, Herbert Products Inc.; Dorothy B. von Steinberg, The Arkansas Co. Inc.; Charles B. Warren, Markem USA; John M. White, Morrison Machine Co.; Arno H. Wirth, Arno H. Wirth Company.

Special thanks and appreciation are extended to the following members of the faculty and staff of the Fashion Institute of Technology for their invaluable assistance: Marvin Feldman, President; Beverly Berke and Nurie Relis, Fashion Design Department; Arthur Price (chairman), George Tay, and Joseph Samuales, Textile Science Department; Robert Riley (director), Laura Sinderbrand, Dom Petrillo and staff, Design Laboratory; Marjorie Miller and Pete Smith, Library Media Service.

My personal gratitude to my daughter Donna Gioello; my friends Josephine DeCaro, Sherri Mannuzza, Gail Monteforte, and Ken Falber for their assistance and William Brown for his assistance for the art work.

1 ~ Fibers

Fibers are the basic units or the basic components in textiles. They are the smallest particles that make up yarn. Yarns used in the production of fabrics use different types of fibers as their raw material.

Textile fibers are found in natural sources or may be manufactured from remains of natural sources or synthesized from chemicals.

All fibers have innate or inherent characteristics and multiple properties. Each textile fiber has its own distinctive structural shape, marking and size. Properties or inherent characteristics of fibers are determined by the fiber's:

- Composition and Origin
- Length and diameter
- Shape/Cross-section Form
- Contour/Longitudinal Form
- Spinnability/Cohesiveness
- Light-reflecting Qualities
- Dyeability

Multiple properties and inherent characteristics of the fiber will affect the fabric's:
- Performance Expectation
- Hand or Feel
- Body or Weight
- Appearance
- Surface Texture
- Luster
- Care
- End Use

Factors influencing the development and utilization of natural or man-made fibers include the:
- Desirability of fiber properties
- Ability to spin fiber
- Availability in sufficient quantities

- Cost and economy of production
- Performance expectation of fiber and fabric
- End use of fabric
- Life and care factors of fabrics

The innate or inherent properties of a fiber can be altered or modified at the stages of raw fiber, yarn or fabric structure.

Fibers can be texturized to produce bulk, crimp or stretch or may be modified to change the hand of the fiber, thereby changing the performance of the yarn and the finished cloth. The ultimate behavior, performance expectation, drapability quality, care and end use of the fiber are not dependent on fiber characteristics or fiber properties alone. These properties are also influenced by the methods used to transfer fibers into yarns, yarns into finished cloth as well as finish and color applications.

Fiber, yarn, fabric structure and finishes are interdependent in the production of fabric. When one or more of the components in the production of fabric is modified or changed, the finished fabric is changed.

Selecting one fiber over the other to produce yarn or fabric depends on:
- Fiber's individual characteristics
- Positive qualities vs negative qualities
- Performance expectations required
- Appearance, feel, hand and texture desired
- Drapability qualities
- Finishing processes
- Weight or opacity
- Care performance
- End use
- Fiber's availability
- Cost

Fiber Composition/Fiber Origin

Fibers are derived from natural and man-made (or synthetic) materials.

Natural Fibers Natural fibers are materials that grow in nature such as cotton, flax, silk and wool. Utilizing various processes of harvesting, sorting, cleaning and milling, natural fibers are made ready for spinning.

Man-made Fibers Man-made fibers are fibers created by man through technology. The fiber-forming ingredients of man-made fibers are extruded, twisted or spun to form a long chain polymer.

Man-made fibers are divided into two groups:
- Regenerated Man-made fibers
- "True" Man-made Fibers

Regenerated man-made fibers are made from cellulosic substances or natural materials such as petrified wood, cotton linters, corn protein, milk or seaweed. The substances are reformed or generated by chemical treatment or may be processed into usable fibers.

"True" Man-made Fibers are synthesized completely from noncellulosic substances or chemical substances such as petroleum derivatives, nitrogen, hydrogen and carbon.

Natural or man-made textile fibers can be classified according to their origin and their chemical constitution.

- Cotton fibers for cotton fabrics and cotton-blended fabrics
- Flax fibers for linen fabrics and linen-blended fabrics
- Jute fibers for burlap fabrics and burlap-type fabrics
- Silk fibers for silk fabrics and silk-type fabrics
- Wool fibers for wool and worsted fabrics and wool and worsted-type fabrics
- Specialty hair fibers/Animal fur fibers
- Man-made fibers (regenerated cellulose fibers or 100% synthetic fibers)

Man-made fibers may be manipulated and finished to simulate natural fibers of cotton, linen, burlap, silk, wool or worsted fabrics. The texture, look, feel and structure that are important parts of any natural-fiber fabric may be copied.

The Federal Trade Commission, under the rules and regulations of the Textile Products Identification Act, has assigned *generic names* and definitions for the various types of man-made fibers according to the chemical composition of the fiber-forming substance. The *generic name* and definition of the fibers are listed according to section 7(c) of the Act. All fibers with the same *generic name* have similar chemical structure, compounds and characteristics. However, characteristics of individual generic fibers differ. Not all fibers possess the same properties.

Composition/Origin of Natural Fibers

	Fiber Type	Origin
Cellulosic/Vegetable Fibers	Cotton Kopak Hemp Jute Flax Ramie Pina Sisal Coir	Cotton boll/Seed hair Kopak tree/Seed hair Hemp or Abaca stalk/Bast fiber Jute stalk/Bast fiber Flax stalk/Bast fiber Rhea or China Grass/Bast fiber Pineapple leaf/Leaf fiber Agava leaf/Leaf fiber Coconut husk/Nut husk fiber
Animal/Protein Fibers	Silk Specialty Fur Fibers Specialty Hair Fibers Wool	Cultivated, doupioni or wild silkworms Selected fur bearing animals Camel and goat family animals Sheep
Mineral Fibers	Asbestos	Varieties of rock Silicate of magnesium and calcium
Rubber Fibers	Natural Rubber	Rubber plant

Composition/Origin of Man-Made Fibers

	Fiber Type	Origin
Cellulosic/Vegetable Fibers	Acetate Rayon Triacetate	Cotton Linters or Wood Cotton Linters or Wood Cotton Linters or Wood
Man-Made/Synthetic Long-Chain Polymer Fibers	Anidex Acrylic Modacrylic Nylon Nytril Olefin Polyester Saran Spandex Vinal Vinyon	Monohydic Alcohol/Acrylic Acid Acrylonitrile (85%) Acrylonitrile (35%–84%) Polyamide Vinylidene Dinitrile (85%) Ethylene or Propylene (85%) Dihydic Alcohol-Terephthalic Acid Vinylidene Chloride (80%) Polyurethane (85%) Vinyl Chloride (50%) Vinyl Alcohol (85%)
Protein Fibers	Azlon	Corn or Soybean
Mineral Fibers	Ceramic Glass Graphite	Minerals Silica, Sand, Limestone Carbon
Metal Fibers	Metallic	Aluminum, Silver, Gold, Stainless Steel
Rubber Fibers	Rubber	Man-made/Synthetic

The Production of Man-made Fibers

The fiber-forming ingredients of man-made fibers are extruded, twisted or spun to form a long chain polymer. The liquid substance, forced through a spinnerette (or spinning jet), hardens to produce a long continuous filament fiber. There are three processes used to produce man-made fibers:

- Dry Spinning Process
- Wet Spinning Process
- Melt Spinning Process

Dry Spinning Process Filaments emerge from the spinnerette and are solidified by being dried by warm air. Process is applicable for producing: acetate, acrylic, modacrylic, triacetate, and vinyon.

Wet Spinning Process Filaments emerge from the spinnerette and are passed directly into a chemical bath where they are solidified or regenerated. Process is applicable for producing: acrylic, rayon, and anidex.

Melt Spinning Process Fiber-forming substance is melted for extrusion and hardened by cool air. Process is applicable for producing: nylon, polyester, olefin, aramid, and glass.

spinnerette/spinning jet

Courtaulds North America Co.

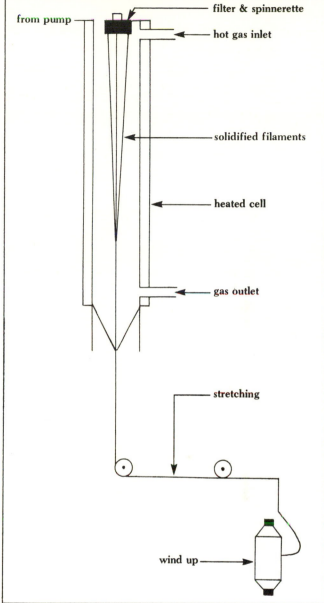

from pump

filter & spinnerette

hot gas inlet

solidified filaments

heated cell

gas outlet

stretching

wind up

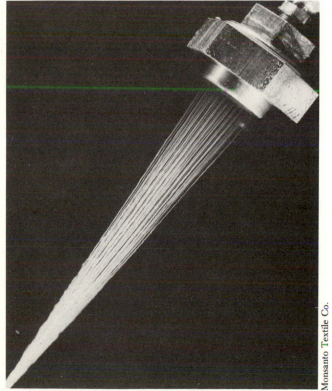

Monsanto Textile Co.

solution emerging from spinnerette to form filament yarns

CLOSE-UP OF SPINNERETTE IN DRY SPINNING PROCESS

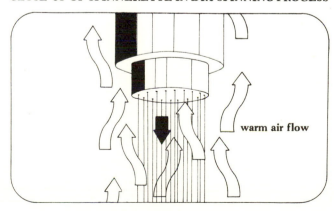

warm air flow

WET SPINNING PROCESS

filter

from pump

solidified filaments

godet wheel

godet wheel

washing & chemical treatment

drying

stretching

coagulating bath

spinnerette

wind up

MELT SPINNING PROCESS

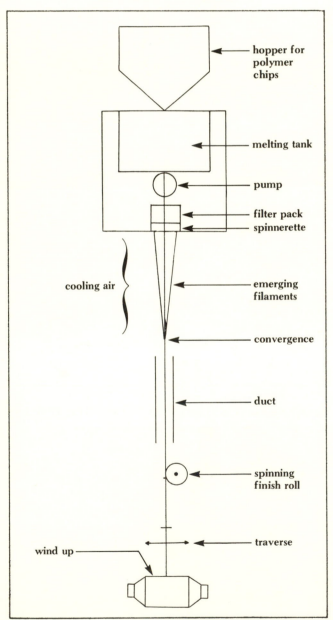

hopper for polymer chips

melting tank

pump

filter pack

spinnerette

cooling air

emerging filaments

convergence

duct

spinning finish roll

traverse

wind up

CLOSE-UP OF SPINNERETTE AND COAGULATING BATH IN WET SPINNING PROCESS

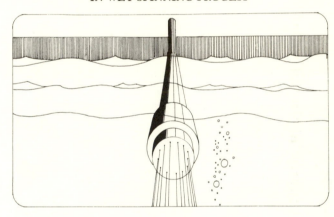

CLOSE-UP OF SPINNERETTE IN MELT SPINNING PROCESS

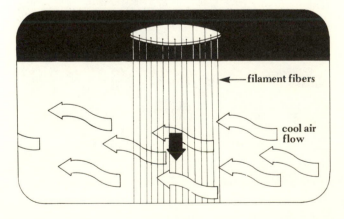

filament fibers

cool air flow

Classification of Natural & Man-made Fibers

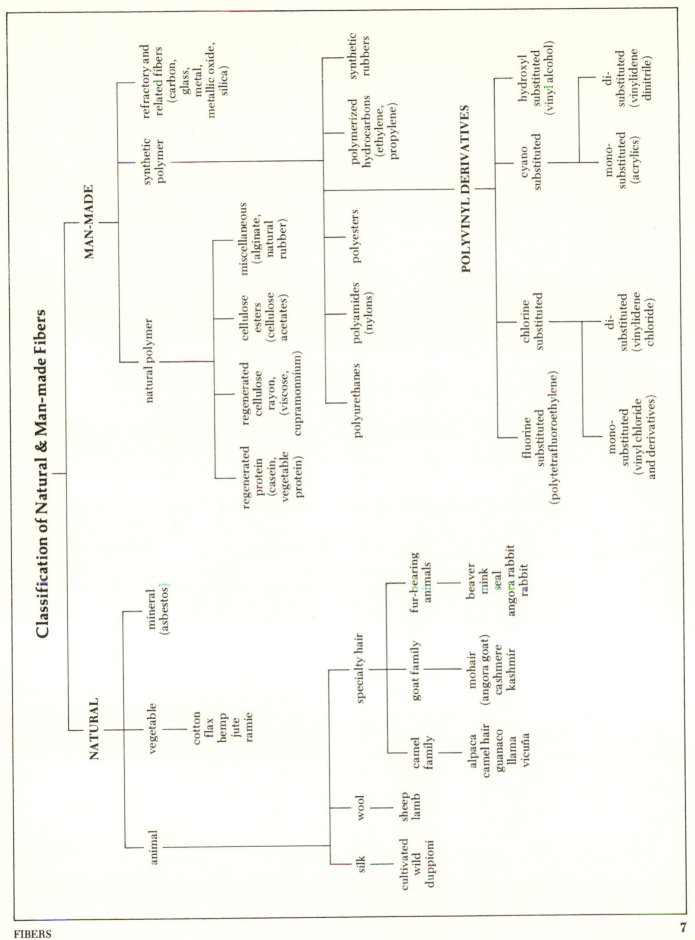

Properties & Characteristics of Man-made Fibers

Modified and improved to build desirable characteristics and eliminate or modify the undesirable characteristics in the finished product.

Special additives mixed into the basic liquid fiber solution may impart special qualities or change one or more characteristics of fiber.

Extruded in different sizes, shapes, and thicknesses to meet special needs of the finished products.

Variations in textiles products.

Engineered and produced to provide specific needs or functions such as:

    Fit a variety of end uses
    Absorb like cotton
    Look like natural-fiber fabrics
    From fine and sheer to thick, strong and opaque
    Stretchy or bulky without additional weight
    Hold pleats permanently
    Flame-retardant
    Mildew and moth resistant
    Formed into filament fibers of any length or cut staple fibers
    Formed into film fiber form
    Monofilament or multifilament yarns
    Tow yarns

Man-made yarns may be texturized to produce bulk, stretch or various surface interests; cut into different lengths; spun, blended or combined.

Advantages & Disadvantages of Man-made Fibers

Advantages

Thermoplasticity. Fiber can be molded or shaped to a desired form. Permanent setting of pleats by heat setting.

Abrasion Resistant. Withstands surface wear; shows minimum wear.

Resiliency. When crushed, springs back quickly; inherent wrinkle resistance.

Strength. A strong fiber; high dry and high wet strength.

Resistance. Resistant to damage by mildew, moths and sunlight.

Easy Care. Washes easily and dries quickly. Surface may be cleaned with damp sponge. Water stains penetrate fiber slowly and can be easily removed. Requires little or no ironing.

Disadvantages

Absorbency. Poor absorbency due to inability of fiber to absorb moisture. Perspiration condenses between body and garment. Fabric feels either cold and clammy or hot and uncomfortable on the body.

Staining. Oil-base stains such as grease, butter or animal fats penetrate the fiber and become difficult or impossible to remove.

Static Electricity. Builds up static electricity causing electric shocks. Fabric clings to body.

Thermoplasticity. Overdrying or high heat sets undesirable creases and wrinkles. High ironing temperatures will melt fabric.

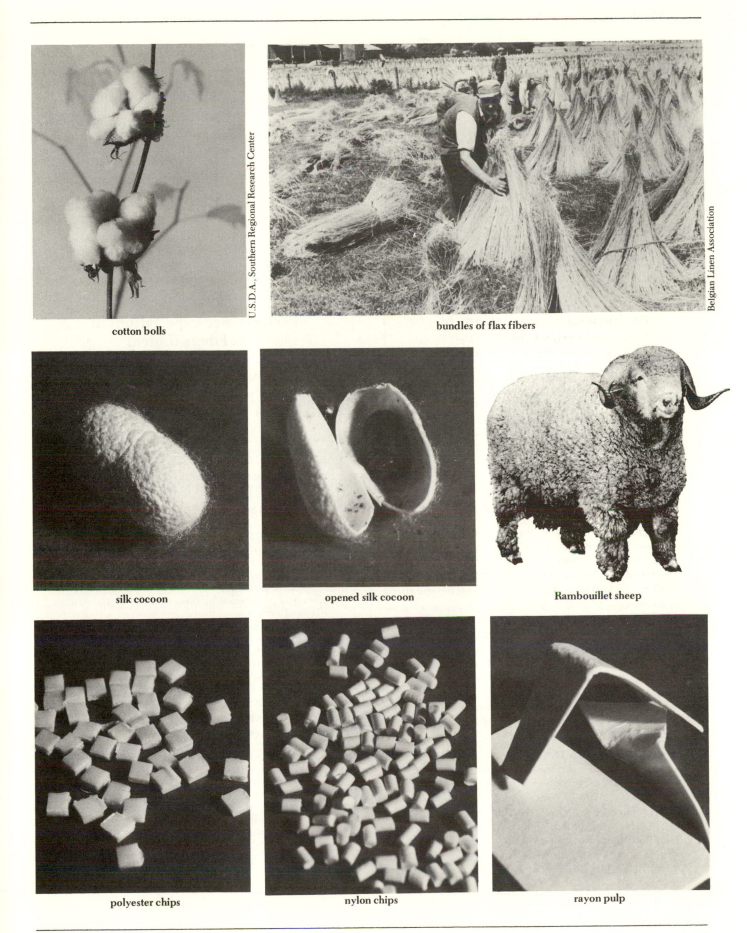

U.S.D.A., Southern Regional Research Center

Belgian Linen Association

cotton bolls

bundles of flax fibers

silk cocoon

opened silk cocoon

Rambouillet sheep

polyester chips

nylon chips

rayon pulp

Properties & Characteristics of Cotton Fibers

Cotton is a natural vegetable fiber composed mainly of cellulose and cultivated from a seed-pod forming plant. Cotton plants yield fibers approximately ½″–2½″ (1.27–6.35 cm) in length (see chart on page 24).

Cotton fiber grades are based on:
- Color—from white to a yellow cast or to gray
- Purity—amount of foreign matter present
- Ginning Process—methods and operations of carding and sorting

Cotton fibers are spun and twisted to form a continuous strand of yarn. Cotton fibers, yarns and/or fabrics may be manipulated and finished to resemble linen, silk or wool fabrics.

Performance Expectations of Cotton Fibers

Absorbency Hydrophilic fiber; 8½% moisture regain
Affinity to Dyestuff High
Covering Power Good
Effect of Heat Withstands high temperatures; can be boiled and hot pressed
Elasticity Poor; 3%–10% elongation at breaking point
Elongation 74% recovery at 2% elongation; 45% at 5%
Luster Little luster unless treated
Pilling No problem
Resiliency/Wrinkle Recovery Poor; wrinkles in use
Resistance
  Abrasion Good
  Biological Resistant to moths and beetles; attacked by silverfish; damaged by fungi causing mildew and bacteria growth
  Chemical Weakened by strong acids; weakened by chemical resins in finishing; high resistance to alkalies
  Flame Burns when ignited and continues to burn
  Sunlight Fair; deteriorates and yellows with prolonged exposure
Shrinkage/Dimensional Stability Has dimensional stability; tends to shrink appreciably when washed unless treated
Static Electricity No problem; no static buildup
Strength/Durability Good; tenacity of 3.0–5.0 grams; increases 10% in strength when wet

SPECIAL COMMENTS
Comfort Factors High absorbency qualities contribute to cooling effect which adds to the comfort of the garment, making cotton a desirable fiber, yarn and/or fabric for hot weather clothing.
Care Factors May be laundered or dry cleaned depending on fabric structure and/or garment construction; withstands strain of frequent launderings; safe ironing temperature limit 400°F (206.1°C).

Properties & Characteristics of Flax Fibers (Linen)

Flax is a natural vegetable fiber composed mainly of cellulose that is processed from the stems of the flax plant. By various environmental, mechanical or chemical "retting" processes the fibers are removed from the stems. The flax plant yields long, fine fibers that are approximately 2″–36″ (5.08–91.4 cm) in length; of medium to medium-heavy weight or density. The natural color of flax varies from light ivory to dark tan or grey.

Flax fibers are spun and twisted to form a continuous strand of yarn and when woven the finished fabric is called *linen*. Flax fibers, yarns and/or linen fabrics usually maintain the characteristics and qualities associated with linen fabrics of the past. However, they may be manipulated and finished to resemble cotton, silk or wool and worsted-type fabrics.

Performance Expectations of Flax Fibers (Linen)

Absorbency Hydrophilic fiber; 12% moisture regain
Affinity to Dyestuff Hard, impenetrable and difficult to dye
Covering Power Good
Effect of Heat Withstands high temperatures; may scorch
Elasticity Poor; 2% elongation at breaking point
Elongation Poor; no recovery
Flexibility Poor; brittle fibers tend to crack and break from bending and creasing
Luster Good; high natural luster
Pilling No problem
Resiliency/Wrinkle Recovery Poor; wrinkles easily and quickly unless treated
Resistance
  Abrasion Fair; abrades at folds and edges
  Biological Resistant to moths; attacked by silverfish; damaged by fungi causing mildew and bacteria growth
  Chemical Weakened by bleaches; resistant to alkalies
  Flame Burns when ignited and continues to burn
  Sunlight Good
Shrinkage/Dimensional Stability Stable; fabric retains shape; tends to shrink when washed unless treated
Static Electricity No problem; no static buildup
Strength/Durability High; fabric wears evenly; twice the strength of cotton; increases 20% in strength when wet

SPECIAL COMMENTS
Comfort Factors High natural absorbency and quick drying qualities contribute to cooling effect which adds to the comfort of the garment; desirable for hot weather clothing.
Care Factors May be laundered or dry cleaned depending on fabric structure and/or garment construction; withstands strain of frequent launderings; safe ironing temperature limit 450°F (234.1°C); sheds dirt and stains from surface due to hardness of fibers; fabrics are lint free.

Properties & Characteristics of Silk Fibers

Silk is a natural animal fiber composed mainly of protein that is derived from the cocoon of cultivated or uncultivated silkworms. A continuous strand of natural filament-form silk fiber, in lengths from 300 to 1600 yards, is reeled from each cocoon.

Reeling is the process of unwinding several unbroken or unpierced cocoons at the same time, drawing the fine filaments together, and binding them with their own natural sericin. Silk fibers are reeled, then *thrown* or spun, and then twisted into yarn with different amounts of thicknesses, plies, and twists. Yarns may be woven, knitted or otherwise structured to form the finished silk fabric. The thrown yarn is referred to as *raw silk*. Silk fibers, yarns, and/or fabrics may be manipulated and finished into any degree of thickness or transparency, crispness or softness.

Silk fibers are categorized with regard to:
- Type of cocoon
- Location of growth and cultivation
- Length and purity of filament
- Smoothness of filament

Silk fibers and yarns may be developed to resemble cotton, linen or wool-type fabrics.

Listing of Silk Terms

Cultivated Silk A term applied to the smooth even textured filament fibers that are processed from silkworms raised under controlled environmental and nutritional conditions.

Doupioni Silk A term applied to the thick-and-thin irregular slub yarns produced by a combination of inseparable or interlocking double filaments that are processed from two silkworms purposely nesting together to form one cocoon.

Pure Silk/Pure Dyed Silk A term applied to the finishing method or process of a superior silk fiber fabric, comprised of 100% silk without metallic weighting. Federal Trade Commission ruling allows alternate finishing materials to give body to the finished silk fabric. Alternate finishing materials are not to exceed 15% for black-colored fabrics and 10% for all other colored fabrics.

Raw Silk A term applied to the filament silk fiber reeled in the *gum* from the unpierced cocoon into the skein formation. The filament-fiber yarns, bound by the natural sericin, are held together with only a slight twist or turn. Raw silk is not a fabric. When stores refer to raw silk, they mean wild silk where the yarns are not highly twisted.

Silk Noil/Silk Waste The waste or end product resulting from the process of spun-silk yarn manufacturing or waste left after the reeling process. The short, uneven, irregular noil fibers produce coarse yarns with a seed-like texture. Silk noil yarns may be used with other fiber yarns to produce fabric.

Spun Silk A term applied to the short ends of silk fibers produced from the outer and inner edges of the cocoon and from imperfect or broken cocoons.

Weighted Silk A term applied to the finishing methods and process for inferior silk-fiber cloth production and to silk fabrics in which metallic salts and other finishing agents are applied to the fabric to replace the weight lost during the fabric production process. Weighting is the cover-up of inferior goods to improve the appearance, feel and hand of the fabric. Federal Trade Commission ruling requires that fabrics and garments made of weighted silk be identified and marked with the percentage of weighting agents used.

Wild Silk/Tussah Silk A term applied to the natural tan or light brown-colored coarse filaments, of irregular dimension, taken from wild uncultivated silkworms.

Performance Expectations of Silk Fibers

Absorbency Hydrophilic fiber; 11% moisture regain

Affinity to Dyestuff Natural affinity to dyestuff

Covering Power Poor; Fibers are thin and more yarns are required to produce cloth.

Effect of Heat Sensitive to heat; turns yellow at 231°F (112.4 °C)

Elasticity Good; 20% elongation at breaking point

Elongation Poor recovery; if stretched beyond 2% elongation

Flexibility Good; pliable and supple fibers and yarns

Luster High luster unless uncultivated silk fibers

Pilling No problem

Resiliency/Wrinkle Recovery Fair; wrinkles usually hang out

Resistance
   Abrasion Fair
   Biological Attacked by moths and other insects; resistant to mildew and bacteria growth; damaged by body oils and perspiration
   Chemical Deteriorates if subjected to chlorine bleaching agents
   Flame Smolders
   Sunlight Poor; weakens when exposed

Shrinkage/Dimensional Stability Good resistance to stretch; tends to shrink when laundered or dry cleaned

Slippage High yarn and seam slippage due to weave

Static Electricity Little

Strength/Durability Good in dry state; weakens and loses 15% of strength when wet

SPECIAL COMMENTS

Comfort Factors Insulatory qualities; warmer than other natural fiber fabrics of comparable weight.

Care Factors Usually dry cleaned; may be laundered depending on finishing agents, fabric structure and garment construction; safe ironing temperature limit 300°F (150.1°C); discolors and changes colors at 231°F (112.4°C); damaged by body oils and perspiration; water spots from steam.

Performance Expectations of Wool Fibers

Absorbency Hydrophilic fiber; 13% moisture regain

Affinity to Dyestuff High

Covering Power Good

Effect of Heat Discolors and scorches under high temperatures

Elasticity Good; 20%–40% elongation at breaking point

Elongation High; 99% recovery at 2% elongation; 65% at 20%

Flexibility Pliable

Luster Varies considerably depending on origin and type and breed of animal

Pilling Fair; susceptible to pilling due to short fibers

Resiliency/Wrinkle Recovery Good in dry state; springs back if creased or crushed; resists wrinkles; wrinkles hang out

Resistance

Abrasion Fair

Biological Damaged by moths unless treated; resistant to mildew and bacteria growth

Chemical Weakened by strong alkalies and acids; yellows and discolors when subjected to chlorine bleaches

Flame Self-extinguishing when source of flame is removed; inherent flame-retardant fiber

Sunlight Fair

Shrinkage/Dimensional Stability Tends to felt and shrink when washed

Static Electricity Fair; easily charged by friction on dry, cold days with low humidity

Strength/Durability Fair; loses 20% strength when wet

SPECIAL COMMENTS

Compressibility Natural crimp allows for production of lofted and bulked yarns

Crush Springs back if crushed or creased

Comfort Factors Due to fiber structure, wool sheds water naturally, absorbs water slowly and dries slowly. Thermal and insulatory qualities contribute to warming effect making wool a desirable fiber, yarn and/or fabric for cold weather clothing.

Care Factors Usually dry cleaned unless labeled "Hand Washable" or "Machine Washable"; resists soil; dirt adheres to fabric surface; fabrics retain odors; safe ironing temperature limit 300°F (150.1°C); yellows and discolors when subjected to chlorine bleach.

Properties & Characteristics of Wool Fibers

Wool is a natural animal fiber composed mainly of protein that is formed by the covering or fleece of the sheep, lamb or goat. The hair covering is clipped or shorn from the animal. The resulting fibers are 1″ to 18″ (2.54 to 45.7 cm) in lengths; light- to medium-weight; ranging in color from natural cream, brown, grey or black shades and tones.

There are approximately 200 different types and varieties of grades of wool fibers that are removed from approximately 40 different breeds of sheep, lambs, goats, etc. Wool fibers are divided into different classes and are classified with regard to:

- Type of animal
- Place of origin in which animal is raised
- Method of removal of fleece from animal
- Type of fleece or staple
- Length and width of staple
- Purity of fiber
- Natural color and shades of the fiber
- Luster of the fiber
- Amount of crimp
- Quality of fiber
- Hardness of fiber

Wool fibers from sheep or lamb may be mixed, blended or combined with different types of wool fibers or hair fibers from other wild or domesticated animal stock in any combination or variety of percentages. The selected blending or mixture is used to modify, change or improve the appearance, hand, drapability qualities, performance expectations, and/or end use of the cloth.

Wool fibers and yarns may be manipulated and finished to add or change the texture, surface interest, or loft. The yarns may be constructed in any variety of fabric structures and finished to provide a hard, smooth, soft or napped surface. Wool fibers, yarns and/or fabrics may be manipulated and finished to resemble cotton, linen or silk fabrics.

Comparison of Woolen & Worsted Fabrics

Worsted woolens are made from a select choice of fine long staple fibers. The worsted process incorporates a carding and combing procedure that removes foreign matter and short fibers from the shorn wool.

Worsted yarns are:

- Composed of long parallel fibers
- Composed of fibers which are uniform in length
- Spun evenly, producing a fine yarn
- Tightly or firmly twisted
- Compactly woven into cloth

The worsted process produces a fabric with a smooth, fine surface texture having crisp hand and firm appearance. The finish of worsted fabrics is hardy and more durable than other woolen fiber fabrics.

Comparison of Woolen & Worsted Fabrics

	Woolen Fabrics	Worsted Fabrics
Fiber	short curly	long straight
Yarn	carded only weak bulky uneven twist slack twist	carded and combed great tensile strength fine, smooth, even even twist tight twist generally yarn dyed
Weave	indistinct pattern usually plain weave sometimes twill weave low thread count loosely woven	distinct pattern usually twill weave sometimes plain weave high thread count more closely woven
Finish	soft fulling, napping steaming napping can conceal quality of construction	hard singeing steaming unfinished worsteds are napped
Appearance	soft fuzzy thick	harsh rough flat
Hand	soft lofty	hard crisp
Characteristics	warmer not as durable nap reduces shine soft surface holds dirt stains easily removed does not hold crease well	less insulatory more durable becomes shiny with use resistant to dust and dirt shows stains quickly holds creases and shape
Cost	generally less expensive to produce	costlier yarns, more expensive to produce

The Wool Products Labeling Act

The Wool Products Labeling Act decreed that the terms:

Wool or Virgin Wool   refers to the unprocessed or unused fiber obtained from the fleece of sheep or lambs, to the hair from goats and rabbits, or to the specialty hair from camels or camel-related animals.

Reprocessed Wool   refers to woven or processed fibers, yarns or fabrics that have *not* been *used* by the consumer, but is reclaimed and subsequently broken down and converted into a fiber state to be made into yarns again.

Reused Wool   refers to the reclaiming of wool, woolens or worsted goods after they have been manufactured, finished, made into garments, and *used* by consumer and subsequently treated, processed, broken down, and converted into a fibrous state.

Listing of Wool Terms

The following woolens are named for the origin or type of sheep from which the fleece is shorn and do not relate to yarn, structure, finish or properties of the fabric.

Merino Wool   A fine soft wool from the Merino sheep.

Australian Wool   Wool from Spanish Merino stock raised in Australia.

Botany Wool   Wool from the Merino sheep raised in the Botany Bay area of Australia.

Saxony Wool   Originally, referred to a wool fabric made from sheep raised in Saxony Germany. Today, the term refers to fine woolens similar to Saxony woolens.

Shetland Wool   The term Shetland should be used only when describing wool or wool products from the Shetland Islands in Scotland.

Lambswool   The first or virgin wool fiber clippings obtained from seven- to eight-month old lambs.

Naked Wool   A general term used to describe lightweight, sheer wool fabric constructed into garments without backing or linings.

Properties & Characteristics of Specialty Hair Fibers

Specialty hair fibers are natural fibers composed mainly of protein that is obtained from several families or species of animals. The hair covering is clipped, shorn, brushed or otherwise removed from the animal. Depending on the type of animal and the location of the hair, the resulting hair fibers will vary in length from 1″ to 15″ (2.54 to 38.1 cm).

Specialty hair or fur fibers are used as a variation of wool fibers and *should not be confused* with pelts or furs.

Specialty hair fibers are available in limited qualities; and may be woven or knitted. Specialty hair fibers may be used alone or in blends with wool or other natural or man-made fibers.

Properties & Characteristics of Acetate Fibers

Acetate is a manufactured fiber in which the fiber-forming substance is cellulose acetate. Where not less than 92% of the hydroxyl groups are acetylated, the term triacetate may be used as a generic description of the fiber.

Performance Expectations of Acetate Fibers

Absorbency Fair/moderate; 6% moisture regain

Affinity to Dyestuff Takes special dyestuff easily; wide range of colors; colorfast if solution- or spun-dyed

Covering Power Poor

Effect of Heat Thermoplastic fiber; heat-set pleats; melts under high temperatures

Elasticity 23%–45% elongation at breaking point

Elongation 94% recovery at 2% elongation; 23% at 20%

Flexibility Soft and pliable

Luster High; wide range of silk-like luster

Pilling No problem

Resiliency/Wrinkle Recovery Fair

Resistance
 Abrasion Poor
 Biological Resistant to moths and mildew growth
 Chemical Subject to atmospheric fumes and gas fading
 Flame Burns slowly; melts at 500°F (260°C)
 Sunlight Weakened when exposed

Shrinkage/Dimensional Stability Resistant to shrinkage

Static Electricity Some problems

Strength/Durability Poor; 30% weaker when wet

SPECIAL COMMENTS

Comfort Factors Retains crispness.

Care Factors Dry cleaning is recommended; some fabrics are washable; fast drying; safe ironing temperature limit 250°F (123.5°C).

Properties & Characteristics of Acrylic Fibers

Acrylic is a manufactured fiber in which the fiber-forming substance is any long chain synthetic polymer composed of at least 85% by weight of acrylonitrile units (—CH₂—CH—).

$$(-CH_2-CH-)$$
$$|$$
$$CN$$

Performance Expectations of Acrylic Fibers

Absorbency Poor; hydrophobic fiber; 1%-2% moisture regain

Affinity to Dyestuff Fair; wide range of colors; color-fast

Covering Power Poor unless bulked, crimped or textured

Effect of Heat Thermoplastic fiber; heat-set pleats; melts under high temperatures

Elasticity 25%-46% elongation at breaking point

Elongation 92%-99% recovery at 2% elongation

Flexibility Good

Luster Dependent on modification

Pilling Subject to pilling

Resiliency/Wrinkle Recovery Good; resists wrinkles

Resistance
  Abrasion Good
  Biological Resistant to moths and mildew
  Chemical Resistant to chemicals, oils and grease
  Crush Springs back readily when crushed
  Flame Melts under high temperatures
  Sunlight Good resistance to chemicals, oils and grease

Shrinkage/Dimensional Stability Good dimensional stability; good shape retention; resists stretching and distortion

Static Electricity Produces static buildup

Strength/Durability Fair; becomes 20% weaker when wet

SPECIAL COMMENTS

Comfort Factors Wicking qualities conduct moisture from body. Acrylic may have a lofted, wool-like hand appearance and may be used as a substitute for wool. Acrylic fiber, yarn and/or fabric produced as thick, fluffy; bulked items are warmer and lighter than other fibers, yarns and/or fabrics.

Care Factors May be laundered or dry cleaned; easily laundered; machine dry at low temperatures; safe ironing temperature limit 300°F (150.1°C).

Properties & Characteristics of Anidex Fibers

Anidex is a manufactured fiber in which the fiber-forming substance is any long chain synthetic polymer composed of at least 50% by weight of one or more esters of a monohydric alcohol and acrylic acid ($CH_2= CH - COOH$).

Performance Expectations of Anidex Fibers

Absorbency Poor

Affinity to Dyestuff Poor; takes on color of companion fibers

Covering Power Used in filament form, assumes hand and covering power of companion fiber, yarn

Effect of Heat Good resistance

Elasticity Elastomeric fiber; high degree of elongation; multidirectional

Elongation High; retains dimensional stability and stretch power

Flexibility Elastomeric fiber

Luster Dependent on companion fibers

Pilling No problem

Resiliency/Wrinkle Recovery High

Resistance
  Abrasion High
  Biological Resistant to moths and mildew
  Chemical Resistant to effects of chlorine bleach; to gas fading and oxidation
  Sunlight Resistant to sunlight

Shrinkage/Dimensional Stability Ability to stretch and snap-back similar to natural rubber; imparts permanent stretch and recovery properties to fabric

Static Electricity No problem

Strength/Durability High

SPECIAL COMMENTS

Comfort Factors Improves fit, comfort and appearance of garment; provides persuasive shape control.

Care Factors May be laundered or dry cleaned; fabric retains dimension and power after repeated launderings.

Properties & Characteristics of Aramid Fibers

Aramid is a manufactured fiber in which the fiber-forming substance is a long-chain synthetic polyamide in which at least 85% of the amide linkages are attached directly to two aromatic rings ($-C-NH-$).
$$\overset{\|}{O}$$

Performance Expectations of Aramid Fibers

Absorbency Fair; regular filament and staple; 5% moisture regain; high tenacity filament—2.7%–7% moisture regain

Affinity to Dyestuff High; takes dyestuff easily

Covering Power Fair

Effect of Heat Heat resistant; no melting point

Elasticity Low

Elongation Low

Flexibility Good

Pilling Nonpilling

Resiliency/Wrinkle Recovery Good

Resistance
  Abrasion Good
  Biological Resistant to moths and mildew
  Chemical Resistant to most chemicals, oils and grease
  Flame Low flammability
  Sunlight Good resistance to sunlight

Shrinkage/Dimensional Stability Good dimensional stability; resists stretching and shrinkage

Static Electricity Good

Strength/Durability High tensile strength; tough fiber

SPECIAL COMMENTS

Care Factors May be laundered or dry cleaned; easy to launder; quick drying; easy to iron; resistant to oil-borne stains and soil.

Properties & Characteristics of Azlon Fibers

Azlon is a manufactured fiber in which the fiber-forming substance is composed of any regenerated naturally occurring proteins.

- No production of fiber in the United States, but produced in foreign countries.
- Treated to resemble wool, cotton and rayon.
- Used in combination with other fibers and provides a soft feel to the touch.

Properties & Characteristics of Metallic Fibers

Metallic is a manufactured fiber composed of all metal, plastic-coated metal, metal-coated plastic, or a core completely covered by metal.

Performance Expectations of Metallic Fibers

Absorbency Nonabsorbent

Affinity to Dyestuff Colorfast

Covering Power Depending on width of cut strands

Effect of Heat Withstands high temperatures

Elasticity None unless blended with elastomeric yarns

Elongation Good

Flexibility Depends on type and method of yarn manufacture

Luster Glitter

Pilling No problem

Resistance
  Abrasion Good
  Biological Resistant to moths and mildew
  Chemical Resistant to chemicals; not affected by salt or chlorinated water
  Flame Flame resistant/nonflammable
  Sunlight Resistant to sunlight and weathering

Shrinkage/Dimensional Stability High resistance

Static Electricity Fair

Strength/Durability Good; high tensile strength

SPECIAL COMMENTS

Care Factors for Coated Metallic Yarns May be laundered or dry cleaned; Unaffected by perspiration and body oils; nontarnishing; plastic-coated yarn melts under high temperatures.

Properties & Characteristics of Modacrylic Fibers

Modacrylic is a manufactured fiber in which the fiber-forming substance is any long chain synthetic polymer composed of less than 85% but at least 35% by weight of acrylonitrile units.

Performance Expectations of Modacrylic Fibers

Absorbency Poor; hydrophobic fiber; 0.4%–4% moisture regain

Affinity to Dyestuff High; easy to dye; wide range of colors

Covering Power Good; yarns are bulked

Effect of Heat Thermoplastic fiber; may be stretched, molded or embossed; sensitive to heat; low melting temperature; shrinks and melts under high temperature

Elasticity 33%–39% elongation at breaking point

Elongation 79%–97% recovery at 2% elongation

Flexibility Good

Luster High

Pilling Fair

Resiliency/Wrinkle Recovery Good; resists wrinkles

Resistance
  Abrasion Good
  Biological Resistant to moths and mildew
  Chemical Resistant to chemicals, bleaches, alkalies and acids
  Flame Inherent natural flame-retardant properties; does not support combustion
  Sunlight Resistant to sunlight and weathering

Shrinkage/Dimensional Stability Produced with controlled heat shrinking capacity; good shape retention

Static Electricity Creates static buildup

Strength/Durability Fair to good; no loss of strength when wet

SPECIAL COMMENTS

Comfort Factors A nonallergenic fiber; used as a substitute for fur; may be produced as a high-pile constructed fabric that is warm; has bulk without added weight; good shape and crease retention.

Care Factors May be laundered or dry cleaned; poor absorbency aids in quick drying qualities. Shrinks and melts under hot iron; safe ironing temperature limit 225°F (108.1°C).

Properties & Characteristics of Novoloid Fibers

Novoloid is a manufactured fiber containing at least 85% by weight of a cross-linked novalac.

Performance Expectations of Novoloid Fibers

Absorbency High

Effect of Heat Does not melt

Pilling Subject to pilling

Resistance
  Abrasion Fair
  Biological Resistant to moths and mildew
  Chemical Resistant to chemicals, acids and alkalies, oils and grease
  Flame Flame resistant
  Sunlight Resistant to sunlight

Shrinkage/Dimensional Stability Good shape retention; resistant to stretching

Strength/Durability Fair

SPECIAL COMMENTS

No production of fiber in the United States, but it is produced in foreign countries. Limited information available at this time

Care Factors Easy to launder and iron.

Properties & Characteristics of Nylon Fibers

Nylon is a manufactured fiber in which the fiber-forming substance is a long-chain synthetic polymer in which less than 85% of the amide linkages are attached directly to two aromatic rings ($-C-NH-$).
$$\underset{O}{\overset{\|}{}}$$

Performance Expectations of Nylon Fibers

Absorbency Fair to poor; hydrophilic fiber; 4%–4.5% moisture regain

Affinity to Dyestuff Good; easy to dye; wide range of colors; colorfast

Covering Power Poor

Effect of Heat Thermoplastic qualities; heat-set pleats and creases; melts under high temperatures

Elasticity 26%–40% elongation at breaking point

Elongation 100% recovery at 8% elongation

Flexibility Good

Luster Naturally lustrous

Pilling Subject to pilling

Resiliency/Wrinkle Recovery Good; resists wrinkles

Resistance
 Abrasion Good
 Biological Resistant to moths and mildew
 Chemical Resistant to most chemicals; deteriorates in sulfuric acids
 Flame Melts at 500°F (260°C)
 Sunlight Poor; fades during prolonged exposure

Shrinkage/Dimensional Stability Resists shrinkage; good shape retention

Static Electricity Subject to static buildup; produces electrical charge

Strength/Durability High; exceptionally strong fiber; loses 15% of strength when wet

SPECIAL COMMENTS

Comfort Factors Nylon is a naturally water repellent fiber, which contributes water and wind resistant qualities to the fabric. Provides high degree of warmth compared to fibers, yarns and/or fabrics of heavier weight and bulk.

Care Factors May be laundered or dry cleaned; easy to launder; quick drying; machine dry at low temperatures; safe ironing temperature limit 350°F (122.1°C).

Properties & Characteristics of Nytril Fibers

Nytril is a manufactured fiber containing at least 85% of a long-chain polymer of vinylidene dinitrile where the vinylidene dinitrile content is no less than every other unit in the polymer chain ($-CH_2-C(CN)_2-$).

Performance Expectations of Nytril Fibers

Absorbency Poor

Affinity to Dyestuff Difficult to dye

Effect of Heat Withstands high temperatures; heat sensitive

Pilling No problem

Resiliency/Wrinkle Recovery Good; resists wrinkles

Resistance
 Abrasion Good
 Biological Resistant to moths and mildew

Strength/Durability Fair to Good

SPECIAL COMMENTS

No production of fiber in the United States, but it is produced in foreign countries. Fiber is used as a substitute of wool, produced with a soft hand to simulate wool. Used in wool blends to control shrinkage and loss of shape. Limited information available at this time.

Properties & Characteristics of Polyester Fibers

Polyester is a manufactured fiber in which the fiber-forming substance is any long-chain synthetic polymer composed of at least 85% by weight of an ester of a substituted aromatic carboxylic acid, including but not restricted to substituted terephthalate units, $p(-R-O-C-C_6H_4-C-O-)$, and para-substituted hydroxybenzoate units, $p(-R-O-C_6H_4-C-O-)$.

Performance Expectations of Polyester Fibers

Absorbency Poor; hydrophobic fiber; 0.4%–0.8% moisture regain

Affinity to Dyestuff Good; easy to dye; wide range of colors; colorfast

Covering Power Poor

Effect of Heat Thermoplastic fiber; retains heat-set pleats and creases

Elasticity 19%–23% elongation at breaking point

Elongation 97% recovery at 2% elongation; 80% recovery at 8% elongation

Flexibility Good

Luster High

Pilling Easily subject to pilling

Resiliency/Wrinkle Recovery High resistance to wrinkling when dry or wet; retains original shape

Resistance
 Abrasion Resistant to wear; colors crock and abrade at garment edges
 Biological Resistant to moths and mildew
 Chemical Resistant to most chemicals
 Flame Difficult to ignite; melts at 480°F–550°F (249°C–288°C)
 Sunlight Resistant to sunlight and weathering

Shrinkage/Dimensional Stability Good dimensional stability; good shape retention; resistant to stretching and shrinking

Static Electricity Subject to static buildup

Strength/Durability High; no loss of strength when wet

SPECIAL COMMENTS

Comfort Factors Nonallergenic fiber. Nonabsorbent qualities hold in body heat producing a fabric that may be uncomfortable in warm, humid weather. Fabric retains crispness and resilient qualities in wet or dry state. Maintains crease retention.

Care Factors Laundered or dry cleaned; easily laundered; quick drying; machine dry at low temperature setting; requires little or no ironing after laundering; safe ironing temperature limit 325°F (163.1°C); attracts lint; oil-borne stains difficult or impossible to remove.

Properties & Characteristics of Rayon Fibers

Rayon is a manufactured fiber composed of regenerated cellulose, as well as manufactured fibers composed of regenerated cellulose in which substituents have replaced not more than 15% of the hydrogens of the hydroxyl groups.

Listing of Rayon Terms

Cuprammonium Rayon/Cupro Rayon Filaments made from regenerated cellulose coagulated from a solution of cellulose in *ammoniacal oxide*.

Viscose Rayon Filaments made of regenerated cellulose coagulated from a solution of *cellulose xanthate*.

Performance Expectations of Rayon Fibers

Absorbency Good; hydrophilic fiber; 13% moisture regain

Affinity to Dyestuff Good; easy to dye; wide range of colors; colorfast when solution dyed

Covering Power Poor

Effect of Heat Melts under high temperatures

Elasticity 15%–30% elongation at breaking point

Elongation 82% recovery at 2% elongation; 30% recovery at 20% elongation

Flexibility Good

Luster High

Pilling No problem

Resiliency/Wrinkle Recovery Poor; wrinkles easily when worn or crushed

Resistance
 Abrasion Poor
 Biological Resistant to moths; susceptible to mildew
 Chemical Affected by chemicals
 Flame Burns readily
 Sunlight Good resistance, but affected by prolonged exposure; resistant to weathering

Shrinkage/Dimensional Stability Poor dimensional stability; shrinks appreciably from washing; shrinks and/or stretches unless treated

Static Electricity No problem

Strength/Durability Fair to good; good tensile strength when dry; loses 30%–40% of strength when wet

SPECIAL COMMENTS

Comfort Factors Absorbency qualities produce a fabric that is considered a comfortable fiber, yarn and/or fabric for warm weather coloring.

Care Factors May be laundered or dry cleaned; easily laundered; dries slowly easy to iron; safe ironing temperature limit 350°F (122.1°C).

Properties & Characteristics of Rubber/Synthetic Rubber Fibers

Rubber is a manufactured fiber in which the fiber-forming substance is comprised of natural or synthetic rubber, including the following categories: (1) a manufactured fiber in which the fiber-forming substance is a hydrocarbon such as natural rubber, polyisoprene, polybutadiene, copolymers of dienes and hydrocarbons, or amorphous (non-crystalline) polyolefins, (2) a manufactured fiber in which the fiber-forming substance is a copolymer of acrylonitrile and a diene (such as butadiene) composed of not more than 50% but at least 10% by weight of acrylonitrile units ($-CH_2-CH-$).
$$\underset{\displaystyle CN}{|}$$

The term *lastrile* may be used as a generic description for fibers falling within this category, (3) a manufactured fiber in which the fiber-forming substance is a polychloroprene or a copolymer of chloroprene in which at least 35% by weight of the fiber-forming substance is composed of chloroprene units ($-CH_2-C=CH-CH_2-$).
$$\underset{\displaystyle Cl}{|}$$

Performance Expectations of Rubber/Synthetic Rubber Fibers

Absorbency Nonabsorbent
Covering Power Depends on size of extruded strip
Effect of Heat Sensitive to extreme temperatures; softens, melts and loses strength in heat
Elasticity High; elastomeric fiber
Elongation High
Flexibility Pliable
Pilling Subject to some pilling
Resiliency/Wrinkle Recovery High
Resistance
    Abrasion Good
    Chemical Resistant to acids
    Flame Melts
    Sunlight Damaged by sunlight
Static Electricity Some static buildup
Strength/Durability Good

SPECIAL COMMENTS
Rubber yarns may be produced as uncovered or bare yarns or as a monofilament core covered with another fiber. Rubber is used with other fiber yarns to produce elastics or fabrics.
Care Factors Washable in cold or warm water with cold water soaps. Extreme *cold* temperatures cause rubber to become brittle and crack. Extreme *hot* temperatures cause rubber to soften, melt and lose strength and elasticity.

Properties & Characteristics of Spandex Fibers

Spandex is a manufactured fiber in which the fiber-forming substance is a long-chain synthetic polymer comprised of at least 85% of a segmented polyurethane.
Spandex is extruded as a monofilament or in a multiplicity of fine filaments which immediately coagulate to form a monofilament.

Performance Expectations of Spandex Fibers

Absorbency Poor; hydrophobic fiber; 0.75%-1.3% moisture regain
Affinity to Dyestuff Good; colorfast
Covering Power Good
Effect of Heat Deteriorates and loses elasticity when subjected to heat
Elasticity High; elastomeric fiber; 440%-770% elongation at breaking point
Elongation 93.5%-96% recovery at 5% elongation
Flexibility Supple; pliable
Pilling No problem
Resiliency/Wrinkle Recovery Good; resists wrinkling
Resistance
    Abrasion Fair to good
    Biological Resistant to moths and mildew
    Chemical Resistant to solvents, sea water, oil and grease; resistant to most alkalies; deteriorates in chlorine bleach
    Flame Melts at 446°F-518°F (230°C-270°C)
    Sunlight Deteriorates when subjected to sunlight
Shrinkage/Dimensional Stability Good resistance; good shape retention
Static Electricity Some static buildup
Strength/Durability Poor strength compensated by high fiber stretch. Able to stretch over 500% without breaking

SPECIAL COMMENTS
Spandex fiber is produced as an uncovered or bare yarn and as a monofilament core covered with other spun or filament yarns. Spandex fiber is used with other fiber yarns to produce fabric.
Comfort Factors Has high stretch and holding power; lends lightweight freedom of movement to garment; improves fit, comfort and appearance of garment.
Stretch and Recovery High stretch and recovery properties; stretches with 100% snap-back to original size and shape
Care Factors May be laundered or dry cleaned; easily laundered; quick drying; deteriorates and yellows when subject to chlorine bleach; safe ironing temperature limit 300°F (200.1°C); not affected by body oils and perspiration.

Properties & Characteristics of Triacetate Fibers

Triacetate is a manufactured fiber in which the fiber-forming substance is cellulose acetate. Where not less than 92% of the hydroxyl groups are acetylated, the term triacetate may be used as a generic description of the fiber.

Performance Expectations of Triacetate Fibers

Absorbency Poor; hydrophobic fiber; 3.2% moisture regain

Affinity to Dyestuff Good; easy to dye; wide range of colors; colorfast

Covering Power Poor

Effect of Heat Thermoplastic fiber; allows for heat-set pleats and creases

Elasticity 25%–40% elongation at breaking point

Elongation 88% recovery at 3% elongation; 65% recovery at 5% elongation

Flexibility Good

Luster Good

Pilling No problem

Resiliency/Wrinkle Recovery Good; resists wrinkles

Resistance
 Abrasion Poor
 Biological Resistant to moths and mildew
 Chemical Dissolves in acetate
 Flame Melts at 575°F (302°C)
 Sunlight Good resistance to sunlight; resistant to fading

Shrinkage/Dimensional Stability Good dimensional stability; shrink resistant; good shape retention

Static Electricity Some static buildup

Strength/Durability Poor; loses 30% of strength when wet; stronger than acetate when wet

SPECIAL COMMENTS

Comfort Factors Maintains crisp finish and retains pleats.

Care Factors May be laundered or dry cleaned; easily laundered; quick drying; easy to iron; safe ironing temperature limit 375°F (192.1°C).

Properties & Characteristics of Vinyl Fibers

Vinyl is a manufactured fiber in which the fiber-forming substance is any long-chain synthetic polymer composed of at least 50% by weight of vinyl alcohol units ($-CH_2-CHOH-$) and in which the total of the vinyl alcohol units and any one or more of the various acetal units is at least 85% by weight of the fiber.

Performance Expectations of Vinyl Fibers

Absorbency Nonabsorbent

Effect of Heat Softens at low temperatures; melts at 425°F (219.1°C)

Elasticity Good

Resiliency/Wrinkle Recovery Poor

Resistance
 Abrasion Good
 Chemical High resistance to chemicals
 Sunlight Resistant to weathering

Strength/Durability Good tensile and tear strength; loses 25% in strength when wet

SPECIAL COMMENTS

No production of fiber in the United States, but it is produced in foreign countries. Manufactured by the Air Reduction Company for use in industrial products.

Properties & Characteristics of Vinyon Fibers

Vinyon is a manufactured fiber in which the fiber-forming substance is any long-chain synthetic polymer composed of at least 85% by weight of vinyl chloride units ($-CH_2-CHCl-$).

Performance Expectations of Vinyon Fibers

Absorbency Poor; hydrophobic fiber; 0.5% moisture regain

Effect of Heat Heat sensitive; thermoplastic resin properties; allows for embossing, molding and bulking effects; low softening and melting temperatures; allows for heat sealing and bonding under controlled temperatures and conditions

Elongation Elongates under stress and contracts under heat

Resistance

Biological Resistant to moths, mildew, perspiration

Chemical High resistance to chemicals; resistant to acids and alkalies

Flame Does not support combustion; nonflammable; melts at 260°F (127°C)

Strength/Durability High wet and dry strength

SPECIAL COMMENTS

Used primarily as bonding agent for nonwoven fabric structure. It has the ability to shrink either alone or in combination with other fibers and yarns. Low moisture absorbency produces water-repellent qualities.

cotton staple fiber

flax staple fiber

silk filament fiber

nylon filament fiber

man-made filament staple

Fiber Length

Wide variations of fiber lengths occur *within* a fiber of the same source as well as *between* varieties obtained from different sources.

Fibers of relatively short length are referred to as *staple fibers* and are measured in inches or centimeters. Staple fibers include all natural fibers *except* silk—silk is a natural filament fiber. Man-made fibers, manufactured in filament form, and silk filament fibers may be cut up to form short staple fibers. Staple fibers must be spun or twisted together to make a long continuous strand of yarn. They may also be used in their staple form to produce nonwoven or felted fabrics.

Fibers of long, continuous length are referred to as *filament fibers* and are measured in yards or meters.

Silk, in filament form, is reeled from cocoons.

Man-made fibers of a chemical composition liquid nature are forced through spinnerettes, hardened and produced into continuous filament strands of a determined length.

When filament fibers are planned to be cut into staple fibers, a large spinnerette with many openings is used. The filament fibers are grouped into a bundle referred to as a *tow* and then cut into the desired staple length.

Line or *tow* man-made fibers are manufactured in continuous strands of any desired length. The tows may be cut into staple lengths, or flocks for specific end use.

Classification of Natural Fiber Lengths

Fiber	Length
Cotton	Very Short/less than ¾″ (1.9 cm) Short/ ¹³/₁₆″ – ¹⁵/₁₆″ (2.06–2.38 cm) Medium/ ¹⁵/₁₆″–1⅛″ (2.38–2.86 cm) Long/1⅛″–1⅜″ (2.86–3.49cm) Extra Long/1⅜″ (3.49 cm) or longer
Flax (Linen)	from 5″–40″ (12.7–101.6 cm) *tow fibers*/11″ (27.9 cm) or shorter *line fibers*/12″ (30.5 cm) or longer
Silk	usually from 1000 to 1300 yards sometimes up to 3000 yards (2700 meters)
Wool	Short/2½″ (3.14 cm) or shorter Medium/2½″–4″ (3.14–10.16 cm) Long/4″ (10.16 cm) or longer

Classification of Specialty Hair Fiber Lengths

Hair from the following animals varies in length from 1″ to 16″ (2.54–40.64 cm) depending on animal and location of hair on animal.

Origin	Approximate Length of Fiber	Characteristics of Fiber
Angora Goat (Mohair)	usually 4″–6″ (10.16–15.24 cm) occasionally 9″–12″ (22.86–30.48 cm)	fine, springy translucent
Angora Rabbit	3″–5″ (7.62–12.7 cm)	fine, soft
Camel Hair	under hairs/1″–5″ (2.54–12.7 cm) outer hairs/up to 15″ (38.1 cm)	short, fine, soft long, coarse, tough
Cashmere Goat	short hairs/1″–3″ (2.54–8.89 cm) long hairs/2″–5″ (5.08–12.7 cm)	fine, soft straight, stiff, coarse

Llama
   Alpaca
   Llama
   Vicuna
	
	up to 16″ (40.6 cm)
	10″–12″ (25.4–30.48 cm)
	up to 5″ (12.7 cm)
		
		fine, soft
		thick, coarse
		extremely fine
		   (finest of all hair fibers)

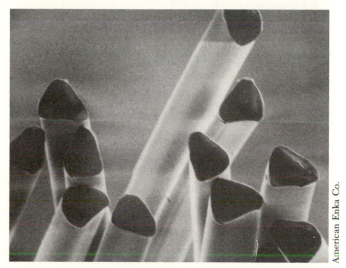

nylon, round/500X

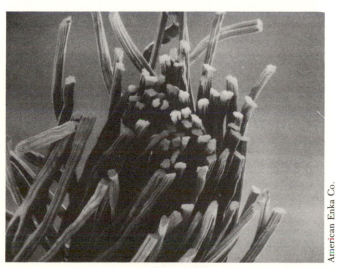

nylon, triangular/500X

rayon, square/200X

Fiber Diameter

The diameter of a fiber is the distance across the fiber's cross section.

The diameter of *natural staple fibers* is irregular and may vary from one part of the fiber to another. Staple fiber diameters are measured in *microns*.

The diameter of the smooth, even *filament man-made fibers* is uniform. The diameter of man-made fibers can be controlled during the manufacturing process by changing the size of the openings in the spinnerette. The sizes of the spinnerette openings range from fine to heavy; small openings produce fine filament fibers. Filament fiber diameters are measured in *denier*.

Natural and man-made fibers may be altered or changed *purposely* to produce irregularities for special or novelty effects.

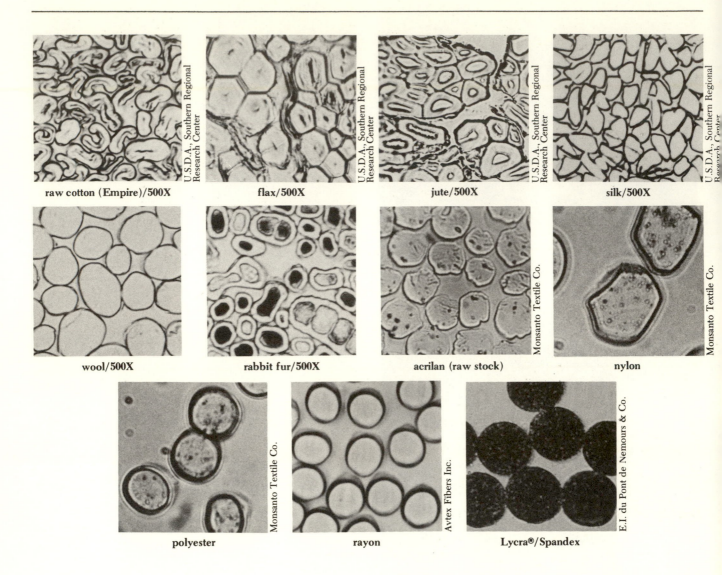

raw cotton (Empire)/500X — U.S.D.A., Southern Regional Research Center

flax/500X — U.S.D.A., Southern Regional Research Center

jute/500X — U.S.D.A., Southern Regional Research Center

silk/500X — U.S.D.A., Southern Regional Research Center

wool/500X

rabbit fur/500X

acrilan (raw stock) — Monsanto Textile Co.

nylon — Monsanto Textile Co.

polyester — Monsanto Textile Co.

rayon — Avtex Fibers Inc.

Lycra®/Spandex — E.I. du Pont de Nemours & Co.

Fiber Shape/Cross-Section of Fibers

The shape of a fiber can be determined by the cross-section form of the fiber when viewed through a microscope. Fiber shape is inherent in natural fibers.

The shape of man-made fibers may be induced or controlled during the manufacturing process by changing the type and the size of the openings in the spinnerette.

Cross-section form of the fiber will vary from fiber to fiber. The variations in the cross-section shapes will produce differences in the characteristics of fibers which will effect the covering power and light-reflecting qualities of the fiber and/or yarn.

Engineered or second-generation fibers have modified cross-section shapes.

Cross-section shapes are modified to:

- Produce higher luster
- Reduce undesired luster
- Induce softer and pliable hand
- Induce better soil cloaking properties

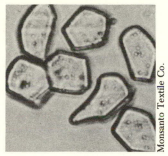
flat

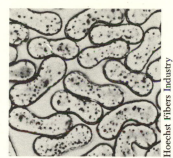
dogbone/peanut

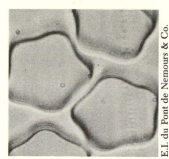
pentalobal

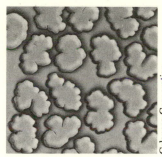
multilobal

Monsanto Textile Co.

Hoechst Fibers Industry

E.I. du Pont de Nemours & Co.

Celanese Corporation

Fiber Shapes & Characteristics of Cross-Sectional Forms

Fiber Shapes	Characteristics of Cross-Sectional Form of Fibers
Round or Oval	Smooth Soft Slippery feel High reflecting pattern High luster (unless treated with delusterants) Fibers packed closely Less surface area; Poor covering power
Flat (spinnerette openings are shaped rectangularly)	Reflects more light than round fibers
Dog Bone/Peanut	Produces a harsh fiber Hand is less smooth than round fibers High luster and glitter luster Excellent covering power
Trilobal (three-sided or three-lobed fiber)	Silk-like feel Reflects more light than round fibers Reflects light from surface and each lobe Produces increased luster Excellent covering power
Pentalobal (five-sided or five-lobed fiber)	Star-shaped effect Produces bulkier fiber Reflects light from each lobe Produces less shiny fabric with soft, subdued sheen
Octolobal (compressed into flat-sided hexagons)	Flat sides reflect light allowing for light to scatter or disperse Reduces objectionable glitter from round fibers Produces subdued luster
Multilobal (any fiber with a number of pentalobals)	Reflects light from each lobe

Fiber Contour

Fiber contour can be determined by the *longitudinal* surface form of the fiber. Fiber contour will vary from fiber to fiber. It is inherent in natural fibers and may be induced or controlled in man-made fibers.

Longitudinal surface form or surface contour is classified:

- Smooth—Even or uniform contour
- Rough—Uneven contour
- Irregular—Nodes or ridges
- Scales—Various sizes from small to coarse
- Twisted—Natural or induced; slight to heavy
- Crimp—Natural or induced; slight to close

twisted (raw cotton)

U.S.D.A., Southern Regional Research Center

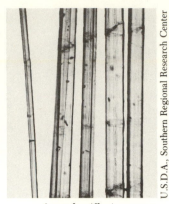

irregular (flax)

U.S.D.A., Southern Regional Research Center

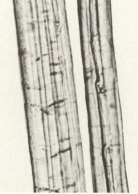

irregular (jute)

U.S.D.A., Southern Regional Research Center

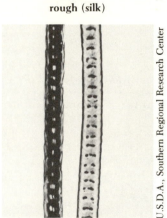

rough (silk)

U.S.D.A., Southern Regional Research Center

scales (wool)

U.S.D.A., Southern Regional Research Center

scales (rabbit fur)

U.S.D.A., Southern Regional Research Center

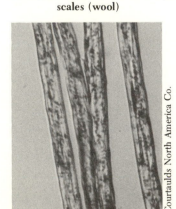

smooth (rayon)

Courtaulds North America Co.

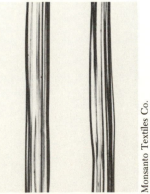

smooth (modacrylic)

Monsanto Textiles Co.

Fiber Spinnability/Fiber Cohesiveness

Spinnability/cohesiveness is the ability of natural and man-made fibers to cling together. The properties of fiber spinnability are dependent on the surface contour and internal structure or shape of the fibers. The natural or induced twist or crimp of a fiber gives the fiber cohesiveness, allowing the fibers to hold together during the spinning process.

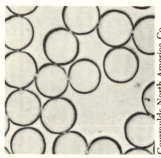

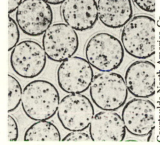

bright (nylon)/300X   semi-matt (nylon)/500X

Fiber Light-Reflecting Qualities

Light-reflecting is a term used to define the fiber's ability to reflect or diffuse light. Natural and man-made fibers vary in light-reflecting qualities, ranging from flat or dull to lustrous or bright. The cross-section shape of the fiber contributes to the fiber's luster or dullness.

Man-made fibers can be changed or modified to achieve the desired dullness, shine, luster or brightness. Titanium dioxide may be added to the fiber to deluster the natural brightness.

Natural fibers may be made more lustrous by various finishing processes during the yarn or fabric stage.

Light-reflecting qualities relate to:

- Origin of fiber
- Shape of fiber
- Natural luster or sheen of fiber or yarn
- Natural dullness of fiber or yarn
- Need for special lusterants, brighteners or delusterants
- Need for special fabric finishes
- Visual appearance of fabric

Fiber Dyeability

Dyeability depends on the fiber's ability to absorb the dye. The ability of the fiber to absorb dyestuff relates to the size of the pore openings on the outer surface of the fiber or the porosity of the fiber.

Fiber Variants/Second Generation Man-Made Fibers

Man-made fibers can be modified both physically and chemically, causing a molecular change, producing a different fiber. Fiber modifications may be made by changing the spinning solution, technique of extrusion or coagulation of the fibers. Fiber modifications are called *fiber variants, second generation man-made fibers* or *fiber types*.

Fiber variants/second generation man-made fibers are a product of a particular company's continous research program. The exploration expands the potential of the original fiber and develops properties and characteristics in the newly developed fibers that are suitable for a new end use. Variants are also developed for a specific or special purpose and are engineered to offer improved performance and aesthetic characteristics such as:

- Greater comfort
- Reduced static or clinging
- Flame resistance
- Dyeability properties
- Greater whiteness
- Luster or delustering
- Special hand
- Better blending with other fibers
- Ready availability
- Consistent quality

Although variants/second generation fibers are similar, each fiber has its own properties and characteristics as produced by the member company. Variants are given a trademark name which is owned and promoted by the individual fiber manufacturers who developed and produced the fiber. Fiber manufacturers may have more than one trademark for the same generic fiber. The variety of trademarks indicate some difference in the manufacturing or production of the fiber. Each trademark name will have different characteristics and must conform to the basic Federal Trade Commission generic family definition.

Cotton, flax (linen), silk, and wool are natural fibers and do not carry a trademark in the way man-made fibers do. However, the following information is important to cotton, linen and wool.

Cotton fibers of longer staple length are referred to by the following:

- Egyptian Cotton
- Pima Cotton
- Pima I
- Pima 32
- Super-Pima
- Sea Island Cotton

Linen fabrics have names that indicate where the linen is produced and the quality of linen:

- Irish Linen
- Belgium Linen
- Moygashel® (made from smoother and harder flax fibers)

In *wool* fabrics the following is important:

- The woolmark symbol identifies fabrics made of 100 percent wool fibers.
- The woolblend mark identifies fabrics made with wool blended with other fibers.

Fiber Trademarks
Listed by Generic Fiber Name*

GENERIC FIBER	TRADEMARK NAME	COMPANY
ACETATE	Acetate by Avtex	Avtex Fibers Inc.
	Ariloft	Eastman Chemical Products, Inc.
	Avron	Avtex Fibers Inc.
	Celanese	Celanese Fibers Marketing Co., Celanese Corporation
	Celacloud	Celanese Fibers Marketing Co., Celanese Corporation
	Celacrimp	Celanese Fibers Marketing Co., Celanese Corporation
	Celafil	Celanese Fibers Marketing Co., Celanese Corporation
	Celaloft	Celanese Fibers Marketing Co., Celanese Corporation
	Celaperm	Celanese Fibers Marketing Co., Celanese Corporation
	Celara	Celanese Fibers Marketing Co., Celanese Corporation
	Celarandom	Celanese Fibers Marketing Co., Celanese Corporation
	Cela Tow	Celanese Fibers Marketing Co., Celanese Corporation
	Celatress	Celanese Fibers Marketing Co., Celanese Corporation
	Celaspun	Celanese Fibers Marketing Co., Celanese Corporation
	Chromspun	Eastman Chemical Products, Inc.
	Estron	Eastman Chemical Products, Inc.
	Lanese	Celanese Fibers Marketing Co., Celanese Corporation
	Loftura	Eastman Chemical Products, Inc.
ACRYLIC	Acrilan	Monsanto Textiles Company
	Bi-Loft	Monsanto Textiles Company
	Creslan	American Cyanamid Company
	Fi-lana	Monsanto Textiles Company
	Fina	Monsanto Textiles Company
	Orlon	E.I. du Pont de Nemours & Co., Inc.
	Pa-Qel	Monsanto Textiles Company
	Remember	Monsanto Textiles Company
	So-Lara	Monsanto Textiles Company
	Zefran	Badische Corporation
ARAMID	Kevlar	E.I. du Pont de Nemours & Co., Inc.
	Nomex	E.I. du Pont de Nemours & Co., Inc.
METALLIC	Lurex	Badische Corporation
	X-Static	Rohm & Haas Co.
MODACRYLIC	SEF	Monsanto Textiles Company
	Verel	Eastman Chemical Products, Inc.
NYLON	A.C.E.	Allied Fibers and Plastics Company
	Anso	Allied Fibers and Plastics Company
	Antron	E.I. du Pont de Nemours & Co., Inc.
	Blue "C"	Monsanto Textiles Company
	Cadon	Monsanto Textiles Company
	Cantrece	E.I. du Pont de Nemours & Co., Inc.
	Caprolan	Allied Fibers and Plastics Company
	Celanese	Celanese Fibers Marketing Co., Celanese Corporation
	Cordura	E.I. du Pont de Nemours & Co., Inc.
	Courtaulds Nylon	Courtaulds North America Inc.
	Crepeset	American Enka Company
	Cumuloft	Monsanto Textiles Company
	Eloquent Luster	Allied Fibers and Plastics Company
	Eloquent Touch	Allied Fibers and Plastics Company
	Enkalure	American Enka Company
	Enkasheer	American Enka Company
	Golden Touch	American Enka Company
	Lurelon	American Enka Company
	Matte Touch	American Enka Company
	Multisheer	American Enka Company
	Natura Luster	Allied Fibers and Plastics Company
	Natural Touch	American Enka Company

GENERIC FIBER	TRADEMARK NAME	COMPANY
	Qiana	E.I. du Pont de Nemours & Co., Inc.
	Shareen	Courtaulds North America Inc.
	Shimmereen	American Enka Company
	Softalon	American Enka Company
	Ultron	Monsanto Textiles Company
	Zefran	Badische Corporation
	Zeftron	Badische Corporation
OLEFIN	Herculon	Hercules Incorporated
	Marquesa	Amoco Fabrics Company
	Marvess	Phillips Fibers Corporation, subsidiary of Phillips Petroleum
	Company	
	Patlon	Amoco Fabrics Company
	Polyloom	Chevron Fibers, Inc., subsidiary of Chevron Chemical Company
	Vectra	Chevron Fibers, Inc., subsidiary of Chevron Chemical Company
POLYESTER	A.C.E.	Allied Fibers and Plastics Company
	Avlin	Avtex Fibers Inc.
	Blue "C"	Monsanto Textiles Company
	Caprolan	Allied Fibers and Plastics Company
	Dacron	E.I. du Pont de Nemours & Co., Inc.
	Encron	American Enka Company
	Encron MCS	American Enka Company
	Encron 8	American Enka Company
	Enka 3	American Enka Company
	Fortrel	Fibers Industries, Inc. Marketed by Celanese Fibers Marketing Co.
	Fortrel 7	Fibers Industries, Inc. Marketed by Celanese Fibers Marketing Co.
	Golden Glow	American Enka Company
	Golden Touch	American Enka Company
	Hollofil	E.I. du Pont de Nemours & Co. Inc.
	Kodel	Eastman Chemical Products, Inc.
	KodOfill	Eastman Chemical Products, Inc.
	KodOlite	Eastman Chemical Products, Inc.
	KodOsoff	Eastman Chemical Products, Inc.
	Matte Touch	American Enka Company
	Natural Touch	American Enka Company
	Plyloc	American Enka Company
	Polyextra	American Enka Company
	Shanton	American Enka Company
	Silky Touch	American Enka Company
	Spectran	Monsanto Textiles Company
	Strialine	American Enka Company
	Trevira	American Hoechst Corporation
	Twisloc	Monsanto Textiles Company
RAYON	Absorbit	American Enka Company
	Avril	Avtex Fibers Inc.
	Avsorb	Avtex Fibers Inc.
	Beau-Grip	North American Rayon Corporation
	Coloray	Courtaulds North America Inc.
	Durvil	Avtex Fibers Inc.
	Enkaire	American Enka Company
	Enkrome	American Enka Company
	Fibro	Courtaulds North America Inc.
	Rayon by Avtex	Avtex Fibers Inc.
	Zantrel	American Enka Company
	Zantrel 700	American Enka Company
SPANDEX	Lycra	E.I. du Pont de Nemours & Co., Inc.
TRIACETATE	Arnel	Celanese Fibers Marketing Company
VINYON	Vinyon by Avtex	Avtex Fibers Inc.

*Based on the listing from Man-Made Fibers Producers Association, Inc. and reflects the additions and deletions of trademarks as developments and improvements allow.

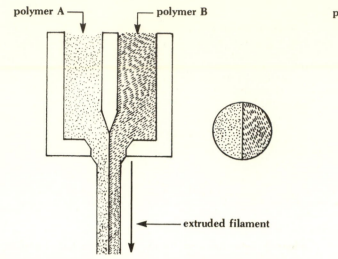

polymer A ⟶   ⟵ polymer B

⟵ extruded filament

BICOMPONENT & BICONSTITUTE FIBERS/SIDE-BY-SIDE

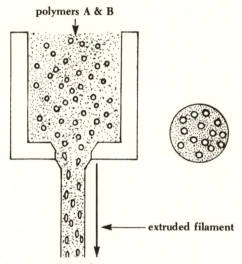

polymers A & B

⟵ extruded filament

**BICOMPONENT & BICONSTITUTE
FIBERS/MATRIX & FIBRILS**

polymer A ⟶   ⟵ polymer B

⟵ extruded filament

**BICOMPONENT & BICONSTITUTE
FIBERS/SHEATH CORE**

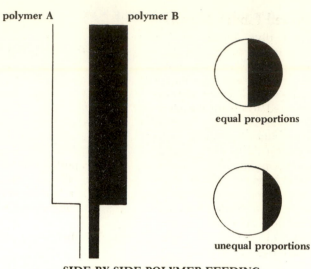

polymer A   polymer B

equal proportions

unequal proportions

SIDE-BY-SIDE POLYMER FEEDING

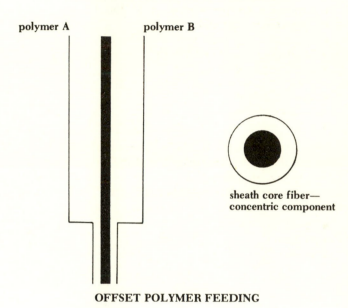

polymer A   polymer B

sheath core fiber—
concentric component

OFFSET POLYMER FEEDING

polymer A   polymer B

sheath core fiber—
eccentric component

OFFSET POLYMER FEEDING

Blended Fibers/Blends

Blended fibers/blends combine two or more fiber substances into a single fiber strand or yarn with modified or changed properties and appearance of the fiber, yarn or fabric. Each fiber has a separate set of physical and aesthetic characteristics inherent in its design. The blended fibers are engineered to create the kind of fibers required to meet specific needs of the industry. Fiber blends have their own characteristics depending on the type and the percentage of the specific fibers used. Each fiber in a blend adds not only favorable properties but also undesirable properties. Fiber blends, however, utilize the advantages of all fibers to counteract the disadvantages of each single fiber. Man-made fibers can be blended with one or more other fibers, either natural or man-made.

Type, quality, and percentage of different fibers selected for blending depends on:

- Positive vs. negative qualities of each fiber
- Performance expectation modification desired
- Appearance, feel and hand desired
- Color and texture effects desired
- Drapability qualities desired
- End use of fabric
- Weight and opacity of fabric
- Care of fabric
- Availability of fibers
- Cost

Blends with regard to the properties of each fiber, enhance the physical characteristics of the fabric, allow for cross dyeing and new color effects and for improved spinning, weaving and finishing procedures. Blends improve the fabric's:

- Hand
- Weight
- Feel
- Texture
- Performance Expectations
- Drapability Qualities
- Appearance

According to the Federal Trade Commission, it is mandatory that each fiber and the percentage of each fiber in the blend be specified by its generic name and trademark.

Blends are defined as: *biconstituted fibers* and *bicomponent* or *bilateral fibers.*

Biconstituted Fiber The process of combining two different polymers homogeneously, mixed or blended together during or before extruding through the spinnerette. Biconstituted fiber blending process combines the characteristics and properties of the two materials or substances into a single filament fiber.

Bicomponent/Bilateral Fibers The process of blending or combining different substances or polymers during the extruding process. Two different polymers, with different heat and moisture properties, may be extruded side by side as it comes from the spinnerette forming a single filament fiber when hardened. Bicomponent fiber blending process produces a bulked, fluffed or textured fiber. The bicomponent blending process:

- Produces finer denier
- Allows for developing crimp, bulked or textured fibers
- Improves colorfastness of fiber
- Changes moisture absorption properties
- Modifies the fiber for antistatic properties
- Allows a wider range of fiber, yarn and fabric development
- Increases the fiber's, yarn's and fabric's resistance to pilling
- Allows for resistance to stitch distortion, for retention of fabric and garment shape
- Provides for softer hand

opening method

roving method

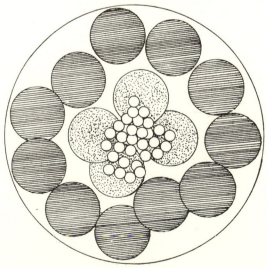

spinning method

Mixed Fiber Yarns

Mixed fiber yarns are the combination of two or more strands of different fibers to form one yarn. Mixed fiber yarns may:

1. be of any conventional or novelty construction;
2. contain two or more plies;
3. contain equal or unequal fiber percentages;
4. be of any twist tension desired.

Mixed fiber yarns are classified as *spun blended yarns*, *blended ply yarns* and *mixture/combination yarns*.

Spun Blend Yarns   Fibers from two or more textile sources are spun into a yarn. Spun blends may be of equal or unequal fiber percentages.

Blended Ply Yarns   Different fiber strands are twisted together to form one yarn.

Mixture/Combination Yarn   Yarns utilizing two or more different types of yarns of different fiber contents.

There are three methods used to blend fibers:
- Opening Method
- Roving Method
- Spinning Method

Opening Method   Fibers are fed into the machine alternately from two or more bales.

Roving Method   Different fiber strands are combined and twisted together drawing the slivers to a size suitable for spinning.

Spinning Method   The combing of two strands twisted into a single yarn. Long fine fibers migrate towards the center while shorter fibers remain to the outside.

2 ~ Yarns

Yarns are the components or materials that are used in the production of fabrics. Yarns are comprised of any variation or combination of staple or filament fibers that have been made into yarn forms by various processes creating different yarn structures.

Yarns may be spun into a continuous strand from staple or filament form fibers or may be extruded directly into monofilament form. Any combination of spun, filament or textured yarns may be used for specific purposes, variation or novelty effect. The variations provide interest and change, producing the different fabrics on the market.

Properties and characteristics of yarns depend on:
- Composition or origin of fiber (natural or man-made)
- Length of fiber (staple or filament)
- Type of yarn (spun or filament)
- Count (thickness, diameter or size of yarn)
- Number of strands of yarn (single, plied or core)
- Construction of yarn (simple, complex or textured)
- Twist of yarn (direction of twist)
- Tension of yarn (degree of twist)
- Yarn dyeability (application of dyestuff)

Yarns and fibers interrelate. Different types of fibers and yarns have basic inherent properties. If the type of fiber or yarn is changed, the basic characteristics of the fabrics will be different causing fabric expectations to be different. Yarn size, count, number of strands, twist and structure also interrelate.

Changing, altering or combining any of the components will affect the appearance, texture and drapability qualities of the fabric.

The type of yarn or yarns selected for fabric structure depends on:
- End use of fabric
- Type of fabric
- Structure of fabric
- Appearance, hand and performance expectation of fabric
- Need or demand of fabric
- Price limit of fabric
- Relationship to brand name requirements:
  - Quality of performance
  - Dependency of performance
  - Reliability of performance

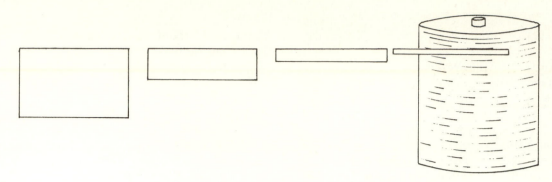

Yarn processing incorporates progressive operations by which a mass
of fiber is gradually converted into finer and finer yarns by
a drawing process.

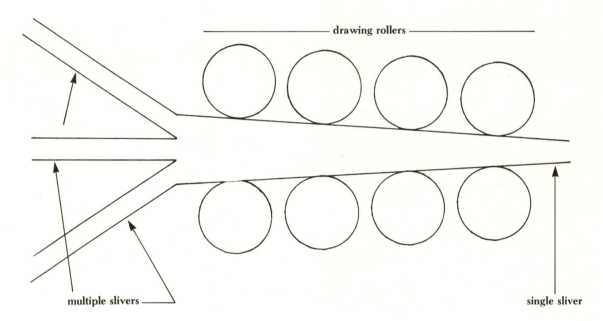

In a drawing process multiple slivers are drawn into a narrower
single sliver.

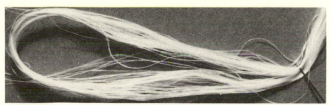
filament tow

monofilament yarn (untextured)/200X

polyester monofilament yarn

rayon monofilament yarn

multifilament yarn

Yarn Type

Types of yarn includes *spun yarns* and *filament yarns*. Yarns may be made by utilizing only staple or filament fibers or strands or by combining both.

Filament tow is a term applied to a long ropelike bundle of raw fibers which has not been cut or processed into staple form. The tow is composed of numerous strands of continuous fibers which are extruded from the spinnerette in preparation of forming a tow to be processed for cutting.

Filament yarns are also classified as *monofilament* and *multifilament*.

Characteristics of Spun & Filament Yarns

Spun Yarns
Composed of short staple fibers of definite length
Made from natural cotton, flax or wool staple fibers
Made from natural or man-made filaments which are chopped or cut into short lengths and referred to as filament staple yarn
Individual fiber lengths vary
Bigger and wider in diameter than filament fiber yarns
Fuzzy appearance and feel; fiber ends protrude from yarn
Uneven number of fibers throughout
Range from soft, loose construction to hard-finished, fine twist yarn
Thick-and-thin areas
Highly twisted
Fall apart when untwisted
Dull or flat in appearance
Rough to the touch
Natural textural appearance and feel
Bulkier to the feel
Provide good covering power
Snagging depends on fabric structure
Pilling depends on fiber content

Filament Yarns
Composed of long, continuous fibers
Made from natural silk fibers
Made from man-made fibers
Fine and smooth
More uniform in diameter than spun yarn
Equal number of filaments throughout
Provides lustrous, shiny or gossamer-sheen appearance
Softer and more pliable than spun yarns
Thick to thin diameters
Light-to heavyweight
Loosely twisted
Do not fall apart when untwisted
Filaments separate when untwisted and can be counted
Stronger than spun yarn of the same diameter
Poor covering power
Produce high seam and yarn slippage
Snagging depends on fiber structure
Pilling depends on fiber content
May be bundled into a "tow" which will be cut into staple size

carded cotton yarn

combed cotton yarn

Cotton Spun Yarns

Cotton fiber and cotton-type fiber spun yarns are classified as *carded yarns* and *combed yarns*.

The fiber mass in *cotton carded yarns* lack uniformity and parallelization. The process of double carding, which is applied to some yarns, produces a more uniform yarn and some fiber parallelization is attempted.

Cotton combed yarns are made of cotton fibers longer in length than those used for carded yarns. During the combing process, the fiber mass is straightened and fibers are parallelized producing yarns that are even, strong, clean and smooth.

Characteristics of Combed & Carded Cotton Yarns

Combed Yarns
Made of the longest staple fibers
Produce even yarns
Close fabric structure
Fine, smooth fabric structure

Carded Yarns
Made of the shortest staple fibers
Produce uneven yarns
Produce thick or coarse yarns
Visible in the fabric structure due to unevenness
Low fabric structure
Loose, coarse or napped fabric structure

Belgian Linen Association

glossy flax emerging from the combing process

Linen Spun Yarns

Flax fibers and linen-type fiber spun yarns are classified as tow yarns and line yarns.

Characteristics of Tow & Line Linen Yarns

Tow Yarns
Made from shorter fibers of various lengths
Thick and coarse
Uneven and irregular
Produce bulkier yarns
Loose, open and rough fabric structure

Line Yarns
Made from longer fibers
Fine
Smooth and even
Fine, lightweight fabric structure

Wool Spun Yarns

Wool staple fiber and wool-type fiber spun yarns are classified as *woolen yarns* and *worsted yarns*.

Characteristics of Woolen & Worsted Yarns

Woolen Yarns
Made from *carded yarns*
Fuzzy; fiber ends protrude from yarn
Uneven diameter
Bulky and thick
Spongy and springy feel
Result in soft, bouncy fabric structure
Hidden weave construction
Allow for napping and brushing finishes
Produce insulating properties providing warmth
Resist wrinkling; wrinkles hang out
Do not hold a crease well

Worsted Yarns
Made from *combed yarns*
Smooth
Even diameter
Tightly twisted
Fine, hard yarns
Distinct weave construction
Do not produce insulating properties
Show undesirable wrinkles
Maintain desired crease

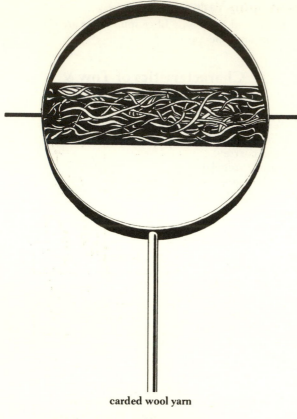

carded wool yarn

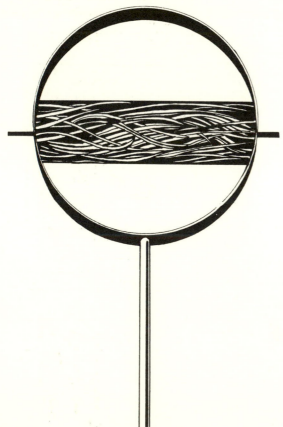

combed worsted wool yarn

Differences in the Manufacturing of Woolen & Worsted Yarns

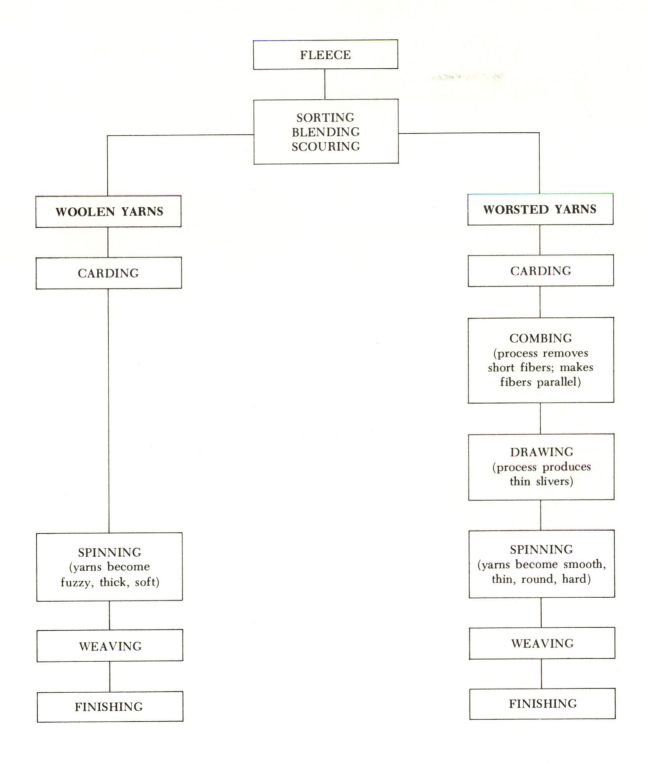

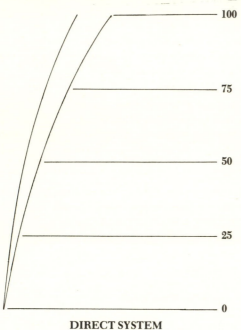

DIRECT SYSTEM

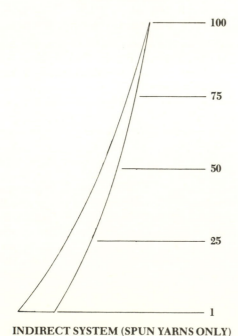

INDIRECT SYSTEM (SPUN YARNS ONLY)

Yarn Count/Yarn Size/Yarn Thickness

Yarn count is the physical thickness, coarseness or fineness of yarn which can be measured and defined as fine increasing in size to thick or coarse.

The size or thickness of the yarn relates to a unit of length and weight of the yarn and also influences the covering power of the yarn. Yarns of finer thickness require a *greater number* of yarns to fill a square-inch measured space of fabric. Yarns of coarse or greater thickness require *less yarns* to fill the same square-inch measured space. High covering power or good covering power translates to mean, *fewer* yarns are required. Low or poor covering power—*many* yarns are required.

Yarn count and yarn thicknesses are measured by a *direct* and *indirect system of measuring*. The direct system is used to measure all filament yarns. The indirect or inverse proportion system is used to measure all spun yarns.

Direct System/Decitex System/dtex   This system measures filament yarns only. The direct system is a direct reading whereby the weight of the fiber is the same as the yarn count. Weight is measured in grams, the grams equal the denier count. The basic unit used for measuring is 9000 meters or one gram.

As the number increases, the physical size of the yarn gets thicker. Fine or thin yarns will have a lower count than coarse, thick yarns.

Indirect System/Yarn Count System   This system measures spun yarns only. The yarn count number is inversely proportioned to the weight of the yarn. As the number increases, the physical size of the yarn gets finer and thinner. A fine, sheer yarn will have a higher count number than a coarse, thick yarn.

Yarn count standards differ for each staple fiber classification. Yarn count standards represent the number of yards in one pound of a number one count of that specific yarn.

Specific	# of Yards in One Pound
Cotton/Cotton Blends	840
Linen/Linen Blends (LEA)	300
Silk (SPUN)	840
Wool/Wool Blends (CUT)	300
Wool/Wool Blends (RUN)	1600
Worsted/Worsted Blends	560
Man-made Fibers (SPUN)	840
100% Acrylic (SPUN STAPLE)	560

Tex System   This is a direct system of measuring. It is used to measure both filament and spun yarns of silk, regenerated cellulosic fibers and man-made fibers. As the numbers increase, the physical size of the yarn gets thicker. The tex system using fixed weights, states the weight of 1000m of a given yarn.

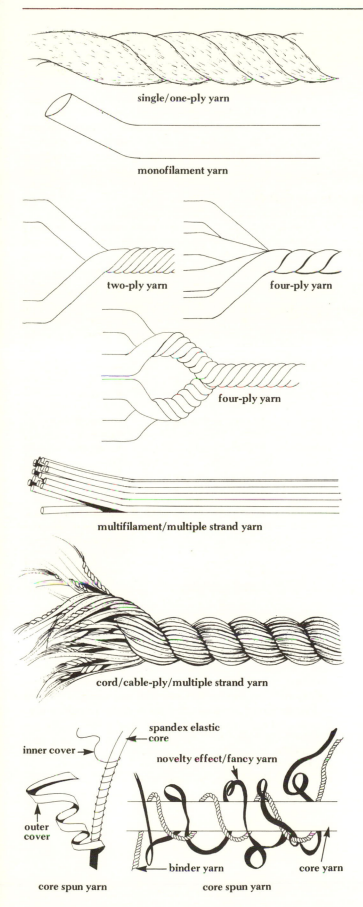

single/one-ply yarn

monofilament yarn

two-ply yarn

four-ply yarn

four-ply yarn

multifilament/multiple strand yarn

cord/cable-ply/multiple strand yarn

inner cover

spandex elastic core

novelty effect/fancy yarn

outer cover

binder yarn

core yarn

core spun yarn

core spun yarn

Number of Strands in a Yarn

Yarns are made up of one or more strands of twisted or bonded fibers. They are classified as *single yarns* or *ply yarns*.

Single One-ply Yarn   A yarn composed of one strand that makes up a single yarn. Single yarn is produced by spinning and is considered an initial twisting operation. When untwisted, the fibers separate and come apart.

Monofilament Yarn   A single strand of filament form yarn. Monofilament yarn cannot be separated, it is an indivisible component. Monofilament yarns include horsehair, raffia, twisted paper, flat-slit film, and plastic yarn.

Plied/Ply Yarn   A yarn composed of two or more single strands that are twisted together to form a yarn. When untwisted the separate strands, which are single yarn strands, can be counted. Plied yarns are identified as two-, three- or four-ply yarns. The number indicates the amount of strands used to make up the yarn.

Yarn is plied to:
- Introduce different fiber yarns
- Combine spun and filament yarns
- Add to or increase the strength of single strand yarns
- Utilize multi-strands of fine yarns to produce a thick strand
- Produce a smoother yarn
- Produce a yarn with uniform diameter
- Introduce textured or novelty yarns
- Add color interest

Characteristics of Plied Yarns:
- Thicker and heavier
- Coarse
- Differ in count
- Less flexible than single yarns
- Affect drapability quality of fabric
- May be constructed with no twist at all
- May be highly twisted
- May differ in tension and direction of twist

Multifilament Yarn/Multiple Strand   Yarns are composed of two or more filament strands twisted, plied or bonded together to form one yarn. When separated, each filament strand can be counted.

Cord/Cable-ply Yarn   A multiple-ply yarn. It is composed of two or more plied yarns twisted together to form a yarn. Cord yarns list the number of single strands that make up each ply. Three, six ply-cord yarn indicates that there are three plies in the yarn construction; each of the three plies contain six single strands.

Core/Core Spun Yarn   A yarn which has one type of fiber twisted or wrapped around another to provide the yarn with strength and/or stretch. A core yarn consists of a core, which could be spandex, rubber or any other type yarn, and an outer shell or layer usually of texturized natural, man-made or blended fiber yarn. The hand, texture and elasticity of the yarn is determined by the covering or outer shell.

Yarn Construction

Yarn count, yarn ply and yarn construction interrelate to form the characteristics of yarn.

Yarn construction is classified as:

- Simple/Conventional Yarns
- Complex/Novelty Yarns
- Metallic Yarns
- Textured Yarns
- Bulked/High Bulked/Lofted Yarns
- Stretch Yarns

SIMPLE/CONVENTIONAL YARNS

Single	Ply	Multiple
One Yarn	Two or More Single Yarns	Two or More Ply Yarns Cable or Cord Yarn

COMPLEX/NOVELTY YARNS

Single	Ply	Multiple	

Stretch
Bare Yarn
	Textured
	Bulked
		Stretch
		Elastic Core
			Novelty
			  Bouclé
			  Brushed
			  Chenille
			  Corkscrew
			  Flocked
			  Loop
			  Nub
			  Ratiné
			  Seed
			  Slub
			  Splash
			  Thick-and-Thin
			Metallic
			  Supported
			  Unsupported

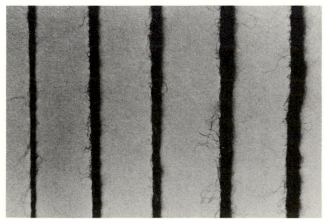

simple/conventional yarn

Simple/Conventional Yarns

Simple/conventional yarns are two or more simple single yarns plied or twisted together. They are referred to as two-, three-, four-, five- or six-ply yarn. Size and number of plies may be changed for different weaves or fabric structures.

- Relatively uniform in size
- Smooth
- Equal number of turns per inch throughout
- Turns per inch are the same from one part to another

bouclé yarn

brushed/napped yarn
(lamb's wool)

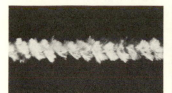

chenille yarn

corkscrew yarn (thin over thick)

flock/flake yarn

loop/curl yarn

noil yarn

nub yarn

ratiné yarn

seed yarn

slub yarn

spiral yarn

splash yarn

thick-and-thin yarn

Complex/Novelty Yarns

Complex/novelty yarns are single or plied yarn structures characterized by intentionally introduced irregularities in size and twist effects. The irregularity of novelty yarns may be uniform or random.

Complex/novelty yarn construction utilizes:
1. *base yarn*—to control length and stability;
2. *effect yarn*—to add aesthetic value and texture;
3. *binder or tie yarn*—to hold the effect yarn to the base yarn.

- Add texture and design to fabric
- Allow for interest, variation and unusual appearance in fabric
- Soft and light to the touch
- Harsh and rough to the touch
- Strength varies from one part to another
- Do not have uniform thickness throughout
- Uneven performance in wear
- Reduced abrasion resistance
- Subject to pilling and snagging

Complex/Novelty yarns may be varied by:
- Changing type and size of yarn
- Changing degree or amount of twist
- Combining simple and complex yarns to form a novelty yarn
- Adding different colored yarns
- Adding metallic yarns

Complex/novelty yarn variations include:
Bouclé Yarn
Brushed/Napped Yarn
Chenille Yarn
Corkscrew Yarn
Flock/Flake Yarn
Loop/Curl Yarn
Noil Yarn
Nub Yarn
Ratiné Yarn
Seed Yarn
Slub Yarn
Spiral Yarn
Splash Yarn
Thick-and-Thin Yarn

Bouclé Yarn A three-ply yarn with small, tight loops protruding from the body of the yarn at widely spaced intervals.

Brushed/Napped Yarn A staple yarn in which the short fibers of the yarn are brushed to the surface to form a soft, bulked effect.

Chenille Yarn A yarn with pile fibers held between plied core yarns producing a hairy or velvety effect.

Corkscrew Yarn A two-ply yarn consisting of one slack-twisted and one hard-twisted fine yarn. The different size yarns are twisted together at a different rate with the thinner yarn twisting around the thicker yarn.

►

Complex/Novelty Yarns (continued)

Flock/Flake Yarn A single yarn in which round or elongated tufts of fibers are inserted at regular intervals. The tufts are held in place by the twist of the base yarn.

Loop/Curl Yarn A core yarn in which the slack-twisted effect yarn has irregularly shaped loops and curls and is held to the core yarn by a fine, tightly twisted binder yarn.

Noil Yarn A yarn characterized by small irregularly sized balls emerging on the surface of the yarn and fabric at irregularly spaced intervals. The noils, or silk waste, are taken from broken or defective cocoons and may be spun with silk or other natural and/or man-made fibers to produce the textured yarn. Man-made fibers may be manipulated to resemble silk noils and may be incorporated into the yarn to produce noil yarn.

Nub Yarn A multiple-ply yarn in which one yarn is twisted around the other yarn several times forming a built-up, enlarged or knotted effect on the surface of the base yarn.

Ratiné Yarn A core yarn with a rough surface effect in an allover appearance in which the small loops are closely spaced and securely twisted to the core yarn.

Seed Yarn A tiny, round or oval enlarged nub produced by crimping and twisting a yarn repeatedly over a base yarn at regular intervals.

Slub Yarn A thick-and-thin yarn with randomly spaced soft, lofty portions produced by irregular intervals of twist and lack of twist in the yarn formation.

Spiral Yarn A two-ply yarn consisting of one slack-twisted soft, thick yarn and one hard-twisted, fine yarn. The thick yarn is twisted and wound spirally around the fine yarn.

Splash Yarn An elongated enlargement or nub produced by crimping and twisting a yarn over a base yarn at regular intervals.

Thick-and-Thin Yarn A yarn that is thicker in some sections than others. *1.* A filament fiber yarn of irregular size produced by pressure forcing the polymer solution through the spinnerette in varying amounts so that the filaments are thicker in some sections than in others. *2.* A natural fiber yarn of irregular size produced by slack and hard carding processes and/or different spinning actions.

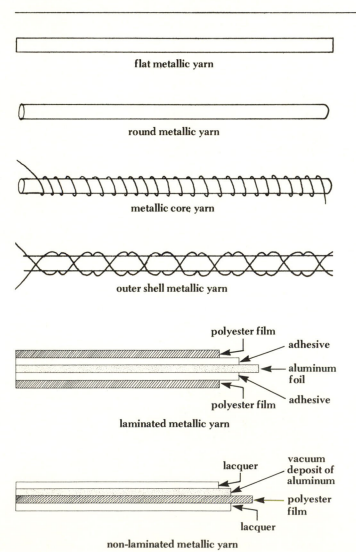

flat metallic yarn

round metallic yarn

metallic core yarn

outer shell metallic yarn

polyester film
adhesive
aluminum foil
polyester film
adhesive

laminated metallic yarn

lacquer
vacuum deposit of aluminum
polyester film
lacquer

non-laminated metallic yarn

Metallic Yarns

A monofilament flat yarn produced by lacquering aluminum pigment or by laminating aluminum foil between layers of plastic. After laminating or lacquering, webs are cut into wide coils and the rolls are slit into fine, ribbon-like yarn. After slitting the yarn is wound onto spools or coils depending on type of ribbon. Since metallic yarns are flat rather than round as most other man-made fiber yarns, the size of the yarn is specified in inches. The denier reference and the cotton count method for sizing yarn have *never* been used for metallic yarns.

The width of the metallic ribbon-like yarn ranges from 1/120th of an inch to 1/4 inch. The most common size for textile production is 1/64 inch. Both laminated and lacquered metallic yarns are produced in a range of metallic colors such as red, blue, green and copper as well as gold and silver. Metallic yarns may be used alone, as laid-in yarns or in a core yarn. Metallic yarns for textiles are produced with the following qualities:

- Dry cleanable or washable
- Nontarnishable and colorfast
- Able to be steamed or ironed
- Flame resistant
- High tensile strength

Lacquered Metallic Yarns Lacquered metallic yarns are produced when plastic film is aluminum metallized under a high-vacuum process and then coated with lacquer. The vacuum deposits of aluminum have a high shine producing a yarn with more luster and metallic-reflecting qualities than laminated metallic yarns.

Laminated Metallic Yarns Laminated metallic yarns are produced when layers of clear plastic are bonded onto aluminum foil. The clear film and the transparent adhesive allow for high-reflecting qualities of the foil to come through.

Textured Yarns

Textured yarns are the end result of physical, chemical or thermal manipulation of fibers and yarns so that they are no longer straight or uniform. The manipulation process of textured yarns results in the modification and altering of the arrangement of fiber and yarn. Texturizing produces a permanent change in the physical structure of the yarn. The fibers no longer lie parallel to the other.

The process changes the properties of the yarn which in turn change the hand, thickness, flexibility, appearance and wear behavior of the finished cloth.

- Texture varies from soft to crisp
- Greater covering power than untextured yarns
- Spongy and springy feel
- Stretch and elongation recovery
- Better shape retention
- Softer than untextured yarns
- Resistance to undesirable creases and wrinkles
- Higher abrasion resistance and strength
- Bulk without added weight
- Warmer than untextured yarns
- Resistance to yarn and seam slippage
- Comfort and versatility
- Improved absorbency
- Improved dyeing properties
- More dimensional, lofty and opaque fabric structure

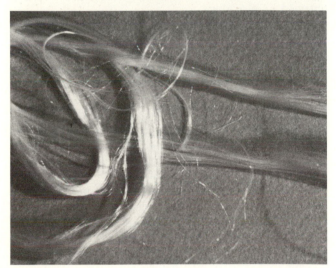

textured yarn

untextured yarn

Bulked/High Bulked/Lofted Yarns

Texturizing of yarns also produce bulked yarns. High bulk yarns are created and processed by nonlinearity and loop formation in individual filaments. The process introduces crimps, loops, curls and crinkles into the yarn. Bulk yarns may also be shrunk and stretched introducing shrink differential. The resulting yarns of these processes are bulked, fluffed, puffed and twisted.

- Made of staple or continuous filament fiber
- Increased loftiness, thickness and volume for given fabric weight
- Cannot be packed close together during fabric structure
- Increased covering power due to fluffed up process
- Retain bulkiness under both relaxed and stress conditions
- Allows for insulating properties in the fabric
- Produces fabric with soft hand
- Process reduces luster and strength of yarn

before bulking

after bulking

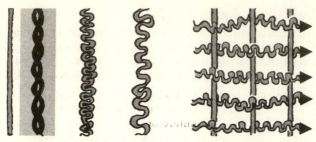

Twist texturing induces a coil or crimp in filament yarns. Yarns then provide stretch characteristics to woven or knitted fabrics.

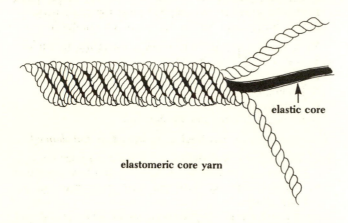

elastic core

elastomeric core yarn

no torque stretch yarn method/knit de knit crimp

Crimp size and frequency can be varied by differences in stitch size and tension.

Stretch Yarns

Almost all natural and man-made fibers can be treated to produce yarns with some degree of stretch and recovery. Stretch properties may be applied to yarns by chemical or mechanical methods. Not all methods or fibers will achieve equally effective stretch properties.

- Both bulk and stretch characteristics
- High stretch and recovery properties
- Produce fabric with elastic/high elasticity and extensibility qualities
- Complete recovery
- Produced with a soft or hard finish
- Elasticity acquired directly from the yarn
- Provide cling and molding qualities without great pressure

Elasticity of stretch yarn is controlled by the amount and type of twist in the yarn. Variation in the stretch may be obtained by changing:
- Amount of false twist
- Heat-set temperatures
- Texturizing thermoplastic continuous filaments
- Degree of tension and feed roll mechanism
- Right- or left-hand twist or alternating both
- Single or plied yarns

Most yarns with high stretch potential and good recovery properties are made with *spandex fibers*. The yarn may be produced with a soft or hard hand.

Forms of Spandex Yarns

Bare Yarn The extruded, fused multifilaments and the monofilament spandex fiber may be used uncovered. The yarn produces a lightweight, sheer, supple, and more elastic fabric.

Covered Yarn The spandex fiber is covered by wrapping a single yarn of any other fiber around it. The stretch of the yarn is limited by the extent of the stretch properties of the covering yarn.

Core-Spun/Double-covered Spandex Yarn A staple fiber is twisted to form a sheath around the spandex core that is held in tension and subsequently relaxed. The hand and texture of the yarn is determined by the covering yarn. Elasticity is limited by the length to which the twisted sheath may be extended.

Type and amount of stretch of the stretch yarn is selected with regard to:
- Area of stretch
- Amount of stretch needed
- Recovery power in the particular garment

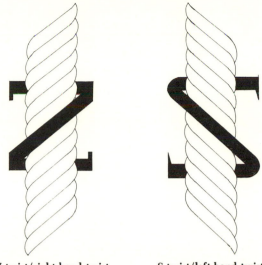

Z-twist/right-hand twist   S-twist/left-hand twist

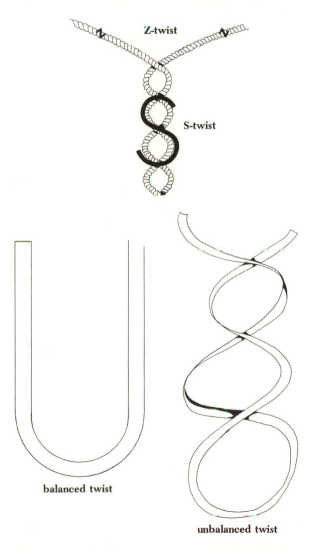

Z-twist

S-twist

balanced twist

unbalanced twist

Yarn Twist & Direction

Simple, complex or textured yarns are twisted to hold them together. Twist controls the cohesive characteristics and strength of yarn. The yarns may be twisted in a right- or left-hand manner for a minimal or maximum twisted structure.

Right-hand twist Clockwise rotation, produces a yarn strand with a "Z" torque or "Z" twist effect.

Left-hand twist Counterclockwise rotation, produces a yarn strand with a "S" torque or "S" twist effect.

Yarn twist direction allows for:
- Cohesiveness between fibers
- Utilization of either "Z" and "S" twist for simple yarns
- Combination of "Z" and "S" twist for plied yarns
- Combination of "Z" or "S" twist for durability

Yarn twist direction produces a variation in surface appearance of fabric structure:
- Affects wear
- Facilitates processing
- Increases bulk
- Reduces picking and/or slippage

Yarn twist is also classified as *balanced* or *unbalanced*.

Balanced Yarns Balanced yarns are twisted so that the yarn does not twist, kink or double upon itself when suspended in a loop. Balanced yarns are used to produce smooth feeling fabrics.

Unbalanced Yarns Unbalanced yarns will untwist and retwist in the opposite direction when suspended in a loop. Unbalanced yarns are used to produce textured and/or pebbly fabrics.

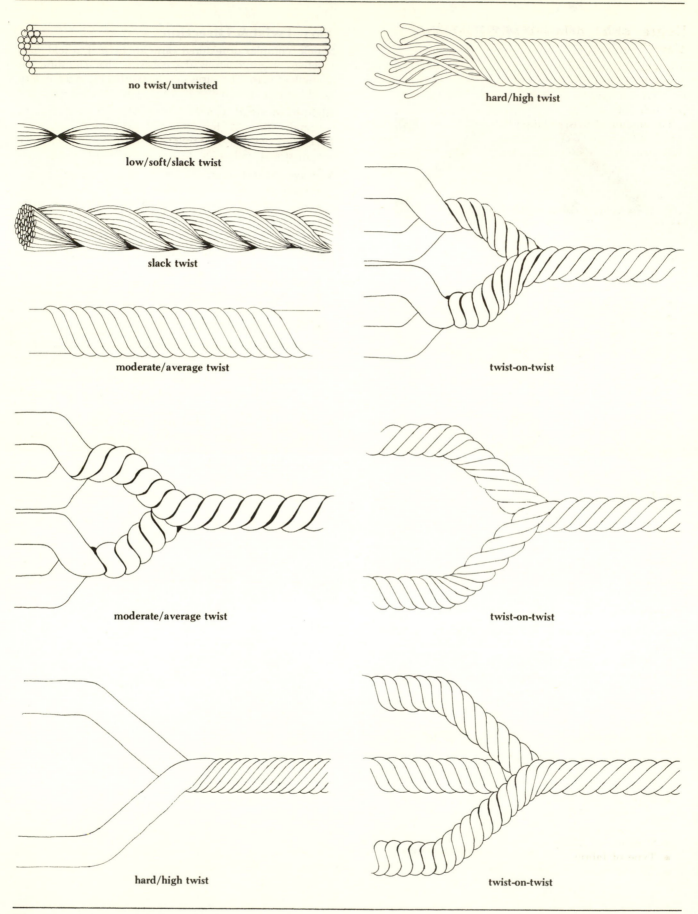

no twist/untwisted

low/soft/slack twist

slack twist

moderate/average twist

hard/high twist

twist-on-twist

moderate/average twist

twist-on-twist

hard/high twist

twist-on-twist

UNDERSTANDING FABRICS

Degree of Yarn Twist/Twist Tension/ Yarn Tension

The degree or amount of yarn twist may vary from slight or almost no twist at all to tightly or highly twisted. The amount or degree of yarn twist is measured in the number of turns per inch (TPI).

The amount of twist required to hold the fibers and yarns together depends on the diameter or size of yarn. Thicker yarns will require less twist to hold them together and are referred to as *low twist yarns*. Finer yarns will require more twist to hold them together and are referred to as *high twist or hard twist yarns*.

Spun yarns are twisted tightly in order to hold the short staple together. Filament yarns do not require high twist unless producing textured or crepe yarns.

Degree of yarn twist affects the *yarn's*:
- Diameter of fineness
- Softness or hardness
- Bending behavior
- Specific volume
- Covering power
- Permeability
- Tensile strength:
  - Strength
  - Stress distribution
- Elastic performance/extension and recovery
- Resistance to creases and abrasion
- Pilling behavior

Degree of yarn twist affects the *fabric's*:
- Hand
- Appearance
- Texture
- Drapability qualities
- Performance expectations
- Durability
- Serviceability

Degree of Yarn Twist & Uses

Degree of Yarn Twist	Uses
No Twist/Untwisted	Novelty fabrics Loosely woven fabrics Damask and brocade
Low/Soft Twist	Soft-surfaced fabrics Napped fabrics As a filling yarn
Slack Twist	Silk filament yarns Man-made filament yarns
Moderate/Average Twist	Staple fibers Warp yarns Most frequently
High/Hard Twist	To produce compact yarns Harder smooth-surfaced fabrics
Twist-on-Twist	To produce yarns with high number of turns per inch Rough, pebbly or crinkled fabric

Yarn Dyeability

Dyestuff or application of color may be added at different times:
1. during the fiber stage;
2. during development and extension in the spinneret;
3. after spinning the yarn.

Yarn-dyed fabrics, when constructed, show an evenness of color and will wear evenly. Color added after the cloth is woven usually will not wear well and will also show grey state color of cloth.

Yarn dyeability depends on:
- Content of fiber
- Type of yarn
- Construction of yarn
- End use of yarn
- Structure of fabric
- Type of fabric
- Cost of fabric

3 ~ Fabric Structure/Fabric Construction

Fabric structure is the result of the process by which fibers become yarns, and yarns become fabric.

Natural or man-made fibers of spun or filament form are cured, twisted, bulked or otherwise manipulated, arranged, and developed into yarns. Yarns utilized for fabric structure may be crimped, textured, creped, plied, loosely or firmly twisted and prepared for fabric construction. In nonwoven or fused fabric structures, the fibers are utilized in fiber form to produce the material. In film or plastic fabric structures, the fibers are extruded and developed into fabrics.

Any combination of finishes or treatments whether functional, decorative or permanent may be applied to the fiber, yarn or finished fabric at one or more stages of development. Type of fibers or yarns, method of fabric construction and finishes applied interrelate in the production of the fabric. When one of the components is changed, the fabric will change and will affect the fabric's:

- Weight
- Hand and feel
- Drapability qualities
- Performance expectations
- Appearance
- Covering power
- Surface texture
- Body
- Thickness
- Luster
- Strength
- Flexibility
- Resiliency
- Warmth
- Affinity to dyestuff
- End use
- Cost

There are basic inherent properties of fibers, yarns, finishes and fabric constructions. Fiber performance and yarn performance may be modified, altered or changed so that fabric expectations may differ. One or more properties may be modified or altered to achieve the desired results for a fabric applicable to a particular end use or design.

Fiber, Yarn & Construction Characteristics that Influence Fabric Structure

Fiber characteristics that influence fabric structure:
- Type—natural or man-made
- Form—spun, filament or combination of both
- Length—long or short
- Diameter—fine or thick
- Shape—natural or induced
- Surface contour—smooth or uneven

Yarn characteristics that influence fabric structure:
- Texture—straight, crimped or curled
- Surface Contour—even, slubbed or uneven
- Size—thin or thick
- Ply—single or multiple
- Twist—loose or tight; simple or complex
- Twist direction—Z- or S-twist
- Hand—soft or crisp
- Covering power—fine or bulked

Construction characteristics that influence fabric structure:
- Composition of yarns needed to produce cloth
- Type of structure—woven, nonwoven, knitted or extruded film
- Type of weave or knit—basic or complex
- Variations within the weave or knit
- Finish applied during or after construction

Felt Fabric Structure

Felt fabric structure is a nonwoven fabric produced directly from fibers forming an interlocking, uniform, compact matted layer or material by either the *traditional form of wool felting*, or the *needle-felting process*. Fibers used in the production of felt include: fine or coarse wool, hair, cotton, sisal, jute, fine rayon and fine or coarse man-made fibers.

Felts may be made in a variety of thicknesses and weights by controlling the buildup and felting process of the superimposed web layers. Thicknesses range from 1/32″–3″ (0.05–7.6 cm) or more. Felts used for garments are produced in thicknesses of 1/16″–1/8″ (0.16–0.32 cm) and from 60″–90″ (1.5–2.3 meters) wide.

- No system of threads
- Does not ravel
- Requires no seam or hem finishes on garment
- High thermo-insulating properties that provide warmth
- Can be blocked and cut into shape
- Retains predetermined or molded shapes
- Good resiliency
- Poor elasticity and poor flexibility
- Does not return to shape if stretched
- Poor tensile strength

RANDOM-LAID WEB PROCESS

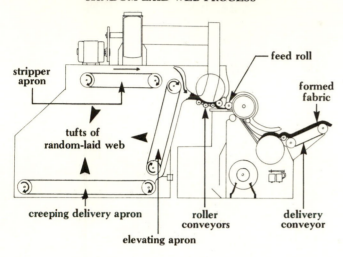

NEEDLE PROCESS

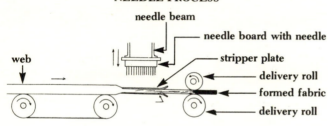

CLOSE UP OF NEEDLE PROCESS

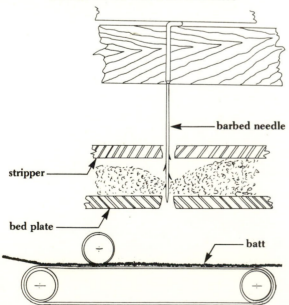

Methods Used to Produce Felt Fabric Structures

Traditional Form of Wool Felting The traditional form of wool felting uses the combination of heat, moisture and pressure to agitate, steam and hammer the web of wool or animal hair fibers into an interlocking mass forming the felt fabric structure.

Wool and other animal fibers used for felting have a natural barb or projection that facilitates fulling and felting by the traditional process.

Needle-felting Process The needle-felting process is a method of mechanically interlocking loose man-made fibers to form a felt fabric structure. The major fibers used in the needle-felting process are the man-made fibers. Man-made or synthetic fibers lack the natural barb of wool and animal fibers. The needle-felting process utilizes barbed needles to interlock the fibers.

The principle of the needle-felting process remains the same regardless of the type of man-made fiber or the type of needle used. A web of fibers from a suitable source is conveyed under the beam which contains the specially designed needles.

The type and size of needles, the specific number of needles and the arrangement of the needles are selected to achieve specific desired results or to produce a particular type of felt fabric. The amount of needling given the web is regulated by synchronizing the number of penetrations per inch in advance to the number of strokes per minute of the needle. The needle pattern is the actual way the needles are drilled in the board and can be adjusted from product to product.

Needled felts are the result of fiber entanglement—the more entanglement taking place and the denser the felt, the stiffer the fabric will be.

Comparison of Weight & Hand in Felt Fabric Structures

100% Wool Fiber Felt

Lightweight
Medium Weight
Heavyweight
Soft Hand
Hard Hand

Wool & Natural Fiber Blended Felt

Lightweight
Medium Weight
Heavyweight
Soft Hand
Hard Hand

Wool & Man-Made Felt Fiber Blended Felt

Lightweight
Medium Weight
Heavyweight
Soft Hand
Hard Hand

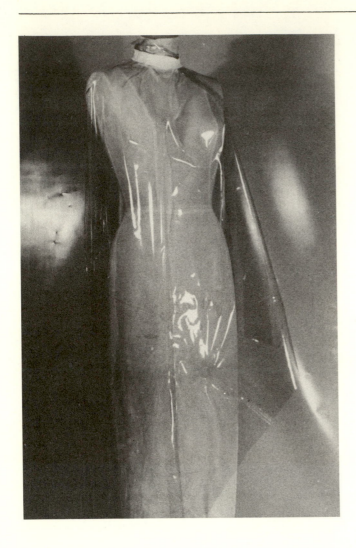

Film/Plastic Fabric Structure

A plain, expanded or supported film fabric produced from resins of polyvinylchloride, polyurethane or polyethylene by calendering, casting, extruding, knife-coating or laminating methods.

- Light to heavyweight
- Thin to thick
- Smooth to sculptured texture
- Transparent to opaque
- Soft to stiff hand
- Supple to rigid drapability qualities
- Waterproof
- Soil resistant
- Easy to clean and maintain
- May be cut into flat untwisted tapes or yarns and used for woven, knitted or embroidered fabric structures
- May by finished to resemble grains and patterns of animal skins

Methods Used to Produce Film/ Plastic Fabric Structures

Calendering Method The vinyl film is made on a large machine known as a *calender*. In one of the later stages of calendering, the fabric is fed into the unit. By means of heat and pressure, the vinyl is impregnated into the fabric.

Casting Method The backing fabric is laid into a liquid film, which has been cast on another film that was originally cast on paper. The wet film acts as a bonding agent between the fabric and the initially cast film. The film and fabric are dried, cured and then stripped from the paper.

Knife-coating Method A thin, viscous vinyl solution is scraped onto fabric and spread with a knife-type blade. The fabric may have to be passed through the knife-coater several times in order to obtain the proper thickness, bulk or cover. The coated fabric is then dried in an oven.

Laminating Method The vinyl formulation is first subject to intense mixing and heat, rolled out and then laminated to the backing fabric. The calender presses the fabrics between rollers laminating the two plies and forming a single fabric.

Knit Fabric Structure

Knit fabric structures are formed through the process of interlocking loops or forming loops with one or more yarns in preceding and succeeding rows. Knit fabrics are produced by hand or on a variety of knitting machines with one or more needles of different types.

Variations of knit fabrics may be achieved by adding, deleting or combining any one or more of the following:

- Content of fiber—natural, man-made, blend or combination
- Type of fiber—filament or staple
- Size or denier of yarn—fine, lofted or bulked
- Type of yarn—twisted, textured, novelty or specialty
- Color of yarn—one color or multicolored
- Type and capability of knitting machines
- Attachments used on knitting machines
- Type and quality of needles
- Size, thickness and length of needles
- Formation of needles—inoperative or selectively operative
- Number and spacing of needle sets
- Size of stitches
- Formation and pattern of stitches
- Number or threading of guide bars
- Finishing processes applied to yarn and/or finished goods

Any variation of the above will affect the appearance, texture, performance expectation, weight, hand and drapability qualities of the fabric.

- Naturally inherent elasticity and/or resiliency
- Provides its own shape and drapability qualities
- Moves easily with body movements
- Stretch qualities not found in woven goods
- Insulating properties in still air
- Easy to care—requires little or no ironing
- Snags and pulls easily
- Poor crease retention because of loop formation
- Shrinks unless stabilized

Knit fabrics are classified and named with regard to the:
- Structure of fabric
- Method or type of production or construction
- Type of machine used for its construction
- Number of guide bars on a machine

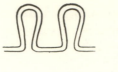

warp knit
loop stitch

weft knit
loop stitch

wale

course

count

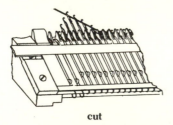

gauge—
fine stitches

gauge—close,
compact stitches

gauge—loose or
open stitches

cut

denier

Parts of Knit Fabric Structure

Stitches The smallest fundamental unit in a knit fabric. Stitches are produced by a knitted loop pulled through a previously formed loop.

Wale The *vertical* succession of loops whereby one loop is formed *under* another in the *lengthwise* direction. The continuous succession of interlocking loops is made by the *same* needle.

Course The *horizontal* succession of loops whereby one loop is formed *next* to the other in the *filling* or *crosswise* direction. Each loop is made by a *different* needle.

Count The number of wales per inch and courses per inch of a knitted fabric. Also referred to as course count or wale count.

Gauge Gauge determines the *fineness* or *density* of the fabric. It is used to evaluate the closeness and compactness of stitches in a knit fabric. Gauge relates to the number of needles to the inch in a knitting machine, which accounts for the number of stitches or loops produced per square inch of fabric. For example:

> Full fashion knits—Numbers of needles per 1½″
> Raschel knits—Number of needles per 2″
> Tricot knits—Number of needles per 1″

Cut The number of needles to the inch (NPI) in a weft knitting machine.

Denier The weight or diameter of the yarn used for knitting.

knit/plain stitch (face)

knit/plain stitch (back)

knit/plain stitch (face)

knit/plain stitch (back)

face and back are same on purl/reverse knit stitch

missed stitch

tuck stitch

two-needle tuck stitch

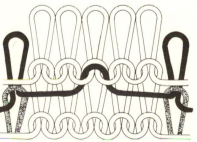

combination missed & tuck stitch

Stitches or Loops Used to Produce Knit Fabric Structures

Knit/Plain Stitch   A stitch showing neck of loop formation on the face of the fabric and head of loop formation on the back of the fabric (reverse). The process produces a fine, thin or sheer fabric with a smooth face. Fabric has a definite face and back or reverse side.

Purl/Reverse Knit Stitch   Successive courses of loops that resemble the reverse of the knit stitch, drawn to the face and back (reverse) side of the fabric. The intermeshing of loops in opposite directions occurs on the crosswise or width of the goods. The process produces a rounder, puffier stitch. The fabric has the same appearance on the face and back.

Missed Stitch   The action of one or more knitting needles that deactivate and do not move into position to accept the advancing yarn. At patterned intervals the yarn passes by forming no stitch. The missed yarn floats unlooped on the reverse side of the fabric.

Tuck Stitch   The process of holding one or more loops on the needle while taking on one or more additional loops, then casting all of them onto another loop. The tuck stitch creates open spaces at regular intervals across the knitted cloth. The process is used to create blister effects, open work, lace effects, mesh and knobby or bumpy textured knit fabrics.

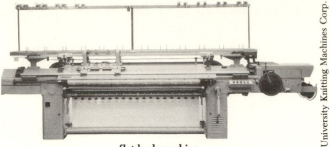

flat bed machine

University Knitting Machines Corp.

narrowing

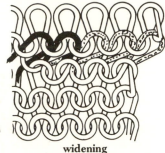

widening

fashion marks

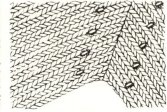

mock fashion marks

circular-type knitting machine

Milan Textile Machines Inc.

Types of Knit Fabric Structures

Flat Knit A flat-formed fabric or yard goods with straight edges or sides produced on a flat-bed machine.

Full-fashioned/Fashioned Knit A fully formed or partially shaped garment or garment component produced by increasing (widening) and/or decreasing (narrowing) the number of wales. The shaping operation is accomplished by controlling the movement of the needles. The needle action may tighten or loosen the stitch form; add or delete stitches; knit two or more stitches as one. Full-fashioned knits may be made on a flat-bed or circular machine.

1. *Widening.* Loops are transferred one at a time—from the center towards the end.
2. *Narrowing.* Four loops are moved across two wales each time—from the edge towards the center.
3. *Fashion marks.* Each time a needle transfers stitches in the widening or narrowing process to an adjacent needle it leaves a distinct mark in the fabric where it was widened or narrowed.

Mock Fashion Marks Artificial or mock fashion marks that may be machined or embossed into the garment at joining areas.

Tubular/Circular Knit A tubular or circular fabric produced on a circular-type knitting machine with the loop-stitch formation process made around the fabric. Needles on the knitting machine are arranged in a circle, producing fabric in tubular form. Goods may be produced as tubular yard goods or circular-shaped components or trimmings.

Methods or Types of Machine Knit Fabric Structures

There are two basic methods or types of knit fabric structure:

- Warp Knit Fabric Structure
  Milanese Knit
  Raschel Knit
  Kettenraschel Knit
  Tricot Knit
  Weft Insertion Warp Knit
- Weft/Filling Knit Fabric Structure
  Double Knit
  Interlock Stitch Knit
  Plain/Single/Jersey Knit
  Purl Knit
  Rib Knit
  Weft Knit Variations

Warp knit fabrics are produced by a system of interlocking loops in a *lengthwise* direction. Fabric is produced by several parallel yarns that form one stitch for each yarn in each course. Each stitch in a course is made by a different yarn. *All the needles move up at the same time* to make the stitch. The stitches are produced in each course simultaneously.

- Mostly flat goods with straight edges
- Variety of stitch patterns and techniques
- Wispy netting to close coating patterns
- Flat, smooth surfaces to erect pile surfaces
- Fine to thick hand
- Light to heavyweight
- Narrow widths to widths up to 168″
- Stretch resistant
- Run resistant
- Does not ravel
- Less susceptible to snagging

Weft/filling knit fabrics are produced by a system of interlocking loops in a *filling or crosswise direction*. The loops are made in horizontal courses with each course built on top of the other. Fabric is produced by adjacent needles which draw a yarn from a creel attached to the knitting machine. *All the needles operate independently* of one another and all the stitches in the course are *made by one yarn*.

The three primary categories of weft knits are:
1. jersey;
2. rib;
3. purl.

Plain, purl, tuck and missed stitches are the basic stitches used in the formation of weft-constructed fabrics. All other stitches used to produce weft knits are a variation or combination of these four basic stitches.

- Simulate hand knitting procedures
- Flat or tubular
- Shaped and full-fashioned
- High elongation and elasticity properties
- Runs or ladders if one stitch is broken

Variations within the warp or weft knit fabric structures may be achieved by:

- Changing or altering the principle stitches or loops by:
  - Casting off, holding, adding or distorting loops or stitches
  - Changing the size, length, number and placement of stitches
  - Changing the arrangement of threading the guide bars
  - Changing the movement of the guide bars
  - Adding patterning mechanisms or wheels to the machines
- Selective programming of needle motion or action
- Changing type, size, ply twist or texture of yarns
- Changing, adding or mixing different colors or patterns of fibers or yarns.

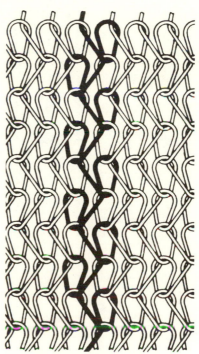

warp knit fabric structure

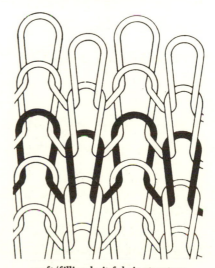

weft/filling knit fabric structure

Milanese Knit

A warp knit process in which stitches are composed of two loops—one from each set of warp thread—both moving diagonally from one stitch to another at each course. The crossing of several sets of yarns create a diamond effect or pattern on the back of the goods and a fine rib-like stitch on the face. Milanese knit construction usually utilizes filament yarns and are made on a straight bed or circular knitting machine.

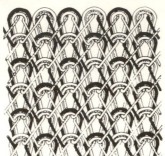

- Fine to lightweight
- High tear and split strength
- Smooth texture
- Soft, pliable, fluid drapability qualities
- Limited pattern designs

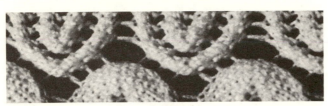

raschel knit

Raschel Knit

A warp knit process utilizing a variety of stitch formations and methods of fed-in or laid-in yarns arranged and manipulated to produce design interest, various surface textures and open work effect.

Variations of raschel machine knits are created by utilizing spun or filament yarns of any fiber, conventional or novelty yarns, colored texture or specialty yarns or specialty yarn materials made of ribbon, straw or braid.

- Fine to heavy gauge
- Compact, close knit to openwork crochet
- Laces and nets
- Power nets and similar elastic-types for foundation garments
- High elasticity for swimwear
- Pile surfaces
- Pronounced dimensional effects
- Ribbed and pleated effects
- Double face and reversible

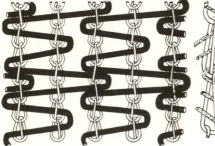

crochet openwork   crochet effect

net

fishnet   power net with   square mesh (marquisette)
               elastomeric yarns

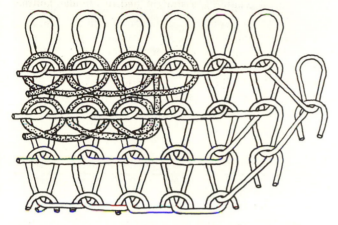

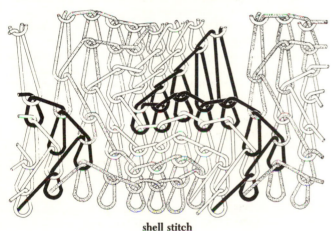

shell stitch

Kettenraschel Knit

The terms *Kettenraschel, cut presser, shell stitch* and *knob effects* are used to describe those fabrics having conspicuous three-dimensional effects and knitted on specific generally coarse bearded needle warp knitting machines. The terms, Kettenraschel and cut presser, in addition to describing certain types of fabric, also refer to the machines employed for the manufacturing of the fabrics.

Kettenraschel A bearded needle warp knitting machine usually built in gauges from 9 to 16 needles per inch and with up to four guide bars. The machine is fitted with one full presser and two cut pressers; all three fitted into one group.

Cut Presser A bearded needle warp knitting machine usually built within gauges ranging from 12 to 28 needles per inch and with two to four guide bars. The machine is equipped with a sinker bar as an ordinary tricot unit, but differs from the normal bearded needle machine in that it has two needle presser bars known as the full presser and the cut presser, each independently controlled.

Shell Stitch A stitch that may be knitted on both the Kettenraschel and cut presser machines. The main requirements are the provision of one guide bar, one cut presser and one warp beam.

Knob Effects Shell stitch fabrics incorporating raised knob effects may be knit using two guide bars and a cut presser.

Kettenraschel knit construction utilizes filament or staple yarns or yarns with high covering power.

- Coarse gauge
- Variations in surface texture ranging from close knit to openwork effects
- Raised pattern or raised knobby effects that are three dimensional
- Pattern effects created by one or more colors
- High elasticity

single guide bar tricot

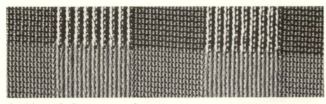

double guide bar patterned tricot

double guide bar tricot/Queenscord

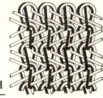

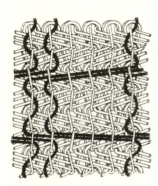

triple guide bar tricot

mesh

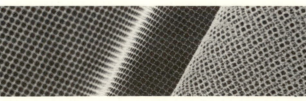

tulle

Tricot Knit

A warp knit process producing a flat, thin textured fabric characterized by fine vertical lengthwise ribs on the face and horizontal crosswise ribs on the back. Differences in gauge and thickness of tricot knit fabrics are produced by varying the size of the yarn, the lightness and compactness of the stitch, the length of the guide bar movement or the finishing process. Tricot knit fabrics are usually made of fine, thin filament yarns and range in gauge from fine (44 gauge) to coarse (14 gauge). Tricot machines may be set up to produce plain, patterned or decorative tricot fabrics. The different tricot knits are identified by the number of yarns and guide bars used for each needle at each repeat and are classified as:

- Single guide bar tricot/One guide bar tricot
- Double guide bar tricot/Two guide bar tricot
- Three guide bar tricot
- Four guide bar tricot

Single Guide Bar Tricot/One Guide Bar Tricot The simplest of the tricot knit fabrics produced by utilizing a single guide bar and one set of yarns. The yarn is knitted in one direction and then in the reverse, producing a striped effect. One bar tricot has limited production usage because it runs and ladders easily.

Double Guide Bar Tricot/Two Guide Bar Tricot A tricot knit utilizing two sets of yarns, one set is knitted in one direction and the other set is knitted in the opposite direction, producing a ribbed surface effect.

Three Guide Bar Tricot A tricot knit of high opacity, maximum weight and in a variety of designs.

The more the number of guide bars used in the manufacturing of tricot fabric, the more intricate the pattern that can be incorporated into the fabric.

Tricot Jersey Two beams of yarn are needed to produce tricot jersey. Characteristics include: no stretch; usually only filament yarns; only solid colors.

Patterned Tricot Three beams are needed to produce patterned tricot. More beams are needed to produce a knit fabric of heavier weight, with rigidity, and with less drapability.

Tricot Mesh Produces tulle, tulle point de esprite and tulle base for embroidered lace.

- Soft and pliable, fluid and flowing drapability qualities
- Does not fray, ravel or run
- Tends to curl at raw or cut edges
- Good abrasion and snag resistance
- Good stability
- Finished to provide high tear and bursting strength
- Crease and wrinkle resistance
- Resilient
- Controlled stretch in the lengthwise direction and no stretch in the crosswise direction
- Less stretch than weft/filling knit fabrics
- Stronger and firmer than weft/filling knit fabrics
- Coated with metallic or colored pigment
- Utilized as backing for bonding, laminated or coated fabrics

Weft-insertion Warp Knit

A warp knit process utilizing a conventional tricot machine providing a method and technique of introducing a filling yarn across the width of the course on a warp knit structure fabric. The filling insertion yarns may be filament or spun, textured, novelty or stretch yarns. They add color, design and pattern variety. The yarns may be raised or dominate, altering the appearance and hand of the fabric and provide versatility to the fabric design and styling.

- Similar to other knits, but lighter weight
- Both properties of knitting and weaving
- Has stability; easier than other knits to cut and assemble
- Subject to less yarn and seam slippage than other knits
- Better abrasion resistance than other knits
- Available in degrees of stretch, depending on type of yarn and finishing processes used

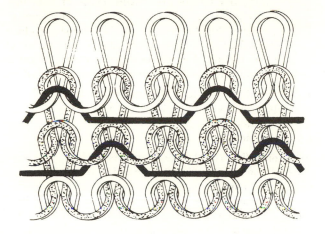

WEFT INSERTION—LAYING-IN TECHNIQUE

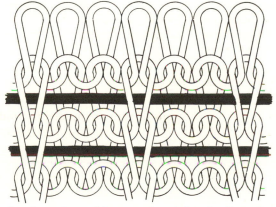

Weft threads are inserted between the stitches that lie on the face and back of the fabric. Threads appear on face of fabric.

Laid-in yarn facilitates the use of extra yarns on a foundation of plain fabric. Knitting and laid-in courses are produced alternately.

blister double knit

face and back are same on double knit.

Double Knit

A weft knit process producing a double constructed fabric. Double knit, a variation of the rib knit process, is made on a circular or flat-bed machine with two sets of needles and yarns. A double layered fabric characterized by fine ribs in the lengthwise direction on both sides of the goods (reversible) and the same stitch as the face of jersey fabrics.

- Same appearance on face and back; double-faced
- Strong and durable;
- Fine to heavyweight
- Heavier than warp or interlock knits
- Firm, closely knit structure; full bodied in hand and appearance
- More body than single knits
- Good stability and shape retention
- Stabilized or heat-set for shrinkage control
- Does not sag, stretch or *sit out*
- Good crease and wrinkle resistance
- Does not curl at raw or cut edges

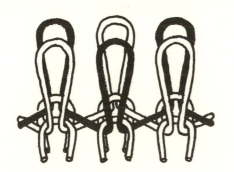

Interlock Stitch Knit

A weft knit process producing a compound fabric. Two separate 1x1 rib fabrics are interlocked or interknitted to form one cloth, and are characterized by fine ribs in the lengthwise direction on both sides of the goods (reversible). The two rib courses are defined as one interlock course, since together they produce one stitch in every wale. Interlock stitch knit process utilizes single yarns in the knitting process.

- Same appearance on face and back; double-faced
- Limited patterns or surface designs
- Smooth-surfaced face and back
- Firm, closely knit structure
- Fine, or sheer to heavier gauges
- Heavier and thicker than other knit stitch fabrics of the same gauge
- High elasticity and stretch in the *lengthwise* direction
- Limited elasticity and stretch in the *crosswise* direction
- High dimensional stability and good shape retention
- Does not curl at raw or cut edges
- One edge tends to run or ladder under tension
- Unravels only from the end knitted last

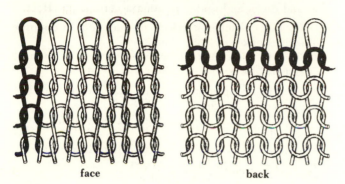

face   back

Plain/Single/Jersey Knit

A weft knit process producing a plain, flat-surfaced fabric with a distinct face and back. A single-faced knitted fabric formed by an intermeshing of stitches in the same direction on the face and a series of semicircular loops produced on the reverse or back. Even-patterned loops or wales are produced in the lengthwise direction on the face of the fabric and even-patterned, wavy loops in the crosswise direction on the reverse. Jersey knit process utilizes both single and double yarn construction.

- Distinct face and back; single-faced
- Flat open fabric or tubular fabric
- Shaped or full-fashioned
- Stretch in both *length-* and *crosswise* directions
- Poor dimensional stability
- Stretches out of shape
- Curls at each selvage edge and where it is cut on a walewise direction
- Drop stitches result in runs or ladders if yarn is broken
- Cut edges unravel from either end
- Sheer or fine to bulked or lofted
- Fine lightweight openwork to heavy furlike piles
- Flat smooth surfaces of raised looped surfaces as in terry cloth or velour

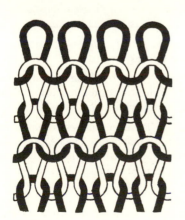

Purl Knit

A weft knit process producing a double-faced fabric. Alternate rows of knit and purl stitches that interlock or intermesh as semicircular loops in the crosswise direction on both face and back of the goods (reversible).

- Same appearance on face and back; double-faced
- Flat or tubular
- Stretch in both *length-* and *crosswise* directions; with high lengthwise extension
- Bulky, heavy-effect knits
- Large loose stitches
- Does not curl at raw or cut edges

3X1 rib knit

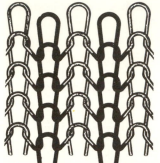

1X1 rib knit

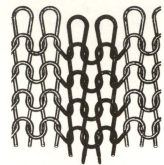

2X2 rib knit

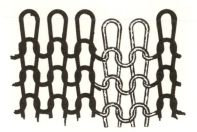

3X2 rib knit

Rib Knit

A weft knit process producing a double-faced fabric. Rib knit is made with two sets of needles producing alternate plain and purl stitches that interlock or intermesh in opposite directions in the *lengthwise* direction and produce distinct vertical ribs on both sides of the fabric. Rib knit process produces high and low areas with stitches alternating up and over and down and under creating a corrugated effect.

1x1 Rib Knit Stitches interlock or intermesh in opposite directions of every *other* wale.

2x2 Rib Knit Stitches interlock or intermesh in opposite directions of every *two* wales.

- Same appearance on face and back; double-faced
- Resilient and high elasticity
- Stretch in lengthwise direction; high extension in crosswise direction
- More elasticity in crosswise direction than plain knits
- Lies flat at both ends and sides
- Does not curl at raw or cut edges
- Unravels only from the end knitted last
- Ladders only towards the end knitted last
- Even or uneven patterned ribs
- Suitable for edges of sleeves, necklines, waistlines, and bottoms of pants legs
- May be planned as part of a plain or full-fashioned sweater knit
- Designed as banding to be attached to other knit or woven fabrics

transfer stitch

intarsia knit

Weft Knit Variations

Weft knit variations may be designed into jersey knit, purl knit or rib knit fabrics by combining any or all of the stitches or introducing methods known as *transfer stitches* or *intarsia*.

Transfer Stitches   Transfer stitches are made by loop transfer on the knitting machines. The needles holding the yarn are emptied by the transfer of loops allowing the loop to intermesh at the next course. The stitches that are transferred create patterns, designs or openwork effects in the finished cloth.

Intarsia   The term intarsia applies to knit fabrics having an isolated design, which resembles a cut-out pattern. The design may be made of a different type or by a colored yarn and of different stitches. The yarns used to form the pattern do not float on the back of the fabric as they do in Jacquard knit fabrics.

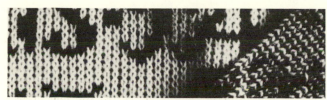

two-colored jacquard knit

floats of yarn on back of jacquard knit

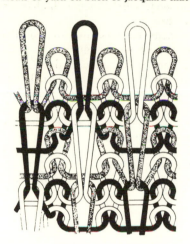

Jacquard Knit

Jacquard knit is a system of producing a patterned knit fabric incorporating the Jacquard system. The system is the individual control of the selection or inhibition of the needles to produce the design or pattern utilizing:

- Punch cards or programmed techniques similar to woven Jacquard fabric
- Electronic or electromagnetic devices
- Coded strips of film of opaque and transparent squares activated by light

Jacquard knit construction:

- May be produced by warp- or weft-type methods of knitting fabric
- Produces single or multicolored designs and patterns
- Designed with a flat or raised surface
- May be hard finished for smooth texture or brushed for napped finish
- Produces Jacquard blister knit, Jacquard jersey knit and jersey knit variations, Jacquard rib knit and rib knit variations

Knit/Knit-type Fabrics

Cotton Knit Fabrics Natural Fibers	Silk Knit Fabrics Natural Fibers	Wool Knit Fabrics Natural Fibers	Knit Fabrics of 100% Man-Made Fibers & Blended Fibers	Stretch Knit Fabrics Natural Fibers	Metallic Fabrics Natural Fibers
Double-faced knit	Crepe	Double-faced Knit	Double-faced Knit	Fiber Stretch	Cire/Metallic-coated Fabric
Double Knit	Lingerie Knit/	Double Knit	Double Knit	Lycra® (180–220%)	Metallic Laid-in
Interlock Knit	Crepe Set®	Medium Knit	Interlock Knit	Lycra® (140–175%)	Yarns in Jersey,
Lightweight	Double Knit	Heavyweight	Fine Weight	Lycra® (110–140%)	Tricot, Raschel
Medium Weight	Interlock Knit	Jacquard Knit	Lightweight	Yarn & Fabric	Knit Fabrics
Jacquard Knit	Fine Weight	Smooth Face/	Medium Weight	Structure Stretch	
Rib	Lightweight	Birdseye Back	Heavyweight	Double Knit	
Jersey Knit	Medium Weight	Napped Face,	Jacquard Knit	(lightweight)	
Lightweight	Heavyweight	Birdseye Back	Flat	(medium weight)	
Striped	Jacquard Knit	Jersey Variation	Single Blister	(heavyweight)	
Novelty Yarn	Jersey Knit	Jersey Knit	Jersey	Stretch Terry	
Tweed Effect	Sheer	Lightweight	Jersey Variations	Cloth	
LaCoste®	Fine Weight	Medium Weight	Rib	Stretch Lace	
Open Effect	Lightweight	Heavyweight	Smooth Face,		
Pleated Effect	Open Effect	Tweed Effect	Birdseye Back		
Purl Knit	Pleated Effect	Open Effect	Napped Face,		
Raschel Knit	Milanese Knit	Purl Knit	Birdseye Back		
Crochet Effect	Purl Knit	Raschel Knit	Jersey Knit		
Dishcloth Effect	Raschel Knit	Crochet Knit	Sheer		
Lace Effect	Crochet Effect	Lace Effect	Fine Weight		
Rib Knit	Lace Effect	Loop Effect	Tweed Effect		
1 x 1	Rib Knit	Double Cloth Effect	LaCoste®		
2 x 2	1 x 1	Tweed Effect	Open Effect		
3 x 3	2 x 2	Rib Knit	Pleated Effect		
Combinations &	Pique Effect	1 x 1	Milanese Knit		
Variations	Open Effect	2 x 2	Purl Knit		
Pique Effect	Combinations &	3 x 3	Raschel Knit		
Open Effect	Variations	4 x 4	Crochet Effect		
Thermo Knit	Tricot Knit	Combinations &	Lace Effect		
Dropped/	Sheer	Variations	Loop Fringe Effect		
Missed Stitch	Lightweight	Pique Effect	Double Cloth Effect		
Transfer Stitch	Medium Weight	Open Effect	Rib Knit		
Tuck Stitch/	Soft Finish	Thermo Knit	1 x 1		
Rib Effect	Crisp Finish	Dropped/Missed Stitch	2 x 2		
Cable Stitch	Patterned	Tuck Stitch	3 x 3		
Sweater Knit	Printed	Rib Effect	4 x 4		
Laid-in-Yarn	Dropped/	Popcorn Effect	Combinations &		
Intarsia	Missed Stitch	Cable Stitch	Variations		
	Transfer Stitch	Intarsia	Pique Effect		
	Tuck Stitch	Sweater Knit	Open Effect		
	Sweater Knit	Laid-in Yarn	Tricot Knit		
	Laid-in Yarn		Sheer		

Knit/Knit-type Fabrics (continued)

Cotton Knit Fabrics Natural Fibers	Silk Knit Fabrics Natural Fibers	Wool Knit Fabrics Natural Fibers	Knit Fabrics of 100% Man-Made Fibers & Blended Fibers	Stretch Knit Fabrics Natural Fibers	Metallic Fabrics Natural Fibers
	Weft-inserted Yarn Intarsia		Fine Weight Lightweight Medium Weight Heavyweight Crisp Finish Polished Cire Patterned Printed Dropped/ Missed Stitch Transfer Stitch Tuck Stitch Rib Effect Popcorn Effect Cable Stitch Intarsia Sweater Knit Laid-in Yarn		

Knit/Knit-type Fabrics with Face Finish

Napped/Sueded Face	Pile Face	High Pile Face

Suede Cloth
  Cotton Fibers
  Silk Fibers
  Wool Fibers
  Man-made Fibers
  Blended Fibers
Fleece
  Cotton Fibers
  Wool Fibers
  Man-made Fibers
  Blended Fibers
  Baby Bunting Fleece
  Sweatshirt Fleece
Plush
	Terry Cloth
	  Terry Velour
	  Sculptured
	Terry Chenille
	  Diagonal Pattern
	  Overall Pattern
	Tufted Cloth
	  Chenille Velvet/Velcle®
	  Chenille Yarn
	Velvet
	  Crushed
	  Panne
	Velour
	Sealskin Velour Velvet
		Astrakhan/Persian
		  Lamb
		Poodle Cloth
		Shag
		Sherpa/Sheared Lamb
		Teddy Bear

Lace Fabric Stucture

Lace is a fragile, fine or elaborately designed openwork fabric structure produced by manipulating a network of thread or yarn, or by the use of caustic chemicals on a base fabric. Lace may be made by hand or by machine. Many of the laces originally made by hand are now made by machine. Machine methods of lace-making can copy, duplicate or simulate the pattern and intricate work of the original handmade lace designs.

Construction techniques and methods of manipulating threads for lace-making include: appliqueing, braiding, crocheting, embroidering, interlacing, intertwining, knitting, knotting, looping, plaiting, stitching, tatting, twining, twisting, weaving.

Lace design is identified by:
- Types of basic stitches
- Use and combination of basic stitches
- Parts of the pattern
- Type of ground or mesh

Parts of Lace Fabric Structure

Appliqué
A separate piece or motif design laid on and applied to a ground fabric.

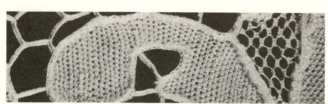
brides overcast with buttonhole stitch

brides with twisted threads

brides with cord strip

Brides/Bars/Ties/Bridges
Connecting threads that link parts and details of the design of the lace. Brides are used to hold together or connect lace designs having no net ground. Brides may consist of:

1. threads overcast with buttonhole stitches;
2. twisted, fully or partially plaited threads;
3. a cord strip or narrow piece of fabric.

Cordonnet
The heavier threads or raised outlines applied around a lace pattern or motif. The cordonnet may consist of gimp braid, heavy thread or yarn.

Filet
A square mesh ground or net of, and on, which darned laces are made.

Fond
Groundwork of lace formed by twisting double threads as opposed to fully or partially plaited grounds.

ground formed by brides

reseau net ground

mesh/machine-net ground

Ground

Background to the pattern. Grounds may be identified as:

1. bride grounds (grounds formed by brides);
2. reseau (net ground);
3. mesh (machine net).

Picot

Small loops that may be:

1. formed on the surface of the design;
2. protrude along the edge;
3. formed as part of the bride.

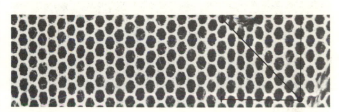

Points

Point is the degree of fineness or coarseness of the lace. To calculate the number of points per inch:

1. count the number of openings per inch in a straight line and in a diagonal 45° line;
2. multiply the straight line count by the diagonal count.

The greater the hole count the finer the lace.

Toile

The solid part of the *design* as distinguished from the ground.

Hand Methods Used to Produce Lace

Bobbin/Pillow Lace Method
Crochet Lace Method
Knotted Lace Method
Needlepoint Lace Method
    Needlepoint Cut Work Lace
    Needlepoint Drawn Work Lace
Appliquéd/Embroidered Lace
Combination Laces

The following terms describe types and varieties of hand-made laces which employ the original methods of lace-making.

tatting   macramé

Knotted Lace Method

A process of knotting threads with fingers, utilizing one or more coarse or thick yarns, in a variety of knot formations to produce the design. Tatted lace utilizes a shuttle wound with a fine single thread worked with the fingers to form a knotted lace with a circular motif.

bobbin/pillow method

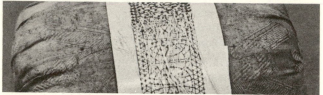

pillow used for handmade bobbin lace

Bobbin/Pillow Lace Method

A process of *interlacing* and *twisting*, in varying sequence, the same thread or threads around pins or pegs. Thread-wound bobbins are manipulated back and forth over a design marked on a pillow forming the pattern and the openwork ground.

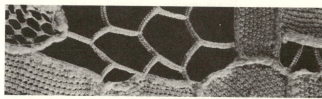

needlepoint lace

needlepoint cut work   needlepoint drawn work

Needlepoint Lace Method

A process of *stitching* utilizing a hand needle, thread and the buttonhole or blanket stitch. The weaving, darning and loop stitching processes fill in and attach a patterned design, which had been drawn on parchment. The term needlepoint applies to laces worked with a needle as distinguished from those made by bobbin, crocheting, knotting, darning or other methods. True *needlepoint* lace is when the needle is used in making a buttonhole stitch. The use of darning and overcast stitches is considered *needlework*.

Needlepoint Cut Work Lace A process of cutting away portions of fabric and outlining the cut edges with buttonhole stitches. Individual motifs are joined by bridges or ties to complete and/or hold the designed areas.

Needlepoint Drawn Work Lace A process of removing, pulling out or drawing threads from a woven cloth. The remaining threads of the drawn area are divided and pulled into groups which are stitched or overstitched to form an open pattern with an embroidered effect. Also considered needlework.

Crochet Lace Method

A process of *looping* a single thread utilizing a hooked hand needle and building the design across and upward.

Appliquéd/Embroidered Lace

A process of securing a design or motif to a sheer fabric or net ground. Motif may be appliquéd by machine or hand using buttonhole, overcast or chain stitches. The ground beneath the design may be left intact or cut away.

Combination Laces

A combination of lace-making methods to produce a new type of lace. Individual designs or motifs of bobbin- or needle-type laces are stitched to a bobbin net ground or may utilize bobbin- and needlework to attach the motifs. Combination lace methods may also include appliquéd lace and embroidered lace.

Machine Methods Used to Produce Lace

Leaver Machine Method
Raschel Machine Method
Nottingham/Bobbinet Machine Method
Jacquard Raschel Machine Method
Schiffli Machine Method
Burnt Out/Simulated Lace Method

The following terms describe methods or categories of machine-made lace that simulate original handmade laces.

Leaver Machine Method

A method utilizing the Leavers machine which incorporates the principles of weaving used by the Jacquard loom attachment. The mechanically controlled bobbins move in all directions and intertwist with the warp threads according to the planned pattern.

- Resembles handmade laces that incorporate knot and tie procedures
- Fine texture
- Lightweight
- Delicate and dainty patterned designs
- Intricate patterns on a net ground

Raschel Machine Method

A method utilizing a raschel warp knitting machine, employing multi-latch needles and guide bars, or limited bars, and incorporating an interlooping method or loop structures the same as in a knitted fabric. Large quantities of lace may be produced in a short time; less expensive than other laces. Method may use laying-in yarn technique for variation.

- Flat-surfaced design
- Variety of net and lace fabrics
- Different effects and variations

Nottingham/Bobbinet Machine Method

A method utilizing a bobbinet lace-type machine with a programmed multicard Jacquard set-up which incorporates a warp and filling thread structure whereby the filling yarns on the bobbins are intercepted between the warp yarns. The filling yarns surface to the face of the fabric between the gate and across the courses, producing a slightly raised surface. Machine may be set up to produce laces of various widths, lengths and shapes.

- Fully framed patterns
- Coarse, heavy, and durable
- Bold, large allover patterns with simple or complex designs
- Figures and wildlife patterns similar to Jacquard woven fabrics
- Dimensional-surfaced design

Schiffli Machine Method

A method utilizing a Schiffli machine employing multi-needle operations controlled by punch cards similar to the Jacquard system of weaving. The embroidery technique is applied to a net fabric base to produce the lace. When Schiffli embroidery is applied to woven goods it is referred to as embroidered fabric.

- Fine and lightweight
- Fine and intricate designs
- Various colored threads or metallic thread may be introduced into the design

Jacquard Raschel Machine Method

A method utilizing a raschel lace-making machine with Jacquard card-controlled pattern procedures. Lace may be produced as completely designed units of definite sizes and shapes, garment components, inserts for various parts of garments, allover patterned fabrics, and as trimmings.

- Heavy, thick yarns or fine, smooth yarns
- Coarse, thick fabric or fine, thin fabric
- Simple or complex designs
- Resembles traditional bobbinet-type lace
- Duplicates handmade knotted macrame

Burnt Out/Simulated Lace Methods

A design or pattern is embroidered on a base fabric which will be removed by heat or caustic chemicals leaving only the stitched embroidered design in relief form. The yarn used for the embroidery is resistant to the level of heat or type of chemicals used to remove the base fabric. Burnt out method is also used to produce cut work designed lace.

Allover Lace
Banding/Lace Ribbon
Beading/Ribboned Lace
Border Lace/Flounce
Edging Lace
Galloon Lace
Insertion Lace
Medallion
Motif
Sprig
Reembroidered/Embroidered Lace

Laces may be produced as fabric goods with an allover design and pattern or as trimmings or edgings with one, both or neither lengthwise edge decoratively finished.

Allover Lace

A term applied to wide laces with the design or motif distributed and repeated throughout the entire surface of the fabric—not confined to a bordered edge. All-over lace is produced in widths of 36″ (91.4 cm) or more and with both lengthwise edges finished the same; usually devoid of scallops. The lace is used as fabric for an entire garment or section of a garment.

Banding/Lace Ribbon

A term applied to laces designed with scallops or picots on one or both lengthwise edges. Banding is produced in widths under 8″ (20.3 cm). The lace is designed for *application* on woven goods or spanning a section of a garment. Banding may be used as a border or edging.

edge-type beading lace

galloon-type beading lace

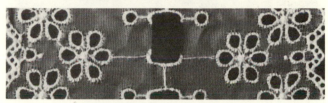

ribbon pulled through beading lace

simulated beading lace

Beading/Ribboned Lace

A term applied to laces designed with perforations or openings through which ribbons can be inserted.

Ribbon/beading lace is designed:
- In a variety of widths
- In a variety of edge finishes
- For a variety of ribbon insertions
- To be left flat or gathered
- To create a ruffled effect when ribbon is pulled through
- To be inserted between fabric layers
- To be used as trimming, banding, edging, straps and ties

Beading Edge Type A ribbon lace with openings at one lengthwise edge.

Beading Galloon Type A ribbon lace designed with openings in the center and a scalloped finish along both lengthwise edges.

Beading Insertion Type A ribbon lace designed with openings in the center and unfinished straight sides along both lengthwise edges.

Simulated Beading Lace A ribbon-type lace designed with raised and recessed areas to create the illusion of openings and inserted ribbons. The openings and ribbon may be of the same or different colors and may be made of elastomeric yarns having stretch properties. ▶

Border Lace/Flounce

A term applied to lace finished with a scalloped edge or decorative border on one lengthwise edge. Border laces are produced in widths of 12″ (30.5 cm) or more. The lace is used as fabric for an entire garment or section of a garment such as a border on mantillas, shawls or scarfs; as a ruffle or flounce to edge a section of a garment.

Edging Lace

A term applied to narrow laces that are designed with one straight edge and one scalloped or picot edge. The lace is used as a trimming or to edge garments. Val or Valenciennes laces are known as edging laces.

Galloon Lace

A term applied to laces designed with a scalloped finish along both lengthwise edges. Galloon lace is produced in widths of 18″ (45.7 cm) or less. The lace is designed to be used as ruffles, banding, applique or insertions.

insertion lace applied to garment

Insertion Lace

A term applied to laces designed with edges that are straight and void of scallops on any lengthwise side. Insertion laces are produced in widths under 4″ (10.2 cm). The lace is designed for application between two pieces of fabric.

Medallion

A term applied to a single unit lace design or a finished motif. The medallion is used as an applique on fabric, net or other laces.

Motif

A term applied to a unit of designed lace that forms a separate pattern or section of a garment such as a collar, cuff, pocket or neckline.

reembroidered lace using gimp

reembroidered lace
using round cord

reembroidered lace
using cellophane

reembroidered lace using sequins

Reembroidered/Embroidered Lace

A term applied to lace fabric in which the design is outlined with any variety of cord, yarn, gimp, ribbon, beading or sequins. The outlines are raised on the surface of the lace.

Lace/Lace-type Fabrics

Cotton/Cotton-type/ Cottony Hand	Silk/Silk-type/ Silky Hand	Wool/Wool-type/ Woolly Hand	Stretch/Stretch-type/ Stretch Qualities	Metallic/ Metallic-type/ Metallic Hand

Cluny-type
Crochet
Cutwork-type
  Eyelet
Duchesse-type
Embroidered-type
Eyelet-type
  Drawn Work
  Burnt-out Method
Filet-type
  Crochet
  Darned Work
Macrame
Nottingham-type
Pt de Venice
Pt Plat de Venice
Shadow-type
Tatting/Tatted
Val/Val-type
Venice/Gros Pt de
  Venice
	Alençon-type
	Binche-type
	Blonde-type
	Brussels-type
	Chantilly-type
	  Reembroidered
	Crochet-type
	Duchesse-type
	Embroidered-type
	Filet-type
	  Crochet
	  Darned Work
	Honiton-type
	Macrame
	Pt de Esprite
	Pt de France
	Pt de Venice
	Pt Plat de Venice
	Rose Point-type
	  Large Motif
	  Small Motif
	Shadow-type
	Tatting/Tatted
	Val/Val-type
	Venice/Gros Pt de
	  Venice
		Blonde-type
		Crochet-type
		Filet-type
		  Crochet
		  Darned Work
		Macrame
		Nottingham-type
		Shadow-type
		Tatting/Tatted
			Yarn & Fabric structure
			  Lace
			  Net
			  Power Net
			Yarn
			  Crochet-type
				Lace
				  Chantilly-type
				    with Metallic
				    Yarn
				  Pt de Esprite
				  Embroidered-type
				    with Metallic
				    Yarn
				  Macrame

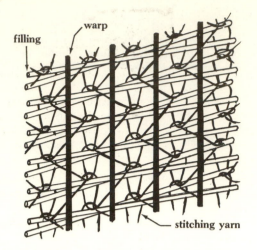

Mali/Stitch-bonded Fabric Structure

Mali fabric structure is a method of producing fabric without utilizing conventional methods of weaving, knitting, felting or bonding. The mali structure utilizes three systems of thread. Two systems are laid one over the other and the third system creates stitches which hold the other together thus forming a stitch-bonded fabric structure.

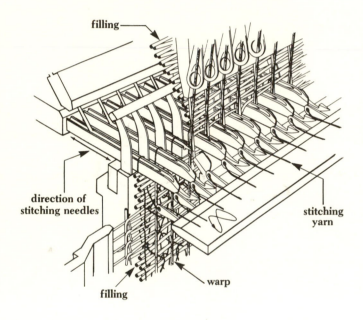

Malimo Fabric Structure

Malimo fabric is a three-dimensional Mali-type or Arachne fabric structure that is neither woven nor knitted; named after the Mali or Arachne machine employed in its manufacturing. Fabric is produced by one or more warp yarns placed over one or more layers of filling yarn. The criss-crossed layers of yarns are locked or held together by an additional thread system and by a multi-needle operation performed by an interlocking tricot or interlocking chain-stitch machine. Variations in malimo construction includes use of two or more yarn systems, different arrangements of warp and filling yarns and use of backing fabric instead of warp yarn.

Variation possibilities of malimo construction:
- A high yarn count in warp and filling and fine stitching thread result in a fabric with a woven look
- An equal yarn count in all three systems results in a fabric with a woven look on underside of fabric
- A fine warp and filling count and prominent stitching thread result in a fabric with a knit look while maintaining a woven fabric's characteristics.
- Behaves like a woven fabric
- Does not ravel

Physical properties and performance expectations of the fabric depend on the fiber and yarn components.

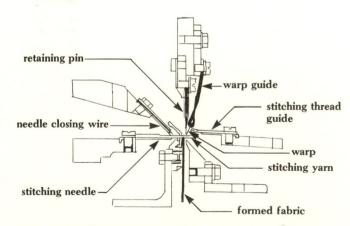

Cross section illustrates how the filling and warp yarns are stitched together by the malimo fabric-forming technique.

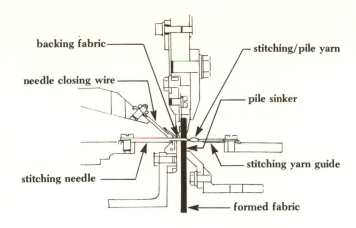

backing fabric

needle closing wire

stitching needle

stitching/pile yarn

pile sinker

stitching yarn guide

formed fabric

Cross section illustrates the malipol technique of stitching loops through a flat backing fabric to form pile fabric.

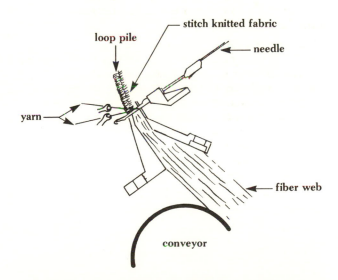

A malipol pile fabric with loops on both face and back formed by combining tufting and knitting processes.

loop pile

stitch knitted fabric

needle

yarn

fiber web

conveyor

Malipol Fabric Structure

Malipol fabric is a Mali-type fabric structure of a malimo variation that forms a single-faced pile fabric. Malipol pile fabric is produced by tufts of thread or yarn punched through a base fabric structure, resulting in a pile surface on the face side of the fabric. Tufts are held in place by closely spaced rows of chainstitching visible on the back of the fabric. A coating of adhesive on the fabric back anchors stitches and tufts. Face side of fabric is polished laying the pile in a lengthwise direction and producing a crushed panne velvet look.

- Crushed velvet with a high glossy, shiny appearance
- Simulated or imitation fur fabric for outerwear and linings
- Poor reaction to cleaning solvents causing changes in appearance and hand
- Poor abrasion causing loss of pile during wear or dry cleaning

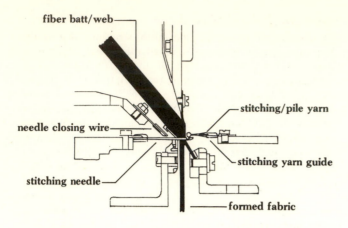

Cross section illustrates the maliwatt technique of stitching a yarn through a batt of loose fibers to form a felt-like fabric.

Maliwatt Fabric Structure

Maliwatt fabric is a Mali-type fabric structure that forms a firm fabric. Malliwatt fabric is produced by overstitching compacted bats or webs of loose fibers and utilizing an interlocking chainstitch or plain chainstitch.

- Retain natural fluffiness of the fiber
- Felt-type fabric without a grain or direction
- Variety of hand and appearances
- Variety of thicknesses and weights

Variations of maliwatt fabrics can be achieved by changing:

- Types or blends of fibers
- Type, size and count of overstitching yarn
- Regulation of stitch formation
- Impregnation of various substances in the fibers or bats
- Type of finishing process

COATING HIGH PILE FABRICS

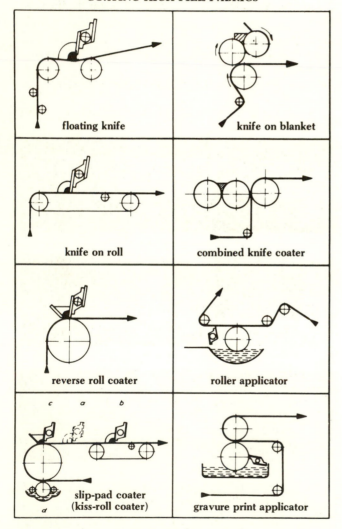

floating knife

knife on blanket

knife on roll

combined knife coater

reverse roll coater

roller applicator

slip-pad coater (kiss-roll coater)

gravure print applicator

net points per inch

Net Fabric Structure

A geometric open mesh fabric structure produced by twisting, knotting or fusing yarns together at each point of intersection. Traditionally, net fabric was made by hand knotting yarns at each intersecting point and was referred to as a netted lace. Nets are now produced commercially on special purpose bobbinet, raschel or tricot knitting machines which can copy, duplicate or imitate hand-knotted net. Net construction is produced in a variety of gauge, denier, weight, hand and flexibility.

Net and net-type fabrics are categorized according to the degree of fineness or coarseness which is stated in *points* or *point count*. Point count, a numbering system used for lace and net fabric structures, indicates the number of openings to the inch. To calculate the number of points per inch:

1. count the number of openings per inch in a straight line and in a diagonal (45°) line and;
2. multiply the straight count by the diagonal count.

The greater the hole count or number of points the finer the net.

- Lightweight
- Airy open construction
- Resilient and strong
- Used for a base/ground for lace, embroidery or beading
- Used for a base/ground for darning and decorative network

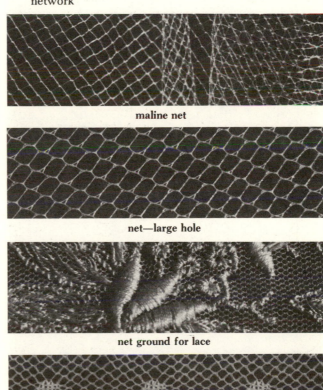

maline net

net—large hole

net ground for lace

pt. d'esprit net

variations in openings/point count

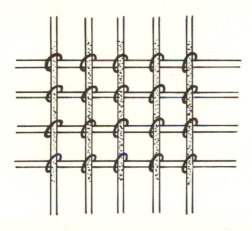

cable/laundry net

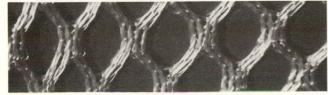

fishnet

Net/Netting/Net-type Fabrics

Cottony Hand	Silky Hand	Stretch Qualities	Metallic Hand

Cable Net/Laundry Mesh
Fishnet
	Cable Net/Laundry Mesh
	Fishnet
	   Fine Hole
	   Small Hole
	   Medium Hole
	   Large Hole
	Maline Net
	   Fine Hole
	   Small Hole
	   Medium Hole
	   Large Hole
	Net
	Pt d'Esprit Net
	Pt d'Esprit Tulle
	Tulle
	Tulle Illusion/Veiling
		Fishnet
		   Medium Hole
		   Large Hole
		Net
		   Stretch Net
		   Power Stretch
			Metallic Fishnet
			Metallic Mesh
			Metallic Net

translucent to opaque

soft to firm

thin to thick

smooth to textured

flat

surface interest

Nonwoven/Fused/Formed Fabric Structure

A fabric structure produced directly from fibers by a process of interlocking or bonding the fibers by any one of the following seven processes:

1. Dry Process—Dry Forming (Carding or Garnetting)
2. Dry Process—Dry Forming (Air-Laid)
3. Spunbonded Process
4. Spunlaced Process
5. Film Extrusion Process
6. Wet Process
7. Needlepunched Process

Fibers used to produce nonwoven fabrics, alone or in combination, include cotton, wool, acetate, acrylic, nylon, rayon and polyester.

- Translucent to opaque
- Soft to firm hand
- Inelastic/rigid to stretchable in one or all directions
- All bias stretch
- Light- to heavyweight
- High porosity permitting air flow to impermeable
- High to low tear and bursting strength
- Fluid to stiff drapability qualities
- Washable to dry cleanable, but may change color or hand during laundering or cleaning process
- No grain or selvage
- Does not ravel or fray
- May be shaped and molded to form
- Uniform in quality throughout
- Provides bulk without increase in weight
- Less expensive to produce than wovens or knits
- Used as fabric goods or as backing for other goods.

Variations in nonwoven fabric structure are produced by:
- Structure of Fiber—natural or man-made
- Type of Fiber—spun, filament or film-formed
- Denier, Length and Crimp of Fiber
- Formation or Orientation of Web—parallel, cross-layered, undirectional, random
- Type of Bonding Agents—adhesives, resins, heat fusion, thermoplastic, thermoplastic stitch through, needle-punching, or needle weave through

Method of Manufacturing—weight, thickness and bulk of fiber, formation and layers of web, content of fiber, type or method of bonding and manufacturing processes used will affect the appearance, hand, characteristics and performance expectations of the finished fabric.

Nonwoven/fused/formed structured fabrics are produced under various company-listed trademark names and include:
- Sew-on application types
- Iron-on/Press-on application types
- Fusible types
- Featherweight, lightweight, medium weight, heavyweight
- Bias featherweights and lightweights
- Stretch nonwovens of one-direction stretch, length- or crosswise stretch, two or more direction stretch
- Special nonwoven finishes of durable press or permanent press

Processes Used to Produce Nonwoven Fabric Structures

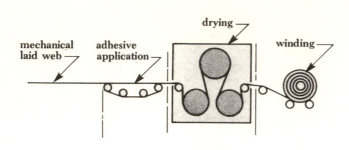

Dry Process—Dry Forming (Carding or Garnetting)

Process   Individual natural or man-made fibers are metered and uniformly distributed by mechanical means to form a moving web. Fiber-to-fiber bonding is then achieved by the addition of binders or by heat fusion. Following drying of the binder chemicals, the resulting web is wound into a roll, ready for post-treatment or conversion into a finished product.

Fabric Characteristics
- Soft hand
- Excellent drape
- Strength is oriented in the direction of web travel through forming process—one directional
- Weights range from 0.3-6 ounces per square yard
- Thicknesses range from 3-15 mils

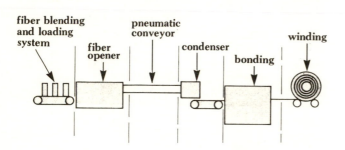

Dry Process—Dry Forming (Air-laid)

Process   Like carding or garnetting, the air forming process meters individual natural or man-made fibers into a finished web. Distribution, however, is accomplished by suspending the fibers in an airstream and then forming them into a continuously moving web. By controlling the characteristics of the airstream, fiber direction can be more randomly oriented than in the previous process. The fibers in the web are then chemically- or heat-bonded and the web is wound into a finished roll.

Fabric Characteristics
- Properties similar to those of carded web, except that machine direction strength and cross-machine-direction strength tend to be more nearly equal—isotropic
- Weights range from 0.5–6 ounces per square yard
- Thicknesses range from 5–70 mils

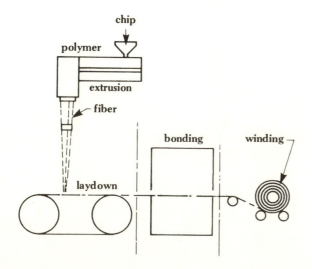

Spunbonded Process

Process   Spunbonding is a continuous process producing a finished fabric from polymer. A polymer, or several polymers, such as polyester, polyamide, polypropylene, polyethylene or others, is fed into an extruder. As it flows from the extruder it is forced through a spinneret, a device with tiny holes, like a shower nozzle. After cooling, the resulting continuous filaments are then laid down on a moving conveyor belt to form a continuous web. In the lay-down process, the desired orientation of the fibers is achieved by various means, such as rotation of the spinneret, electrical charges, introduction of controlled airstreams or varying the speed of the conveyor belt. The fabric is then bonded by thermal or chemical treatment before being wound up into finished roll form.

Fabric Characteristics
- Wide range of characteristics can be achieved by controlling the various elements
- High performance-low weight fabrics because of the continuous nature of the fibers
- Weights range from 0.3-6 ounces per square yard
- Thicknesses range from 3-25 mils

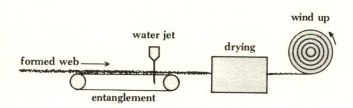

Spunlaced Process

Process   In this system, a fibrous web is subjected to high-velocity water jets that entangle the fibers and achieve mechanical bonding. The fabric then travels through conventional drying and wind-up operations.

Fabric Characteristics

- Very soft and drapable fabrics because of the substitution of mechanical bonding of fibers
- Weights range from 0.7–2.2 ounces per square yard
- Thicknesses range from 3.5–25 mils

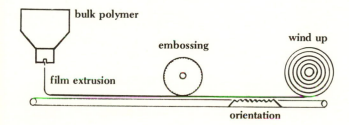

Film Extrusion Process

Process   Film extruded nonwovens are formed in a continuous process from a polymer melt of polypropylene, polypropylene copolymers or polyethylene. The web is formed by extruding the melt through a slotted film die. Any one of several patterns may then be cut into the web by an embossing roll. When the web is biaxially oriented, it opens up into a network structure or nonwoven fabric.

Fabric Characteristics

- Excellent uniformity in lightweight nonwovens
- Embossing pattern, type of polymer, film thickness and degree of orientation determine characteristics
- Weights range from 0.2–1.6 ounces per square yard
- Thicknesses range from 2–20 mils

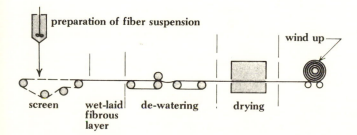

Wet Process

Process   In wet forming of nonwoven fabrics, individual natural or man-made fibers are suspended in water to obtain a uniform dispersion. As the fiber-and-water suspension flows onto a moving screen, the water passes through, leaving the fibers laid uniformly in the form of a web. Additional water is then squeezed out of the web and the remaining water is removed by drying. Bonding may be done completely during the drying step, or further bonding may be achieved through the use of rolls. Following bonding, the fabric is wound up into a finished roll ready for subsequent operations.

Fabric Characteristics

- Water suspension of fibers results in generally random orientation of fibers
- Weights range from 0.3–16 ounces per square yard
- Thicknesses range from 2.3–190 mils

Needlepunched Process

Process A needlepunched fabric is produced by introducing a fibrous web—already formed by cards, garnetts or air-laying—into a machine equipped with groups of specially designed needles. While the web is trapped between a bed plate and a stripper plate, the needles punch through it and reorient the fibers so that mechanical bonding is achieved among the individual fibers. Often, the batt of fibers is carried into the needlepunching section of the machine on a lightweight support material or substrate. This is done to improve finished fabric strength and integrity.

Fabric Characteristics
- High density yet retains some bulk
- Weights range from 1.7–10 ounces per square yard
- Thicknesses range from 15–160 mils

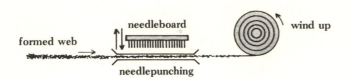

formed web   needleboard   wind up

needlepunching

Nonwoven Fabric Structure Needling Systems

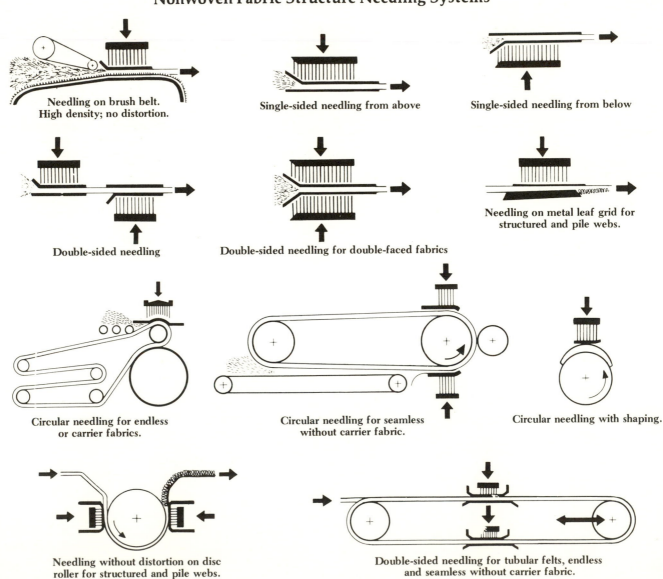

Needling on brush belt. High density; no distortion.

Single-sided needling from above

Single-sided needling from below

Double-sided needling

Double-sided needling for double-faced fabrics

Needling on metal leaf grid for structured and pile webs.

Circular needling for endless or carrier fabrics.

Circular needling for seamless without carrier fabric.

Circular needling with shaping.

Needling without distortion on disc roller for structured and pile webs.

Double-sided needling for tubular felts, endless and seamless without carrier fabric.

W-pile formation utilizing three-yarn interlacing.

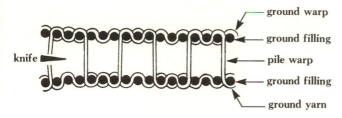

W-pile formation for double cloth pile weaving. Knife cuts pile to make two separate fabrics.

V-pile formation utilizing one-yarn interlacing.

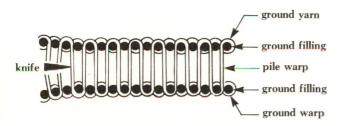

V-pile formation for double cloth pile weaving. Knife cuts pile to make two separate fabrics.

Pile Surface Fabric Structure

A pile-surface fabric structure is formed by any one of a variety of different techniques which utilize three sets of yarns: the warp and filling yarns are the base or ground yarns and an additional set of yarns introduced into the warp or filling yarns of a woven or knit fabric form the pile or loop surface. The additional yarns forming the pile may be cut, clipped or sheared to produce a pile which stands erect on the face of the fabric or may be left uncut to form loops on one or both sides of the fabric.

Pile-surface fabrics may be produced by one of the following methods:
1. double-cloth method
2. slack tension or loop method;
3. wire method.

Pile-surface fabrics can also be produced on a Mali, Arachne or Arallop machine. The process produces pile fabrics utilizing a nonwoven fiber web through which the loops or tufts are stitched or punched in place (see Mali Fabric Structure).

A Kraftamatic machine combines a tufting and knitting technique, locking the loops in place. With this process, the loops may be formed on one or both sides of the fabric.

- V or W construction
- Different woven or knitted ground or base fabric
- Tight, loose or stretchy knit or woven ground structures
- Cut or uncut loops or any combination
- Pile may be of a different fiber or yarn than ground
- Pile may be cut alternately high or lower for decorative effect
- Pile may be brushed, crushed or patterned
- Uncut loops may vary in height
- Surface may have an "up and down" direction; brushed *downward* produces a lighter, dull-toned grey-colored pile; brushed *upward* produces a dark, deep-colored pile
- Brushed upward exposes pile to rubbing forces or abrasion
- Entraps air and holds in body heat

Pile surface fabrics may be classified as *warp pile fabric or filling pile fabric*. *Warp pile fabrics* are made with two warp yarns and one filling yarn. The pile is formed in rows that run across the fabric. *Filling pile fabrics* are made with two filling yarns and one warp yarn. In filling pile fabrics, the pile forms rows that run the warp or length of the fabric.

Terms Related to Pile Surface Fabric Structures

level loop pile

multilevel loop pile

Loop/Uncut Pile

The base cloth is fed through the machine in the direction indicated at the same time as the needles are being reciprocated vertically, so as to penetrate the cloth at regular intervals. The loops are shed from the hooks after they are formed. They remain uncut forming a loop pile.

Loops may all have the same height, which produces a smooth level surface, or they may be staggered at two or three different heights to create a sculptured surface.

velvet—yarns with very little twist

plush—yarns in a range of twist

friezé—tightly twisted yarns

Cut pile fabrics are constructed with yarns of varying amounts of twist.

Cut Pile

On cut pile machinery the hook itself is one element of the cutting shears and works with a cooperating *knife to cut* the formed loops producing *cut pile*. The cut yarns untwist slightly or "bloom when cut."

Combinations of cut and uncut pile can offer a wide variety of sculptured effects.

chenille/candlewick

Tufted Fabrics

Tufted fabrics are made in two basic constructions:
1. cut pile
2. loop pile

In both cases an endless strand of needle-thread (yarn) for each needle in the machine is inserted into a base fabric at regular intervals and looped around cooperating hooks on the back side of the fabric to form tufts. Tufted fabric is distinguished by the individually spaced tufts that form the pile design. Heavily plied yarns are needled into the base fabric forming loops on the surface. The loops are cut, sheared, and brushed to give the fuzzy cut yarn the effect of chenille.

Weight and density of tufted goods depend on:
- Gauge of machinery
- Length of nap or pile
- Number of stitches per inch
- Type and size of yarns
- Type of backing or base fabric

LOOP PILE TUFTED FABRIC STRUCTURE

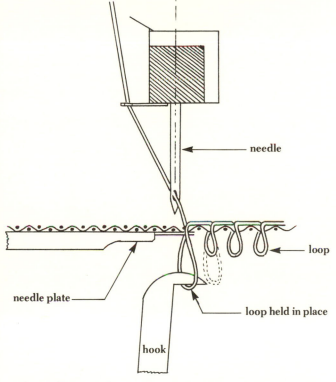

The needle inserts the yarn through the fabric to form a loop pile. The hook catches the loop and holds it in place as the needle retracts. Height of loop may be varied depending on effect desired.

CUT PILE TUFTED FABRIC STRUCTURE

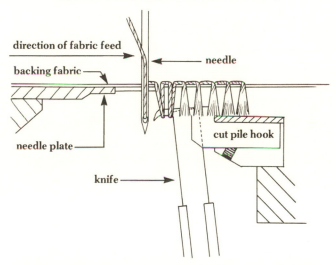

Each time the fabric is fed forward, the tufting needle pushes the yarn through the fabric to form a loop pile. The pile hook moves in a forward progression; the knife moves with it to cut progressively the rearmost loop on the hook.

Velvet Fabric Structure

1. Two layers of fabric are woven simultaneously on a double-action shuttle loom.
2. As the fabric leaves the loom, the vertical filling yarns are severed forming two separate fabrics—each with upright pile surfaces. The lengthwise warp yarns form the pile in the weaving of velvet.
3. The pile fabric is passed under shears to even and level the pile to a predetermined height forming a smooth, uniform surface.

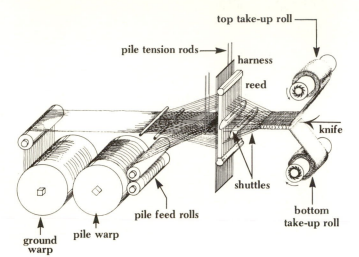

Friezé Fabric Structure

Friezé fabric is constructed by raising supplementary warp yarns into a loop pile by means of wires inserted during the weaving process.

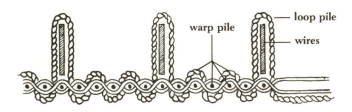

Corduroy Fabric Structure

1. Base of ground of the fabric is woven at the same time as the pile.
2. Each supplementary filling yarn that floats over the woven ground is slit.
3. When cut the fibers spring up and stand erect.
4. Cut fibers are brushed together to form the pile in ribs, cords or wales.
5. The crosswise filling yarns form the pile in weaving corduroy. The width of the rib will be governed by the length of the float.

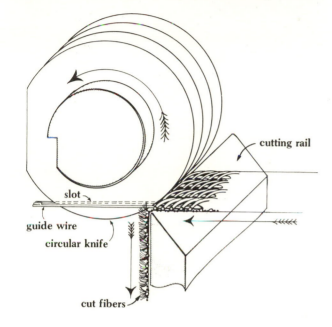

woven terry cloth (filling pile)

terry cloth (knit base)

Terry Cloth

A woven or knit uncut loop structure produced as single faced with loop formation on face or double faced with loop formation on face and back. Size, shape and density of loop formation may vary.

face of cloth

base of cloth

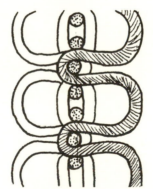

loop formation of
single-faced terry cloth

loop formation of
double-faced terry cloth

Pile Surface/Pile-type Fabrics

Cotton-type/ Cottony Hand 100% Natural or Man-made Fibers, Blended Fibers	Silk-type/ Silky Hand 100% Natural or Man-made Fibers, Blended Fibers	Wool-type/ Wooly Hand 100% Natural or Man-made Fibers & Blended Fibers	Metallic-type Man-made Fibers & Blended Fibers	Stretch-type/ Stretch Qualities 100% Natural or Man-made Fibers, Blended Fibers	Knit Base 100% Natural or Man-made Fibers, Blended Fibers
Corduroy	Fleece	Astrakhan/Poodle Cloth	Brocade Velvet	Yarn & Fabric Structure	Fleece
Feathercord	Velvet	Fleece	Metallic Pile	Stretch	Cotton
Fine Wale	Brocade	Tufted Cloth		Stretch Terry Cloth	Silk
Mid Wale	Crushed	Chenille Velvet/			Wool
Thick-set	Cut	Velcle®			Baby Bunting
Wide Wale	Embossed	Chenille Yarn Fabric			Sweatshirt
Broad Wale	Lyons	Simulated Fur Pile			Plush
Novelty Wale	Panne	Beaver			Terry Cloth
Fleece	Transparent	Chinchilla			Terry Velour
Frieze	Velour/Sealskin Velour	Ermine			Sculptured Terry
Terry Cloth	Simulated Fur Pile	Fox Red			Terry Chenille
Single-faced	Poodle Cloth	Silver Fox			(diagonal &
Double-faced	Shag	White Fox			overall pattern)
Tufted Cloth	Teddy Bear	Blue Fox			
Chenille Candlewick	Ocelot	Giraffe			
Chenille Velvet/Velcle®	Poney	Astrakhan/Persian			
Chenille Yarn Fabric	Seal	Lamb			
Velvet	Tiger	Broadtail			
Cotton	Zebra	Sherpa/Sheared Lamb			
Flocked		Leopard			
Lyons		Lynx			
Velvet Cord		Mink			
Velveteen		Muskrat			
Simulated Fur Pile		Opossum			
Shag		Rabbit			
		Raccoon			
		Squirrel			
		Skunk			
		Teddy Bear			

Stretch/Stretch Yarn Fabric Structure

A woven or knitted fabric constructed with specially prepared yarns or mechanically/chemically finished yarns to produce the characteristics of stretch and recovery to its original state on release from tension.

Stretch characteristics can be developed at the fiber, yarn or fabric structure stages.

- Increased comfort to the wearer
- Used for action and comfort stretch garments
- Used for well-fitted and attractive garments
- Improved and unrestricted form-fitting qualities to the body
- Greater and easier stretch
- Allow for greater and freer movement of the body
- Action and give needed when flexing elbows and knees
- Provide stretch across hips, shoulder, and seat of garments
- Higher elongation factor than any other fabric
- Extension and recovery for garment
- Shape retention and wrinkle resistant
- Wide range of designs

Types of fiber and/or yarns, finishes or structure used for stretch fabrics depend on the:

- Desired amount of elasticity
- Desired amount of power
- Yarns resemblance to other fibers
- Sheerness and hand of fiber, yarn or fabric
- Type of fabric structure
- End use of fabric
- Style and end use of garment

Amount of stretch and power or strength of stretch and recovery of the fabric depend on the types of fibers, the ply

knitted stretch fabric structure

knitted stretch fabric
with elastomeric fibers

Helenca® nylon stretch yarn

back twisting stretch yarn

heat-set crinkle stretch finish

and method of yarn process, the structure of the fabric, and the types and methods of finishes employed.

Stretch fabrics range from soft, pliable lightweights to firm, closely woven heavyweights with smooth, textured or pile surfaces.

Fibers for stretch fabrics include:
- Elastomeric fibers such as rubber or spandex
- Heat-set thermoplastic fibers with memory
- Modified version of filament fibers

Yarns for stretch fabrics include:
- Modified version of filament yarns
- Stretch, textured or high-bulked yarns
- Core-spun yarns with spandex or rubber core
- Conventional or false-twist-type yarns

Fabric Structures for stretch fabrics include:
- Knit fabrics made with elastomeric or core-spun yarns
- Most knit fabric structures with stretch in one or both directions (controlled by method or type of knitting process)
- Crepe fabrics made with high-twist yarns

Finishes for stretch fabrics include:
- Mechanical or chemical stretch
- Slack mercerization process
- Crinkle heat-set finish

Most fibers, natural or man-made, can be treated to produce a yarn with some degree of stretch and recovery. Variations of fibers and in methods of applying stretch properties will result in different built-in stretch and recovery properties.

When fabrics made with twist-textured yarns are stretched, the yarns extend; when fabrics relax, the yarns recoil to the heat-set shorter length.

Degree of stretch is referred to as the elongation factor of stretch fabrics. Stretch fabric elongation or degree of stretch may be measured as:
1. 5%–8% elongation—(woven fabric comfort stretch);
2. 400%–500% elongation—(Lycra® power stretch).

Stretch fabrics can be produced with:
- Horizontal stretch
- Vertical stretch
- Two-way stretch
- Power stretch
- Comfort stretch

Horizontal Stretch Stretch yarns are used as the filling yarns providing stretch in the crosswise direction, from selvage to selvage.

Vertical Stretch Stretch yarns are used as the warp yarns providing stretch in the lengthwise direction.

Two-Way Stretch Stretch yarns are used as both the filling and the warp yarns providing stretch in *all* directions.

Power Stretch
- With 10%–200% extensibility
- With spandex, lastril or rubber fibers and yarns
- Composed of heavy yarns
- For garments with holding power
- For garments with support and hold in body and muscles

Comfort Stretch
- With 15%–50% extensibility
- With textured nylon or polyester fibers and yarns
- Composed of core-spun spandex yarns
- May be made with regular yarns with special finishes
- Contain fine- to medium-sized yarns
- For garments with more give to body

PARTS OF THE LOOM

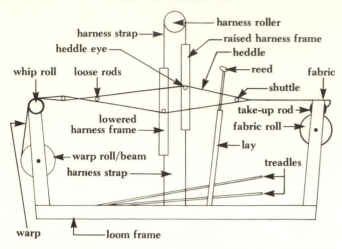

The movement of the harnesses produce the shed or opening through which the filling yarn is passed.

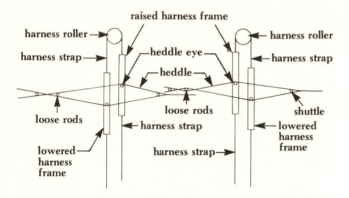

To permit the insertion of the filling pick and to have the filling interlace with the warp, it is essential to raise and lower the harnesses systematically.

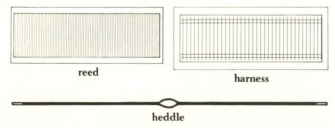

Each harness holds many heddles. The heddle is a thin metal or wire strip with an eye in the center. The reed is similar to a comb. Warp ends are threaded through the eye of the heddle and through an opening in the reed.

Woven Fabric Structure

Woven fabric structure constitutes one of the most widely used methods of fabric construction. Woven fabrics are produced on any one of a variety of simple or complex looms, which interlace or intersect one or more warp (length) and filling (cross) yarns at right angles.

Warp Yarns   Warp yarns run the length of the fabric and are referred to as the lengthgrains or length yarns in the finished cloth.

Filling or Pick Yarns   Filling or pick yarns run the width of the fabric from selvage to selvage and are referred to as the crossgrains or cross yarns in the finished cloth.

The three basic weaves used to produce woven fabrics are:
1. plain weave;
2. twill weave;
3. satin weave.

Within the structure of these basic weaves are variations. Other weaves are variations and/or combinations of the basic weaves and are classified as *complex or novelty weaves*.

Weave variations are produced by :
- Different ply, count or texture of yarns
- Equal or unequal size and count of yarns
- Equal or unequal yarn count for warp and filling
- Equal yarn size and unequal or dented spacing
- Equal yarn count for warp and filling and unequal yarn size
- Interlacing different patterns and weave effects
- Interlacing different colored yarns

Type of weave selected to achieve the desired effect is determined by:
- Ply or texture of thread
- Count of thread
- Luster desired
- Strength required
- Pattern produced
- Surface textures
- Color effect
- End use
- Cost

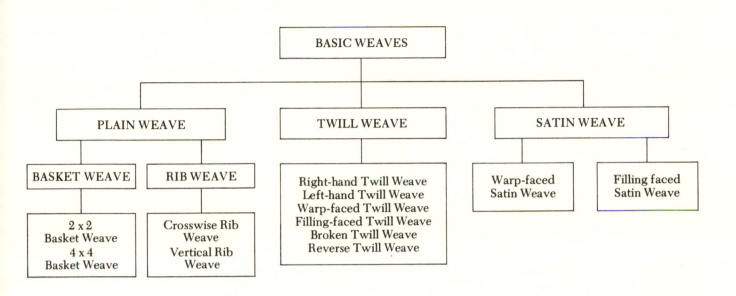

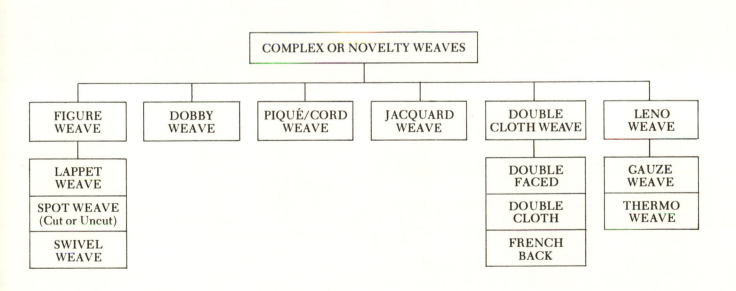

basket weave (mock up)

1X2 basket weave

2X2 basket weave

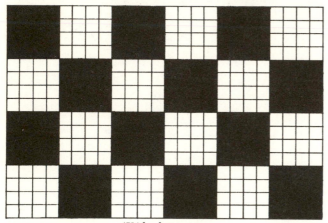

4X4 basket weave

Basket Weave

Basket weave is a variation of the plain weave. Two or more warp end yarns, functioning and interlacing as one yarn, are interlaced over and under two or more filling/pick yarns, which are also functioning and interlacing as one. Variations within the basket weave structure are produced by the quantity and thickness of yarns within the group. Yarns used may:

1. be the same in the warp and in the filling;
2. vary in the warp and in the filling;
3. vary within the warp and filling.

- Decorative weave
- Flat weave effect
- Coarse looking
- Loose-type goods
- Porous
- Shed wrinkles
- Do not hold creases
- Not durable
- Do not withstand chafing, friction or abrasion
- Tend to snag easily
- Yarns move and shift
- Poor shape retention
- Shrink when laundered

Basket Weave/Basket Weave Variations

Cotton/ Cotton-type Fabrics	Silk/ Silk-type Fabrics	Wool/ Wool-type Fabrics
Hopsaking Monk's Cloth Oxford Oxford Stripe	Hopsaking	Hopsaking

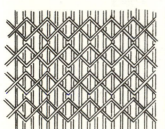

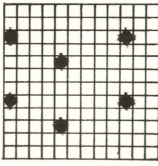

dobby weave (mock up)

Dobby Weave

A flat or raised, small floral, dotted or geometric patterned weave produced with a dobby attachment on a loom. Patterned designs woven repeatedly throughout the fabric are referred to as: *birdseye, nailhead, dots, squares, diamonds, honeycombs.*

- Decoratively woven patterns or designs
- Dull and shiny surface effects
- Tone-on-tone effects using the same yarn color
- Small patterns in geometric forms in a sequence

double cloth

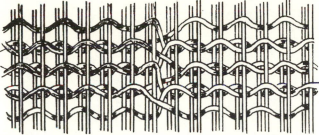

double cloth with two sets of warp yarns and two sets of filling yarns

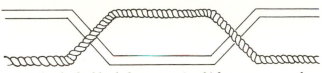

matalassé—double cloth structure in which crepe yarns and conventional yarns crisscross

Double Cloth

A single-ply fabric produced by two sets of filling and one set of warp yarns or two sets of warp and one set of filling yarns. The extra warp or filling yarns are interlaced in a satin or twill weave construction to form the fabric. Double cloth *cannot* be separated into two distinct fabrics. The extra (binding) yarn is *part* of the weave structure. If cut the fabric will be damaged. Wool, worsted, silk, cotton or man-made fiber yarns may be used as extra set of yarns.

- Increased weight
- Warm and insulatory

two-ply double-faced cloth

Double-faced Cloth

A woven or knitted fabric constructed with more than one set of warp and filling yarns, producing two fabrics with two distinct faces. An extra set of warp or filling yarns, referred to as the *binder* yarn, interlace between both fabrics and bind the fabrics together. The fabric *can* be separated by clipping the joining or binder yarn or thread. Double-faced cloth-constructed fabrics include:

1. a fully constructed top or face fabric;
2. a fully constructed back fabric;
3. a binder yarn interlacing the two fabrics.

- Heavy and thick
- Double-faced
- Self insulating
- Strong and resilient
- Warm
- Requires no lining
- Two-ply, reversible; one or both sides may be used in designing
- Different woven or knitted face and back
- Different colored or patterned face and back

Double Cloth/Double-faced Double Cloth Weave

Cotton/ Cotton-type Fabrics	Silk/ Silk-type Fabrics	Wool/ Wool-type Fabrics	Specialty Hair/ Hair Blends	Stretch/ Stretch-type Fabrics	Knit/ Knit-type Fabrics
Double Cloth Double-faced Cloth	Crepes Bark Crepe Matalessé Crepe Meteor Crepe/ Satin-Faced Chiffon Matalessé Hammered Satin	Cloqué Double Cloth Albatross Double Gauze French Back Kersey Loden Cloth Melton Double-faced cloth Lightweight Medium Weight Heavyweight Coating Blanket Cloth/ Plaid Back	Mohair Cloth Napped Face Napped Double-faced Mohair Gauze	Stretch Finish Crinkled Double Cloth	Double Cloth Double-faced cloth Raschel Knit Double Cloth Effect

Figure Weave

Ornamental embroidered effects are produced by introducing additional warp or filling yarns at regular intervals during the weaving process. Looms are adapted to accommodate the additional yarns. Variations are produced by floating the yarns between the designs. The floats may be cut, clipped or uncut. Variations of figure weaves are defined as: *lappet weave, spot or dot weave (uncut or cut)* and *swivel weave.*

lappet weave (mock up)—face   lappet weave (mock up)—back

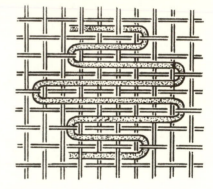

Lappet Weave

A figure weave or embroidery weave design produced by a needle on the loom, which weaves additional warp yarns into the plain woven background base cloth at fixed or patterned intervals repeating the design from selvage to selvage.

The needle attachment carries its own supply of warp yarn across the fabric creating a design similar to embroidery. The design is fastened or knotted to the base fabric. Trail threads, formed on the back of the fabric from one design to the next in the row, are cut.

- Superimposes designs over predetermined portions of the base fabric
- Designs resemble hand embroidery or drawn work
- Ornamentational design that is permanent
- Durable and expensive figure weave types
- Floats on back of cloth may be cut if too long or left as floats if short (uncut remaining floats are subject to snags)

spot/cut dot/clipped dot weave

spot/cut spot/clipped dot "eyelash" fabric

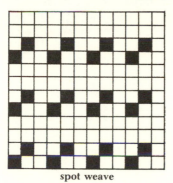

spot weave

Spot/Dot/Clipped Spot Weave

A method of producing decorative designs and patterns on the entire width or length of the fabric in predetermined areas. Additional warp and/or filling yarns interlace with the regular yarns producing the design with thread floats on the back of the fabric between the patterned areas. The floating threads may be cut or remain as is when the fabric is completed. Each produces different design effects. Extra threads may be different in weight or color from base fabric. Durability depends on closeness or looseness of base fabric.

Clipped Spot/Cut Spot Weave

The floats between the patterned areas *are* cut to produce fringed effects and eyelash fabrics.

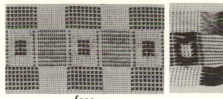

uncut spot design

face   back

spot/uncut dot/uncut spot weave

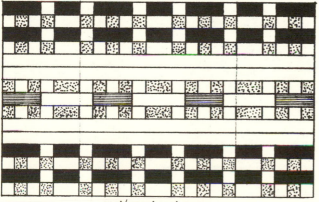

spot/uncut spot weave

Uncut Spot/Uncut Dot Weave

The floats between the patterned areas *are not* cut:

- Form border designs
- Repeated pattern usually close together
- Reversible pattern
- Floats may remain on back of fabric
- Floats may be used as face of fabric to form an embroidered effect

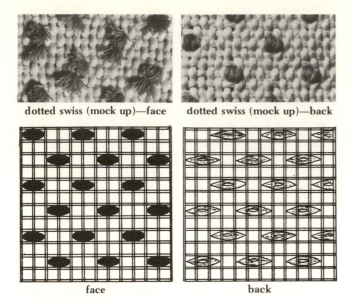

dotted swiss (mock up)—face   dotted swiss (mock up)—back

face   back

Swivel Weave

A method of producing decorative dots, circles or squares on the surface of the fabric. While the fabric is being constructed, additional filling yarns interlace separate designs on a small area of the base cloth. The design threads float on the back of the fabric from one design to the next. The floating threads are cut when the fabric is completed.

- Different colored design yarn from base cloth
- Multicolored designs in the same row
- Prominent designs and raised appearance
- Do not have float yarns on back
- Not durable—yarns pull out easily

Figure Weave/Figure Weave Variations

Cotton/ Cotton-type Fabrics	Linen/ Linen-type Fabrics	Silk/ Silk-type Fabrics	Wool/ Wool-type Fabrics

Boucle Yarn Fabric
  Dobby
Double Weave Effect
Dotted Swiss
Embroidered Fabrics
Spot/Clip Spot
  Lightweight
  Medium Weight
  Heavyweight
  Eyelash Fabric
Swivel Weave
Lappet Weave
Surface Fringe
	Dobby Weave
	Linen
	Surface Fringe
		Crepe de Chine Dobby
		Honan/Pongee Dobby
		Spot/Clip Spot
		  Eyelash Effect
		Satin
		  Charmeuse Dobby Stripe
		Surface Fringe
			Tweed
			  Birdseye Tweed
			Surface Fringe

JACQUARD MACHINE PROCESS

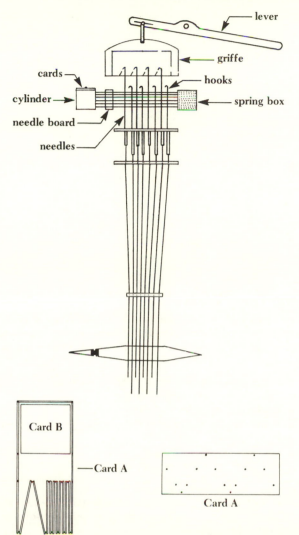

- lever
- griffe
- cards
- hooks
- cylinder
- spring box
- needle board
- needles

Card B

— Card A

Card A

Card (A) fits on the cylinder (B) and moves into position to control movement of warp yarn.

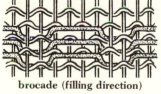

heavyweight brocade lightweight brocade lightweight reversible damask

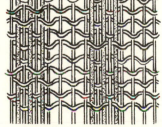

brocade (filling direction)

brocade (warp direction)

Jacquard Weave

Jacquard is the name of an attachment for a weaving loom which enables the loom to make complicated patterns during the process of weaving a Jacquard fabric. Fabrics produced on the Jacquard looms incorporate any or all of the three basic weaves and their combination on one fabric.

On the Jacquard loom, each warp yarn is separately controlled by a punch card. The punched card fits on the cylinder and controls the rods that raise the designated warp yarns creating the shed. Filling yarns are passed through the shed.

- Intricate design
- Use multiweaves and colored yarns
- Poor abrasion
- Long floats snag easily
- Difficult to clean—weave scratches and abrades during spot and stain removal
- Lack dimensional stability in laundering and dry cleaning

Brocade: Raised designs are woven in colors that contrast to the background color. Colors not used in the design are floated across the back of the fabric.

Tapestry Designs are woven in multicolors interspersed with metallic yarns. Designs include figures, flora and fauna.

Damask Designs are usually of the same color or filling yarns white and an alternate color. Warp design is a high-gloss thread; filling threads are dull. Creates a reversible fabric.

Matelassé Surface effect of quilted, blistered, puckered or wadded designs on double cloth or compound fabric.

Jacquard Weave/Jacquard Weave Variations

Cotton/ Cotton-type Fabrics	Linen/ Linen-type Fabrics	Silk/ Silk-type Fabrics	Wool/ Wool-type Fabrics	Metallic/ Metallic-type Fabrics

Bouclé Yarn Fabric
Brocade
  Lightweight
  Heavyweight
Damask
  Medium Weight
  Heavyweight
Embroidered Fabrics
Jacquard Cottons
Jacquard Piqué
	Jacquard Linen
	Linen Suiting
		Brocade
		Damask
		  Lightweight
		  Heavyweight
		Taffeta Jacquard
		Satin
		  Brocaded Satin
		  Jacquard Stripe
		    Satin
		  Jacquard Floral
		    Satin
			Cloqué
			Jacquard Wood
				Jacquard Woven with
				Metallic Yarns

leno weave (mock up)

gauze weave (mock up)

Leno/Doup Weave

A set or pair of warp threads are half turned, interlocked or partially twisted to encircle a filling yarn. A doup attachment on the loom is used to form the pattern for the warp yarn twisting.

- Warp yarns do not lie parallel to each other
- Filling yarns are held in place
- Openmesh-type construction
- Reduced yarn slippage in sheer openweave fabric types
- Does not sag
- Loosely woven, but firm
- Stronger than plain weave fabric

Variations of leno weave construction include:

Gauze Weave The filling yarns are encircled by two warp threads crossed or twisted around each other forming a figure eight.

Thermal Weave Low-twist plied yarns are used to produce a fabric with a recessed and raised ridge pattern. Thermal weave fabrics have insulatory qualities.

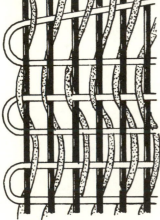

The second of each of the two warp yarns pulls around the first yarn.

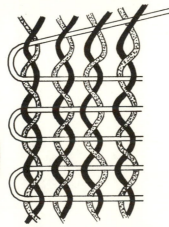

Filling yarns are encircled by two warp yarns twisting around each other.

Leno/Gauze Weave

Cotton/ Cotton-type Fabrics	Linen/ Linen-type Fabrics	Silk/ Silk-type Fabrics	Wool/ Wool-type Fabrics	Metallic/ Metallic-type Fabrics	Novelties

Gauze Cloth/Cotton Net
Leno
  Lightweight
  Heavyweight
  Open Effect
	Linen Leno
	Linen Gauze
		Grenadine
		Marquisette
		Mousseline de Soie/
		  Silk Gauze
			Fancies
			Gauze/Open Weave
			  Effect
				Metallic Gauze
				Gauze with Metallic
				  Laid-in Yarns
					Mesh
					Nettings
					Open Effects
					Fancies

waffle piqué

bull's eye piqué

ladder piqué

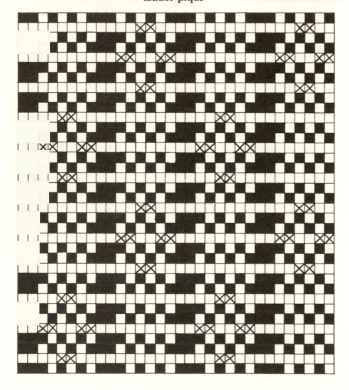

Piqué/Cord Weave

A fabric characterized by wales or cords on the face of the fabric, which are held in place by floats on the back of the fabric. A dobby attachment on the loom is used to provide for as many as thirty different interlacing arrangements of the warp yarns. As many as thirty filling yarns are utilized to produce the variety of designs. Two-ply yarns are used for face and a heavy single-ply for back.

- Wales/cords in various widths
- Raised- or quilted-effect surface
- Wales/cords may be planned in the length- or crosswise direction
- Definite right or wrong side

Piqué Weave Variations

Cotton/Cotton-type Fabrics	Wool/Wool-type Fabrics

Birdseye Piqué
Bullseye Piqué
Corded Pique/Cords
Crow's Foot Piqué
Diamond Piqué
Embossed Piqué
Honeycomb Piqué
Jacquard Piqué
Ladder Piqué
Square Piqué
Waffle Piqué
	Fancies
	   Waffle Cloth
	   Cloqué

plain weave (fine, thin yarns)

plain weave (medium yarns)

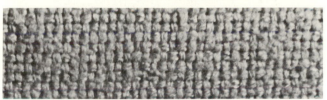

plain weave (heavy yarns)

Plain Weave

One filling yarn and one warp yarn are constructed at right angles to each other whereby the filling yarn passes alternately over and then under one warp yarn. Variations may be introduced within the plain weave by changing the size, ply, twist or texture of the yarns and by weaving the yarns loosely or tightly.

- Firm and wears well
- Ravels less than comparable fabrics
- Used as background for printing or embroidery designs
- Snag resistant
- Tends to wrinkle more than other weaves
- Lower tear strength than other weaves

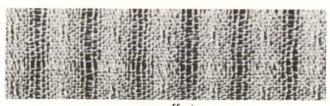

open effect

warp threads omitted

Skip Denting Weave/Openweave Effect

A plain weave variation with predetermined warp or filling threads eliminated during the weave-form operation. The skip-denting method produces the openweave effect, which is often referred to as *leno fabric* although it is not constructed of a true leno weave.

- Air permeable
- Open and porous
- Loose and pliable, unless crisply finished
- Available in a variety of conventional and novelty yarns
- Allows for laid-in yarn effects

Plain Weave Fabrics with Novelty Yarns, Special Effects & Embroidery

Cotton/ Cotton-type Fabrics	Linen/ Linen-type Fabrics	Silk/ Silk-type Fabrics	Metallic/ Metallic-type Fabrics
Bark Cloth	Butcher Linen	Silk Embroidered Fabrics	Metallic Embroidered Fabrics
Bouclé Yarn Fabric	Cambric Linen with Cord	Georgette	Sheer
Chambray with Cord	Embroidered Fabrics	Skip Denting/Open Effect	Lightweight
Dimity	Skip Denting/Open Effect	Leno Effect	Medium Weight
Embroidered Fabrics	Handkerchief Linen with Cord	Shantung	Heavyweight
Eyelet	Homespun Linen	Soft Finish	
Seersucker		Crisp Finish	
Skip Denting		Shantung Georgette	
Open Effect			
Corded Effect			

Plain Weave Fabrics with Special Finishes

Cotton/ Cotton-type	Linen/ Linen-type	Burlap/ Burlap-type	Silk/ Silk-type	Wool/ Wool-type Fabrics	Specialty Hair/ Blends	Stretch/ Stretch-type	Metallic/ Metallic-type
Airplane/Byrd Cloth®	Art Linen	100% Natural Fiber	Broadcloth	Baize	Alpaca Cloth	Yarn Stretch	Lamé
Batiste	Bisso Linen	Man-made Fiber	Chiffon	Broadcloth	100% Natural Fibers	Canvas	Sparkle Glitter
Beach Cloth	Butcher Linen	Blended Fiber	China Silk	Clear Finish	Blended Fibers	Stretch Finish	Adhesive Bonded
Broadcloth	Cambric Linen		Crepe	Napped	Lightweight	Crimped Cloth	Sheer
Calcutta/Bangladesh Cloth	Crash		Albatross Crepe	Wool Crepe	Medium Weight		Crepe
Cambric	Soft Finish		Bark Crepe	Doeskin	Heavyweight		Printed Crepe
Canvas	Crisp Finish		Canton Crepe	Eiderdown	Camel Hair Cloth		
Chambray	Dress Linen		Chiffon Crepe	Etamine	100% Natural Fibers		
Chameleon/Irides- cent Cloth	Soft Finish		Crepe de Chine	Homespun Wool	Blended Fibers		
Chintz	Crisp Finish		Creponne/	Homespun Coating	Lightweight		
Clokay	Handkerchief Linen		Crinkled Crepe	Iridescent Wool	Medium Weight		
Embossed Cotton	Soft Finish		Flat Crepe	Kasha Cloth	Heavyweight		
Dotted Swiss	Crisp Finish		Pebbly/Mossy Crepe	Sheers	Cashmere Cloth		
Dotted Flocked Swiss	Homespun Linen			Batiste	100% Natural Fibers		
Duck	Linen Suiting			Challis	Blended Fibers		
				Voile	Lightweight		
					Medium Weight		

Plain Weave Fabrics with Special Finishes (continued)

Cotton/ Cotton-type	Linen/ Linen-type	Burlap/ Burlap-type	Silk/ Silk-type	Wool/ Wool-type Fabrics	Specialty Hair/ Blends	Stretch/ Stretch-type	Metallic/ Metallic-type
Embroidered Fabrics				Tweeds	Coating		
End & End Cloth				Donegal-type	Mohair Cloth		
Topweight				Heather-type	100% Natural Fibers		
Bottomweight				Oatmeal	Blended Fibers		
Flannel				Salt & Pepper	Hard Finish		
Dommet/Outing				Heavy Textured	Clear Finish		
French				Fancies	Single-faced		
Gauze/Bunting Cloth				Gauze	Napped		
Gingham				Tropical Worsted	Double-faced		
Homespun				Unfinished	Napped		
Lawn				Worsted	Fancies		
Glazed-faced					Looped Face		
Madras					Novelty Yarns		
Muslin					Rabbit Hair Cloth		
Organdy					Blended Fibers		
Osnaburg					Lightweight		
Percale					Medium Weight		
Plissé					Heavyweight		
Polished Cotton							
Pongee							
Poplin							
Medium Weight							
Medium-							
Heavyweight							
Heavyweight							
Printcloth							
Ratiné							
Sailcloth							
Sheeting							
Tattersall							
Ticking							
Voile							
Crinkled Voile							

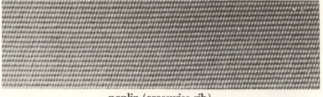
poplin (crosswise rib)

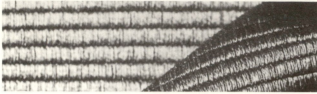
ottoman (crosswise rib)

filling-faced (crosswise) rib   filling-faced (crosswise) rib

seersucker cord (lengthwise rib)

bedford cord (lengthwise rib)

warp-faced (lengthwise) rib   dimity cord

COMPARISON OF RIB WEAVES

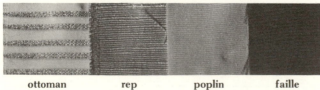
ottoman   rep   poplin   faille

Rib Weave

Heavy or thick yarns, or groups of yarns, are used in one direction and fine yarns in the other direction, producing a rib effect in the length- or crosswise direction on the surface of the fabric.

Variations within the rib weave are produced by:

- Using heavier or thicker yarns in the filling direction only
- Grouping or spacing yarns in specific areas of filling
- Arranging more warp than filling yarns

Rib Weave/Rib Weave Variations*

Cotton/ Cotton-type Fabrics	Silk/ Silk-type Fabrics	Wool/ Wool-type Fabrics	Stretch/ Stretch-type Fabrics

Bedford Cord (L)
  Crisp Finish
  Sueded Finish
Bengaline (C)
Bouclé Yarn Fabric (L & C)
Dimity (L)
Poplin (C)
  Medium Weight
  Medium-heavyweight
  Heavyweight
Seersucker (L)
Seersucker with Checkered
  Effect (L & C)
	Bengaline (C)
	Crepe (C)
	  Canton Crepe
	  Crepe Faille
	Faille (C)
	  Silk Faille
	  Moiré Faille
	  Tissue Faille
	Grosgrain (C)
	Ottoman (C)
	  Suiting
	  Coating
	Poplin (C)
	Rep (C)
	Seersucker (L)
	Seersucker with Checkered
	  Effect (L & C)
	Sharkskin (C)
	Taffeta (C)
	  Antique Taffeta
	  Faille Taffeta
	  Moiré Taffeta
	  Warp-dyed/Warp-
	    printed Taffeta
	  Yarn-dyed Taffeta
		Bengaline (C)
		Ottoman (C)
		Poplin (C)
			Yarn Stretch
			  Poplin (C)

*L—Rib in lengthwise direction.
 C—Rib in crosswise direction.

Satin/Satin-type Weave

Cotton/ Cotton-type Fabrics	Silk/ Silk-type Fabrics	Wool/ Wool-type Fabrics	Specialty Hair/ Blended Fabrics	Stretch/ Stretch-type Fabrics

Cretonne
Dimity Stripe
Dimity Satin Stripe
Sateen
	Crepe
	  Satin-backed Crepe/
	    Creped-backed
	      Satin
	Peau de Soie
	Satin
	  Antique Satin
	  Baronet Satin
	  Bridal Satin
	  Charmeuse
	  Ciré Satin
	  Creped Satin
	  Duchesse Satin
	  Hammered Satin
	  Messaline Satin
	Thermo Satin
	  Napped-back
	  Coated Satin
	Satin Novelties
		Duvetyn	Mohair
			  Zebaline®
				Yarn Stretch
				  Satin
				  Sateen

floats formed by warp yarns (mock up)

satin weave as part of brocade fabric

duchess satin

Satin Weave (warp-faced)

Warp-faced satin weave fabrics are characterized by warp floats across the surface of the fabric due to the action of the filling yarns passing over one and under several warp yarns. Warp-faced satin weave, with the warp floats on the surface, produces a shiny surface.

- Utilizes natural and man-made filament fiber yarns
- High luster on face of fabric
- High light-reflection
- Smooth slippery fabric that slides easily over other garments
- Nondurable
- Floating yarns subject to snagging, pulling, or breaking during wear
- Floating yarns subject to snagging or scarring when rubbed during spot or stain removal
- Poor wearing fabric susceptible to abrasion
- Long floats shift and produce wavy areas or promote slippage

Variations within the satin weave are produced by:
- The differences in the weight and texture of the fiber
- The differences in the twist and combination of the yarns
- The order of the under and over count of the satin-weave formation

The term *satin* refers to a fabric as well as to a weave. There are many fabrics made utilizing the satin weave that are not called satin.

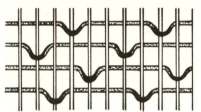

5-end repeat:
Under 4 yarns/over 1 yarn

5-shaft construction:
Black squares indicate where filling yarns pass under warp yarns.

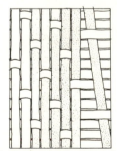

5-shaft construction/Yarn layout:
Filling floats interlace every
5th warp yarn.

8-shaft construction/Yarn layout:
Filling floats interlace every
8th warp yarn.

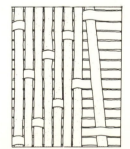

12-shaft construction/Yarn layout:
Filling floats interlace every 12th warp yarn.

floats formed by filling yarns (mock up)

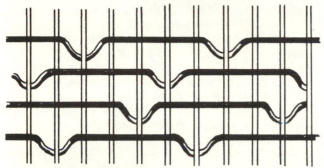

5-end repeat: Over 4 yarns/under 1 yarn

Satin Weave (filling-faced)

Fabric with long floats *across* the surface of the filling direction of the weave characterized by the floating *filling* yarns visible on the surface of the fabric.

- Utilizes cotton or wool staple fiber yarn
- More filling yarns on face as compared to satin with more warp yarns on face
- Shiny, but less lustrous than warp-faced satin
- Produces sateen and base for heavily napped wool fabrics

5-shaft construction: White squares indicate where warp yarns pass under filling yarns.

5-shaft construction/Yarn layout: Warp floats interlace every 5th filling yarn.

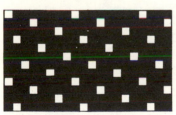

8-shaft construction: White squares indicate where warp yarns pass under filling yarn.

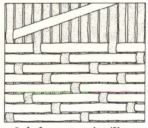

8-shaft construction/Yarn layout: Warp floats interlace every 8th filling yarn.

12-shaft construction: White squares indicate where warp yarns pass under filling yarns.

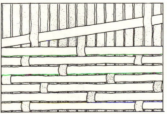

12-shaft construction/Yarn layout: Warp floats interlace every 12th filling yarn.

Twill Weave

Filling yarns are interlaced over and under two or more warp yarns in a fixed staggered manner, forming a diagonal line or ridge on the fabric surface. The direction of the diagonal may be formed from right to left, from left to right, or a combination of both.

- More yarns packed into a given area
- Dense, compact and closely woven
- Heavier, durable and wears well
- Does not show dirt readily
- Softer and more pliable
- Good wrinkle recovery
- Definite right (face) and wrong side
- Diagonal design on the surface
- Diagonal ridge so pronounced at times as to limit choice of garment styling

Variations within the twill weave are produced by:
- Varying the prominence, direction, degree or angle of the diagonal line
- Varying the number of harnesses, producing different surface designs
- Changing the *direction* of the heddle during the weaving process
- Changing the *order* of the heddle during the weaving process
- Changing or reversing *both the direction and the order* of the heddle
- Using different colored yarns for the warp and filling, producing a fabric with different colors on each side

Twill weave construction utilizes plied yarns or yarns with a high degree of twist. Yarns with a high degree of twist:
1. reduces possibility of snagging floats;
2. increases strength and durability of fabric.

Twill weaves are classified as even or uneven according to the number of warp and filling threads or yarns visible on the face of the fabric. Twill weaves are also named with regard to the number of harnesses or shafts required to produce the diagonal design.

Simple twills require three to seven harnesses. Complex or novelty twills require eight or more harnesses.

By changing the order or direction, or both, of the heddle the following twills are produced:
- Herringbone twill, double-point twill (changing *direction* of the heddle)
- Broken twill, stockinette twill, wave twill (changing *order* of the heddle)
- Fancy twills, steeper twills, lined work twills, patterned twills (changing or reversing *both the direction and the order* of the heddle)

Warp-faced Twill   The predominance of warp yarns float over two or more filling yarns and then under one filling yarn. Fabric shows more warp than filling yarns on the face of the fabric.

Filling-faced Twill   The filling yarns float over two or more warp yarns and then under one warp yarn. Fabric shows more filling yarn on the face of the fabric.

Right-hand Twill   The diagonal runs upward to the right of the fabric.

Left-hand Twill   The diagonal runs upward to the left of the fabric.

Balanced Twill   A 2/2 or even-sided twill with the same number of warp and filling yarns exposed on the face and back. Fabric is reversible and looks the same on both sides, except the direction of the diagonal lines reverse. Balance twill weave shows a 45° diagonal line.

Unbalanced Twill   Fabric shows a warp-faced side and a filling-faced side. The floats interlace the yarn in an under two and an over one progression.

Broken Twill   The diagonal of the twill is interrupted or disguised purposely to form a random design.

Herringbone Twill   Both a right- and left-hand twill reversing direction at regular intervals, producing a pattern of "V" in a vertical stripe design. Herringbone twills may be constructed as warp-faced herringbone, filling-faced herringbone and reversed herringbone.

Pointed/Double-pointed Twill   A twill structure forming a chevron design.

Interlacing Sequences & the Different Angles & Degrees

Most twills interlace at a 45° angle, but interlacings can be formed in other sequences producing different angles or degrees.

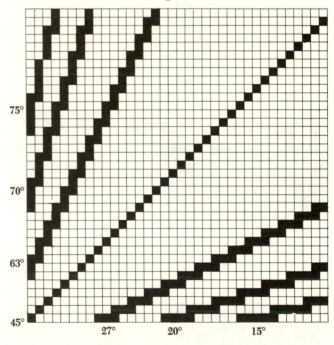

Key: 75° Twill: 4 filling yarns higher (RHT) lower (LHT).

    70° Twill: 3 filling yarns higher (RHT) lower (LHT).

    63° Twill: 2 filling yarns higher (RHT) lower (LHT).

    45° Twill: 1 filling yarn higher (RHT) lower (LHT).

    27° Twill: 2 filling yarns across to right (RHT) to left (LHT).

    20° Twill: 3 filling yarns across to right (RHT) to left (LHT).

    15° Twill: 4 filling yarns across to right (RHT) to left (LHT).

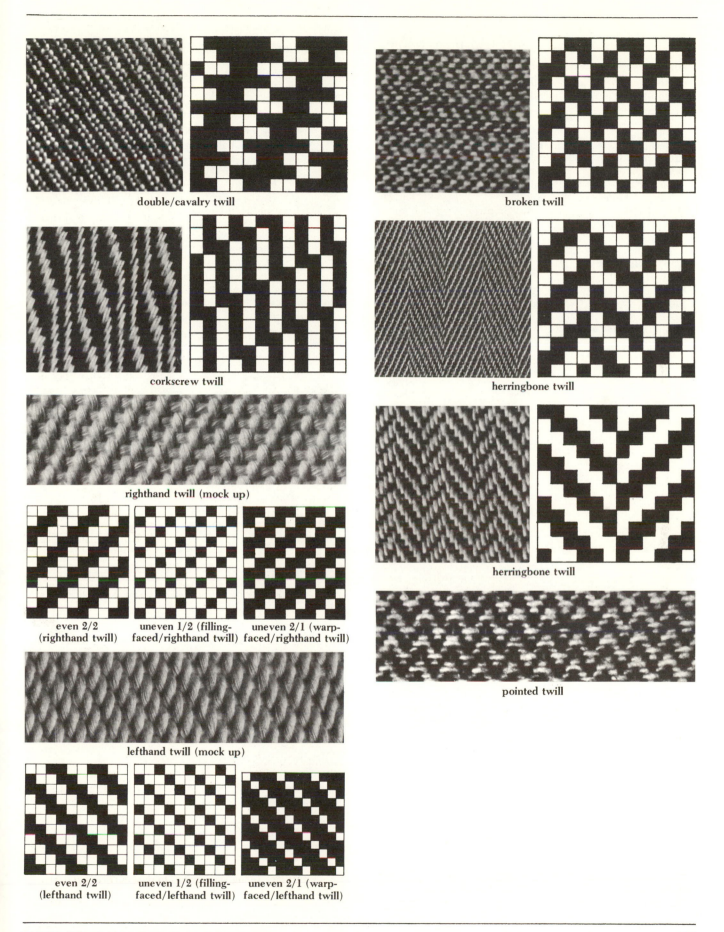

double/cavalry twill

broken twill

corkscrew twill

herringbone twill

righthand twill (mock up)

even 2/2
(righthand twill)

uneven 1/2 (filling-
faced/righthand twill)

uneven 2/1 (warp-
faced/righthand twill)

herringbone twill

pointed twill

lefthand twill (mock up)

even 2/2
(lefthand twill)

uneven 1/2 (filling-
faced/lefthand twill)

uneven 2/1 (warp-
faced/lefthand twill)

Twill Weave/Twill Weave Variations

Cotton/ Cotton-type Fabrics	Silk/ Silk-type Fabrics	Wool/ Wool-type Fabrics	Specialty Hair/ Blended Fabrics	Stretch/ Stretch type Fabrics
Chino Cloth	Barathea	Bolivia	Alpaca Cloth	Yarn Stretch
Covert	Barathea Suiting	Cassimere	100% Natural Fibers	Chino
Cretonne	Silk Canvas	Cheviot	Blended Fibers	Denim
Denim	Charvet	Covert Suiting	Lightweight	Gabardine
Clear Face	Silk Suiting	Covert Coating	Medium Weight	Twill
Napped Face	Surah	Duvetyn	Heavyweight	Whipcord
Drill Cloth	Surah Suiting	Flannel	Camel Hair Cloth	
Dommet/Outing		Wool	100% Natural Fibers	
Flannel		Worsted	Blended Fibers	
Gabardine		French	Lightweight	
Jean Cloth/Middy		Gabardine	Medium Weight	
Twill		Wool	Heavyweight	
Khaki		Worsted	Cashmere Cloth	
Ticking		Summerweight	100% Natural Fibers	
Tricotine		Coating	Blended Fibers	
Twill/Reverse Twill		Iridescent	Lightweight	
Whipcord		Kersey	Medium Weight	
		Polo Cloth	Coating	
		Serge	Mohair Cloth	
		Sharkskin	100% Natural Fibers	
		Sheers	Blended Fibers	
		Challis	Hard Finish	
		Tartans	Clear Finish	
		Blackwatch	Brushed Face	
		Glen Plaid	Fancies	
		Hound's-tooth	Rabbit Hair Cloth	
		Check	Blended Fibers	
		Tricotine/Cavalry	Lightweight	
		Twill	Medium Weight	
		Tweeds	Heavyweight	
		Heather		
		Wool & Worsted		
		Herringbone		
		Oatmeal		
		Heavy Textured		
		Whipcord		
		Fancies		
		Corkscrew		
		Twill		
		Broken Twill		
		Reverse Twill		

Compound Fabric Structure/Fabrics with Additional Processes to Complete Structure

Compound fabrics are base fabrics with additional processes applied to complete the structure. The base fabric may be of any weave or knit formation and of any type of fiber or yarn. Each fabric has its own specific process of construction and each fabric has its own particular characteristics.

These compound fabrics are referred to as novelty fabrics and are usually included in more than one fabric group with regard to fiber content, yarn construction, fabric structure or finishing process.

Compound fabrics structures include:

- Embroidered/Cut Work Fabric Structure
- Flocked Fabric Structure
- Tufted Fabric Structure
- Napped/Brushed Fabric Structure

eyelet/cutwork

Schiffli embroidery on sheer fabric

sequin-embroidered fabric

re-embroidered lace

Embroidered/Cut Work Fabric Stucture

An additional process utilizing the Jacquard card system to operate a multi-thread and multi-needle machine, producing a fabric with fine and intricate designs, appliqués or cut work.

Embroidered fabrics may be created by hand utilizing a one needle and one yarn system to create the designs.

Embroidered fabrics include:

- Eyelet/Cut Work/Open Work
- Schiffli Embroidery
- Pavé Beading/Bead Work/Sequins
- Re-embroidered Lace
- Motif or Repeated Motif Designs
- Allover Embroidered Designs

flocked fabric (woven base)

flocked fabric (knit base)

face   back
allover flocked fabric

Flocked Fabric Structure

A mechanical vibrating or electrostatic technique utilizing adhesives or resins to apply minute pieces of natural or man-made fibers to a woven, nonwoven or knitted base fabric, producing a raised, textured or pile surface in an overall patterned design.

- Imitation figure weaves and dotted Swiss
- Imitation pile fabric structures and suede cloth
- Allover or patterned design
- Poor abrasion resistance—flocks rub off

Mechanical Flocking The beater bars' vibration of the fabric causes the flock to flow over the surface of the fabric, to stand erect and to penetrate into the adhesive-coated fabric. An inexpensive pile design is produced.

Electrostatic Flocking Adhesive-coated fabric is passed over an electric field, which establishes an atmosphere that forces the loose fibers in the area away from one electric field and towards the second.

Ground Flocking Tow is fed into a channel of predetermined width where a knife slices uniform lengths of flock, which are forced into a vertical position along the fiber guide. Adhesive coating is applied to the fabric and the coated fabric meets the fiber, which adheres to the cloth. The flocked fabric is subsequently returned and fed into a curing oven.

Adhesives may change the hand and drapability qualities of the base fabric and may dissolve during the cleaning of the fabric resulting in dislodging of flocks.

MECHANICAL FLOCKING PROCESS

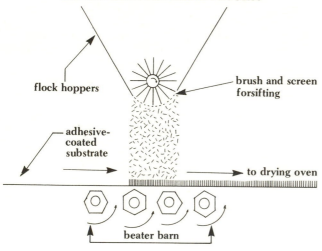

flock hoppers

brush and screen forsifting

adhesive-coated substrate

to drying oven

beater barn

ELECTROSTATIC FLOCKING PROCESS

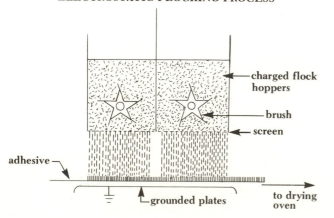

charged flock hoppers

brush

screen

adhesive

grounded plates

to drying oven

GROUND FLOCKING PROCESS

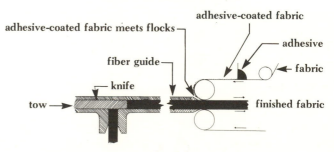

adhesive-coated fabric meets flocks

adhesive-coated fabric

adhesive

fiber guide

fabric

knife

tow

finished fabric

high-napped fabric

napped fabric (face & back)

napped fabric (knit base)

Napped/Brushed/Sueded Fabric Structure

Napping is a finishing process utilizing a mechanical cylindrical revolving brushing action applied to a woven or knit fabric structure raising the fiber ends to the surface. Raised fiber ends may be clipped to a uniform length, brushed to lay flat or maintained in a raised, upright position.

Napping changes the texture, appearance and hand of the fabric. The surface may vary from a slight fuzz to a thick nap and from compact to loosely formed. Process may be applied to a plain or twill weave constructed base fabric.

- Produces air space which entraps still air and increases warmth of fabric
- Provides softness to fabric
- Creates natural water- and stain-repellent qualities
- Conceals a loosely woven, flimsy or inferior construction
- Process weakens the fabric when overbrushed
- Produces light-reflecting qualities—nap has up and down direction
- Nap sheds on other garment surfaces during wear and laundering
- Nap flattens with wear.

SINGLE-ACTING NAPPER

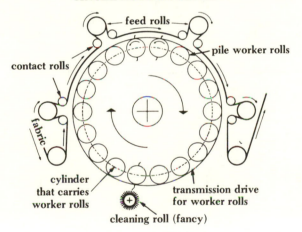

feed rolls

pile worker rolls

contact rolls

fabric

cylinder that carries worker rolls

transmission drive for worker rolls

cleaning roll (fancy)

DOUBLE-ACTING HOPPER

transmission drive for worker rolls

counter pile   pile

cylinder that carries worker rolls

fabric

feed roll

feed roll

C.P.   P

cleaning rolls (fancy)

KNIT-GOODS NAPPER

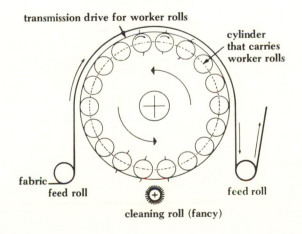

transmission drive for worker rolls

cylinder that carries worker rolls

fabric

feed roll

feed roll

cleaning roll (fancy)

Napped/Brushed/Sueded Fabrics

Cotton/ Cotton-type Fabrics	Wool/ Wool-type Fabrics	Specialty Hair/ Blended Fabrics	Knit/ Knit-type Fabrics	Pile/ Pile-type Fabrics	Stretch/ Stretch-type Fabrics
Bedford Cord 　Napped Face 　Sueded Face Denim 　Brushed Face Flannel 　Dommet/Outing Suede Cloth	Astrakhan/Karakul Baize Broadcloth 　Napped Face Covert Coating Doeskin Double Cloth Double-faced Suede 　Cloth Double-faced Wool Blanket Cloth/ 　Plaid Back Duvetyn Eiderdown Étamine 　Napped Face Wool Flannel Worsted Flannel French Flannel Fleece Homespun Iridescent Wool Kasha Cloth Loden Cloth Melton Polo Cloth Serge Suede Cloth Tartans 　Clan Plaids 　Glen Plaid 　Hound's-tooth Check Tweed 　Wool Herringbone 　Heather 　Fancies 　Gauze Tropical Worsted	Alpaca Cloth 　100% Natural Fibers 　Blended Fibers 　Lightweight 　Medium Weight 　Heavyweight 　Coating Camel's Hair Cloth 　100% Natural Fibers 　Blended Fibers 　Lightweight 　Medium Weight 　Heavyweight 　Coating Mohair 　100% Natural Fibers 　Blended Fibers 　Lightweight 　Medium Weight 　Heavyweight 　Gauze 　Single-faced 　Double-faced 　Looped-face 　Zebaline® Rabbit Hair Cloth 　Blended Fibers 　Lightweight 　Medium Weight 　Heavyweight	Jacquard Knit 　Napped Face Jersey Knit Variation 　Napped Face Rib Knit Variation 　Napped Face, 　Birdseye Back Laid-in Yarn	Corduroy 　Feathercord 　Fine Wale 　Mid Wale 　Thick-set 　Wide Wale 　Broad Wale 　Novelty Wale Fleece 　Baby Bunting Fleece 　Sweatshirt Fleece 　Tufted Cloth 　Chenille Candlewick 　Chenille Velvet/ 　Velcle® Velvet 　Brocade 　Cotton 　Cut 　Embossed 　Pamne 　Transparent 　Velour 　Velvet Cord Velveteen	Yarn Stretch 　Satin 　Sateen 　Twill Yarn & Fabric 　Structure Stretch 　Double Knit (napped 　face & back)

Tufted Fabric Structure

Tufting is a process using additional yarns, carried by needles, that are forced through a finished base fabric and formed into loops on the surface of the fabric. Base fabric may be of woven or knitted fabric structure and composed of natural or man-made fibers. Yarns for tufting may be the same or different from base fabric.

- Allows for surface variation, which can be achieved by varying the size and number of loops, by combining cut and uncut loops or by cutting tufts into different lengths
- Covers an entire surface
- Forms a design

Tufting can be held in place by:
- Stitching tufting with chain stitch
- Intertwisting tufting yarns
- Shrinking base fabric after tufts are inserted
- Coating back of base fabric to hold tufts in place
- Bonding back of base fabric to another fabric increasing stability and preventing damage to tufts

Weight and density of tufted fabrics depend on:
- Gauge of machinery
- Length of nap or pile
- Number of stitches per inch
- Type and size of yarns
- Type of backing or base fabric

For illustration of tufting process, refer to pages 89–94.

Multicomponent/ Layered Fabric Structure

Multicomponent fabric structure includes components of face and lining fabrics, plastic film, wadding or batting, which produce double-faced cloth of two or more piles. The fabric components are sealed or bonded together by adhesives, foam- or flame-bonding, machine-stitched quilting or ultrasonic fusing.

Multicomponent fabric structure includes:
- Bonded Fabric Structure (adhesive and laminated)
- Coated Fabric Structure
- Quilted Fabric Structure

►

printed vinyl _____
"stop light" _____
scrim _____
plain vinyl _____

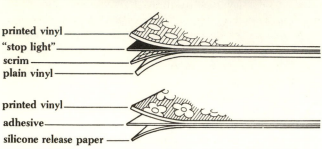

printed vinyl _____
adhesive _____
silicone release paper _____

Adhesive-bonded Fabric Structure

A fabric joined by a bonding process in which an outer or face fabric is joined or welded to a backing or lining ply by an adhesive agent. Bonding is referred to as a wet-adhesive method of permanently bonding a face and lining fabric back to back. Bonding process is applied to a wide variety of fabrics of different fibers, structure and textures. Adhesive may deteriorate in dry cleaning or laundering. Some plastic films discolor and yellow after exposure to light.

- Changes the hand of the outer or face fabric
- Stabilizes an open weave
- Reinforces a stretchy pliable surface
- Stabilizes outer or face fabric
- Resists stretch or deformation
- Acts as a backing or self-lining and saves cost in garment construction
- Reduces or eliminates raveling
- Enhances the hand, appearance and performance of a flimsy fabric
- Provides a comfortable backing to plastic or outer face fabric
- Produces a double-faced cloth of two or more plies
- Stiffens permanently collars, cuffs, flap and other design details
- Contributes to opacity of fabric
- Creates wet-look or see-through look

Adhesive-bonded fabric structure includes:
- Woven to knit
- Woven to woven
- Knit to knit
- Malimo structure to knit or woven
- Lace structure to knit or woven
- Clear and opaque film to knit or woven
- Plastic binder between two layers of goods
- Fabric layer to layer of fiber or web

FABRIC-TO-FABRIC BONDING PROCESS

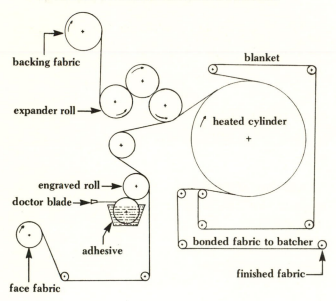

backing fabric

expander roll

blanket

heated cylinder

engraved roll
doctor blade

adhesive

bonded fabric to batcher

finished fabric

face fabric

ADHESIVE-BONDED FABRIC PROCESS

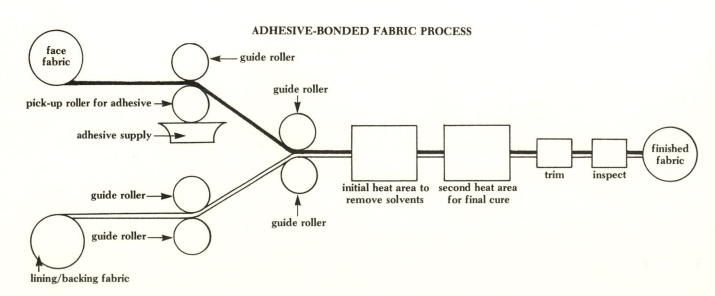

face fabric

guide roller

guide roller

pick-up roller for adhesive

adhesive supply

guide roller

guide roller

guide roller

initial heat area to remove solvents

second heat area for final cure

trim

inspect

finished fabric

lining/backing fabric

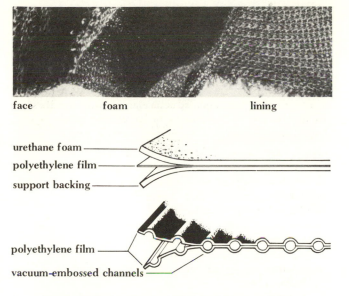

face   foam   lining

urethane foam ———
polyethylene film ———
support backing ———

polyethylene film ———
vacuum-embossed channels ———

BONDED KNIT-TO-KNIT LAMINATED PROCESS

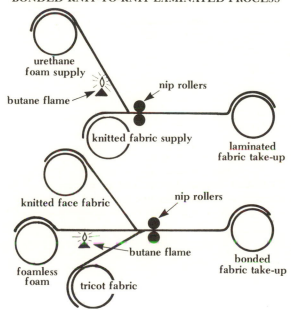

urethane
foam supply

butane flame

nip rollers

knitted fabric supply

laminated
fabric take-up

knitted face fabric

nip rollers

foamless
foam

tricot fabric

butane flame

bonded
fabric take-up

Laminated-bonded Fabric Structure

A fabric consisting of two plies, a face fabric and a lining fabric, made to adhere together by a flame foam bonding process, in which polyurethane foam acts as the adhesive center filling between the fabric plies. Foam may deteriorate or dry out during dry cleaning or laundering of garment. Fabric may de-laminate by abrasion during wear and cleaning. The two fabrics may shrink in varying degrees causing a puckering or waving surface.

- Gives body to face fabric
- Adds dimension to weak or poorly structured garments
- Stabilizes face fabric
- Produces a springy, spongy fabric
- Allows fabric to maintain shape or silhouette of garment design
- Enhances the hand, appearance and performance of a flimsy fabric
- Produces fabric with thermal qualities
- Produces fabric with a finished appearance on face and back
- Acts as a backing or self-lining and saves cost in garment construction.
- Produces a double-faced cloth of two or more plies

Laminated-bonded fabric structure includes:
- Woven to knit
- Woven to woven
- Knit to knit
- Film to woven or knit
- Film to foam

FOAM-FLAME BONDING PROCESS

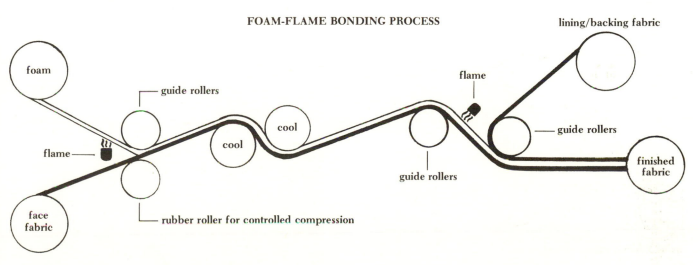

foam

guide rollers

flame

cool

cool

flame

lining/backing fabric

guide rollers

finished
fabric

face
fabric

guide rollers

rubber roller for controlled compression

face   back

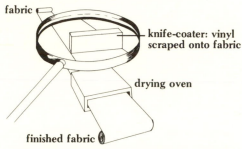

face   back

KNIFE COATING METHOD

fabric

knife-coater: vinyl scraped onto fabric

drying oven

finished fabric

A thin, viscous vinyl solution is scraped onto fabric and spread with a knife-type blade. The fabric may have to be passed through the knife-coater several times in order to obtain the proper thickness, bulk or cover. The coated fabric is then dried in an oven.

CALENDERING METHOD

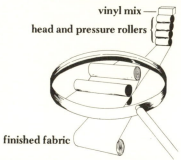

vinyl mix

head and pressure rollers

finished fabric

The vinyl film is made on a large machine known as a calender. In one of the later stages of calendering, the fabric is fed into the unit. By means of heat and pressure, the vinyl is impregnated into the fabric.

LAMINATING METHOD

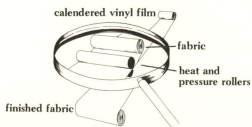

calendered vinyl film

fabric

heat and pressure rollers

finished fabric

The vinyl formulation is first subject to intense mixing and heat, rolled out and then laminated to the backing fabric. The calender presses the fabrics between rollers laminating the two plies and forming a single fabric.

Coated Fabric Structure

A fabric produced by the process of impregnating, coating, covering, treating, spraying or otherwise sealing the face or back of a woven, nonwoven, felt or knitted base fabric with various substances. Coating agents include lacquer, varnish, pyroxylin, rubber, resins, plastics, plastic films, melamines, oil compounds and metallic particles or platings.

- Seals the fabric pores and imparts water repellent qualities
- Creates a waterproof, non-air permeable fabric
- Utilizes metallic agents, producing reflecting linings
- Utilizes metallic-plated process, creating high-gloss fabric
- Allows fabric to maintain soft and pliable hand
- Produces a fabric that resists slippage
- Reduces fraying
- Stabilizes fabric
- Produces a fabric that may stiffen or change hand during cleaning process
- Produces a fabric that may crack or yellow with age
- Produces a fabric that may become brittle and cold to wear in cold temperatures

Types and methods of coating processes include:
1. knife coating;
2. solid film coating;
3. transfer coating;
4. utilization bonding and laminating methods.

Coating may be applied to any variety of fiber content fabrics. It may be embossed or textured, smooth with matte or shiny face or made to simulate any animal skin.

Top-coated Fabric   Coating is applied to face of goods.
Bottom-coated Fabric   Coating is applied to back of goods.

CASTING METHOD

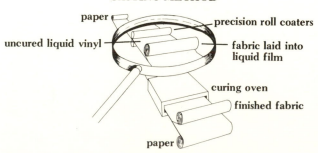

paper

precision roll coaters

uncured liquid vinyl

fabric laid into liquid film

curing oven

finished fabric

paper

The backing fabric is laid into a liquid film, which has been cast on another film that was originally cast on paper. The wet film acts as a bonding agent between the fabric and the initially cast film. The film and fabric are dried, cured and then stripped from the paper.

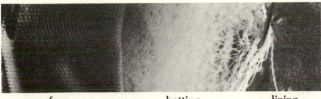

face   batting   lining

stitched process

stitchless process/Chem-stitch®

Quilted Fabric Structure

A fabric consisting of two or more plies of fabric above and/or below a layer of wadding or batting, held together as one fabric by machine stitching, Chemstitch® or sonic-fusion processes.

Quilted fabrics may be produced with a face front and back lining or with two faces resulting in a reversible fabric.

- Provides insulating qualities
- Produces a warm fabric without weight
- Produces lightweight fabrics for use in outerwear
- Acts as a self-lining

Machine-stitched Quilting Quilting process is completed with multi-needle lockstitch or chain-stitch pattern of lines.

Stitchless Quilting Quilting process utilizes ultrasonic vibration and fusion, pressing fabric components together producing a permanently embossed pattern or crinkled or rippled effect (trademark—Chemstitch®). High percentage of thermoplastic fibers, fabrics of one-hundred percent thermoplastic fibers or polyurethane foam, are used to properly complete fusion.

4 – Finishes/Finishing Processes

Classification of Finishes
Absorbent Finish
Ammoniating Finish
Beetling Finish
Bleaching Finish
Brushing Finish
Burling/Specking Finish
Calendering Finishes
  Regular/Simple Calendering Finish
  Schreiner Calendering Finish
  Moiré Calendering Finish
  Friction/Polishing Calendering Finish
  Cire Calendering Finish
Carbonizing Finish
Coating Finishes
  Thermal-Insulative Metallic Coating Finish
  Metallic-Plated Coating Finish
  Plastic-Film Coating/Waterproofing Finish
Crabbing Finish
Creping Finish
Decating Finishes
  Decating/Decatizing Finish
  Full-Decating Finish
  Semi-Decating Finish
  Continuous-Decating Finish
Decurling Finish
Degumming Finish
Denier Reduction Finish
Embossing Finish
Flocking Finish
Fulling
Glazing
Mercerizing Finish
Napping/Brushing Finish
Optical Finishes
  Lustering
  Delustering
  Optical Brighteners
Parchmentizing/Transparency Finish
Permanent Press/Durable Press/Wash-and-Wear
  Wash-and-Wear/Drip Dry

Resistant Finishes for Specific Properties
  Abrasion-Resistant Finish
  Bacterial-Resistant/Antiseptic/Antimicrobial Finish
  Crush-Resistant Finish
  Flame-Fire Resistant/Flame-Fire Retardant Finish
  Gas-Fading/Fume-Fading Resistant Finish
  Mildew-Resistant/Rot-Repellent Finish
  Moth-Resistant/Moth-Repellent Finish
  Slip-Resistant/Anti-Slip Finish
  Snagging-Resistant/Anti-Snag Finish
  Static-Resistant/Anti-Static Finish
    (chemical process)
    (mechanical process)
  Soil- and Stain-Resistant Finish
  Water-Resistant/Water-Repellent Finish
  Wrinkle-Resistant/Crease-Resistant Finish
Sanding/Sueding Finish
Shearing/Cropping Finish
Shrinkage Control/Stabilizing Finish
  Compressive Shrinkage Control Finish
  Heat-Set Shrinkage Control Finish
  Resin Treatment/Shrinkage Control Finish
  Sponging Shrinkage Control Finish
Singeing/Gassing
Stiffening Finishes
  Permanent Stiffening Finish
  Temporary Stiffening Finish
Stretch/Slack Mercerization Finish
Softening Finish
Soil Release Finish
Wool Presensitizing
Operations that are Part of Other Finishes
  Cooling Operation
  Chlorine Retention Operation
  De-sizing Operation
  Drying Operation
  Souring Operation
  Steaming Operation
  Straightening Operation
  Tentering Operation
  Washing/Scouring Operation

Finishing processes are the additional processes applied to fabric after the fabric is produced. Finishing processes are needed to allow the fabric to perform in a predictable manner, making it more serviceable, acceptable, attractive, and better suited for a specific use. Specific finishes are applied to the constructed cloth while the cloth is in the greige or grey stage. A fabric in its grey state is not considered ready for consumer usage; a newly constructed fabric will have to be converted or be passed through various finishing processes before it is considered complete.

    Finishes take many forms and are selected or applied with regard to the:
- Type of fiber and yarn
- Thread count
- Method of fabric construction
- Federal Trade Commission Rulings

- Hand, weight, drapability qualities desired
- Anticipated end use of the fabric or garment

All finishing processes are not applicable to all kinds of goods. Finishes vary in their effectiveness and durability. Some fabrics require more than one finishing process to achieve the characteristics or performance expectations desired. Mechanical or chemical finishing processes may be applied to a fiber, yarn, fabric or garment in one or more stages of application and at different stages of fabric production. The processes applied in the finishing of the fabric may impart two or more properties to the fabric.

Treatment or finishing operations accomplished during post-production processes to ready the fibers will not be discussed. Finishes included in this text are those applied to the woven, knitted, constructed, dyed or printed cloth *after initial preparations* and/or cleaning of the fiber or yarn.

Finishes affect the look, hand and behavior of a fabric or garment as well as influencing the drapability qualities, performance expectations and care of fabrics or garments. Fabrics made of identical fibers, yarns and fabric structure will react differently depending on the type and method of finish applied.

Finishes:
- Change and alter the fabric
- Modify or improve the hand of the fabric
- Make fabric attractive and serviceable
- Produce a change in behavior or service characteristics
- Provide specific characteristics and desired properties
- Control instability or shrinkage of fabric
- Provide aesthetic value to fabric
- Are used to conceal inferior structure
- Are used to simulate superior quality goods

Recognizing and understanding the function of finishes is necessary in order to select the proper fabric suitable for the following specific or particular considerations.
- Climate conditions
- Work-related activities
- Sports-related activities
- Care factors
- Construction procedures
- Design and end use of the fabric and garment
- Life of garment
- Federal Trade Commission Rulings

Classification of Finishes

Mechanical Finishes Finishes are applied to fabric by mechanical equipment such as copper plates, perforated cylinders or tentering frames. They are dry-finishing operations, which refer to the handling of cloth in its dry state. Mechanical finishes cause a physical change in the fabric.

Chemical Finishes Finishes in which acids, alkalies, bleaches, detergents, resins and other chemical substances cause a reaction and produce a permanent change in the fiber, yarn or fabric.

Basic Finishes Basic finishes are considered general or routine procedures and are added to most fabrics by mechanical or chemical means as a normal or regular process. Basic finishes are used to produce certain characteristics associated with definite fabric construction. They impart the desired end use properties in finished goods. Basic finishes usually cannot be seen or felt in the finished goods, and may or may not influence the performance of the fabric during wear or cleaning.

Some basic finishes are cleaning operations done by a wet or dry process to rid fabric of soil, oil or additives before dyeing, printing or application of other finishing processes.

Special Finishes Special finishes change, modify, alter or improve the behavior or service characteristics of a fabric to produce certain specific properties. Special finishes affect the performance of the fabric. Special finishes may or may not be permanent or durable.

Functional Finishes Functional finishes alter or improve the wearability and performance of a fabric or garment and provide for:

- Additional comfort
- Safety measures
- Environmental and biological resistance
- Durability for wear life of garment
- Improved care performance

Aesthetic Finishes Aesthetic finishes change or modify the appearance and/or hand of the completed garment. Aesthetic finishes give fabric a distinct surface effect and are pleasing to both hand and eye.

Internal Finishes Internal finishes are deposited and absorbed within the fiber to modify or inhibit inherent faults or weaknesses.

Internal finishes are applied to porous-surfaced fibers, combined chemically, and produce cross-linkage of fiber molecules. These finishes do not alter the appearance of the fabric, but usually modify the hand and drapability qualities.

External Finishes External finishes are additives to coat the surfaces of yarn, fabric and/or garment. External finishes may alter or improve the appearance and hand of the fabric.

Permanent Finishes Permanent finishes usually involve a chemical change in the fiber structure and will not change, alter or reverse the process desired throughout the life of the garment. Permanent finishes are applied to withstand wear without injury or deterioration and are considered durable.

Temporary Finishes Temporary finishes are not durable. They rub off during wear, diminish gradually or are removed completely the first time the garment is washed or drycleaned. Temporary finishes add body and are used to enhance and improve the appearance and hand of the fabric. They increase the salability of an inferior fabric.

Absorbent Finish*

A chemical finish applied to increase the moisture holding power of cotton, linen, and rayon fabrics. This chemical process changes the molecular structure of nylon and other man-made fiber fabrics.

- Aids in the affinity for dyestuff
- Increases drying action of fibers, yarns, fabrics
- Increases capability of fabric to absorb moisture
- Provides added comfort to individual wearing garment
- Reduces static electricity
- Corrects hardness and lack of water absorption of nylon
- Improves appearance, comfort and salability of nylon

*Refer to page 204 for photographs illustrating end result of finish on fabric.

Ammoniating Finish

A chemical finish for cotton or rayon in which the fabric is immersed into a weak solution of ammonia, and passed through a hot-bath stretching and drying process.

- Increases luster, dimensional stability, and affinity for dyestuff
- Produces 40–50 percent more strength over untreated goods
- Produces a higher strength than mercerized goods
- Less expensive than mercerization
- Fewer fabric imperfections
- Increases smoothness of yarn
- Fabric retains smooth appearance
- Abrasion resistant
- Increases absorbency
- Better heat resistance
- Wrinkle-shed ability to fabric
- Effective permanent-press characteristics

Sanfor-Set® is a registered trademark of The Sanforized Company, a division of Cluett, Peabody & Co., for an ammoniating finish.

LIQUID AMMONIA RANGE

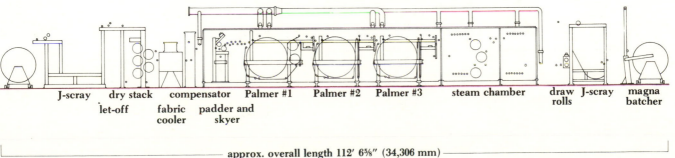

J-scray | dry stack let-off | compensator / fabric cooler / padder and skyer | Palmer #1 | Palmer #2 | Palmer #3 | steam chamber | draw rolls | J-scray | magna batcher

— approx. overall length 112′ 6⅝″ (34,306 mm) —

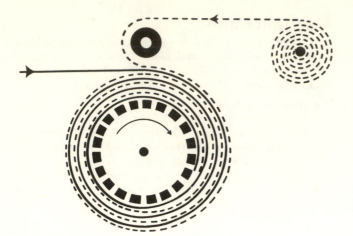

Beetling Finish

A mechanical finish that utilizes beetlers or wooden mallets to flatten the yarns in a cloth.

- Closes the weave of the fabric
- Imparts firm appearance
- Increases luster
- Produces bright and dim effects
- Flattens yarn providing more area of light reflection
- Provides simulated linen-look to cotton fabrics

Bleaching Finish

A controlled chemical finish that removes natural and other types of impurities and blemishes from yarns and fabrics. Bleaches may be acid or alkaline in nature. Most bleaches are oxidizing agents, some are reducing agents. The same type of bleaching chemical or agent is not suitable for all fabrics. Agent, type and method of bleaching used depends on type of fiber used to make the fabric and other finishing processes applied.

Bleaching chemicals used include: chlorine bleaching compounds, peroxide bleaching compounds, a combination of chlorine and peroxide, sodium chlorite, sodium perborate, sodium hypochlorite, citric acid, hypochloric acid, oxalic acid, sulfuric acid, peracetic acid, reducing bleaches, and optical bleaches or brighteners.

- Is considered a general or routine finish used on most fabrics
- May be performed in rope or open width processes
- Removes coloring matter that may be present
- Whitens fabric
- Prepares the yarn or fabric for clearer dyeing and printing
- Aid in the affinity of dyestuff
- Reduces the fiber's strength

ROPE BLEACHING RANGE

washer   J-box   washer   J-box   washer   scray

caustic saturator   peroxide saturator

cloth to white bins

OPEN WIDTH BLEACHING RANGE

scray   desize steamer   desize saturator   desize washer   caustic saturator   caustic steamer   caustic washer   peroxide steamer   peroxide saturator   peroxide washer   scray

cloth to white bins

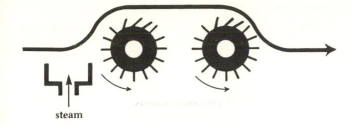

steam

Brushing Finish

A mechanical finish applied to woven, knitted, formed or lace-structured fabrics. Brushing utilizes multiple brush rollers and a revolving action which abrade yarns raising the fiber ends thus producing a low or short nap.

- Creates a short brushed surface texture when surface yarns are roughened
- Improves hand of the fabric by imparting softness
- Produces brushed denim and flannel fabrics
- Lifts nap of cut and uncut pile-surface fabrics

Brushing finishes may be used as cleaning processes to remove lint and to brush away unwanted materials adhering to the fabric following a shearing/cropping finish.

process of mending wool

Csiro Division, Textile Industries

Burling/Specking Finish

A hand-finishing operation performed during the fabric examining procedure utilizing tweezers and/or burling irons to remove burrs, knots and other detrimental or protruding yarns or threads created during the weaving process. The burling tool is used to push the knot or irregularity through to the back of the goods.

This is a selective process applied to fine woolen and worsted goods and also may be applied to fine spun rayon and cotton fiber fabrics.

- Improves final appearance of fabric
- Mends wool fabric

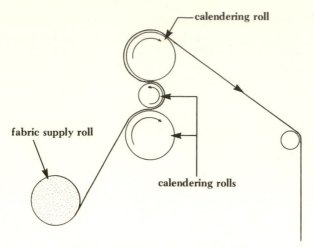

calendering roll

fabric supply roll

calendering rolls

fabric passes between and around rolls

Regular/Simple Calendering Finish

A routine or general mechanical finish applied to natural and man-made fiber fabrics. Calendering utilizes different types and number of heavy rollers arranged above and below the fabric. The rollers and different combinations of heat, pressure and surface friction closes or tightens the pores of the fabric making the cloth compact and imparting different degrees of luster to the cloth.

- Flattens round yarns, compresses fabrics and reduces thickness
- Produces a smooth surface with silken hand
- Imparts a soft, full, thready feel to fabric
- Gives cotton fabric the appearance and feel of linen or silk
- Produces a fabric with more light reflection, sheen and luster
- Reduces yarn slippage
- Process is similar to ironing but done with greater pressure
- Adds aesthetic value and imparts a good appearance
- Requires renewal after *each* laundering or cleaning (pressing or ironing)

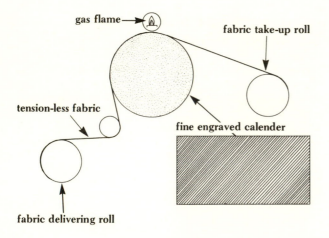

gas flame

fabric take-up roll

tension-less fabric

fine engraved calender

fabric delivering roll

Schreiner Calendering Finish

A milling or pounding calendering method utilizing metal rollers engraved with fine diagonal lines. Schreinering changes and/or modifies the appearance and/or hand of a finished fabric.

- Imprints microscopic, fine ridges allowing for light reflection
- Produces a deep-seated lustrous surface
- Flattens yarns reducing openness and creating a smooth, compact fabric
- Flattens yarns producing a fabric more opaque than unfinished fabric
- Upgrades a sleazy or flimsy fabric
- Produces a soft luster on cotton and linen
- Along with other finishing processes produces a "silk finish" on cotton
- Produces an opaque finish on nylon and polyester fabrics
- May be used on tricot knit and lingerie fabrics of nylon and polyester
- Produces a highly lustrous finish on tricot knit goods

Moiré Calendering Finish

A watermark-design effect achieved by passing fabric between engraved rollers utilizing steam, moisture and pressure. Chemicals may or may not be used. Permanency and durability of finish depends on thermoplastic inter-reaction of the resins and fabrics. Nonpermanent on rayon and silk fiber fabrics; permanent on chemically treated cotton fiber fabrics and on acetate and nylon.

Bar Moiré Wavy design forming rows and bars utilizing mechanical method, heat, moisture, and pressure. Ninety-five percent of all designs.

Scratch Moiré Yarns are deflected to produce a variety of designs utilizing mechanical method, heat, moisture and pressure.

Patterned Moiré Relief design produced by engraved rubber roller.

Hot Process Larger and more complicated designs utilizing a combination of chemicals and mechanical processes.

- Imparts design to the surface of the fabric
- Changes and modifies the appearance and hand of finished goods
- Usually applied to fabrics of fillingwise rib weave
- Produces crushed and uncrushed patterns
- Produces light and dim effects
- Creates design effects by diverting reflection of light on patterned lines of design
- Produces a fabric with luster

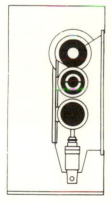

Friction/Polishing Calendering Finish

A calendering finishing process applied to woven and knitted fabrics that mercerizes and then friction calenders fabric utilizing wax, starches or thermoplastic resins; heat and high friction.

- Produces fabrics with a softer hand than chintz which is glazed
- Produces a sheen on face of fabric
- Allows fabric to shed dirt and resist water
- Reduces air permeability of a fabric by changing porosity
- Used on simulated fur and high pile fabrics to produce shine

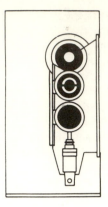

Ciré Calendering Finish

A calendering finishing process utilizing wax and wax compounds on a fabric, then processing the fabric through hot calenders.

- Produces a super gloss or metallic appearance on face of fabric
- Creates a high luster or lacquer finish on face of fabric
- Produces a highly glazed and patent-leather look
- Changes porosity of fabrics and reduces air permeability

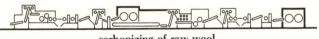

carbonizing of raw wool

carbonizing of woolens

Carbonizing Finish

A controlled chemical finish applied to woolens to remove vegetable matter. Wool fabric is immersed in a solution of sulfuric acid, subjected to high temperature and dried. Vegetable matter carbonizes and dusts off.

Thermal-Insulative Metallic Coating Finish*

The application of aluminum spray or thin layer of aluminum foil to fabric, which acts as an insulatory agent to reflect or retain heat.

- Increases warmth or coolness of fabric and adds to comfort in wear year-round
- Conserves body heat when coated surface faces the body
- Protects the body from heat when coated surface faces away from the body
- Retains softness and pliability of fabric
- May change appearance and serviceability of fabric when drycleaned

Quality and durability of metallic coating depends on quality of aluminum spray or film applied. Degree of air permeability depends on closeness of fabric weave.

Metallic-Plated Coating Finish*

The process of coating silver, gold or colored pigment, in a resin binder, to man-made fiber knit fabrics.

- Imparts heat- and light-reflecting qualities
- Maintains the softness of the base fabric
- Fabric loses air permeability qualities
- Creates a fragile fabric that:
  1. requires care during finishing process;
  2. may abrade during removal of spots and stains;
  3. surface may deteriorate or dissolve from cleaning agents;
  4. loses shine and brightness with wear and cleaning;
  5. light-streaking or fading may result from abrading and creasing;
  6. produces color changes due to perspiration;
  7. cannot be ironed directly because iron adheres to metallic face.

Plastic-Film Coating/ Waterproofing Finish*

A coating process using one or a combination of compounds to coat or seal a fabric by:
  1. spraying or brushing solution of coating substance to the fabric;
  2. immersing fabric in plastic-coating materials;
  3. utilizing extrusion or heat annealing to fuse plastic film to fabric;
  4. bonding or laminating plastic film to fabric.

Waterproofing finishing agents include: insoluble metallic compounds; paraffins, waxes or lacquers; asphaltum or tar materials; linseed and other drying oils; rubber or synthetic resins; microporous film.

- Produces a fabric impervious to rain, snow or water
- May be applied to woven, nonwoven or knitted fabrics
- Closes the pores of the fabrics
- Renders the original fabric nonporous and non-air permeable
- Changes hand and appearance of fabric
- Fabric stiffens when drycleaned
- Fabric requires wet cleaning or laundering
- Finish become brittle and cracks when subjected to cold, ageing, and wear

Plastic-film coated/waterproof-finished fabrics include:

- Pyroxylin coated oilcloth
- Slicker rainwear
- Oiled-skin rainwear
- Simulated leather

*Refer to page 126 for illustration of coating process.

Crabbing Finish

A mechanical stretching finishing process applied to woolens and worsteds utilizing cylinders, rollers, hot water or steam, a cold water bath and pressing.

- Stretches and loosens the fabric where necessary
- Prevents uneven shrinkage during subsequent finishing processes
- Sets or fixes yarn twist permanently
- Permanently sets the weave reducing offgrain fabric
- Prevents creasing of fabric

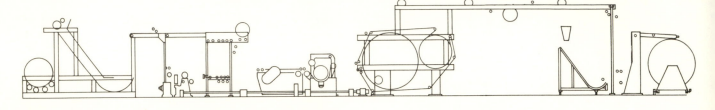

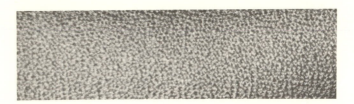

Creping Finish

A mechanical finishing process producing a textured, pebbly or crinkly effect on fabrics and plissé fabrics. Finish is accomplished by one of the following methods.

1. Passing cloth between hot rollers in the presence of steam, matching roller designed with indentations. This method is nonpermanent and will wash out or iron out.
2. Rolling caustic soda paste onto cloth in striped or figured patterns and subjecting fabric to wash bath. Treated areas create a puckered or crepe effect; untreated areas will shrink. Degree of permanency depends on thermoplastic qualities of the fabric.

Csiro Division, Textile Industries

Decating/Decatizing Finish

A wet or dry mechanical finishing process, similar to steam ironing, utilizing perforated cylinders or rollers, water, steam, moisture and pressure, which refinishes fabric after sponging or cold water shrinkage and assists in setting the finish. Finish is general or routine and applied to most fabrics.

- Helps even the yarn and set the grain or nap of fabric
- Produces a smooth, wrinkle-free fabric
- Reduces shine
- Enhances and sets the natural luster of fabrics
- Helps overcome uneven and blotched dyeing
- Softens the hand for softer drapability qualities
- Delays appearance of breaks and cracks on silk, blends, and man-made silk-type fiber fabrics

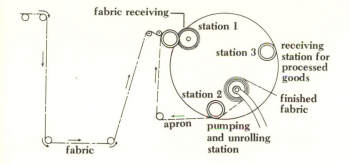

Full-Decating Finish

A permanent finish applied to both woven and knitted fabric structures and done in a closed high-pressure chamber, either dry in live steam or wet in hot and cold water. Permanent finish on woolens, worsted and worsted-blend fabrics.

- Is most vigorous of all decating processes
- Applied in a batch process
- Imparts crisp hand to fabric
- Greatest degree of fixing and stabilizing minimal residual shrinkage
- Adds maximum luster of all processes

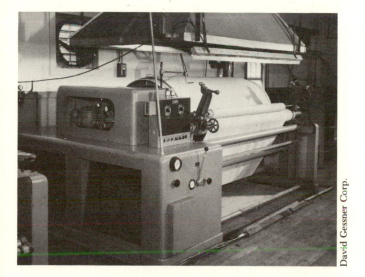

David Gessner Corp.

Semi-Decating Finish

A decating process performed open to the atmosphere and processed in separate steaming and cooling cycles. Semi-decating process does not produce a permanent finish on all fabrics.

- Is not as severe or as durable as full-decating finish
- Applied in a batch process
- Used on knitted fabric structures especially double knit and jerseys
- Processes woven or knitted woolen and worsted yarn fabrics without shrinking
- Used on man-made fiber fabrics
- Special adaptation used to handle fragile and special fabrics

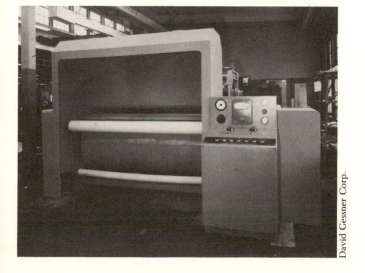

David Gessner Corp.

Continuous-Decating Finish

A decating process utilizing an endless apron which carries a layer of open-width fabric around the steaming and cooling cylinders. Steam penetrates rapidly, exposing fabric to steaming operation for a limited amount of time.

- Least severe of all decating processes
- Degree of finish can be varied with regard to fabric and end use
- Used on man-made fiber and blended fiber fabrics
- Used on knitted fabric structures that do not require lengthy processing
- Used on sensitive fabrics where crushing is objectionable

decurling with overfeed pinning wheel and post pinning

Decurling Finish

A finishing process applied to the selvages of knitted goods, which tend to curl at the edges. Stiffening agents are applied to the selvages of the goods as they pass through the gumming unit of the machine.

- Prevents edges of knitted goods from rolling and curling
- Allows fabric to lay flat for layout and cutting operations
- Allows knit goods to lay flat for laminating
- Prevents fabric from adhering to each other
- Allows for ease of wind-up on fabric roll
- Prevents fabric in a layout from adhering to each other

DEGUMMING RANGE

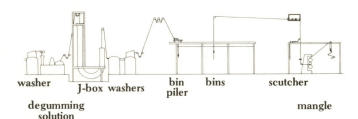

washer   J-box washers   bin   bins   scutcher
piler
degumming   mangle
solution

Degumming Finish

A scouring operation that removes the natural gum (sericin) from silk. The fabric or yarn is submerged in a hot soap solution. Degumming may take place after the silk is thrown or during any finishing process after the fabric is woven.

- Brings out natural luster of silk
- Softens hand of silk
- Restores natural creamy-white color of silk
- Prepares silk yarns for yarn-dyeing process
- Applied prior to dyeing and printing of silk
- Reduces weight of fabric up to 25 percent

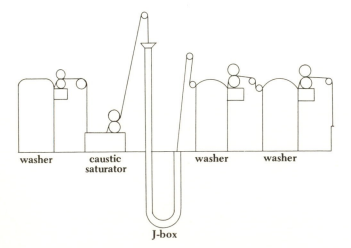

washer   caustic   washer   washer
         saturator

J-box

Denier Reduction Finish

A caustic solution applied to man-made fibers to reduce the weight and denier of man-made fiber fabrics.

- Controls character of the fabric
- Gives fabric silk-type hand
- Softens fabric
- Adds to the lightweightness of fabric
- Can make the fabric too tender if improperly applied

Embossing Finish

A finishing process used to create a flat or raised decorative design or a three-dimensional design effect on fabrics by one of the following methods.

1. A mechanical process utilizing engraved rollers, heat, moisture and steam.
2. A chemical process changing the molecular fiber structure of fabrics before processing fabric through heat-engraved rollers.
3. Utilizing the thermoplastic qualities of man-made fiber fabrics and heat-setting designs in fabric.

Degree of permanency depends on thermoplastic qualities of the fabric.

- Applied to woven and nonwoven fabrics
- Changes hand and appearance of fabrics
- Allows for a variety in patterns and depth of embossing

CALENDERING EMBOSSING

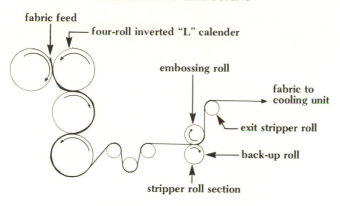

EXTRUSION EMBOSSING

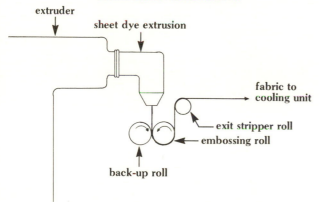

ANGLE-MOUNTED EMBOSSING

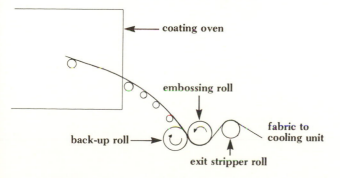

Flocking Finish*

A mechanical process utilizing adhesive and a vibrating, electrostatic or electrocoating technique to attract short fibers, hairs or metallic particles to the fabric.

The flocking operation consists of using a high-voltage electromagnetic field to "shoot" short-length monofilaments *(flocks)* with a given conductivity onto the fabric precoated with a layer of adhesive. These flocks align themselves at right angles to the surface of the adhesive layer to form a uniform dense pile.

- Changes the appearance, hand and weight of the fabric
- Produces a raised or textured surface design
- Applied to one or both sides of the fabric
- Used to simulate suede and pile fabrics
- Applied in a pattern or motif design during the printing stage
- Applied as an allover surface to the fabric
- Produced as yardage, ribbon or yarn

*Refer to page 120 for illustration of flocking process.

pressure

before fulling   finished fabric

Fulling

A general or routine finishing process applied to 100 percent wool fabrics or fabrics containing wool fibers. Utilizing the action of water moisture, friction and pressure, the woolen fabrics are alternately compressed and extended.

- Applied to carded or worsted yarn, to woven or knitted fabrics
- Action causes fibers to swell and thicken
- Shrinks yarns
- Closes weave
- Produces a fabric with close, full hand and body
- Produces a soft and more compact fabric

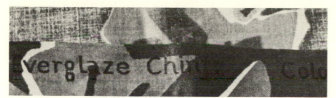

chintz/glazed cotton

Glazing

The application of wax, starch, glue, mucilage, shellac or resin to fabric prior to or during the friction-calendering process. Permanent glaze finish impregnates fabric yarn and fiber with resin. Nondurable glaze uses soluble glue, starch or shellac.

- Changes and/or modifies appearance or hand of fabric
- Produces high sheen, shiny or polished face of fabric
- Produces stiffened fabric
- Fabric is resistant to dust, soil and water spotting
- Reduces air permeability of fabric by changing porosity

Mercerizing Finish

A chemical finishing process that causes the physical properties of cotton or linen fiber fabrics to change while under tension. Fabric is impregnated with a cold, strong sodium hydroxide (caustic acid) solution. Mercerization is an important preliminary finish.

- Considered a routine or general finish for natural cellulosic fiber fabrics
- Swells the flat cotton fibers to round shapes
- Contracts the length of cotton fibers
- Promotes stabilization
- Produces silk-like appearance in cotton
- Increases strength of fabric
- Provides greater absorbency
- Improves dyeing characteristics
- Increases affinity for dyestuff thus producing brighter colors
- Allows fabric to take resin finishes better
- Increases luster of fabric when done under high tension

Slack Mercerization A method of introducing elasticity and stretch properties to 100 percent cotton fabric (for more information see page 160).

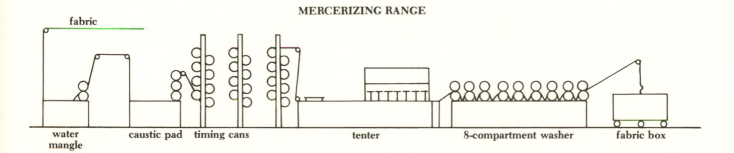

MERCERIZING RANGE

fabric

water mangle   caustic pad   timing cans   tenter   8-compartment washer   fabric box

Napping/Brushing Finish*

A mechanical finishing process that raises the short fibers on the face of the fabric by utilizing teasels, rollers or revolving cylinders with fine bristle, wire or metal points. Protruding nap is clipped or sheared to a uniform length and brushed. May be referred to as: *genapping*, *raised surface*, *gigging* (gentle napping process) and *teaseling* (gentle process).

- Applied to woven, knitted, tufted or nonwoven fabric structures
- Produced on one or both sides of the goods
- Surface may be brushed in one direction (single napping) or in opposite directions (double napping)
- Changes and/or modifies appearance or hand of fabric

*Refer to page 121 for illustrations of napping/brushing process.

- Softens fabric
- Increases durability
- Creates insulating air cells in the nap, increasing warmth of fabric
- Hides the weave of the fabric
- Hides weaving imperfections and defects in the cloth
- Cotton or man-made fiber fabrics may be treated to resemble wool texture
- Increases pilling action
- May abrade with wear and cleaning
- Flattens with wear

Brushing finish combined with steam is used to fix in position or lay the nap or pile of napped and pile structure fabrics in one direction.

Georgia synthetics

close-up of delustering stand

Optical Finishes

Due to inherent qualities of natural or man-made fibers the shape, configuration and surface transparency of fibers, light deflects or reflects from the surface of the fabric. Chemical and/or mechanical finishes are applied to enhance or modify the light-reflecting or deflecting qualities of the fabric.

- Permanently or temporarily dulls luster and sheen
- Changes or modifies the hand and/or appearance of fabric
- Changes translucent fibers into opaque fibers
- Causes breakup of light reflection

Lustering A mechanical process of adding luster by utilizing heat and pressure, with or without chemicals.

- Improves hand of fabric
- Mercerizing, calendering and glazing processes
- May be durable or renewable

Delustering A process of eliminating luster, dulling sheen or reducing brightness of fibers or yarns of a fabric by:
1. applying heat treatment to soften yarns and fabric surfaces causing a change in light reflection;
2. coating surface of yarns with oil and dulling the surface;
3. introducing titanium dioxide (white pigment) in the fiber solution which becomes an integral part of the fiber creating an opaque fiber;
4. adding a chalk finish—a temporary finish which deposits dulling materials on the surface of the fabric.

Optical Brighteners A whitening compound applied to the fabric to create an illusion of whiteness or brightness by means of light-reflecting qualities of the whitening compound under specific lighting conditions. Brightening agent composition is similar to dyestuff. The same dye becks or machines used to dye fabrics are also used to apply brighteners.

- Agent changes ultraviolet light wavelengths into visual wavelengths and produces a fluorescent effect
- Fluorescent agents mask natural yellow cast of fabrics
- Produces a brighter looking fabric

Parchmentizing/Transparency Finish

A controlled chemical process using sulfuric acid solution bath and neutralizing bath.

- Makes cotton fabrics transparent
- Produces permanently stiffened cotton
- Used to produce organdy

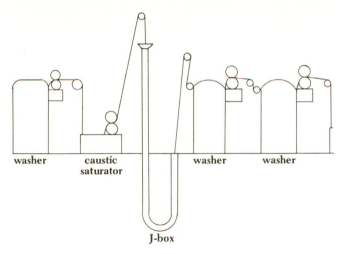

washer   caustic
      saturator   washer   washer

J-box

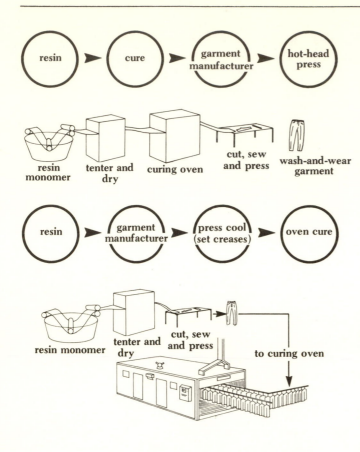

Permanent Press/Durable Press/ Wash-and-Wear/Drip Dry

Fabric is saturated with resins, silicone emulsion softeners, reactants, catalysts, optical whiteners, and thermoplastic polymers, then subjected to a *heat-curing process*. Effectiveness and end result of finishing process depends on particular process and agents selected and the inter-relationship of fibers, percent of fiber blends, and structure of fabric.

Heat-curing procedures refer to the following.

Cure/Curing A process applied to a fabric or garment. The application of heat, by baking or pressing, to cause a reaction in the finishing agents applied to the cloth.

Pre-cured A process applied to set or cure the fabric *prior to cutting* the garment. Fabric is treated with chemical resins and cured at a high heat. Garment is constructed then pressed on high pressure press with a high temperature. Heat from pressing reactivates the permanent-press finish, permanently setting the fabric.

Post-Cured/Deferred Cure A process completed *after garment is constructed*. Fabric is impregnated with resins and catalyst and dried at low temperatures. Garment is constructed and completed garment is put through a baking process. Permanent-press agents are activated while baking and the garment assumes the constructed shape.

Batch Cure One group of garments of a fabric is placed in the oven to cure at one time.

Advantages & Disadvantages

Advantages

Imparts wrinkle resistance to fabric

Eliminates or reduces need for ironing or pressing

Improves care performance of garment

Allows garment to be worn, washed, tumble dried and worn again

Sets the shape of the garment

Provides shape retaining qualities, sharp creases, flat seams and smooth-surface textures

Disadvantages

Stiffens fabric, but becomes progressively softer as resin wears off

Stiff/crisp drapability because of high percentage of resin used

Poor moisture absorption due to percent of resins and content of hydrophobic fibers

Not comfortable to wear in warm climates

Oil-born stains are difficult to remove

Treatment reduces strength and durability

Reduces abrasion resistance

Produces color change or degradation

Weakens structure of cellulosic fibers (man-made fibers are added to improve strength)

Presents problems with selecting compatible components and findings (interfacings, thread, zippers, fasteners)

Presents problems with garment construction such as seams may pucker during sewing or during laundering

Garments cannot be altered successfully as seam and hem creases cannot be pressed out

Shrinkage occurs in curing and shrinks further durin washing

Wrinkles occurring during process will be set and are not removable

Improperly applied finishes leave residual odor

Formaldehyde-type resin compounds may cause allergic reaction

Type of Finish	Trademark	Manufacturer
Durable press (home-sewn garments)	ALMI-Set Lifetime-Pressed	Ameritex Div. of United Merchants and Manufacturers, Inc.
Durable press	Coneprest	Cone Mills
Durable press	Dan-Press	Dan River Mills
Durable press	Koratron	Koratron Co.
Durable press (cotton knits)	Pat-Nit RX	Pak-Nit Compax Corp.
Durable press	Penn Prest	J.C. Penney Co.
Durable press	Perma Press	Sears Roebuck & Co.
Wash-and-wear	Everglaze	Joseph Bancroft & Sons
Wash-and-wear	Minicare	Joseph Bancroft & Sons
Wash-and-wear	Bates Disciplined	Bates Fabrics, Inc.
Wash-and-wear	Coneset	Cone Mills, Inc.
Wash-and-wear	Wrinkl-Shed	Dan River Mills
Wash-and-wear	Belfast	Deering Milliken, Inc.
Wash-and-wear	Super Kwik Care	Reeves Brothers Inc.

Resistant Finishes for Specific Properties

The following processes are used for specific purposes and may be applied during different stages of finishing operations. Chemical formulations may be applied during, prior to, or after other selected finishes and/or dyeing processes.

Several or all chemicals may be applied together insofar as they fit and work together and are compatible to produce the desired effect. Special equipment is not necessary as multi-purpose ranges facilitate all operations. The same machine used to perform different finishing and dyeing processes may be used. Products are applied by conventional wet-processing operations using roller, exhaust, dye beck or rotary methods and also by paddle or extraction machines.

Specific chemical agents or resins and the type of application are selected with regard to:
- Fiber content of fabric
- Yarn construction and fabric structure
- Performance expectation desired
- End use of fabric and/or garment

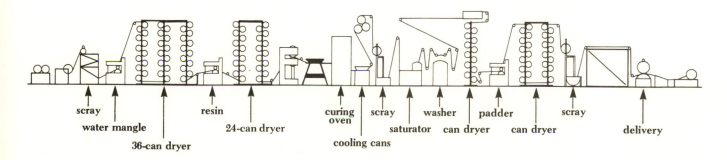

scray · water mangle · 36-can dryer · resin · 24-can dryer · curing oven · cooling cans · scray · saturator · washer · can dryer · padder · can dryer · scray · delivery

Abrasion-Resistant Finish*

Soft thermoplastic resins or a silicone-base chemical is applied to a finished fabric thus binding the fibers together. Nylon, acrylic, and polyester have inherent resistance to abrasion, and may be blended with fibers with low abrasion resistance, reducing the need for abrasion-resistant finishes.

- Increases the resistance to snags, pulls, abrasion damage
- Strengthens the fabrics
- Produces a soft velvety or silk-like hand
- Increases water repellency
- Increases sewability
- Decreases needle-hole fusion on man-made fiber fabrics during high-speed sewing
- Promotes anti-crush properties to pile fabrics
- Does not effect lightfastness of dyes or tensile strength of fabric.

Abrasion-resistant finishes are applied in the water bath in conjunction with a catalyst; dried and cured at 320°F.

*Refer to page 203 for photographs illustrating end result of finish on fabric.

Bacterial-Resistant/Antiseptic/Antimicrobial Finish*

A process of impregnating the fabric with bacteriostatic formulations designed for use on wool, cotton, linen, rayon, man-made and thermoplastic fiber fabrics.

Depending on the chemical formulation of the agent and the fiber content of the fabric, bacteriostatic agents may be applied by one of the following methods:

1. alone or in a mixture with many different types of finishing agents;
2. exhaust or padding methods in a batch process, dye beck or kettle;
3. poured directly into the application bath;
4. applied to the final wash;
5. applied prior to or after dyeing process.

Bacteriostatic agents include durable or renewable germicidal chemicals applied to fabric. Germicidal chemicals include: phenols, alcohol; iodine; chlorine and chlorine compounds; mercury, silver or copper compounds; quaternary ammonium compounds.

- Controls and reduces the development of unpleasant odors caused by bacteria, perspiration and soil deposited on fabric or garment
- Resists acids or alkalies associated with deterioration of fabric
- Reduces damage to fabric as a result of mildew- and mold-producing fungi
- Reduces bacterial growth and action
- Reduces danger of infection following injury
- Controls spread of germs

Durable Finish Insoluble surface coating that remains on the yarn or fabric.

Internal Durable Finish Insoluble within the fabric structure.

Renewable Finish External finishes that produce resistance to micro-organisms, but must be applied after each laundering or cleaning.

*Refer to page 217 for photographs illustrating end result of finish on fabric.

Crush-Resistant Finish*

A resin treatment applied to pile fabrics to enable the erect pile to recover when crushed.

- Provides resiliency
- Reduces flattening of pile
- Reduces shine and abrasion of pile

*Refer to page 207 and 216 for photographs illustrating end result of finish on fabric.

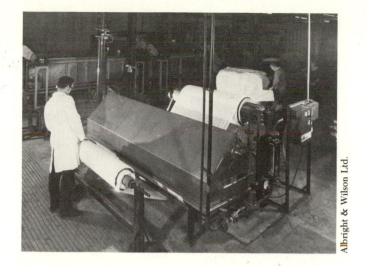

Albright & Wilson Ltd.

Flame-Fire Resistant/Flame-Fire Retardant Finish

A chemical applied to reduce the afterglow properties, charring or flammability of fibers and fabrics. *Durable finishes* withstand to wear-life of the garment. *Water-soluble finishes* must be replaced after laundering or dry-cleaning.

Wool fabrics have built-in flame-retardancy properties; they are self-extinguishing. Man-made fibers with flame resistant/retardant properties include: aramid, asbestos, chloride, glass, modacrylic, novoloid, polyvinyl and special formulas of acetate, nylon, polyester, rayon and triacetate.

- Provides factor of safety to fabric thus to article and person
- Allows the fabric to be self-extinguishing upon removal of fire source
- Provides resistance to after-flaming
- Reduces complete destruction of article
- Non-penetrating coating applied to cellulosic fibers cuts off supply of oxygen
- Changes look, hand, durability, touch and smell of fabric
- Produces crisp, harsh feel to fabric

Fireproofing According to the Federal Trade Commission, Washington, D.C.—a fabric must be 100 percent fireproof to carry the fireproof label. Only *asbestos*, *glass*, and *fiberglass* are truly fireproof. They will not burn in the path of direct flame.

Type of Finish	Trademark	Manufacturer
Flame retardant	Pyroset	American Cyanamid Co.
Flame retardant	Firestop	Ameritex Div. Of United Merchants and Manufacturers, Inc.
Flame retardant	Pyrovatex Cp	Ciba-Geigy Corp.
Flame retardant	THPC	Hooker Chemical Co.
Flame retardant	Fire-Guard	Polymer Research Corp. of America
Flame retardant	Saniflamed	Sanitized Inc.

GAS FADING RANGE

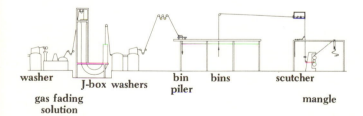

washer J-box washers bin piler bins scutcher

gas fading solution mangle

Gas-Fading/Fume-Fading Resistant Finish

A chemical finish applied to change the physical surface properties, providing resistance to the environment and fading.

- Prevents color change caused by nitrogen oxides in the atmosphere
- Protects dye colors used on acetate and triacetate
- Reduces color breakdown of nylon and polyester fabrics

Mildew-Resistant/Rot-Repellent Finish*

A process that coats cellulosic and protein fiber fabrics by impregnating the fabric with a metallic salt or resin.

- Prevents formation of mildew and mold on damp fabrics
- Prevents mildew and mold from penetrating fabrics thus reducing rot or deterioration
- Prevents growth or parasitic fungus that grows in warm humid weather

Depending on the chemical formulation of the agent and the fiber content of the fabric, mildew agents may be applied by one of the following methods:

1. alone or in a mixture with many different types of finishing agents;
2. exhaust or padding methods in a batch process, dye beck or kettle;
3. poured directly into the application bath;
4. applied to the final wash;
5. applied prior to or after dyeing process.

*Refer to page 217 for photographs illustrating end result of finish on fabric.

Moth-Resistant/Moth-Repellent Finish*

A durable or renewable chemical finish applied to wool, wool blends, and animal hair fiber fabrics to protect against moth attack and damage.

Depending on the chemical agents used:
1. Chemicals added to fulling or dyeing process will permanently change the fiber composition, making fibers unpalatable to the larvae, producing *permanent* moth resistance.
2. Chemicals applied during or after water bath of fabrics are temporary and need to be renewed after laundering and drycleaning.

Moth-proofing agents include: dieldrin (chlorinated hydrocarbon), dichlore-diphenyl, chlorophenol urea, sodium salts of pentachloro, dihydroxy, triphenyl, methane, sulfonic acids; various types of fluorides.

- Impervious to moth larvae
- Reduces or prevents damage by moths and other insects
- Gives off an odor and prevents deposit of eggs
- Gives off gas fumes which are toxic to insects

*Refer to page 217 for photographs illustrating end result of finish on fabric.

Slip-Resistant/Anti-Slip Finish*

A mechanical action and the application of chemical agents to coat or impregnate the fabric, depositing the chemical substance at points of interlacing in the fabric structure. Slip-resistant finishing agents include: resins, rosins and hard waxy substances.

- Prevents shifting or slippage of yarns in fabrics made with filament yarns or low thread count
- Reduces seam slippage at point of strain
- Reduces seam fraying
- Prevents warp and filling yarns in fabric structure from slipping out of place
- Adds durability
- Provides permanent firmness on yarns and fabrics
- Changes hand of fabric

*Refer to page 223 for photographs illustrating end result of finish on fabric.

Snagging-Resistant/Anti-Snag Finish*

A multi-action application of chemicals applied by exhaust or padding methods then heat cured at specific levels.

Snagging-resistant/anti-snag finishing chemicals include: modified acrylic resin emulsion, reactive resins, synthetic wax emulsions, modified polyvinyl acetate emulsions and fluorchemicals.

- Curbs and contols snagging
- Reduces picks and pulls
- Provides anti-snag properties
- Provides stain resistance
- Adds water-repellency
- Adds durability

*Refer to page 223 for photographs illustrating end result of finish on fabric.

Static-Resistant/Anti-Static Finish (chemical process)*

A chemical process that develops an electric charge opposite that of the fiber and neutralizes the electrostatic charge build-up on the fiber by attracting molecules of water to the surface of the fabric, improving surface conductivity.

Chemicals of quaternary ammonium compounds, cationic organic compounds or a blend of cationic surface-acting agents are applied to the fabric by conventional wet-processing operations utilizing padding, spraying or exhausting methods. The surface-acting agents of anti-static finishes vary in effectiveness and are not durable or permanent.

Some producers of man-made fibers are modifying the chemical properties of the fiber, building in anti-static properties.

Household anti-static and anti-cling products may be used during or after laundering or drycleaning to reduce static build-up.

- Applied to noncellulosic man-made fiber fabrics
- Aids, reduces or eliminates static electricity
- Reduces the degree of crackling and sparkling that occurs during fabric friction
- Prevents garments from riding up
- Prevents clinging characteristics of garment to body or other garments
- Reduces static attraction of dirt or lint

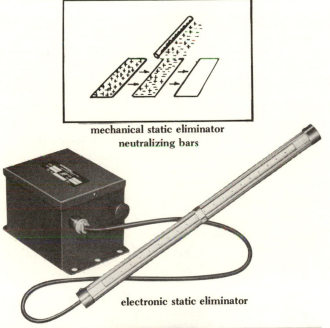

mechanical static eliminator
neutralizing bars

electronic static eliminator

electrical static resistance tester

Custom Scientific Instruments Inc.

Static-Resistant/Anti-Static Finish (mechanical process)*

A mechanical process utilizing an anti-static mechanical eliminator to remove dust or other particles from the fabric. The static eliminator bar ionizes the air around it producing enough ionization to neutralize many different types of materials.

In the *ionization process*, air molecules are broken up into positive and negative ions. Because opposite charges attract, any *positive* charged material passing through ionized air will attract free *negative* ions until it becomes neutralized. *Negative* charged materials will attract positive ions to neutralize.

Anti-static mechanical eliminators include:
- Shockless static bars
- Enclosed static bars
- Metal-encased static bars
- Explosive-proof bars
- Circular static bars
- One-point static bars
- Induction static bars
- Environstat static bars

*Refer to page 224 for photograph illustrating end result of finish on fabric.

soil tester

Soil- & Stain-Resistant Finish

The application of an emulsion consisting of a silicone plus a reactive hydrophilic polymer. Soil-release finishes are used in the durable-press finishing of cotton and cotton/polyester blend fabrics. They are applied on conventional pad frames and curing equipment. The chemical compounds form a layer of film around the fiber or yarn and act as a barrier.

Soil- and stain-resistant finishing agents include: fluorocarbons, fluorochemicals, pyridinum compounds, resins, silicone, triazine compounds, wax and wax-like derivatives.

- Adds to care of garment
- Creates fabric with smooth surface
- Repels or reduces rate of soil absorption, deposit and detention in fabric.
- Provides for good soil-release properties
- Prevents stains from spreading
- Allows water and spills to form globules on fabric surface preventing penetration into the fiber
- Resists water and water-born stains
- Adds soft, silicone hand
- Improves tear strength

resin on the surface of the fabric only

resin penetrating the yarns and on the surface

Water-Resistant/Water-Repellent Finish

A chemical penetration that coats and adheres to the fibers and yarns of fabric, or a wax-coating treatment for fabrics that resist or repel the absorption or penetration of water under certain conditions for a given period of time.

Non-Durable—loses repellency, diminishes with each washing, not dry cleanable.
Semi-Durable—loses repellency if washed but can be dry-cleaned.
Durable—endures dry-cleaning and laundering processes

Water-resistant/water-repellent finishing agents include: resin mixtures, wax emulsion mixtures, aluminum salts and compounds, silicone compounds, fluorochemicals, pyridinum compounds, methylol stearamides, ammonium compounds, metallic salts and surface acting agents.

- Used on woven and knitted porous fabrics
- Allows fabric to shed rain, snow, water
- Allows water to remain on the surface reducing fabric's affinity to absorb water
- Does not close the pores of the fabric
- Retains air permeability, permits body to breathe
- More comfortable to wear than waterproof non-air permeable fabrics
- Retains hand and appearance of fabric
- Allows fabric to be pliable
- Renders fabric spot- and stain-resistant
- Renders fabric water- and oil-born-stain resistant
- Renders fabric wrinkle-resistant

Type of Finish	Trademark	Manufacturer
Water- and oil-resistant	Zepel	E.I. du Pont de Nemours & Co.
Water- and oil-resistant	Scotchgard	Chemical Div. of Minnesota Mining & Manufacturing Co.

Wrinkle-Resistant/ Crease-Resistant Finish

The process of applying resins and reactants to a fabric that combine chemically to change the molecule structure of the fiber by one of the following methods:

1. immersing fabric in a resin solution, impregnating the cloth and permeating the fibers;
2. applying resins during or immediately following the drying process.

Finishes may be durable or semi-durable, effectiveness is dependent on:

- Fiber content
- Fabric structure
- Particular chemical formation
- Care and application process
- Fabric saturation; percent of resin take-up of fabric

Wrinkle resistant/crease resistant finishing agents include: synthetic resins, melamine, epoxy, urea, formaldehyde, vinyl, oxidized starches, thermoplastic resins, linear reactants, and chloro-alkyl compounds.

- Changes hand and weight of fabric
- Adds body and produces stiffer fabric
- Improves care performance, ensuring minimum care of fabric and garments
- Allows for wrinkles to hang out
- Allows for wrinkle recovery during wear
- Provides minimal wrinkling after washing and drying
- Reduces the retention of undesirable folds and creases
- Produces flat, smooth surface
- Imparts dimensional stability
- Fabric remains the same after washing
- Reduces tensile and tear strength of fabric
- Reduces absorbency qualities, abrasion resistance, and elongation factors of the fabric
- Produces non-removable creases when altering fabric
- Produces "Wash-and-Wear, Permanent Press/Durable Press" garments

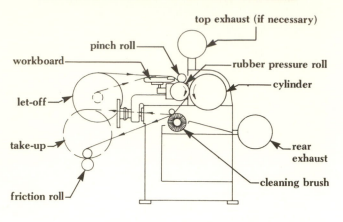

THE CURTIN-HEBERT 710 SANDING MACHINE

top exhaust (if necessary)

pinch roll

workboard

rubber pressure roll

let-off

cylinder

take-up

rear exhaust

friction roll

cleaning brush

Sanding/Sueding Finish

A surface finish imparted to fabric as it passes over rapidly revolving rollers covered with abrasive paper of desired grit for the fabric being processed. The height and direction of the low pile created on the surface of the fabric depends on the selection and manner of programming the multi-cylinder or a single-cylinder sanding/sueding machine.

- Used on both woven and knitted fabrics
- Softens hand of fabric

The degree of roughening the surface is determined by the:
1. speed of the sandpaper roller;
2. coarseness of the sandpaper;
3. speed at which fabric is passed between the rollers;
4. amount of space between the rollers.

Hand of fabric after processing differs depending on the:
- Fiber content of the fabric
- Filament count in the yarn
- Intensity with which fabric is worked

David Gessner Corp.

Shearing/Cropping Finish

A mechanical process applied to natural or man-made staple length fiber fabrics. Utilizing a multi-blade machine, undesirable loose surface fibers are cut or sheared producing different surface looks.

- Evens and levels the surface of the fabric producing a uniform appearance
- Applied to one or both sides of fabric
- Allows weave of fabric to show
- Produces uniform pile for plushes, velvets, velours and cut-loop fabrics
- May be manipulated to produce cut designs and sculptured effects
- Changes hand, drapability and creasing properties of fabric
- Improves color and appearance of fabric

close-up of shearing cylinder and shearing table

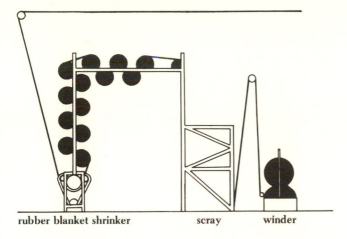

SANFORIZING RANGE

rubber blanket shrinker   scray   winder

Shrinkage Control/Stabilizing Finish

Mechanical stretching or compressing, chemical or resin treatment, steaming, sponging, cold and hot water baths or any combination applied for the control of shrinkage, swelling or stretching of yarns and fabrics.

Shrinkage is the reduction of the length and/or width of a fabric that takes place when laundered, wet-cleaned, dry-cleaned, tumble-dried or steamed during pressing.

Fabrics or garments that have received a pre-shrunk treatment must conform to rulings on shrinkage issued by the Federal Trade Commission in order for garments to carry pre-shrunk or minimal shrinkage labels indicating percent of residual shrinkage.

- Shortens deliberately the length and width of a fabric before consumer consumption
- Restrains dimensional changes in the fabric
- Minimizes subsequent shrinkage
- Relaxes stress and strain left in fabric construction process
- Mechanically compresses fabric to remove relaxation shrinkage, reducing residual shrinkage to less than 1%
- Mechanically and chemically controls progressive shrinkage to reduce or eliminate residual shrinkage to less than 2%
- Reduces tendency for cotton, linen or rayon cloth to shrink when washed or laundered
- Prevents further shrinkage of woolen and worsted fabrics or garments
- Allows for washable woolens
- Provides dimensional stability of knits
- Adds luster and softens hand

Type of Finish	Trademark	Manufacturer
Shrinkage control	Sanforized	The Sanforized Co., Div. of Cluett, Peabody & Co.
Shrinkage control (cotton knits)	Sanfor-Knit	The Sanforized Co.
Shrinkage control plus crease recovery	Sanforized-Plus	The Sanforized Co.
Shrinkage control on durable press	Sanforized-Plus-2	The Sanforized Co.
Shrinkage control (cotton knits)	Shrink-No-Mor	The Sanforized Co.
Shrinkage control	Tebilized	Avondale Mills
Shrinkage control (blended fabrics)	Perma Press	Avondale Mills

PRINCIPLES OF COMPRESSIVE SHRINKAGE

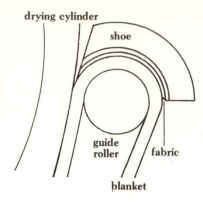

drying cylinder

shoe

guide roller fabric

blanket

Compressive Shrinkage Control Finish

A multi-step mechanical shrinking operation consisting of a water spraying unit which mists and dampens the fabric. Shrinking unit is a large steam heated cylinder with rubber or wool felt blankets, and a drying and finishing unit.

- Considered a relaxation shrinkage method
- Used on woven fabrics of cotton and linen
- Used on cotton-fiber tubular knits and underwear fabrics
- Used on high-wet modular rayon fiber fabrics

blanket surface is stretched at A

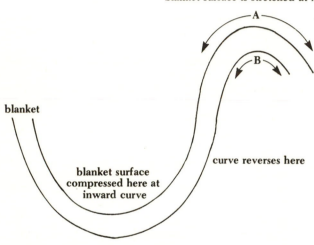

A

B

blanket

curve reverses here

blanket surface compressed here at inward curve

Diagram illustrates how the reversal of curves can cause a change in size, which compresses the fabric.

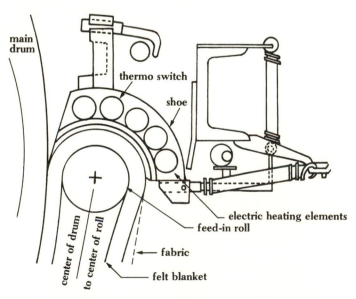

main drum

thermo switch

shoe

electric heating elements

feed-in roll

center of drum

to center of roll

fabric

felt blanket

Cross section of diagram at the point in the compressive shrinkage process where length shrinkage is obtained. The electrically heated shoe holds the fabric firmly on the outside of the blanket so that when the blanket collapses in straightening out, the fabric is shrunk accordingly.

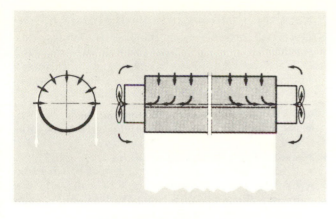

The suction drum "draws" the processing agent through the fabric.

Heat-Set Shrinkage Control Finish

A treatment given to thermoplastic heat-sensitive fibers. Heat causes an internal molecular rearrangement of the fibers, relieving stress, and bringing about molecular crystallinity. The fabric assumes the structural arrangement in which they were held during the finishing process.

- Considered a routine or general finish for man-made fiber fabrics
- Improves dimensional stability, eliminating subsequent shrinking
- Sets the fabric for minimal residual shrinkage and stretch recovery
- Provides resiliency and wrinkle resistance
- Sets the grain of fabric made of nylon and polyester fibers
- Permanently produces desired shapes and sizes
- Permanently sets design detail and surface embroidery
- Provides for a method of permanently pleating or embossing fabrics
- Fabrics may be set into flat surfaces or predetermined shapes
- Provides permanent setting and finishing of:
    Fabrics with mechanical stretch
    Elastic or elastomeric fabrics
    Knit fabrics of wool, wool blends and 100 percent man-made fibers
    Woven fabrics of man-made fibers

chemical foamer and feed system

Gaston County

Resin Treatment/Shrinkage Control Finish

A process of impregnating or applying synthetic resins to fabrics which are then processed by curing producing polymerization of the resin imparting permanent dimentional stability. Resins used are urea formaldehyde, phenol formaldehyde and melamine formaldehyde.

- Used on rayon-fiber fabrics
- Stabilizes the fabric
- Reduces distortion of the fabric
- Provides crease- and crush-resistance
- Produces stiffness thus changing the hand and drape of the fabric
- Provides hand laundering and machine washability of fabric at gentle cycle

Photomicrograph of wool fibers in fabric, which have been treated by a shrink-resistant process

Sponging Shrinkage Control Finish

A process of controlled steam shrinkage for fabrics as they pass through various operations. Fabric in a relaxed state is lead into a continuous chamber, saturated with water or steam; slowly hot-air dried in the drying chamber and wound on rolls without creasing or folding.

- A relaxation shrinkage method
- Fabric achieves dimensional stability prior to cutting and assembling of garment
- Used on woven or knitted fabrics
- Used on woolen and worsted and wool-blended fibers
- Used for controlled stability of 100% man-made fibers
- Recognizied as London Shrunk®, cold water shrunk, and open-steam sponged

SINGEING RANGE

cloth→

scray   singer saturator

Singeing/Gassing

A dry-finishing process that burns off protruding fibers from yarn and fabric by passing them over a gas or jet flame or heated copper plates.

- One of the first essential preparatory processes used on most fabrics
- Removes lint, thread and other detrimental matter from fabric
- Produces a clear, smooth and uniform appearance
- Imparts crispness to fabric
- Prepares fabric for printing and dyeing processes

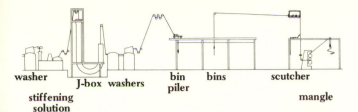

STIFFENING RANGE

washer

stiffening
solution

J-box washers

bin
piler

bins

scutcher

mangle

Permanent Stiffening Finish

An acid or resin chemical process that changes the cellular structure of the fiber and provides the fabric with a *permanent* crispness or stiffness. Finish does not dissolve in laundering and fabric returns to original crisp appearance after ironing.

Permanent stiffening finishes include: thermosetting resins, sulfuric acids, ethyl compounds, cellulose compounds, vinyl acetate, polyacrylates, and plastic compounds.

- Changes hand and appearance of fabric
- Insures permanent crispness without further starching
- Used on sheer and medium-weight cotton or linen fabrics
- Applied to stiffen collars and cuffs of shirts permanently
- Prevents garment from appearing wilted during or after wear
- Smooth fabric surface
- Garments stay clean longer—resists soiling
- Reduces formation of lint
- Provides snag and abrasion resistance
- Increases tensile strength of fabrics
- Contributes to dimensional stability of fabric—reduces shrinkage
- Provides permanent luster

Temporary Stiffening Finish

A sizing or dressing mixture applied to cotton, linen, and rayon fabrics to add a *temporary* firmness or crispness. Finish will wash out after one or more washings. Temporary sizing and dressing mixtures include:

- Starches—to increase weight
- Glue—to provide stiffness
- Fats and oils—to soften or modify the starch
- Wax and paraffins—to produce luster
- Clay, chalk, barium sulfate, calcium sulfate, magnesium sulfate—to increase weight and compactness of weave
- A clear gelatin substance, which does not detract from natural luster, is used on rayons

- Finish flakes off when rubbed between fingers
- Improves appearance and adds luster
- Increases weight
- Improves the hand of limp fabric
- Prevents edges on sheer or thin fabrics from rolling
- Increases strength and smoothness of yarns
- Fills in openings in the constructed fabric creating a more compact appearance
- Adds to appearance of inferior or flimsy fabrics

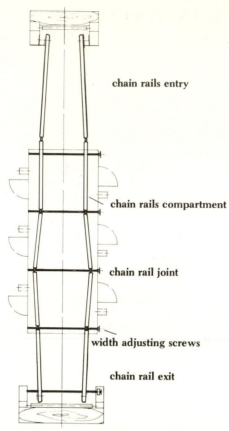

chain rails entry

chain rails compartment

chain rail joint

width adjusting screws

chain rail exit

Fabric can be shrunk in the filling or width direction. Tension applied as required

Stretch/Slack Mercerization Finish

A shrinking process by chemical or mechanical means which imparts stretch properties to a fabric after it has been woven.

Stretch finishes may also be referred to as *slack mercerization*, *mechanical stretch*, and *chemical stretch*. Slack mercerization is applied to fabrics made of 100% cotton fiber and to fabrics made of cotton and man-made fiber blends.

- Usually produces a horizontal stretch
- Shrinks and sets the filling yarns of the fabric permanently

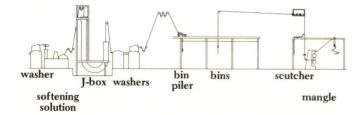

SOFTENING RANGE

washer

softening
solution

J-box   washers

bin
piler

bins

scutcher

mangle

Softening Finish

The application of chemical compounds to change and/or modify the characteristics of a fabric *permanently* or *temporarily*. Softening agents may be applied by padding, dye beck, or washer operations.

Softening agents include: sulfonated oils, fats, wax emulsions, soaps, glycerine/synthetic detergents, substitute ammonium compounds, silicone compounds, lanolin, and cationic softeners.

- Changes the hand and appearance of fabrics
- Improves the drapability qualities of fabrics
- Provides fabrics with a soft mellow hand
- May add body to some fabrics
- Improves sewability and tear strength
- Subdues coarseness imparted during processing and fabric construction
- Facilitates the application of subsequent finishes
- Increases life and utility of the fabric
- Prevents fabrics from soiling and spotting

SOIL RELEASE RANGE

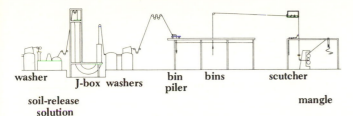

washer

J-box washers bin bins scutcher
piler

soil-release
solution   mangle

Soil Release Finish

Additives that impart a chemical change to fibers and yarns or that provide a protective coating to fabric to prevent or resist staining and deep penetration of soil.

- Adds to care of garment
- Permits better wearability for improved soil release or removal
- Permits relatively easy removal of oil-borne stains from permanent press garments
- Resists redepositing of soil when laundering
- Aids in making the fabric more absorbent
- Provides greater comfort in hot weather
- Provides improved anti-static properties

Type of Finish	Trademark	Manufacturer
Soil release	Visa	Deering Milliken, Inc.
Soil release	Zelcon TGF	E.I. du Pont de Nemours & Co., Inc.
Soil release	Dual Action Scotchgard	Chemical Div. of Minnesota Mining and Manufacturing Co.
Soil release	Rhoplex SR-488	Rohm and Haas Co.

WOOL PRESENTIZING RANGE

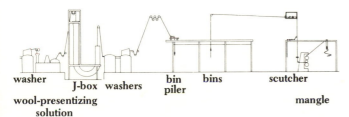

washer

J-box washers bin bins scutcher
piler

wool-presentizing
solution   mangle

Wool Presensitizing

The application of monoethanolamine sulfite to wool fabrics while still in the mill state. The non-resinous wool-setting chemical when activated by water and steam sets formed pleats and creases permanently.

- Provides woolens and worsteds with crease-retention properties
- Provides dimensional stability

Operations that are Part of Other Finishes

Cooling Operation

An air-circulation operation that shock cools the fabric following other processes. An air-circulation system is used consisting of an enclosed compartment with jets or nozzles aimed at both sides of the fabric, allowing for uniform circulation of cool air over the length and width of the fabric.

Chlorine Retention Operation

A resin chemical treatment given to cotton, rayon, nylon, and blended-fiber fabrics. Chlorine retention may cause:
- Goods to retain varying amounts of chlorine
- Discoloration and/or yellowing of some fabrics
- Degradation and weakening of some fabrics

Chlorine-retention application should not be applied to fabrics requiring bleaching agents during laundering process. Fabrics containing chlorine-retention applications should be labeled accordingly for proper care factors of fabric or garment.

De-sizing Operation

De-sizing operation is part of a washing treatment for fabrics to remove the previous sizing or dressing compounds applied to yarns prior to the construction of the fabric. De-sizing is necessary to remove sizes, waxes, oils, and other impurities that were added to the fibers during the spinning and warp preparation.

The type of de-sizing process used depends on the types of sizes on the fabrics. Enzyme treatment removes water-insoluble sizes. Water-soluble sizes are used primarily on polyester/cotton fabrics.

Drying Operation

A drying operation used to evaporate wetness and to provide for uniform drying of yarns; woven, knitted or coated fabrics. Heat, steam, and/or dry air is evenly distributed across the full width of the yarn or fabric.

Drying operation may utilize any one of the following with regard to the specific drying process and type of fabric:
- Loop ager
- Drum dryer
- Roller dryer and curer
- Loop dryer and curer
- Infra-red dryer and curing oven

Souring Operation

Souring operation is applied to stop the bleaching finishing action. A chemical treatment using a weak acid solution to neutralize any alkali content remaining in cellulosic fiber fabrics.

Straightening Operation

The straightening process equalizes the fabric eliminating bow and skew distortion. The finishing unit contains concave and convex, adjustable, rubber-covered, flexible rollers. The straightening rollers are divided into sections, each of which is separately driven and adjusted.

- Applies minimal tension to fabrics
- Used on delicate woven and knitted fabrics
- Straightens and sets the grain of fabrics

Steaming Operation

Steaming processes utilizing steaming chambers are used prior to, in addition to, or after various stages of finishing. During the steaming operation the fabric is fed over a steam box containing a perforated cover, then the steam is forced through the fabric.

- May be applied to woolen fabrics after drying to partially shrink and condition the fabric
- Accompanies the final pressing process for woolen and worsted fabrics
- Reduces undesired glaze imparted by decating process
- Stabilizes the colors of dyes after printing and dyeing processes

▶

vertical return chain rail with graphite wear strips/pins

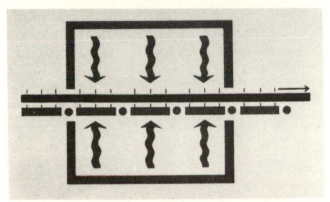

selvages of fabric are held by tentering needles

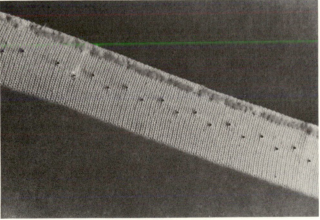

tentering frame mark

Tentering Operation

A mechanical process, which is a routine or general operation, applied at various stages of finishing, coloring or printing goods. The selvages of fabric in open-width form are held onto the tentering frame by hooks, pins or clips as the fabric moves into the drying stage. In the drying stage, a chamber of hot air blows against the top and bottom sides of the fabric. By controlling the feed of the fabric through the chain mechanism of the tenter machine, the fabric can be contracted or stretched during drying.

- Maintains specific dimension of fabrics
- Pulls out creases and wrinkles
- Straightens the weave of fabrics
- May contribute to progressive and relaxation shrinkage of fabrics
- Improperly done, causes offgrain fabric ("bowing and skewing")

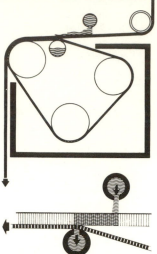

JET WASHER **VACUUM MESH WASHER**

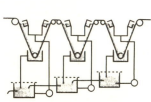

A slot jet forces water to penetrate fabric pile. The water then cascades through pile to collecting tank.

Residual dyestuff thickens and additives are diluted by a film of hot water. Fabric is carried on a mesh over a vacuum slot. Any nonfixed dyestuff is vacuum-extracted and drained.

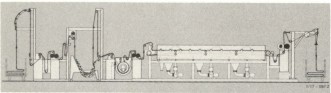

Open-width washing range for crease-prone knit fabrics and stretch-sensitive crease-prone woven fabrics.

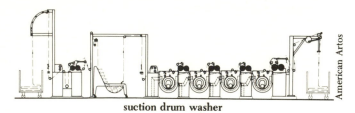

suction drum washer

American Artos

pressure

Wool fabrics are scoured in this machine. They are stitched together, end to end, making a continuous "rope." The fabric is run for a given time using soap and soda solution or other detergents. The suds box below the squeeze rollers is used to dispose of the used scour liquor.

Washing/Scouring Operation

Washing/scouring processes are necessary for all stages of textile finishing as yarns and fabrics must be washed many times. The cleansing process utilizes chemicals, solvents, hydrogen peroxide, soaps, and synthetic detergents. Cleanser is selected with regard to type of fabric and cleaning process required.

During the washing process the fabric is saturated with washing liquor and manipulated to allow for thorough penetration of the solution, removing all unwanted substances, then dewatered in the squeezing unit.

Washing/scouring operation removes substances of:
- Dirt in raw fabrics
- Sizing and dressing agents
- Scouring and mercerizing liquids
- Unfixed dyes and print thickeners
- Residuals after printing
- Residual auxiliary agents after crease- and wrinkle-proofing finishes are added.

Used in pretreatment or aftertreatment of fabrics:
- After dyeing and printing
- In wash-and-wear finishes
- After resin applications
- To remove water soluble substances
- To remove emulsifiable substances and pigments of all types
- To stop or fix action of previous process
- Neutralizing of carbonized goods

Types of Dyes
  Acid Dyes
  Azoic/Napthol/Ice Dyes
  Cationic/Basic Dyes
  Chrome/Mordant/Metallic Dyes
  Direct/Substantive/Commercial Dyes
  Direct-Developed/Developed Dyes
  Dispersed Dyes
  Fluorescent Dyes
  Metal Complex/Metallized Dyes
  Pigment Colors
  Reactive/Fiber-Reactive Dyes
  Solution/Dope Dyes
  Sulfur Dyes
  Vat Dyes
Methods & Techniques of Dyeing
  Fiber Stage Dyeing Methods
    Solution/Dope/Spun Dyeing
    Stock/Raw Stock Dyeing
    Top Dyeing
    Tow Dyeing
  Yarn Stage Dyeing Methods
    Package/Cake Dyeing
    Skein/Hank Dyeing
    Random/Space Dyeing
  Yarn & Fabric/Piece-Goods Stage Dyeing Methods
    Beam Dyeing
  Fabric/Piece-Goods Stage Dyeing Methods
    Beck/Reel/Winch/Box Dyeing
    Jet/Pressure Jet Dyeing
    Jig Dyeing
    Molten Metal Dyeing
    Pad Dyeing
    Continuous Dyeing
    Thermosol Dyeing
  Special Fabric/Piece-Goods Stage Dyeing Methods
    Bale Dyeing
    Burl/Speck Dyeing
    Polychromatic/Multicolor Dyeing
  Product Stage Dyeing Methods
    Extract Dyeing
    Paddle Dyeing
  Hand-Dyeing Methods
    Dip Dyeing
    Tie/Resist Dyeing
  Terms Related to Fiber/Yarn/Fabric Dyeing
    Methods
    Batch Dyeing
    Cross Dyeing/Cross-Dyed Effect

Dip/Test Dip/Sampling
  High-Temperature Dyeing
  Solvent Dyeing
  Tone-on-Tone Dyeing
  Union Dyeing
  Vat Dyeing
Methods & Techniques of Printing
  Direct Printing Methods
    Direct Printing
    Blotch Printing
    Overprinting
    Photographic/Photo Printing
    Print-on-Print
    Transfer/Heat Transfer Printing
    Warp Printing
    Label Printing
  Discharge Printing Methods
    Discharge Printing
    White Discharge/Extract Printing
    Color Discharge Printing
  Resist Printing Methods
    Resist Printing
  Roller Printing Methods
    Roller Printing
    Gravure Printing
    Register/Duplex Printing
  Screen Printing Methods
    Screen Printing
    Manual/Automated Screen Printing
    Flat-Bed Screen Printing
    Rotary Screen Printing
  Special Effects Printing Methods
    Burnt-out Printing
    Flock Printing
    Polychromatic/Jet Printing
    Shadow Printing
    Stipple Printing
    Vigoureaux/Melange Printing
  Methods and Techniques of Hand-Printing
    Batik Printing
    Block Printing
    Iron-on/Press-on Printing
    Hand Painted Designs
    Hand Screen Printing
    Stencil Printing
  Terms Related to Printing Methods
    Pigment Printing
    Wet/Dry Printing

Decoration of fabric by adding color and design is an important visual factor in the development and manufacture of textile fabrics. Fabrics may be colored or printed by various types of dyes and dyestuffs used for dyeing and printing fabrics and by the methods of dyeing or printing.

Colored, printed or otherwise patterned and decorated fabric:

- Adds to its aesthetic qualities
- Appeals to an individual's visual sense
- Provides interest and variation
- Allows for coordinating different solids and patterns within a color story
- Allows for planned selection of particular fabrics
- May induce impulse buying on the consumer level
- May limit serviceability in wear and care

Other than the application of color and design by dyeing and printing methods, pattern design or motifs may be applied to a fabric by the:

- Construction and type of yarn (slubbed, irregular, textured)
- Pattern of fabric structure (twill weave, basket weave, damask or knitted loops)
- Dimension of the fabric (pile, loops, sculptured surfaces)
- Finishing processes (plissé, moiré, embossing, frosting, flocking, glazing, burnt-out methods, napping)
- Additional applications and processes (embroidery, drawn-out work, quilting, appliqué, beading, trapunto, tucking)

This unit will include information on:

- Types of dyes
- Methods and techniques of dyeing fabric
- Methods and techniques of printing fabric

Types of Dyes

Color is transferred to fabrics by *dyeing* fibers, yarns or fabrics or by *printing* or painting using dyestuffs themselves or combinations of other chemicals with dyes in the dyebath. Dye colors or dyestuff used for coloring or printing fabrics are derived from natural sources or may be synthesized from chemicals or chemical compounds. Dyes of natural sources are obtained from vegetation, animals, fish, insects, and minerals. Synthetic dyes composed of chemicals or chemical compounds are categorized into different classes. The classification is based on the particular type of chemical composition of the dye and method of dye application.

Different classes of dyes may be applicable to one or more types of fibers and one or more types of coloring or printing. Some dyes are more widely used and recognized than others.

The development of each type of man-made fiber and blends of man-made and/or natural fibers has necessitated the development and improvement of special dyestuff for the stock fiber, yarn and fabric of the particular fiber or fabric.

The selection of dyes and dyestuffs depend on:
- Suitability of dye to various uses of fabric
- Cost of the dyestuff and the method of application
- Purpose or end use of fabric
- Type of fiber or fibers
- Type of fabric structure
- Methods of dyeing or printing
- Penetration and absorption of dyes
- Deteriorating effect of dyestuff on fabric
- Deteriorating elements of finished fabric
- Anticipated method of maintaining fabric or garment
- Good fastness or required colorfastness

The term *colorfastness* refers to the assurance of the dye or dyestuff to maintain a lasting color for the anticipated life of the garment when exposed to various elements or conditions. Colorfastness of all dyestuff will vary to some degree. Dyes differ in colorfastness resistance and relate to:
- Perspiration and body oils
- Light, gas fumes, and fading
- Crocking or abrading
- Maintenance of fabric or garment
- Reaction of alkalies, acids or bleaches
- Reaction of cleaning agents—wet or dry
- Procedures for pressing—wet or dry

Colorfast rating of dyestuff is based on testing done by the National Bureau of Standards, U.S. Department of Commerce; the A.A.T.C.C. and the U.S.A. Standards Institute.

Dyestuff absorption and variation to colorfastness depends on:
- Size of molecular structure of dyestuff
- Size of pore openings in the outer surface of the fiber
- Differences in chemical structure and content of dyestuff
- Properties of the fiber
- Solubility; acceptance or resistance of dyes
- Affinity of fiber, yarn or fabric to the dyestuff
- Penetration or effectiveness of the dyestuff
- Methods and types of dyeing application
- Manufacturing conditions
- Control of the dyeing procedure

Acid Dyes

Dyes of organic acids that attract and attach the color to the fiber. Available in the form of salts. Acid dyes are water soluble and are applied from an acid medium.

- Produce a complete color range except for bright red and greenish-blue
- Application is made directly to the fabric
- Used on protein fibers such as wool or silk
- Used on acrylic, nylon and some modified polyester fibers
- Applied to spandex
- Varying degree of fastness: some colors have *good* fastness to light, drycleaning and crocking; some colors have *poor* fastness to laundering
- Bright colors tend to bleed

Application processes include:
- Beck and beam dyeing
- Package exhaust dyeing
- Continuous dyeing
- Printing on chlorinated wool
- Printing on silk and acetate fiber fabrics

Cationic/Basic Dyes

Dyes are derived from salts or from the formulations of triphenyl methane derivatives, thiazine, oxazine and azines which produce color as a result of a chemical reaction.

- Produce a complete range of bright colors
- Used on protein fibers such as wool and silk
- Effective for coloring acrylic and modacrylic fibers
- Used on modified nylon, cationic dyeable nylon and modified polyester fibers
- Used on wool as topping color to increase brilliance or brightness of fabric
- Used on cotton when it has been previously treated with a mordant
- Poor colorfastness to light, laundering and drycleaning when used on cellulosic or protein fibers
- Good colorfastness to light and laundering when used on acrylic fibers

Application processes include:
- Top dyeing
- Direct printing on acetate
- Discharge printing on cotton

Azoic/Napthol/Ice Dyes

Dyes derived from the formulation of arylamides and orthophydroxycarloxylic acid and acylacetic arylamides which produce color as a result of a chemical action in the fiber. The final color is formed on the fiber by combination of two chemicals. The process is carried on at low temperatures, sometimes in the presence of ice.

- Produce brilliant colors of red or yellow or deep black
- Used on cellulosic fibers of cottons, linen and viscose rayon
- With special application methods may be used on acetate, acrylic, nylon, polyester and polypropylene fibers
- Preferred for printing—colors are interchangeable and work with other groups
- Good colorfastness to laundering, dry cleaning, alkalies and sunlight.
- Fastness to light varies from poor to excellent depending on fiber.
- May bleed in peroxide bleach
- Dark shades tend to crock and rub off onto other fabrics or body
- Relatively low cost to produce

Chrome/Mordant/Metallic Dyes

A metal or metallic salt of cobalt, aluminum, nickel or copper added to the dye molecules for fixing dyes and dyestuff. Chrome dyes are water soluble and are applied from an acid medium.

- Produce a fairly complete color range
- Colors are fast and duller than acid dyes
- React to form insoluble dyestuff
- May be used in fiber, yarn or fabric dye application
- Effective on protein fibers such as wool and silk
- Used on woolens and worsteds requiring maximum fastness
- Used on acrylic, nylon, some modified polyester and spandex fibers
- Used for printing on wool worsteds and silks
- Requires time-consuming dyeing process and additives in the dyebath or after dyeing
- Good colorfastness to light, laundering and dry cleaning
- Excellent fastness to perspiration
- Used almost exclusively for men's wear
- Specifications require the dyestuffs for many types of government materials such as blankets and overcoatings

Application processes include:
- Raw stock dyeing of wool
- Piece goods dyeing

Direct/Substantive/Commercial Dyes

Dyes derived from the formulation of benzidine and its substitute derivative and amines from polyazo dyes. Direct dyes are so named because the dyestuff colors material *directly* without pre-treatment or preparation in a neutral or alkaline bath. Direct dyes are water soluble.

- Produce a wide range of colors and shades
- Colors are duller than basic or acid dyes
- Applied primarily to cellulosic fibers of cotton
- Most widely used of all dyestuff for viscose rayon fibers
- Used to a limited extent on protein fibers such as wool and polyamides
- Simple to apply and require no special equipment of fixative
- Applies colors to fabric *directly* with one application or impregnation and without preliminary treatment
- Requires no fixative agents or mordant to adhere or fix colors
- Used as background color for discharge printing
- Not as colorfast to light, perspiration, crocking and laundering as other dyes
- To improve colorfastness, an aftertreatment of resins may be applied (label must state additional process)
- Tend to bleed readily
- Least expensive to produce and easy to apply

Application processes include all methods of yarn and piece goods dyeing.

Direct-Developed/Developed Dyes

Direct-developed dyes belong to the group of direct dyes requiring a base to be dyed on the goods during the diazotizing process. Copper salts, copper-resin compounds chemically interact to produce the completed dye. Chemical coupling is needed to complete color transaction.

- Produces a complete range of colors and shades
- Colors are duller than basic or acid dyes
- Applied primarily to cellulosic fibers
- May be used on wool, silk and nylon
- Colorfast to light, laundering, dry cleaning and perspiration

Dispersed Dyes

Dyes derived from the formulation of azo, nitrodiphenylamide and anthroquinones which produce color by attaching themselves to the fiber surface and then dissolving into the fiber. Dispersed dyes are insoluble compounds and are kept dispersed in the dye bath by suitable dispensing agents.

- Produce a good color range except dark blue and black
- May be more absorbent or more effective on one type of fiber than another
- Effective on acrylic, polyester, nylon and polyamide fibers
- Not as effective on acetate as it is subject to gas fading
- Easily dispersed throughout the fiber solution
- Used for dyeing and printing
- Used for transfer printing techniques due to sublimation characteristics
- Fair colorfastness to light, laundering and drycleaning
- Good colorfastness to perspiration and crocking

Application processes include:
- Yarn dyeing
- Piece goods dyeing
- Batch dyeing
- Continuous dyeing
- Roller printing
- Screen printing

Fluorescent Dyes

An organic dyestuff that produces bright and illuminating colors to fabric both under daylight and black light conditions. Illuminating color is not obtainable with conventional dyes.

Metal Complex/Metallized Dyes

Dyes resembling chrome dyes except that the complex-forming metal—chromium—is anchored in the dye molecules prior to dyeing. Metal complex dyes are classified as Group I and Group II with regard to method of use.

- Do not require after-chroming
- Group I must be applied from a strong acid medium
- Group II must be applied from a neutral to weak acid medium
- Do not attain high colorfastness of chrome dyes

Pigment Colors

A source of color made from both organic and inorganic compounds derived from formulations of cobaltous aluminate, azo compounds, phthalocyanines, dioxazines, and triarylmethan.

Pigment colors are true dyes which penetrate the cloth. Color is mechanically bound to fiber by resins. Pigments are primarily used for printing surface color.

- Mixed with binders and thickened to form a paste
- Completely insoluble in water or in solvents
- No affinity for any fiber
- Require fixative or adhesive, resin or bonding agents to adhere color to fabric surface
- Produce a complete range of bright and metallic colors
- Color produced is permanent
- Used on rayon, acetate, nylon and polyester
- Primarily used for printing cotton of all weights
- Good colorfastness to light, laundering and dry cleaning
- Dark colors may crock or wear off when resin or bonding agents wear away
- Used on all natural and man-made fiber fabrics
- Lighter shades have good colorfastness to light, laundering and dry cleaning

Reactive/Fiber-Reactive Dyes

Dyes derived from the formulation of anthraquinoid and phthalocyanine which combine and react chemically with the molecules of the fibers. Reactive dyes are water insoluble.

- Produce bright colors in brilliant shades
- Absorb rapidly
- Used primarily on cellulosic fibers of cotton and linen
- May be used on wool, silk, acrylic, nylon and blended-fiber fabrics
- Relatively expensive to use, due to dye assistants required
- Colorfast to laundering, cleaning, light, crocking, fume-fading and perspiration
- Susceptible to chlorine bleach damage

Application processes include:
- Stock Dyeing
- Piece Goods Dyeing
- Printing methods

Solution/Dope Dyes

Pigment colors are added to and are mixed thoroughly with the fiber solution or molten polymer. Dyes become an integral part of the fiber.

- Produce a fiber which is already colored when extruded
- Effective on rayon fibers
- Used on acetate, olefin and other man-made fibers that accept color during solution stage
- Colorfast to laundering, drycleaning, light, crocking and perspiration

Sulfur Dyes

Dyes derived from the formulation of compounds containing either sulfur or a mixture of the color component of sulfur. There are two groups of sulfur dyes:
1. water insoluble—applied primarily by exhaust dyeing methods;
2. water soluble—applied primarily by continuous dyeing methods.

- Produce a complete range of colors in dull shades except for true red
- Used mainly to produce shades of brown, khaki, blue and black
- Used primarily on cellulosic fibers of cotton, linen and rayon
- Penetrate more thoroughly than other dyes due to high temperature and alkalinity of dyebath
- Good colorfastness to laundering, drycleaning, light and perspiration
- Loses color when subjected to chlorine bleach
- Weakens fabric when garment or cloth is stored for any length of time.

Application processes include:
- Stock dyeing
- Yarn dyeing
- Piece goods dyeing
- Printing methods

Vat Dyes

Dyes derived from the formulation of indigo and anthraquinoid which are attracted to the fiber. Vat dyes are insoluble in water and require an alkaline reduction apply.

- Produce a good color range but limited selection of orange, bright green and blue
- Adaptable to all cellulosic fibers of cotton, linen and rayon
- Primarily used for cotton
- Used for some man-made fibers such as acrylic, modacrylic and nylon
- Not applicable for protein fibers because of alkaline bath during process
- Provides best colorfastness of all dyestuff to laundering, light and perspiration
- Do not run or bleed when laundered
- Resistant to oxidizing bleaches and chlorine
- Expensive, due to initial cost of dye and methods of application

Application processes include:
- Package dyeing
- Beam dyeing
- Continuous dyeing
- Printing methods

Methods & Techniques of Dyeing

Color application by dyeing involves the impregnation of color into fiber, yarn, fabric or product by machine or hand methods. Dyeing is the process of applying color in any one of a variety of methods and techniques using any one or more of the different dyes and dyestuff. Types of dyes selected and methods of application used differ with regard to type of fiber, yarn and fabric structure. Saturation level for each dye differs due to the fiber's affinity for the dyestuff. Some methods of applying color are more widely used and recognized than others. Dyeing may be done in the fiber stage, yarn stage, fabric or piece-goods stage, or product stage.

Fiber Stage Dyeing Method   The application of dyestuff in the chemical solution during the production of man-made fibers. The filament fibers emerge fully colored when they are extruded through the spinnerette.

Yarn Stage Dyeing Method   The total or partial immersion of yarns in the dyebath after the fibers have been spun into yarns. Dyestuff is applied to the formed yarns prior to weaving or knitting the cloth. Yarn dyeing permits use of various colored yarns in the structure of the fabric producing a stripe, check, plaid, tweed, iridescent and multicolored design fabric.

Fabric/Piece-Goods Stage Dyeing Method   The application of color to the fabric after the fabric has been structured. A bolt or piece of finished fabric is subjected to the dyestuff in the dyebath. Yardage is continuously submerged and dyed to achieve desired color, shade or effect. Fabric piece dyeing allows for mechanical or hand operations of applying color and includes conventional and special processes.

- Allows for immediate color changes dictated by fashion or styles
- Color or shade can be applied to fabric on short notice
- Allows for matching color to other stock fabric
- Usually utilized for a single color or limited amount of goods
- Method may be used for blended fibers requiring union-dyeing or cross-dyeing procedures
- More economical method to produce color than yarn-dyed method
- Method or machine selected for dye operation depends on type of fabric, dye and effect desired.

Product Stage Dyeing Method   The application of dyestuff to the finished product.

Hand Dyeing Method   A hand operation for limited quantity dyeing that may be applied to yarn, fabric or completed garment.

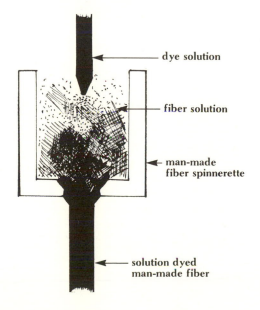

- dye solution
- fiber solution
- man-made fiber spinnerette
- solution dyed man-made fiber

Solution/Dope/Spun Dyeing

A fiber-stage dyeing method in which dye or dyestuff is put into the man-made chemical liquid solution. The dyestuff mixes and bonds with the chemical solution and when extruded, the filament fibers emerge colored.

- Dyestuff penetrates fibers thoroughly
- Filament is impregnated with pigment or color
- Colors of the fiber are the same throughout
- Provides colorfast coloring of fiber

Process may also be referred to as *muff dyeing*.

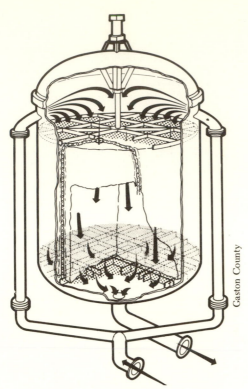

(rotated) Gaston County

cross section of raw stock dyeing machine

Stock/Raw Stock Dyeing

A fiber-stage dyeing method in which the fibers are dyed in the raw state. The dyestuff is applied to loose fibers after degreasing and drying operations, but before blending, combing, carding or spinning.

- Usually applied to woolen and worsted stock
- Dyestuff penetrates fibers thoroughly
- Produces best colorfastness and luster for fiber type
- Allows for mixing of two or more colors of stock when producing yarn
- Permits for wide variation of cast, shade, tone or hue of color
- Allows for fixing colors in yarn or fabric
- Used to produce heather, tweed, checks, plaids, stripes as well as solid-colored fabrics

tops carriers used to dye all fibers in top form

Top Dyeing

A fiber dyeing method in which the dyestuff is applied to carded and combed wool fibers while in the form of a loose rope or a semi-twisted state, also referred to as a sliver. The dyeing process of the sliver is completed prior to spinning fibers into worsted yarn to make worsted fabric. The partially spun yarns are wound into a ball or into a loose ball effect in preparation for top dyeing.

- Dyestuff penetrates fibers evenly and thoroughly
- Allows for permanency of color
- A process for dyeing the slub of sliver of worsted fibers in the top state
- Sliver may be printed with dyestuff at desired intervals for variation
- Allows for different color mixture in yarn construction

Top dyeing is often referred to as *vigoureux printing*—the application of color by dyeing or printing to worsted top or sliver.

tow

Tow Dyeing

The process of dyeing tow fibers or yarns prior to processing before the fibers are stretched and broken for spinning. Tow dyeing is one process used for coloring high-bulk yarns. Dyeing of tow can be done in raw stock, top yarn and beam dyeing equipment.

closed cloth beam dyeing machines

Gaston County

warp beams

Beam Dyeing

A method of dyeing yarns or full-widths of woven or knitted fabrics. Yarn or fabric is wound onto perforated, cylindrical beams and enclosed in a container. Dyestuff is circulated under pressure through the perforations. Yarn or fabric is saturated repeatedly to allow for even penetration of dyestuff.

As *yarn-stage* dyeing method:

- Warp yarns are dyed a solid color prior to weaving
- Utilized when fabrics are to be woven with dyed warp yarns
- Dyestuff penetrates yarns adequately and thoroughly
- Provides for good color absorption
- Better colorfastness than piece-dyed methods
- Produces deep, rich colors
- Allows for different colored yarns to be used to produce stripes, checks and plaids
- Used to produce iridescent fabrics

As *fabric-stage* dyeing method:

- Used on lightweight and open-construction fabrics
- Often used for tricot and other knit fabrics
- Does not subject fabric to stress or tension
- Rapid and economic dyeing method

Dyed yarn being removed from an automatic dye machine after package dyeing process. Yarns are used in both knitted and woven fabrics.

American Textile Manufacturers Institute

Package/Cake Dyeing

A yarn-stage dyeing method in which yarns are spun or wound onto carriers referred to as cones, cakes, cheeses, tubes or muffs and mounted on a perforated rod or frame. The loaded packages are lowered into a package-dyeing machine where the dye solution is forced under pressure through the packages from the center to the inside and then from the outside to the center. The movement is continued until the desired color is achieved.

- Utilizes different packages for different yarn types
- Carriers are selected for fiber content of yarn or yarn treatment
- Dyestuff penetrates yarns thoroughly
- Provides for thorough color absorption
- Produces variations in color and design
- More than one color yarn, can be used in fabric structure
- Large lot dyeing operation due to large capacity of machine
- Large uniform dye lots or batch coloring
- Better colorfastness than piece-dyed methods

yarn in hanks

Skein/Hank Dyeing

A yarn-stage dyeing method in which the loose arrangement of yarns in skein or hank form are hung over a ring and immersed into a large container, which holds the dyestuff. The yarns in skein form are dyed prior to weaving or knitting the fabric.

- Used on wool and some man-made fiber yarns
- Deep color penetration
- Produces uniform color
- Reduces glazing of color on yarns
- Does not distort yarns during dyeing process
- Yarns are not subject to stress or tension
- Minimum quantity of yarns may be processed
- More expensive than package-dyeing

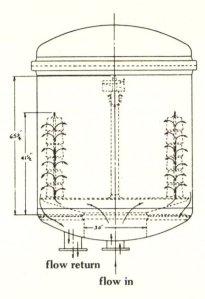

cross section of random dyeing machine

Random/Space Dyeing

A yarn-stage dyeing method in which dyestuff is applied to predetermined portions of yarn. One strand of the yarn receives more color or more than one color of dyestuff at regularly or randomly spaced intervals. Random-dyeing effects may be achieved by:

1. cones or packages or yarns processed by compression effect;
2. treating portions of yarn with resist substance prior to dye bath;
3. dyeing surfae of the goods. When knit is unraveled, dye color is randomly spaced.

- Applied to wool and wool-blended fiber yarns
- Variation in hue produces tweed or heather fabrics
- Produces an abstract design effect when yarn is woven or knitted into fabric

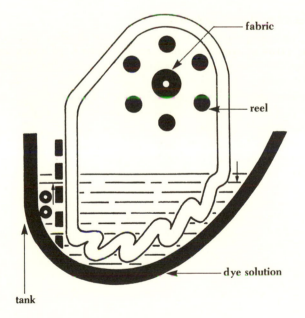

Beck/Reel/Winch/Box Dyeing

A fabric-stage dyeing method in which fabric with ends stitched together to make a continuous rope form is passed through the dye bath and submerged repeatedly. The fabric is held in a slack or loose condition and is lifted in and out of the dyebath by a reel.

- Dyestuff is introduced uniformly across the tube of the box
- Color penetration and desired shade is obtained by continued submersion
- Used on delicate and lightweight fabrics that cannot withstand tension of other methods
- Used on fabrics of crepe-weave structure as it will not flatten crepe effect
- Used on loosely woven and heavyweight woolens

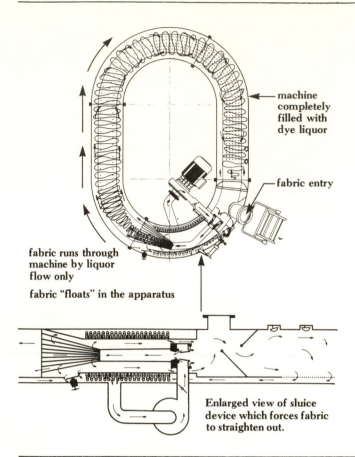

machine completely filled with dye liquor

fabric entry

fabric runs through machine by liquor flow only

fabric "floats" in the apparatus

Enlarged view of sluice device which forces fabric to straighten out.

Jet/Pressure Jet Dyeing

A fabric-stage dyeing method in which fabric, tied in rope form, is place in a high-temperature tube-like container. Dyestuff is forced through pressure jets. The dye is continuously re-circulated as the cloth moves or floats in a tension-free condition along the tube container at rapid speed.

- Movement of fabric in the dyebath is controlled by the propulsive action of the dye liquid as it is forced through the jets
- Tube container that holds fabric may be positioned vertically or horizontally
- Jets that emit dyestuff may be cylindrical or tubular
- Fabric flows through the machine without forming hard crease
- Fabric entanglement is reduced to a minimum
- High-pressure jet dyeing machine designed to handle most fabrics
- Low-pressure jet dyeing machine designed to handle sensitive and woven or knitted fabrics with surface effects

FABRIC MOVEMENT IN JIG DYEING

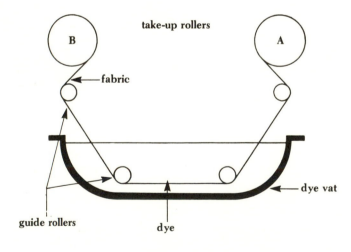

take-up rollers

B   A

fabric

guide rollers

dye

dye vat

Jig Dyeing

A fabric-stage dyeing method in which an open width of fabric, held on rollers, is submerged repeatedly into dyestuff. The rollers move and guide the cloth back and forth through a jig dyeing machine that consists of a large tub holding the dyestuff. The back and forth process in the open vat is repeated until the desired color or shade is obtained.

- Places fabric under stress and tension
- Flattens fabric
- Changes hand of fabric making it less pliable and soft
- Used on medium-weight woven fabrics
- Modifications of the jig have been developed for various weight cotton, rayons or special fabrics
- May produce shade variations in fabric due to uneven tension
- Used for dark-colored direct dye application
- Large quantities of cloth may be dyed at one time
- Not economical for dyeing short lengths of cloth

Molten Metal Dyeing

A fabric-stage dyeing method in which vat dyes inter-react with the molten metal alloys. During the process the fabric and the vat dyes are passed into a tank containing molten metal alloys maintained at 200°F–250°F (99.3°C–122.1°C). The dyes are reduced under pressure, metal is rinsed out, and the fabric is oxidized, scoured and rinsed.

- Used to obtain even-level dying of dense fabrics
- Allows for the same shade throughout on highly textured fabrics
- Used on slub-yarn constructed fabrics and embroidered fabrics

American Artos

Pad Dyeing

A fabric-piece dyeing method in which an open width of fabric is submerged in the trough containing the dye solution and passed through rollers, which repeatedly force the dyestuff into the cloth and squeeze out the appropriate excess dyestuff. Utilizing different types of padders and padding units for the type of fabric, the rollers hold the fabric under tension and subject it to pressure.

- Provides uniform concentration and penetration of dyestuff
- Box holds limited amount of dyestuff
- Flattens fabric
- Reduces soft hand of fabric
- Used on medium-weight woven fabrics

Continuous Pad Dyeing   Used for dyeing large yardages of piece goods. Equipment for continuous method includes: pad mangle, hot flues, steamers and open-width washers.

Semi-Continuous Pad Dyeing   Fabric may be padded with dye solution on a mangle, developed and completed on a jig referred to as *pad/jig method*.

roll dye padder—part of continuous dyeing operation

Morrison Machine Co.

Continuous Dyeing

A fabric-stage dyeing method in which the fabric is processed in a continuous sequential manner and, when completed, the fabric emerges completely dyed. The process utilizes continuous process machines referred to as ranges which consist of compartments for wetting out, dyeing, padding, aftertreatment, washing, rinsing and drying.

- Places fabric under tension throughout
- Flattens fabric
- Changes hand of fabric
- Used on medium-light to medium-heavyweight fabrics and large lots of goods
- Not suitable for production of deep shades

CROSS SECTION OF POLYESTER FIBER IN DYE MOVEMENT

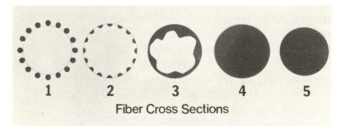

Fiber Cross Sections

1. Dye is dispersed into dyebath—dye particles adhere to fiber surface.
2. Liquid in dyebath and thermosetting temperature soften the fiber, enlarge it slightly—dye starts to penetrate.
3. As dye particles penetrate they begin to dissolve into fiber molecules.
4. Entire fiber is colored.
5. Fiber molecules are cooled—as the fibers cool they become firm, return to their original size and trap the dye.

Thermosol Dyeing

A continuous-dyeing method applied to fabric containing polyester fiber. The fabrics are dyed following the continuous dyeing methods in ranges and then are heat-set for 30 seconds to 1 minute at 350°F (178.1°C).

- Produces colors for polyester-fiber fabrics that are colorfast to machine washing

Bale Dyeing

A fabric-stage dyeing method in which cotton fabric, constructed with sized warp yarns and natural wax-filled yarns, is subjected to a cold water dyebath. The dyestuff adheres to the sized yarns and resists the waxed yarns.

- Inexpensive method of coloring cotton fiber fabrics
- Produces two color effects in the finished cloth
- Simulates fabrics that use yarn-dyed yarns for two color effects
- Produces simulated chambray and iridescent fabrics

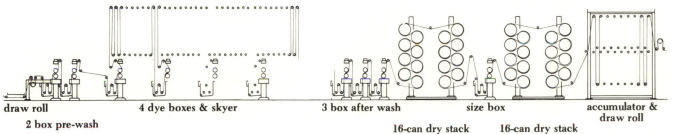

draw roll   4 dye boxes & skyer   3 box after wash   size box   accumulator & draw roll

2 box pre-wash   16-can dry stack   16-can dry stack

Burl/Speck Dyeing*

A fabric-stage dyeing method utilizing special colored inks applied by hand. This hand operation covers small areas or specks and blemishes which did not receive full-cover penetration during the fabric/piece-goods dyeing procedures.

- Used mostly on woolen and worsted fabrics
- Process is done while fabric is rolled on fabric-examining machine
- Tedious hand operation, slow and expensive

*Refer to page 133 for illustration.

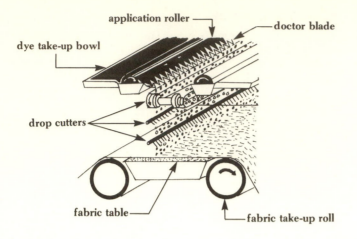

application roller ——— ——— doctor blade
dye take-up bowl

drop cutters

fabric table ———

——— fabric take-up roll

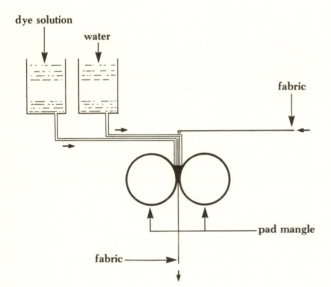

dye solution

water

fabric

pad mangle

fabric ———

Polychromatic/Multicolor Dyeing

A fabric-stage dyeing method in which dyestuff is applied to an open width of fabric through the use of jets in a *dye-weave method* or in a *flow-form method*. Polychromatic dyeing allows different color dye solutions to intermingle across the width of the fabric. Dyes and dyestuffs appropriate to the fiber content of the fabric are used.

Dye-Weave Method Dye is forced through jets onto a metal plate at a 45° angle to the fabric. The dye runs down the plate and onto the fabric.

Flow-Form Method Dye is forced through jets and fed onto a roller, which then rolls the color onto the fabric.

- Produces predetermined multicolors and patterns visible on the face and back of the fabric
- Produces spots of different colors in a solid shade base
- Provides for wide variety of differential coloring and flushing effects
- Produces designs with marbleized effect, random splashes, and multicolored stripes
- Produces multicolored dyeing combinations of distinct and blurred design effects
- Produces batik and tie-dyed abstract, ombre and degrade effects
- Effects resemble printing, but method does not utilize printing machines, screens, etched rollers or other printing equipment

Polychromatic dyeing allows for different effects by varying and combining the:

- Number and size of jets
- Arrangement and placement of jets
- Amount of dye applied and color extruded
- Movement of fabric and color jets
- Rate of speed fabric moves

Polychromatic dyeing is also referred to as *polychromatic printing*.

extracting dyeing machine

Pellerin Milnor Corp.

Extract Dyeing

A product-dyeing method utilizing a compact product dyeing machine which automatically performs scouring and cycled dyeing, followed by automatically extracting the dye lot and directing the dyed lot through the drying cycle. Dyeing extract machine provides precise shade repetition from lot to lot.

Dyeing extract machine is used for lot dyeing hosiery and socks, pantyhose, body shirts and T-shirts, sweaters and scarfs.

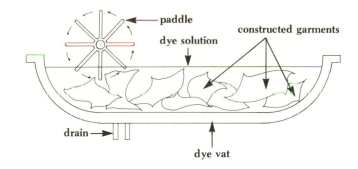

paddle

dye solution

constructed garments

drain

dye vat

Paddle Dyeing

A product-, garment- or component-dyeing method in which dyestuff is applied to the item utilizing a paddle machine with wide, short blades affixed to a circular drive. A limited number of select-type garments are packed loosely into a large tub containing the dyestuff. The dyestuff and items are agitated continuously and circulated by the motor-driven paddle allowing for even penetration.

There are two types of paddle-dyeing machines.

1. *Overhead Paddle*   The paddles or blades extend the width of the machine.
2. *Side Paddle*   The paddles operate from an island position in the oval-shaped machine.

- Offers a wide range of colors
- Reduces need for large stock or inventory
- Fashion color risks are minimized
- Allows garment or item to be dyed with regard to purchase order
- Used for dyeing completely assembled sweaters, scarfs, hosiery and socks
- Tends to misshape the garment during process
- Cannot be used on intricately constructed garments due to problems with shrinkage and distortion

Mix dye powder as directed.

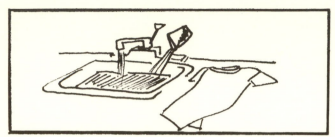
Fill sink, pot or basin with dye solution.

Immerse garment until all areas are saturated.

Dip Dyeing

The hand-dyeing process of applying color to yarn, fabric or garment by manually submerging item into a tub or basin containing prepared dye solution. Follow instructions on dye package for:

- Results in subtle shading of color from light to dark ombré colors
- Specific color shade or strength and effect desired
- Cold or hot dyebath requirements
- Submersion for long or short periods of time
- Agitation by stirring or dipping in an up-and-down motion
- Special preparations for sizing, finishing and removing color
- Restrictions and limitations of dye affinity for some fiber types

TO ACHIEVE OMBRÉ EFFECTS

Immerse entire garment into dye solution of lightest shade desired. Remove garment.

Immerse two-thirds of garment into dye solution of next shade. Remove garment.

Immerse remaining part of garment into dye solution of darkest shade.

TIE DYEING TECHNIQUES

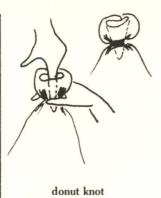

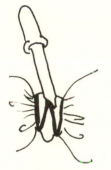

rosette knot (basic)

donut knot

squeeze additional color
into banding with eyedropper

folding and pleating
fabrics before tieing

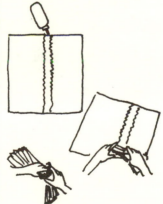

block dyeing—
sandwiching fabric

stripe effect

Tie/Resist Dyeing

A multi-step hand-dyeing method that utilizes string, waxed cord, elastic bands to tie off desired areas of fabric or yarn in order to resist dyestuff when fabric, section of fabric, or yarn is subjected to dyebath. After dyeing, the fabric is rinsed and then untied. The protected or tied area resists the dyestuff and produces a diffused burst of color and design effects. The tieing, dyeing, untieing, and drying cycle can be repeated as often as necessary to complete effect desired.

- Applied to yarns, fabrics or completed garments
- May be planned to produce color bursts, irregular dots or stripes
- Effect may be utilized in reverse and color may be removed from previously colored fabric with a dye remover
- Effect obtained may vary due to the fiber's affinity for dyestuff, the finishes on the fabric, or the fabric structure
- Process may be machine simulated by polychromatic dyeing methods

Batch Dyeing

A term applied to a group of materials which are to be processed as a unit. One batch of fabric is dyed at a time.

- Applied to yarn, fabric or product-dyeing processes
- Processed in same dyebath
- Assures uniformity of tone and shade of a particular color
- Batch is given to batch-dyeing number which indicates it was processed at the same time in the same dyebath

Cross Dyeing/Cross-Dyed Effect

Fabrics containing yarns of various and different types of fibers are subjected to one dyebath. Each fiber in the cloth absorbs or adsorbs the dyestuff at a different rate allowing the color to adhere in varying quantity and quality.

- Applied to fabric-dyeing method
- End product depends on arrangements of fibers in the fabric
- Dyebath solution may be planned so that some fibers do not accept color
- Effects may simulate chambray, stripes or checks
- Allows for variation in shade and color of fabric
- Produces frosted, iridescent and mottled effects
- May combine stock-dyed fibers, yarn-dyed and subsequent piece-dyeing methods.

Dip/Test Dip/Sampling

A term applied to the sample dyeing of the yarn or grey goods to test or match a color for color selection.

High-Temperature Dyeing

The technique of dyeing yarn on a dye tube at temperatures above boiling point and at high pressure. Because of the low swelling capacity of some man-made fibers, they can be dyed only at temperatures above 100°C. High-temperature dyeing is done in suitable pressure vessels.

Solvent Dyeing

The use of liquids such as ammonia, and perchlorethylene as dye solvents on man-made fiber fabrics.

Tone-on-Tone Dyeing

A dyeing method in which fabrics containing yarns of the same generic fiber but of different types or variants are subjected to one dyebath. Due to the planned differential or affinity to dyestuff, each type of the same generic fiber will absorb the dye color at a different rate.

- Used on acrylic, nylon and polyester fiber fabrics
- Produces: monochromatic-shaded effects, ombré effects, iridescent effects, tweed-dyed effects and stripes

Union Dyeing

A dyeing method in which fabric containing different fibers, of two or more origins and composition, is submerged into one dyebath which contains selected dyes appropriate to each type of fiber. The fabric absorbs the dyestuff with the same shade and color throughout.

- Applies dyestuff to the different fibers simultaneously or individually
- Allows fabric of mixed fibers to emerge in a single, uniform color
- Selection and application of dyestuff must be properly applied to insure uniform shading

Vat Dyeing

A method whereby insoluble vat colors are applied to fabric and color is processed by oxidation.

- Utilizes vat dyes and fabric-dyeing method
- Fabrics are colorfast to laundering and cleaning
- Fabrics offer more resistance to sunlight color fading than any other dyeing methods

Methods & Techniques of Printing

Printing is the process of transferring color, design, pattern, motif or decoration of one or more colors in any one of a variety of methods or techniques to fabric. Printing involves the surface application of color in a predetermined pattern, design or motif by manual or mechanical directed discharge, direct or resist methods. The various hand or machine processes, each with specific properties, are capable of transferring designs by one or more of the printing methods. Printing may be applied to yarns prior to structuring the fabric, after the fabric is constructed or after the garment is completed. Some methods of printing are more widely used and recognized than others.

A yarn or fabric is printed after it has gone through singeing, bleaching, cleaning, and other finishing processes. Some fabrics due to the fiber content, structure, finishing agents or dyestuff may show areas where color or design is not evenly or equally distributed.

Printing methods include *direct, discharge,* or *resist.* Any of these three methods may employ roller printing or screen printing techniques.

The method of printing selected depends on:
- Fiber or fibers in the yarn or cloth
- Fabric structure
- Finishing process
- Dyes, dyestuff and colors used
- Colorfastness properties of the dye
- End use of goods
- Mechanical or hand operation
- Cost of process or method

Special Effects Printing Methods

Special-effects printing employs a variety of manual and automated techniques and different printing methods to impart design and/or color to slivers, fibers, yarns, or fabrics creating unusual effects.

Methods & Techniques of Hand Printing

Printing or transferring designs by hand is a process of preparing or transferring designs to implements which will be manually manipulated during the operation of transferring color and design to cloth.

Although the process is slow and the production is expensive, hand-printed or hand-designed fabrics allow for the individual expression on unique and customized designs in limited edition or yardage.

Many of the hand-printing techniques were the inspiration or background for the mechanically and electrically controlled printing methods used today.

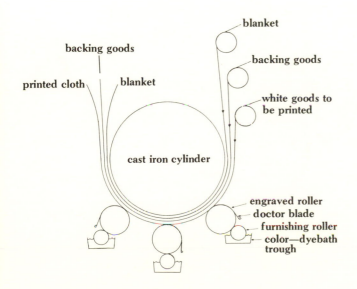

backing goods
printed cloth
blanket
blanket
backing goods
white goods to be printed
cast iron cylinder
engraved roller
doctor blade
furnishing roller
color—dyebath trough

Direct Printing

Direct printing employs a variety of individual or mechanical techniques to print or apply color to white, solid-dyed or preprinted fabrics in a direct manner. The direct manner of printing may be referred to as application printing or commercial printing. A direct print may be produced by roller printing techniques or by screen printing techniques.

- Uses up to 65-line definition for fineness of detail
- Produces fine-line designs
- Method cannot produce large blotches and halftone designs

Blotch Printing

Blotch printing is the method of printing the base or ground color on the fabric instead of applying color by dyeing methods. The color adheres to the surface or face of the fabric—the reverse or back of the fabric remains uncolored. Direct-printing techniques utilize block, screen or roller methods.

- May be applied by roller- or screen-printing methods
- May be hand or mechanically produced
- Used on cotton and linen
- Printed ground color may be overprinted with design in one printing operation
- Large areas of background color do not always print evenly

Photographic/Photo Printing

A method of printing in which fabric is coated with chemicals which are sensitive to light. The photographic prints are transferred onto fabric utilizing photoengraving photography techniques of color printing on paper. A direct-printing technique that does not utilize a roller or screen.

- Allows for black and white and full-color designs
- Produces permanent designs

Overprinting

A direct printing method in which a pre-dyed fabric is printed with a colored print paste different than the color of the ground shade. The addition of the color to the ground color and that of the print yields a final shade for the design. Example: ground color is yellow, overprint color is blue—design shade is green.

- Darkens or adds tonal qualities
- Alters dark or light shades of ground color
- Tones down undesirable vivid colors
- Utilizes a previously dyed fabric for a new end use
- Creates a variety of color and design shades by using individual rollers for each color application
- Salvages a poorly printed or unevenly dyed fabric

Overprint may also be referred to as *topping/printing topping*. Topping is a term that refers to a second printing of a fabric; the topping colors applied after the initial color dye is dyed and fixed.

Print-on-Print

A direct printing method that applies additional and/or different colors, patterns and motifs over preprinted goods.

- Alters or produces prints of splash designs that overlap
- Creates allover designs or large floral designs delineating the outline
- Creates a variety of effects utilizing individual rollers for each color
- Prints or outlines a design on a splash of color

lifting exhausted transfer paper from printed fabric

Sublistatic Corp.

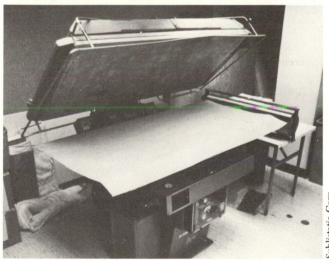

calender press

Sublistatic Corp.

plate press

Sublistatic Corp.

Transfer/Heat Transfer Printing

Transfer printing is the application of a design to fabric by using a paper substrate preprinted with a design made with disperse dyes, which are capable of sublimating and vaporizing. The disperse dyes are converted from a solid into a gaseous state when subjected to roller pressure and processed at high temperatures. During the heat and pressure process, the dyes diffuse or sublimate, and the design is transferred from the paper to the fabric. Transfer printing method may employ dry heat or wetting-out process or special calenders or flat-bed presses.

- Allows for production of a wide variety of designs
- Used on fibers, yarns or fabrics that will accept disperse dyes
- Used on fabrics containing 50 percent or more man-made fibers
- May not be used on 100 percent cellulosic or protein-fiber fabrics
- Used on yardage, garment components or assembled garments
- Used on both woven and knitted goods
- Prints fabrics faster and less expensively than screen printing
- Requires no further processing after printing as in roller- or screen-printing methods
- Allows for rapid changeover of design by changing paper
- Produces clear designs that retain bright coloring
- Colorfastness of print varies with regard to fiber content of fabric, type of dye used, shade or color selected and wear of garment

Sublistatic printing® is a trademark for a heat-transfer printing process.

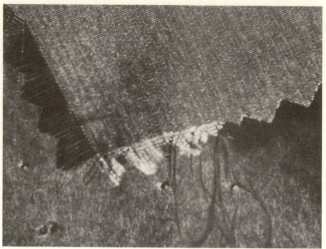
warp-printed taffeta

Warp Printing

A multi-operation of printing color and/or design only to the warp yarns prior to the weaving operation of the fabric. Printed warp yarns are interlaced with white, plain or light-colored filling yarns.

- Incorporates direct method of printing
- May be applied by roller or screen printing
- Produces a fabric with a melange, mottled, blurred or indistinct design or color effect

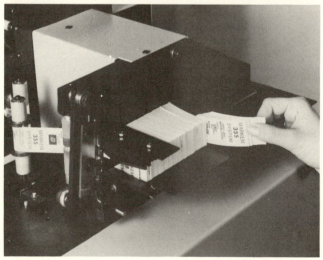

Label Printing

A direct-printing method utilizing narrow label-sized fabric and small rollers incorporated into a compact automated printing machine. Label printing unit prints and cuts labels to specific sizes.

Discharge Printing

Discharge printing is a method of extracting color from a pre-dyed fabric by printing it with a chemical which will destroy, bleach or discharge the color during subsequent steaming leaving the design area different than the dyed cloth. Discharge prints may be produced by roller- or screen-printing methods.

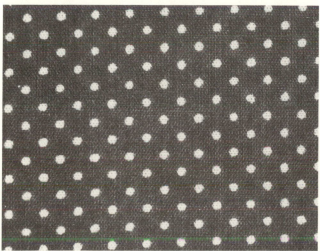

blue ground - white dot

White Discharge/Extract Printing

The process of discharge printing with chlorine or other color-removing chemicals, which are applicable to removing previously used dyestuff. Color on selected areas is bleached out or discharged producing a fabric with a white pattern design or print on a colored ground.

- Produces white dots or other silhouettes on dark ground color
- Used on previously dyed fabric to produce desired print
- Type of design less expensive to produce than direct-, roller- or screen-printing methods
- Same depth of color appears on both sides of the cloth

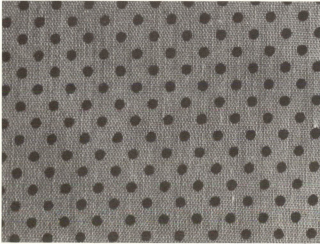

green ground - blue dot

Color Discharge Printing

The process of discharge printing with bleaching agents or other color-removing chemicals and the addition of a selected dye not affected by the discharge process. Example: ground or background shade is blue, discharge shade/design shade is green.

- Utilizes vat dyes which are not destroyed by color-removing chemicals
- Colors on selected area are bleached out and dyed/printed simultaneously
- Produces a fabric with colored pattern design different than colored ground
- Produces dots or other silhouette designs

second color may be applied in subsequent operation

resist did not allow printing color to penetrate

printed color did not penetrate back of cloth

Resist Printing

Resist printing utilizes engraved rollers and a resist paste. Fabric is subjected to a dyebath and emerges completely colored except where it has been printed to resist the color. A white-colored design is produced on a dyed background. The reverse of discharge printing, design is printed first and then dyed.

- Printing paste contains chemicals which resist dyeing
- Colored pigment may be added to the resist paste forming a colored design

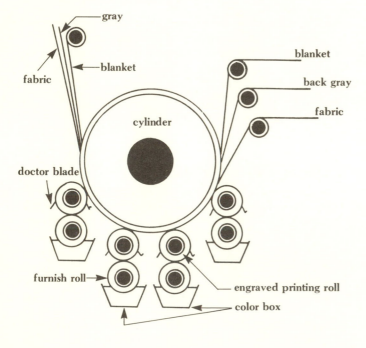

gray

blanket

fabric

blanket

back gray

fabric

cylinder

doctor blade

furnish roll

engraved printing roll

color box

Roller Printing

Roller printing applies design, pattern or motif to fabric using etched or engraved rollers. Rollers are engraved utilizing pantographs or photo-engraving techniques to transfer the design. Each part of the design using a different color requires its own etched roller.

The engraved rollers are arranged around a main cylinder on the printing machine. Each roller has its own dye dispensing unit and blade to scrape away surface dye. With each revolution of the rollers a repeat of the etched design is printed.

Machines may handle from one to as many as sixteen rollers to imprint all the colors required to complete a complex design.

Roller printing is also referred to as *calender* or *cylinder printing*.

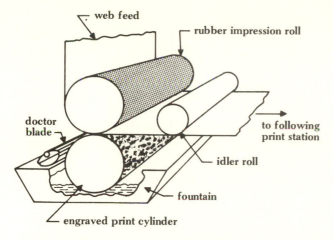

The pressure applied by the impression roll must be great enough to force ink out of the many small holes engraved into the surface of the print cylinder.

Gravure Printing

A printing method that rotates an etched or engraved copper gravure roller in a fountain of ink; a doctor blade wipes the cylinder clean, leaving ink in the depths of the etched or engraved design. As the fabric passes through the roller printing machine, the gravure rollers transfer the design and color sequentially and directly. Gravure printing utilizes as many etched rollers as is necessary to complete the design and color pattern.

Differences in the depth of the etched or engraved design allow for variation in tones.

Gravure printing utilizes:

U-Type Presses Cylinders are arranged around a central point. U-type presses may have a two to six station operation

In-Line Presses All sections sequentially arranged on the same plane. In-line presses may have a two to twelve station operation.

- Design repeat is limited to circumference of the printing roller
- Uses up to 150-line definition for fineness of detail
- Produces finer lines than roller printing
- Allows for printing halftones or fall on colors
- Produces smoother solid areas of color than screen printing
- Relatively inexpensive to produce for vast quantities of printed fabric
- Allows for printing paisley or other intricately printed fabrics
- A machine counterpart of hand-block printing techniques

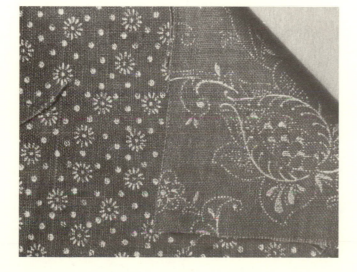

Register/Duplex Printing

In register printing fabric is passed through a roller-printing machine in a single operation or in two separate and distinct operations. Both sides of the goods are printed with the same or with different designs and/or colors.

- Utilizes modified direct roller-print equipment and techniques
- Used to duplicate or simulate woven pattern designs
- Produces clear design outlines on both sides of the fabric
- Offers contrasting designs on either face of the fabric
- Offers advance and receding pattern on different faces of the fabric

Screen Printing

Screen printing is a manual or mechanical method of printing which utilizes flat or rotary screens and squeegees. Using the squeegee, ink or dyestuff penetrates specific areas of the prepared screen, transferring the design to the fabric. The design may be sketched or photographed on prepared silk, nylon, polyester, vinyon or metal screens; separate screens are necessary for each color in the design. During the printing process, screens or fabric are moved manually, mechanically or electrically to continue the repeat of the pattern. The placement and movement of the screens are registered so that the color and design are aligned and will fit together accurately.

Screen printing allows for a wide variety of color and design possibilities and may be used to produce large patterns as well as fine-line designs.

sidewinder manual screen printer

Precision Screen Machines Inc.

four to six color pre-registered screen printer

Precision Screen Machines Inc.

Manual/Automatic Screen Printing

A screen-printing method that utilizes flat screens mounted on a rotary or circular drive. The flat screens contain the dye color and squeegees and rotate to the garment part, transferring design and multiple colors in a sequential operation.

- Preregisters four to eight color applications
- Allows for quick design changeover and production flexibility
- Used for sampling, garment components, garment sections, and completed garments

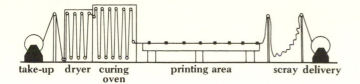

take-up   dryer   curing   printing area   scray delivery
                  oven

Flat-Bed Screen Printing

A screen-printing method that utilizes mechanically or electrically controlled flat-bed screens and squeegees in a continuous operation. During the printing process, the movement of the fabric, the raising and registration of the screens, the dispensing of dyestuff and the operation of the squeegees is mechanically and electrically controlled.

The flat-bed printing method is composed of five basic components. Fabric enters the unit from the J-scray; moves onto the printing table where actual printing is done; moves to the drying oven where it is dried; to the curing oven where colors set; then delivered to rolls or to batching bins.

- Screens are made utilizing photo-chemical techniques
- Fabric moves to the screen intermittently and stops in preparation for next operation
- Utilizes one or more screens for single- or multicolored application
- Allows for design repeat of large-sized range; larger than roller printing methods
- Holds fabrics tautly during operation avoiding distortion of design
- Used on whole rolls of woven, nonwoven and knitted fabrics
- Offers defined colors and delineation same as hand screen printing
- Cannot produce halftone or fall on colors
- Process not applicable to garment components or garment sections

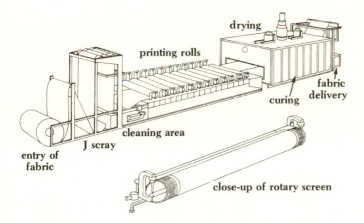

entry of fabric   J scray   cleaning area   printing rolls   drying   curing   fabric delivery

close-up of rotary screen

Rotary Screen Printing

A screen-printing method that utilizes electrically controlled rotary-screen cylinders which are designed to hold the dyestuff and automated squeegee. Fabric anchored to a printing blanket or bed moves along in a continuous process to the mounted screens; ink is pumped inside the rotary screen and the squeegee inside each cylinder forces the printing paste through the openings onto the fabric. Continuous and sequential operations apply different colors for each part of the design. The cylindrically shaped perforated screens on which the design is transferred are made of copper, nickel or metal foil.

- Roller screens may be arranged horizontally, vertically or centrally
- Uses 80-line definition for fineness of detail
- Cannot produce very fine lines
- Allows for stripe effects and fall on designs
- Produces large blotches of dark colors
- Amount of dyestuff, automatically fed, can be controlled for thick or thin color applications
- Fastest of all screen-printing operations and methods
- Allows for continuous movement of fabric and simultaneous printing
- On whole rolls of woven, nonwoven, printed fabrics
- Prints fabrics as wide as 90″ with large 36″ pattern repeat
- Preferred for printing knits as distortion is limited
- Not applicable to garment components/sections

Burnt-Out Printing

A special-effects printing method achieved with chemicals which will react with fibers and dissolve pattern or design in the fabric. By using two or more rollers, process may combine fiber destroying chemicals and color application in sequential order.

- Used to produce simulated eyelet or other openwork-type fabrics
- Creates openweave designs in blended fiber fabrics
- May be applied to produce raised pattern or design on sheer ground
- May be applied by roller-printing methods

Flock Printing*

A special-effects printing method utilizing adhesives or an electrostatic charger to adhere or affix short fibers or flocks to the surface of the fabric in predetermined shapes, sizes of patterns.

- Attracts and adheres flock to adhesive or electrostatic charge
- Produces a raised surface design
- Used to simulate woven dotted Swiss fabric and brocaded velvet fabric
- Process tends to stiffen the hand of the fabric
- Surface design may abrade during wear
- Adhesives may dissolve during laundering or dry-cleaning
- Process may be applied to woven, knitted or formed-fabric structures
- Allover flocking used to simulate suede, plush or pile fabrics (discussed as a fabric finish in the finishing unit)

*Refer to page 120 for illustrations of this process.

Shadow Printing

A special-effects printing method that:
- Produces ombré effect colors ranging from dark to light shades on the same cloth
- Produces fabrics with ombré effects in monochromatic, complementary or contrasting colors
- Simulates hand-dipped multicolored dyed fabrics

The effect may be achieved utilizing different printing methods:
- *Direct printing method*—ombré effects achieved by preparing engraved rollers to print colors from dark to light shades
- *Roller printing method*—ombré effects achieved by using deeper etched and flatter gravure rollers
- *Screen printing method*—ombré effects achieved by dotting the areas to be printed on the screen in different gradations for ink penetration

Polychromatic/Jet Printing*

A process of applying patterns and designs to fabric while the fabric moves in a continuous motion through a machine housing jets through which dyestuff is fed and projected onto plates or rollers; transferring dyestuff onto the fabric and then passes the fabric between heavy rollers allowing the dyestuff to penetrate throughout. Polychromatic printing does not utilize printing machines, screens, etched rollers or other printing equipment. Affinity for dyestuff depends on the fiber content and fabric structure as well as the type of dyestuff used.

- Applies one or several dyes in one operation
- Repeat of the design is controlled by required factor combination
- Design is controlled by movement and position of jets
- Action and speed of fabric creates different design effects
- Color penetrates cloth in varying degrees and quantity
- Produces designs or random splashes in various colors
- Method allows for machine-made tie-dyed and batik hand printing effects
- Pattern is visible on both sides of the fabric.

Polychromatic printing is also referred to as polychromatic multicolored dyeing.

*Refer to page 180 for illustrations of this printing method.

Stipple Printing

A special-effects printing method where chemicals are added to the printing paste which allows the dyes to agglomerate producing small dashes or splashes of color on the fabric. The end result displays dark splashes of color on a light-colored ground or light splashes of color on a dark-colored ground.

- Used to create novelty effects in planned or splattered arrangements
- May be produced as a step in overprinting technique
- May be planned as an additional operation for discharge-printed fabrics
- Technique may be applied to yarns producing stippled yarn

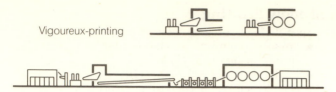

Vigoureux-printing

Vigoureaux/Melange Printing

A printing or dyeing method applied to wool rope-form, fiber top, slub or sliver prior to spinning the yarn utilizing direct-, roller- or screen-printing methods.

- May be applied to worsted yarns prior to weaving
- A variation of warp printing for wool fiber mass and worsted sliver
- May apply color to sliver used for warp or filling yarns
- Color is printed in a striped pattern
- Provides a wide variety of color tones, hues and shades in the finished cloth
- Produces mixed color effects in the woven cloth
- Effect may produce scattered flecks of color recognized in some tweed fabrics

Spelling variations include vigoureaux, vigoureux and vigoreux.

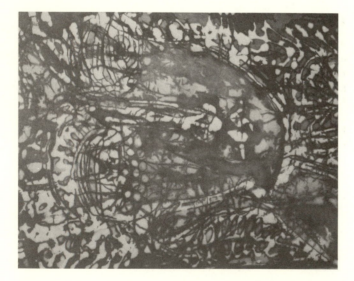

Batik Printing

A multi-step hand printing technique that includes the application of a substance to protect or limit desired areas of the base fabric from coloring by resisting dyestuff. When fabric is submerged in the dyebath, the chemical- or wax-protected areas resist the dyestuff; dyestuff adheres to or penetrates untreated areas. The waxing, dyeing and wax-removal processes are repeated until design or desired effect is completed. White areas may be left white, dyed or over-printed.

- A resist printing or dyeing method
- Usually hand done producing one-of-a-kind pattern and design
- Crazed and diffused flow of color is part of the process
- Type of dyestuff and resist material used depends on the fiber content of the fabric
- Process may be applied to sliver, fiber, yarn, fabric or completed garment
- May be machine-produced by polychromatic dyeing or printing methods

Block Printing

Design is engraved or carved on wooden, linoleum or copper blocks; dye is applied to the raised areas of the designed blocks; block is pressed on the fabric; desired color and design is transferred to base fabric. Procedure is repeated as many times as design is desired. Multicolored patterns require separate blocks for each color.

- A form of direct printing utilizing manual operations
- Separate blocks allow for a variety of design and color effects
- Produces slight irregularities in detail and repetition of design
- Used on comparatively short lengths of cloth
- Process is slow and production is expensive
- Method employed and adapted in countries where labor costs are low and printing machinery is not available
- Method used on authentic Indian and African prints
- Design achieved by hand process and operation, but may be duplicated by roller-printing methods

Iron-on/Press-on Printing

A transfer or heat-transfer printing method that utilizes emblems or individual isolated design decorations which are transferred to the garment by heat of manually operated irons or portable flat-bed presses. The predesigned or formed decals are composed of pigment colors mixed with wax or thermoplastic substances which melt when activated by heat and pressure, therefore binding the design to the fabric.

- Not colorfast to repeated launderings
- Colors fade, crock and abrade
- Colorfast to drycleaning
- Allows for design application to selected area of garment
- Allows for selection of type and style of design by individual
- Requires no after wash or fixatives

hand painted design by Michaele Vollbracht

Hand Painted Designs

A creative method of imparting designs directly to cloth or by outlining the design on fabric with wax that may or may not contain a dye color different from the design. Outlined design, pattern or motif may be colored in by airbursh or brush work utilizing specially prepared thickened dyestuff or thinned acrylic or oil paints.

- A hand-technique imparting singular or insolated designs to fabric
- May be applied to fabric, garment components or finished garment
- Allows for original, one-of-a-kind or copied designs
- Produces designs in limited edition and yardage
- Airbrush may be used directly to impart design and color to fabric
- Design may be painted with brush directly without outlining
- Expensive and slow process because of artistic labor involved

distributing ink on screen

forcing ink through screen with squeegee

complete hand-screened design

Hand Screen Printing

A screen-printing method that utilizes portable flat screens and portable hand-held rubber-edged squeegees to transfer dyestuff and design to the cloth.

The placement of the fabric, the movement of the screens, the application of dye ink to the screen, and the manipulation of the squeegee are all done manually.

- Process is slow and expensive to produce
- Allows for rapid and individualistic changeover of design and/or color
- Used to transfer solo- or multicolored designs or motifs to fabric
- Used on:
  - Garment components prior to construction
  - On selected areas of completed garment
  - On limited yardage for sample cuts or sample runs
  - Finished items such as t-shirts, scarfs, sashes, belts, neckties, handbags

Technique produces bright clean shades of color and clear definition of design.

fountain brushes

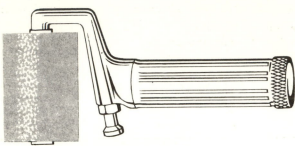

fountain stencil roller

spray ink

Stencil Printing

A design or pattern is made on a base of cardboard, wood or metal and then cut out producing a template or stencil. Color is applied over the stencil with a brush, airbrush, roller or sponge. Open, cut out areas of the stencil allow the ink or dyestuff to penetrate to the cloth while solid areas resist penetration. When stencil is lifted, the cut-out design is transferred to the cloth. Operation is repeated manually to repeat design. Separate stencils are needed for different colors and varied design effects.

- Produces large areas of color
- Limited to the application of one color per stencil
- Used on narrow width and limited yardage fabrics
- Used on garment components or completely assembled garments
- May be planned as a series of designs or as a singular isolated design
- Expensive to produce
- Process is slow and limited

Stencil printing method to transfer design was the fore-runner of the development of screen printing.

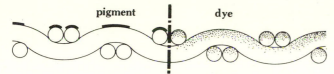

Pigment applied to surface. Dye penetrates surface.

Pigment Printing

A label on fabric or garments that indicates the design or pattern printed on the fabric is made with insoluble pigment colors. The insoluble pigment colors are fixed to fabric with resins then subjected to heat treatment which sets the colors and makes them insoluble.

Print is produced by using pigments during a direct printing process. When completed, the design-printed portion of the garment is stiffer than the non-printed areas.

- Stiffens the fabric
- Effects hand and drapability qualities of the fabric
- Not colorfast to laundering, crocking or abrasion
- Colorfast to drycleaning
- Least expensive printing method, requiring no after-fixing

Wet/Dry Printing

Printing and dyeing both require the same dyestuff to color fabrics. The following describe the differences.

In printing:
- Dyestuff is applied to the surface
- Dyestuff is applied as decorative design
- The fabric is dyed on localized areas

In dyeing:
- Dyestuff combines chemically with fiber and yarn
- Dyestuff saturates and penetrates the entire fabric

Printed fabric *made with dyes* is referred to as *wet-prints* or *wet-printing* methods.

Printed fabric *made with pigment colors* is referred to as *dry-prints* or *dry-printing* methods.

Characteristics of Wet/Dry Printing

Wet-Prints/Wet Printing
Utilizes many steps
Requires steaming, scouring, rinsing
More expensive to produce

Dry-Prints/Dry Printing
Utilizes limited steps
Ages with heat
Less expensive to produce

Steps in Wet/Dry Printing

Wet Printing: Printing/Drying/Steaming/Washing/Framing/Finished Fabric
Dry Printing: Transfer/Finished Fabric

6 – Performance Expectations

Abrasion Resistance/Effect of Abrasion
Absorbency/Porosity/Capillarity/Moisture Regain
  Characteristics of Absorbent and Adsorbent Fabrics
  Standard Moisture Regain of Natural & Man-Made
    Fibers (chart)
Air Permeability/Thermal Conductivity
Compressibility/Crushing/Effects of Crushing
Covering Power
Effect of Heat
  Heat Sensitivity
  Thermoplasticity
  Effect of Heat on Natural Fibers (chart)
  Effect on Heat on Man-Made Fibers (chart)
Elasticity
  Elasticity/Elastic Recovery
  Percentage of Immediate Recovery at 2% Stretch or
    Elongation of Natural & Man-Made Fibers (chart)
  Creep/Delayed Elasticity
  Stretch & Recovery
Elongation/Extensibility
  Percentage of Elongation at Breaking Point of
    Natural & Man-Made Fibers (chart)
Flexibility/Pliability
  Measurement of Stiffness of Natural & Man-Made
    Fibers (chart)
Luster
Pilling
Resiliency/Wrinkle Recovery
Resistance
  Biological Resistance
    Biological Resistance of Natural & Man-Made
      Fabrics (chart)

Chemical Resistance/Chemical Reaction
  Chemical Resistance of Natural & Man-Made
    Fibers (chart)
Flame Resistance
  Flame Resistance of Natural & Man-Made Fibers
    (chart)
  Burning Characteristics of Natural & Man-Made
    Fibers (chart)
Sunlight Resistance
  Sunlight Resistance of Natural & Man-Made
    Fibers (chart)
Dimensional Stability/Shrinkage
  Dimensional Stability/Shrinkage
  Progressive Shrinkage
  Relaxation/Consolidation Shrinkage
  Felting Shrinkage
  Dimensional Restorability
Slippage
  Yarn Slippage/Yarn Shifting/Seam Slippage
Snagging
Static Electricity/Electrical Conductivity
Strength/Durability
  Strength/Durability
  Tenacity/Breaking Tenacity
    Standard or Dry/Wet Strength of Natural &
      Man-Made Fibers (chart)
  Tensile Strength
  Tear Strength
  Bursting Strength
  Peel-Bond Strength

Performance expectations is a term that relates to the predictable or determined behavior of a fabric. The usefulness and the performance of a fabric are dependent on the physical and chemical properties of fibers, yarns, fabric structure, the type and method of finishing processes and color and/or design application and the interrelationship of these components. If one or more of the components is changed, the fabric will be changed and the difference will affect the behavior or performance expectations of the fabric.

Performance expectations of fabric depends on:

- Fiber properties such as: origin and quality, length and diameter, density, crimp, surface characteristics, luster, toughness, elongation, elasticity, resiliency, moisture regain, conductivity, dimensional stability, strength; resistance to heat, fire, sun; climate conditions, micro-organisms, insects, acids, alkalies and other solvents
- Yarn properties such as: manufacturing influences, compactness of fiber within yarn; shape, dimension and diameter; type and structure, ply and twist, crimp, texture and hand, covering power
- Fabric structure such as: manner and type, texture and surface interest, appearance, durability
- Finishing processes that aid, alter or change the fiber, yarn or finished fabric
- Type and method of color and/or design application

The performance of a fabric will affect the wear, care and drapability qualities of the fabric and finished garment. The wear, care and drapability qualities will determine the fabric's end use and its potential for the type, style and design of garments.

abrasion on silk

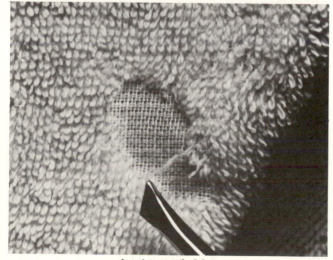

abrasion on corduroy

abrasion on pile fabric

Abrasion Resistance/Effect of Abrasion

Abrasion resistance refers to the ability of a fabric to resist wear and deterioration caused by surface friction resulting from fabrics rubbing against themselves, other fabrics, the body, and other obstructions during wear.

Flat Abrasion The rubbing away of fibers from a flat surface occurring in wear, stain and spot removal and laundering. Flat abrasion is usually associated with pile or flocked fabrics.

Edge Abrasion The removal or wearing down of fibers along the edges of collars, cuffs, flaps, pockets, hems, closures, folds and flat-felled seams.

Flex Abrasion The removal or wearing away of fibers, color or sizing from the fabric by a flexing or folding action on other fabrics, during wear, laundering or dry cleaning. Flex abrasion occurs at elbow, knee, underarm, inner leg and seat areas. The result is a formation of a worn spot, light streaks or crow's-feet" on the surface of the fabric.

Some fibers have an inherent resistance to abrasion. Fibers of high abrasion resistance may be blended with fibers of low abrasion resistance to produce fabrics of good durability.

Abrasion resistance depends on:
- Content of fibers
- Type and quality of fibers
- Type, size and twist of yarns
- Type and density of fabric structure
- Type and method of finishing processes

Abrasion resistance relates to:
- Durability of fabrics and garments
- Length and frequency of wearability of garments
- Ability to resist wear or broken areas on garments

fabric prior to wetting

fabric after wetting/absorbs moisture

adsorbent properties/hydrophobic fabric

Absorbency/Porosity/Capillarity/Moisture Regain

These terms refer to the capacity or ability of a fiber or fabric to take up moisture. As a laboratory determining factor, moisture regain is the amount of water a bone dry fiber will absorb from the air under standard conditions at 70°F and 65 percent relative humidity.

Terms relating to absorbency:

Absorb The fabric's ability to take up moisture.

Adsorb The fabric's ability to hold moisture. Moisture or water is held on the surface of the fiber rather than absorbed into the fiber.

Wicking The fabric's ability to give up moisture by capillary action. The moisture travels to the surface of the fabric where it rolls off or evaporates. Wicking occurs in some man-made fibers.

Hydrophilic/Hydroscopic A property of *absorbing* moisture; affinity for water; moisture absorbing.

Hydrophobic A property of *resisting* absorption of water; water resistance; water repellent.

Absorbency depends on:
- Content of fiber
- Type and construction of yarn
- Type and density of fabric structure
- Type and method of finishing processes

Characteristics of Absorbent & Adsorbent Fabrics

Absorbent Fabrics

Comfortable to wear in hot weather

Provide skin comfort

Reduced electrostatic build-up and pilling

Accept dyes and special finishes easily

Provide ease of laundering and stain removal

Poor elasticity and resiliency

Poor dimensional stability in water

Do not hold a sharp crease

Adsorbent Fabrics

Not comfortable to wear in hot weather

Dry quickly

Stain less readily

Standard Moisture Regain of Natural & Man-made Fibers

The moisture regain of a fiber expressed as a percentage of the moisture free weight. Tested at 70° and 65 percent relative humidity.

Fibers	Percentage of Standard Moisture Regain
Natural Fibers	
Asbestos	1.0
Cotton	8.5–10.3
Flax (Linen)	12.0
Jute	12.0
Silk	11.0
Wool	13.3–2.5
Man-made Fibers	
Acetate	6.0
Acrylic	1.3–2.5
Modacrylic	0.4–4.0
Nylon 6	4.5
Nylon 66	4.5
Polyester	0.4 or 0.8°
Rayon	13
Spandex	.75–1.3
Triacetate	3.2
°Depending on fiber type	

Percentage data given in ranges may fluctuate according to introduction of fiber modifications or additions and deletions of fiber types.

  Charts and tables are offered as guides. Variations in percentages and variables are due to information regarding fibers from different companies and the differences in the fiber type.

loose weave

moderately closed weave

tightly constructed weave

Air Permeability/Thermal Conductivity

Air permeability and thermal conductivity refer to the ability of air to pass through fibers, yarns, and structure of the fabric and also, the result of trapping or emitting air that passes from the body. Air permeability and thermal conductivity are influenced by the fibers, yarns, structure, and finishes of the fabric.

Fabrics with *low thread count*, *openweave construction*, and of *fine yarns* are *more* air permeable. Air moves over and around the body carrying the heat away from the body. Fabrics with *high thread count* and *dense construction* allow for *less* air permeability, offering resistance which may be desirable for special end-use fabrics.

Finishes, such as air-cooled finishes, make the fabric more porous allowing the air to circulate through the fabric. Finishes, such as bulking yarns or napping fabric surfaces, entrap still air and provide warmth by insulating the body.

Air permeability relates to:
- Absorbency and cooling qualities of fibers
- Ability of fabric structure to admit air flow
- Thickness or fineness of yarns and fabrics
- Combination of high and low air-permeable fibers and yarns
- Air-cooling finishes applied to yarns
- Coating finishes applied to fabrics

Thermal conductivity relates to:
- Heat conductivity of fibers
- Fusibility of fibers and yarns
- Ability of fabric structure to trap air flow
- Thickness or layers of fabrics
- Combination of high and low air-permeable fibers and yarns
- Finishes applied to fibers, yarns, or fabrics
- Coating finishes or resins applied to fabrics

compressing pile fabric

pile fabric that does not withstand compressing

Compressibility/Crushing/Effects of Crushing

Compressibility The measure of ease with which a fiber mass or yarn can be crushed with the application of pressure and regain its original position. Compressibility relates to the loft of a fiber, yarn or fabric. Lofted yarns are yarns with increased bulk and thickness, but without added weight. When compressed, lofted yarns spring back to their original thickness and bulk.

Compressibility depends on:
- Type of raw materials used
- Resiliency of yarn
- Type of fabric structure
- Softness and loftiness of yarn and fabric
- Thickness and height of pile

Crushing/Effects of Crushing The property of a pile fabric to recover from crushing or flattening. A fabric's ability to withstand crushing is aided by the application of a wrinkle-resistant finish.

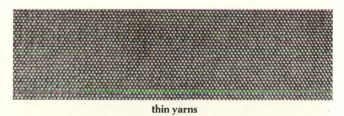

thin yarns

medium-sized yarns

thick yarns

Covering Power

Covering power refers to the ability of fibers or yarns to occupy an area when woven or knitted in the fabric. Covering power is determined by the type, length, size, shape, cross section and surface contour or configuration of fibers. Thick or bulked fibers and crimped or curled yarns will provide better covering qualities than straight or smooth fibers and yarns of small diameters. The thinner or finer and the more transparent the fiber or yarn the less covering power it has.

Geometric Covering Power The quality of a fiber required to make a yarn that will cover a specific area. Geometric covering power is measured by filling a standard size container with yarns, then weighing the amount of yarn required to fill the container.

Visual Covering Power The ability of the fiber or yarn to hide what is underneath it.

Fibers and yarns denoted as having "good covering power":
- Require fewer fibers or yarns to produce a fabric
- Produce a warmer fabric
- Feel and look substantial
- Bulked or high-bulked for increased volume without added weight
- Produce thick yarns and fabrics

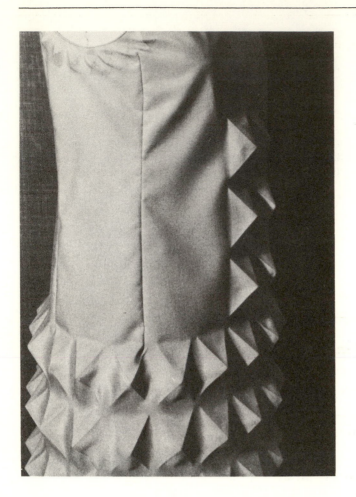

Heat Sensitivity

Heat sensitivity is the chemical composition of a fiber, yarn or fabric in response to the application of heat. Man-made fabrics soften or melt at various temperatures. Cellulosic and protein fabrics scorch or turn brown under high temperatures.

Specific heat behavior of fibers, yarns or fabrics determines manner of handling during:

- Fabric structure
- Finishing processes
- Coloring or printing application
- Garment construction
- Care of garment (laundering and drycleaning)
- Selection of drying or pressing temperatures

Thermoplasticity A term used to describe the properties of a fiber or a fabric to become *plastic* or to *soften* under heat and ability to *retain* a predetermined shape, size or design when cooled.

Thermoplastic fibers are heat sensitive. The control of heat causes physical changes of fibers which alter their forms, thereby establishing permanent shapes. Man-made thermoplastic fibers include: acetate, acrylic, anidex, modacrylic, nylon, olefin, polyester, rubber, saran, triacetate, vinyl, and vinyon.

Thermoplasticity allows for:
- Heat-setting of pleats and creases
- Molding shapes
- Dimensional stability/shrinkage control
- Low melting temperatures

Effect of Heat on Natural Fibers

Fibers	Decomposing Point	Scorching Point	Safe Iron Temperature Limit
Cotton	464°F (241.9°C)	450°F (234.1°C)	400–425°F (206.1–220.1°C)
Flax (Linen)	500°F (262.1°C)	475°F (248.1°C)	450°F (234.1°C)
Jute	500°F (262.1°C)	475°F (248.1°C)	400°F (206.1°C)
Silk	400°F (206.1°C)	325°F (164.1°C)	300°F (149.7°C)
Wool	266–400°F (131–206.1°C)	325°F (164.1°C)	300°F (149.7°C)

Effect of Heat on Man-made Fibers

Fibers	Melting Point	Softening/Sticking Point	Safe Iron Temperature Limit
Acetate	500°F (262.1°C)	350°F (178.1°C)	250–350°F (122.1–178.1°C)
Acrylic	Indeterminate	420–490°F (217.3–156.8°C)	350°F (178.1°C)
Modacrylic	390–400°F (200.1–206.1°C)	250°F (122.1°C)	225°F (108.1°C)
Nylon	480–500°F (250.9–262.1°C)	445°F (231.3°C)	300–350°F (149.7–178.1°C)
Polyester	480–550°F (250.9–290.1°C)	440–455°F (228.5–236.9°C)	325°F (164.1°C)
Rayon	350–464°F (178.1–241.9°C)	Burns	325°F (164.1°C)
Spandex	446–518°F (231.8–272.2°C)	325°F (164.1°C)	300°F (149.7°C)
Triacetate (treated)	575°F (304.1°C)	450°F (234.1°C)	375°F (192.1°C)
Vinyon	260°F (127.7°C)	225°F (108.1°C)	200°F (94.1°C)

Data given in ranges may fluctuate according to introduction of fiber modifications or additions and deletions of fiber types.

Charts and tables are offered as guides. Variations in percentages and variables are due to information regarding fibers from different companies and the differences in the fiber type.

ELASTICITY OF TWO-WAY STRETCH ACTION FABRICS

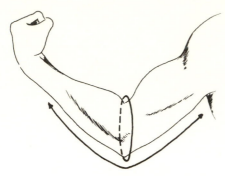

elbow flex: vertical stretch (lengthwise) 35–40%; horizontal stretch (crosswise) 15–22%

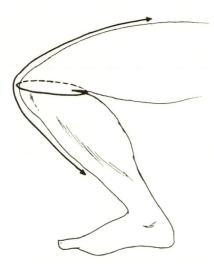

knee flex: vertical stretch (lengthwise) 35–45%; horizontal stretch (crosswise) 12–14%

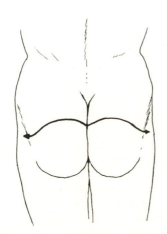

seat flex: horizontal stretch (crosswise) 4–6%

Elasticity/Elastic Recovery

Elasticity is the characteristic of a fiber, yarn or fabric to increase in length under tension and to recover to its original length when released. The elasticity of a fiber is measured as the recovery at 2-percent elongation.

Elasticity of fibers vary due to the type, structure, shape and size that are inherent or manufactured. *Spandex* is highly elastic and recovers almost immediately on the release of stress. *Wool* and *silk* are considered relatively elastic. *Cotton, linen* and *jute* have only a small degree of elasticity.

There is an interdependency of fiber, yarn construction, fabric structure, and finishes to produce a fabric with good elasticity.

Fabrics with elasticity/elastic recovery:
- Produce comfortable garments
- Contribute to comfort and ease in body movements
- Contribute to shape of garment when worn
- Allow garments to be molded to the body contours
- Eliminate bagging at elbows, knees, and seat areas
- Prevent garments from becoming loose fitting with wear
- Reduce seam stress
- Increase breaking strength

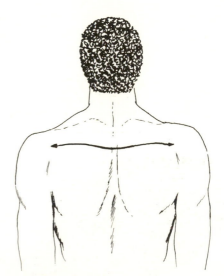

back flex: horizontal stretch (crosswise) 13–16%

Percentage of Immediate Recovery at 2% Stretch or Elongation of Natural & Man-made Fibers

Fibers	Percentage of Recovery
Natural Fibers	
Cotton	75%
Flax (Linen)	65%
Jute	74%
Silk	92%
Wool	99%
Man-made Fibers	
Acetate	94%
Acrylic	92–99%
Modacrylic	79%
Nylon	100%
Rayon (Regular)	82%
Rayon (High Tenacity)	70%–100%
Rayon (High-Wet Modulus)	95%
Spandex	100%
Triacetate	90%–92%

Data given in ranges may fluctuate according to introduction of fiber modifications or additions and deletions of fiber types.

Charts and tables are offered as guides. Variations in percentages and variables are due to information regarding fibers from different companies and the differences in the fiber type.

Creep/Delayed Elasticity

Creep or delayed elasticity is the action of a fiber that does not recover immediately from strain but will recover gradually. Amount of recovery is determined by measuring fiber or yarn length a specific amount of time after removal of stress or stretching action.

Creep in a fiber depends on:
- Molecular structure of the fiber
- Lack of side chain in the fiber structure
- Crosslink in the fiber structure
- Strong bonds inherent in the fibers
- Poor orientation of the fibers

Stretch & Recovery

Stretch and recovery refers to the property of a knit fabric when bonded to a tricot knit.

It is measured by the ability of the fabric to return *quickly* to its original position after stretching and being released from tension.

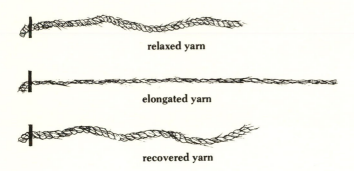

relaxed yarn

elongated yarn

recovered yarn

Elongation/Extensibility

Stretching, extending or lengthening a fiber, yarn or fabric under tension or stress up to a breaking point will determine its elongation or extensibility. The deformation or change in length is measured as a percentage of the original length of the fiber, yarn or fabric after application of tensile force. A minimum of 10 percent elongation in a fiber is desired. Stress beyond maximum elongation or extensibility capacity causes breakage of the fiber, yarn or fabric.

Elongation of fabric depends on:
- Type and content of fibers
- Configuration of yarns
- Fabric structure

Elongations vary at different temperatures and when fiber, yarn or fabric is wet or dry.

Crimped and textured yarns are used to produce fabrics with high elongation performance. The greater the yarn crimp, the more elongation/extensibility the fabric possesses.

Elongation in fabrics is necessary for:
- Strength
- Reduction of brittleness
- Comfort when garment is worn (the garment provides "give")
- Strength in seams
- Prevention of bagginess and sagginess at flex positions (elbows, knees, seat areas)

Percentage of Elongation at Breaking Point of
Natural & Man-made Fibers

Percentage of elongation at breaking point using a load rate of 10 grams per denier per minute for a 30 second duration of load at one minute recovery.

Fibers	Percentage of Dry Elongation
Natural fibers	
Cotton	3%–10%
Flax (Linen)	2.7%–3.3%
Jute	1.7%–1.9%
Silk	10%–25%
Wool	20%–40%
Man-made fibers	
Acetate	23%–45%
Acrylic	25%–46%
Modacrylic	33%–39%
Nylon (Regular)	26%–40%
Nylon (High Tenacity Filament)	16%–20%
Nylon (High Tenacity Staple)	23%–58%
Polyester (Regular)	19%–23%
Polyester (High Tenacity)	11%–28%
Rayon (Regular)	15%–25%
Rayon (High Tenacity)	6%–20%
Rayon (High-Wet Modulus)	9%–15%
Spandex	440%–700%
Triacetate	25%–40%

Data given in ranges may fluctuate according to introduction of fiber modifications or additions and deletions of fiber types.

Charts and tables are offered as guides. Variations in percentages and variables are due to information regarding fibers from different companies and the differences in the fiber type.

stiff

springy

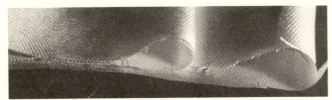

supple/pliable

Flexibility/Pliability

Flexibility/pliability refers to the property of a fiber that permits it to be bent or folded repeatedly without breaking and that allows a garment to withstand the action of flexing during wear when walking, bending or sitting. Fibers with poor flexibility are stiff and rigid, producing a fiber too difficult to spin into yarns and therefore, limited in usefulness.

Flexibility of fibers is important in that it:
- Allows fabrics to be supple, bendable and pliable
- Affects the durability of fabrics
- Affects the strength of fabrics
- Influences drapability qualities of fabrics
- Determines if fabrics can be creased or pleated
- Affects aesthetic qualities of fabrics

Measurement of Stiffness of Natural & Man-made Fibers

Fibers	Grams per Denier
Natural Fibers	
Cotton	57–60
Flax (Linen)	Not available
Jute	Not available
Silk	Not available
Wool	3.9
Man-made Fibers	
Acetate	3.5–5.5
Acrylic	4–18
Modacrylic	Not available
Nylon 6	29–48
Nylon 66	5–58
Polyester	6–80
Rayon	6–50
Spandex	0.11–0.16

Data given in ranges may fluctuate according to introduction of fiber modifications or additions and deletion of fiber types.
   Charts and tables are offered as guides. Variations in percentages and variables are due to information regarding fibers from different companies and the differences in the fiber type.

plastic sequins   shiny

glazed finish

Luster

Luster is the amount of light reflected from the surface of the fabric which is measured by the degree of brightness or dullness.

Degree of surface luster varies with regard to origin type and fineness of fiber, construction of yarn and fabric, and finishes.

The degree of luster in natural or man-made fabrics can be controlled or altered by:

- Changing the shape of the fiber
- Using chemicals in the fiber or yarn state
- Adding pigment to the fiber
- Changing the yarn structure or construction
- Varying the twist of the yarn
- Utilizing a long fiber length and flat cross section shapes
- Selecting weaves which reflect light
- Selecting different finishing processes

The following terms relate to luster and the light-reflecting character of fabrics:

bright	semi-dull
shiny	downey
lustrous	greyed
sheen	uneven
glaze	grainy
waxy	dark
dull	light

Pilling

Pilling is the formation of small balls or tufts on some fabrics resulting when short or broken fibers emerge on the fabric's surface. Pilling:

- Forms on soft fabrics made of wool, cashmere or other hair fibers which break away from the fabric
- Forms on man-made fabrics, adhering to the surface and becoming difficult to remove
- Is more noticeable on knit structures than on woven structures
- Occurs more often on fabrics of spun fibers or yarns than on fabrics of filament fibers or yarns.

Pilling may occur during wear, laundering or dry cleaning or when a fabric has been subject to abrasion that causes ends of fibers to break and surface.

Fabric Pills Pills contain fibers from the garment itself. Fabric pills occur on fabrics made of staple or short hair fibers.

Lint Pills Pills contain fibers acquired in washing or through contact with other garments. Lint pills occur on fabrics made of thermoplastic or electrostatic-type fibers.

fabric that does not wrinkle

fabric that does wrinkle

Resiliency/Wrinkle Recovery

Resiliency is the ability or degree of fabric to recover its shape (to spring back to shape) after being folded, compressed, distorted or twisted due to wearing or laundering.

Fibers differ in their *natural* resiliency. There is inherited resiliency in some fibers and in some fabric structures. *Wool* and *silk* are considered resilient. They may be deformed, crushed or wrinkled, but upon hanging deformations or wrinkles hang out. *Acrylic, modacrylic, nylon* and *polyester* have high resiliency. *Worsted wool* has a fair resiliency. *Cotton* and *linen* have poor resiliency unless chemically treated with a wrinkle-resistant finish.

A resilient fabric will create a problem if a sharp crease is desired in a garment. Wool fabrics resist being bent or creased and purposely designed creases will straighten out or flatten during wear.

Resiliency contributes to:
- Wrinkle resistance
- Wrinkle recovery
- Crease resistance
- Retention of good appearance
- Ease of care

moth hole on wool fabric

Staphylococcus aureus, a bacteria, grows in untreated fabric (left) and is prohibited from growing in treated fabric (right).

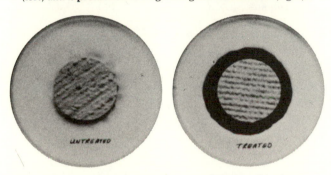

Trichophyton Mentagrophytes Var Interdigital, a white fungus, grows in untreated fabric (left) and is prohibited from growing in treated fabric (right).

Biological Resistance

Biological resistance is the ability of a fiber, yarn or fabric to resist damage caused by insects, climate or bacteria.

Moth Resistance   The chemical composition of a fiber, yarn or fabric that will not attract or be damaged by moths or silverfish.

Mildew/Rot Resistance   The chemical composition of a fabric that attracts or resists fungi causing deterioration or decomposition due to moisture, dampness or mildew.

Bacteria Resistance   The chemical composition of a fabric that will not attract or be damaged by bacteria.

Biological resistance relates to:
- Garment care during dry cleaning, laundering and storage
- Fabric selection for garments worn in warm, humid climates

Biological Resistance of Natural & Man-Made Fabrics

	Excellent	Good/Fair	Poor
Moths	Metallics Nylon Polyester Rayon	Cotton Linen Silk Acetate Acrylic Modacrylic Spandex Triacetate	Wool

	Excellent/ Good	Poor
Mildew & Rot	Acetate Acrylic Metallics Modacrylic Nylon Polyester Spandex Triacetate Vinyon	Cotton Linen Rayon Silk Wool

Chemical Resistance/Chemical Reaction

Chemical resistance is the effect of acids, alkalies, oxidizing agents, and solvents on a fiber, yarn or fabric. The chemical properties of a fiber, yarn, and/or fabric react to: bleaching agents such as peroxide or chlorine, reduction bleaches, strong acids, volatile organic acids, inorganic acids, mild or strong alkalies, dyes, metallic salts, oxidizing agents, cleaning solvents, water temperature, and swelling or matting capacity ability.

Understanding how a fabric reacts to chemicals:
- Allows for bleaching or whitening of fibers, yarns or fabrics
- Affects ability of fabric to take acid or alkali finishes
- Affects types of dyes and method of dyeing and/or printing of yarns and fabrics
- Helps determine the care factors for cleaning of garment

Chemical Resistance of Natural & Man-Made Fibers

Fibers	Dissolved/Disintegrated by Chemicals
Natural Fibers	
Cotton	Strong acids
Flax (Linen)	Strong alkalies; light rays
Jute	Strong alkalies; light rays
Silk	Acids; light rays
Wool	Strong alkalies
Man-Made Fibers	
Acetate	Acids; alkalies; light rays
Acrylic	Strong alkalies
Modacrylic	Strong alkalies
Nylon 6	Strong acids
Nylon 66	Oxydizing agents
Polyester	Strong acids
Rayon	Acids; strong alkalies
Triacetate	Acetones; acids; alkalies; light rays
Asbestos	Resistant to acids and alkalies
Spandex	Resistant to acids and alkalies

Flame Resistance

Flame resistance is the ability of fibers, yarns or fabrics to ignite, burn or extinguish when the source of the flame is removed. Flame resistance and flammability of fibers, yarns or fabrics relate to their selection for uses in particular products.

Some fibers, yarns or fabrics:
- Ignite and continue to burn
- Smoulder
- Are noncombustible
- Are self-extinguishing
- Require finishes to make them flame resistant or flame retardant

Flame resistant finishes change the look, hand, touch, durability, and cost of a fabric.

Flame Resistance of Natural & Man-Made Fibers

Excellent	Good/Fair	Poor
Modacrylic	Acetate	Cotton
Saran	Acrylic	Linen
Asbestos	Metallic	Silk
	Nylon	Rayon
	Polyester	
	Spandex	
	Triacetate	
	Vinyon	
	Wool	

Charts and tables are offered as guides. Variations in percentages and variables are due to information regarding fibers from different companies and the differences in the fiber type.

Burning Characteristics of Natural & Man-Made Fibers

Fibers	Approaching Flame	In Flame	Removed from Flame	Odor	Residue
Natural Cellulosic					
Cotton	Does not shrink away; ignites upon contact	Burns quickly	Continues to burn; afterglow	Similar to burning paper	Light; feathery; light to charcoal gray
Flax	Does not shrink away; ignites upon contact	Burns quickly	Continues to burn; afterglow	Similar to burning paper	Light; feathery; light to charcoal gray
Natural Protein					
Wool	Curls away from flame	Burns slowly	Self-extinguishes	Similar to burning hair	Brittle, small black bead
Silk	Curls away from flame	Burns slowly and sputters	Usually self-extinguishes	Similar to burning hair	Crushable, black
Weighted Silk	Curls away from flame	Burns slowly and sputters	Usually self-extinguishes	Similar to burning hair	The shape of fiber or fabric
Natural Mineral Asbestos	Does not melt (safe fiber)	Glows red if heat is sufficient	Returns to original form	None	Same as original form
Man-made Cellulosic					
Rayon	Does not shrink away; ignites upon contact	Burns quickly	Continues to burn; afterglow	Similar to burning paper	Light; fluffy; very small amount
Man-Made Modified Cellulosic					
Acetate	Fuses and melts away from flame; ignites quickly	Burns quickly	Continues to burn rapidly	Acrid (hot vinegar)	Hard; irregular-shaped, black bead
Man-Made Noncellulosic					
Acrylic	Fuses and melts away from flame; ignites readily	Burns rapidly with hot flame and sputters; melts	Continues to burn and melt; hot molten polymer will drop off while burning	Acrid	Hard, irregular-shaped black bead
Modacrylic	Fuses and melts away from flame (considered safe)	Burns slowly if at all; does not feed a flame; melts	Self-extinguishes	Acrid, chemical	Hard, irregular-shaped black bead
Nylon	Fuses and melts away from flame; shrinks	Burns slowly and melts	Self-extinguishes	Similar to celery	Hard, tough, gray or tan bead
Polyester	Fuses and melts away from flame; shrinks	Burns slowly and continues to melt	Self-extinguishes	Chemical	Hard, tough, black or brown bead
Olefin	Fuses, shrinks and curls away from flame	Burns and melts	Continues to burn and melt, gives off black sooty smoke	Chemical	Hard, tough, tan bead

Burning Characteristics of Natural & Man-Made Fibers (continued)

Fibers	Approaching Flame	In Flame	Removed from Flame	Odor	Residue
Man-Made Noncellulosic					
Saran	Fuses and melts away from flame; shrinks	Melts; yellow flame	Self-extinguishes	Chemical	Crisp, irregular-shaped black bead
Vinal	Fuses, shrinks and curls away from flame	Burns and melts	Continues to burn and melt	Chemical	Hard, tough, tan bead
Vinyon	Fuses and melts away from flame	Burns slowly and melts	Self-extinguishes	Acrid	Hard, irregular-shaped black bead
Elastomers Spandex	Fuses but does not shrink away from flame	Burns and melts	Continues to burn and melt	Chemical	Soft, sticky; gummy
Rubber	Shrinks away from flame	Burns rapidly and melts	Continues to burn	Sulfuric or chemical	Tacky; soft black
Man-Made Protein					
Azlon	Curls away from flame	Burns slowly	Self-extinguishes	Similar to burning hair	Brittle, small, black bead
Man-Made Mineral					
Glass	Does not burn	Softens; glows red to orange	Hardens; may change shape	None	Hard, white bead
Metallic	*Pure* metal no reaction	Glows red	Hardens	None	Skeleton outline
	Coated metal melts, fuses	None	Burns according to behavior of coating	None	Hard, black bead

Sunlight Resistance

Sunlight resistance refers to the ability of a fabric to withstand degradation and damage from direct or from prolonged exposure to sunlight. Fibers, yarns or fabrics are weakened due to exposure to light and heat from the sun.

Sunlight resistance relates to:
- Durability of a fabric or garment
- Colorfastness of a fabric
- End use of fabric or garment

Sunlight Resistance of Natural & Man-Made Fabrics

Excellent	Good	Fair	Poor
Acrylic Metallic Modacrylic	Acetate Linen Rayon Polyester Triacetate Vinyl	Cotton Wool	Nylon Rubber Spandex
Charts and tables are offered as guides. Variables are due to information regarding fibers from different companies and the differences in the fiber type.			

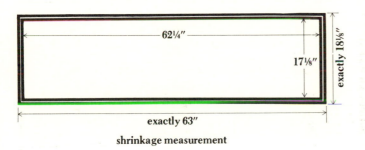

shrinkage measurement

Dimensional Stability/Shrinkage

Dimensional stability is the ability of a fabric to maintain its original shape, length and width when subjected to heat, moisture, water and cleaning.

Dimensional stability relates to:
- Comfort and care of a garment
- Shape retention
- Shrinking or deformation of the fabric
- Resistance to sagging and stretching

Dimensional stability depends on:
- Type and content of fibers
- Inherent characteristics of fibers
- Surface characteristics of fibers
- Morphological structure of fibers
- Physical and chemical properties of fibers
- Friction or interreaction between fibers and yarns
- Twist ply of yarns
- Processes applied to yarns
- Thread and yarn count of a fabric
- Structure and geometry of fabric
- Compression of fibers and yarn weave
- Types and methods of mechanical and/or chemical finishes applied

Progressive Shrinkage

Progressive shrinkage is the continued shrinkage a fabric undergoes each time it is laundered or dry cleaned.

Relaxation/Consolidation Shrinkage

Relaxation shrinkage is the result of stretching and distorting the fabric during manufacturing whereby it becomes elongated during weaving and/or coloring and finishing and then relaxes to its natural size and position held before garment construction procedures, laundering or dry cleaning.

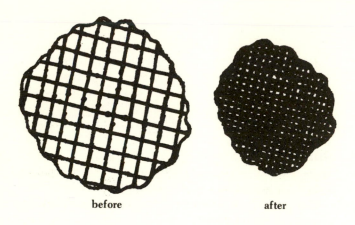

before   after

Felting Shrinkage

Felting shrinkage is the subjection of fabrics of wool and hair fibers to hot water, steam, laundering agents, and agitation resulting in the migration of individual fibers to form a matted mass. During the felting action the scale structure of the woolen fibers overlap, interlock, and thicken.

Felting shrinkage occurs on:

- Knitted and woven garments made of wool and animal hair fibers
- Garments that are laundered or dry cleaned improperly. Garment loses all its air permeability, softness and loftiness causing fabric to become hard and thick—an irreversible condition.

A special finish utilizing a coating or blunting process may be applied to the barb or projection ends of the wool-fiber structures to prevent interlocking and undesirable felting shrinkage. Treated woolens are labeled to identify the finish.

Dimensional Restorability

Dimensional restorability is the ability of a fabric, which has been shrunk, stretched or distorted temporarily, to return or to be restored to its original dimension by stretching, pressing and/or blocking.

seam slippage

Yarn Slippage/Yarn Shifting/Seam Slippage

Slippage refers to the sliding or shifting of yarns following the application of a rubbing action or force during wear or laundering. Shifting occurs when lengthwise yarns slip away from filling yarns causing distortion in yarn or weave. Seams hold firm, but adjacent yarns pull away or yarns move from side to side.

Yarn slippage and shifting is affected by the type of fiber, yarn, weave and/or finish used to produce the cloth. Finishes can affect or control yarn movement.

Yarn slippage occurs:
- When man-made or silk filament yarns are used
- More frequently with smooth surface yarns
- With smooth mercerized yarns
- When yarns are woven or interlaced far apart
- On long float satin weaves
- When number of yarns per inch (thread count) is low

Yarn slippage occurs on areas of the garments where there is wear and strain such as at the hips, thighs and armholes, across the shoulder, on center back and at inseam of trousers.

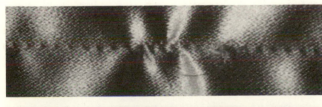

Snagging

Snagging results when a yarn protrudes from the fabric's basic background, but does not break.

The snagged or pulled yarn may be brought back into position or alignment by:
- Applying pressure
- Pressing
- Pushing or pulling raised yarn to back of fabric

Snagging occurs more often on knit fabrics or on loosely woven fabrics with long floats in the weave.

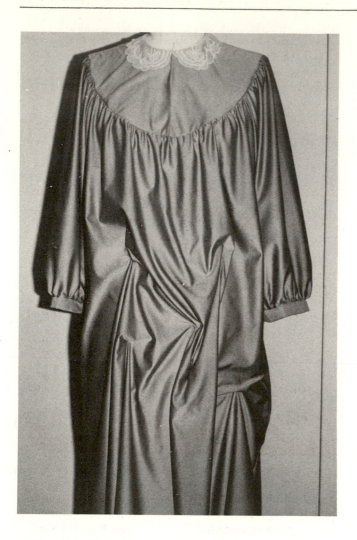

Static Electricity/Electrical Conductivity

Static electricity is the ability of fibers to draw and retain electrical charges from the air resulting in a build up on the fabric's surface. The electricity is generated by friction of a fabric against itself or against another fabric or object. Some fibers are inherently static.

Fabrics with static electricity:
- Produce shocks
- Cause garments to cling together or to the wearer
- Attract dirt and lint
- Allow dirt to adhere to the fabric muting colors and brightness

Hydrophobic fabrics (man-made except acetate and rayon) are more prone to static electricity than *hydrophilic* fabrics (vegetable and animal). Most man-made fabrics have poor conductivity. Poor conductivity is related to low moisture regain. Moisture in fabrics acts as a conductor to remove the charges and to prevent static buildup.

There is no permanent finish that can be applied to fabrics to reduce or control static electricity. Fibers may be modified by using a variant to reduce static; the modified fiber undergoes a change in its molecular structure which causes a change in the fiber's properties.

Anti-static sprays applied to fabrics during the cutting and sewing procedures for garments or during the use of the garment pulls moisture from the air and reduces static temporarily. Anti-static products used during the care or laundering of a garment reduces static, but must be repeated with each laundering to be effective.

Anit-static rods are used in the manufacturing processes of fabrics as an aid to reduce static due to heat buildup and friction and also to deter dust and dirt from settling on newly finished and printed fabrics.

Strength/Durability

The wear-life of a fabric or garment is referred to as durability. Fiber properties related to durability are those which allow the fabric to perform satisfactorily for a long period of time allowing garments to be long wearing. Some fibers are considered strong due to inherent factors. Weak fibers may be made into durable fabrics by selection of yarn construction and/or fabric structure.

Properties of fibers, yarns or fabrics related to durability include:
- Toughness
- Strength
- Resiliency
- Elasticity
- Abrasion resistance
- Elongation
- Thermoplasticity

Durability depends on:
- Type and quality of fibers
- Tensile strength of yarns
- Amount of twist in yarns
- Number and type of ply in yarns
- Type of fabric structure
- Compactness of fabric structure

Tenacity/Breaking Tenacity

Tenacity is the ability to resist stress or the breaking strength of a fiber, filament, yarn or cord. Tenacity is measured either in terms of grams per denier or grams per tex and expressed in force per unit yarn number. *Breaking tenacity* is the stress at which a fiber breaks.

Fiber strength varies from one fiber to another and may also vary *within* one fiber. A weak fiber can be made into a strong yarn or strong fabric by combinations of fibers or yarns, different weaves, application of finishes or any combination of all factors.

Terms related to tenacity:

Denier   The number of grams or weight required to break a fiber one denier.

Tex   The number of grams of weight to break a fiber one tex.

Dry Strength   The measure of a fabric's strength at the point of rupture or tearing in the dry state.

Wet Strength   The measure of a fabric's strength at the point of rupture or tearing in the wet state.

Standard or Dry/Wet Strength of Natural & Man-Made Fibers

Fibers	Standard or Dry	Wet
	(grams per denier)	
Natural Fibers		
Asbestos	2.5–3.1	—
Cotton	3.0–4.9	3.3–6.4
Flax (Linen)	2.6–7.7	8.4
Jute	3.0–5.8	6.8
Silk	2.8–5.2	2.5–4.5
Wool	1.0–1.7	0.8–1.6
Man-made Fibers		
Acetate	1.2–1.5	0.8–1.2
Acrylic	2.0–3.5	1.8–3.3
Modacrylic	2.0–3.5	2.0–3.5
Nylon 66 Regular Tenacity Filament	4.0–5.0	4.0–5.0
Nylon 66 High Tenacity Filament	6.3–9.5	6.2–9.4
Nylon 66 Staple	3.5–7.2	3.2–6.5
Nylon 6 Filament	6.6–9.5	5.0–8.0
Nylon 6 Staple	2.5	2.0
Polyester:		
Regular Tenacity Filament	4.0–5.0	4.0–5.0
High Tenacity Filament	6.3–9.5	6.2–9.4
Regular Tenacity Staple	2.5–5.0	2.5–5.0
High Tenacity Staple	5.0–6.5	5.0–6.4
Rayon:		
Regular Tenacity	0.73–2.6	0.7–1.8
Medium Tenacity	2.4–3.2	1.2–1.9
High Tenacity	3.0–6.0	1.9–4.6
High-Wet Modulus	2.5–5.5	1.8–4.0
Spandex	0.6–0.9	0.6–0.9
Triacetate	1.2–1.4	0.8–1.0

Data given in ranges may fluctuate according to introduction of fiber modifications or additions and deletion of fiber types.

Charts and tables listed are offered as guides. Variations in percentages and variables are due to information regarding fibers from different companies and the differences in the fiber type.

Tested at 21° (70°F) with relative humidity at 65%.

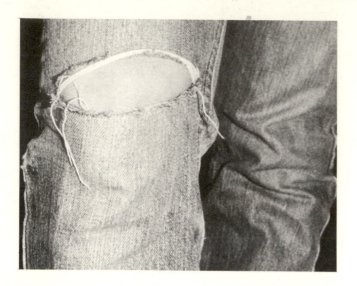

Tensile Strength

Tensile strength is the resistance of a fabric to a pulling force. It is measured in pounds per square inch and force per cross-section area; expressed in terms of units per pound number. Different fibers, yarns, and fabrics vary in tensile strength.

High tensile strength in fabrics is necessary for:

- Strength
- Durability
- Resistance to tearing or splitting at elbows, knees or inseam/crotch areas
- Resistance to wear

Bursting Strength

Bursting strength refers to the punching force necessary to cause a rupture in a fabric, and the ability of a fabric to resist breaking under specific conditions.

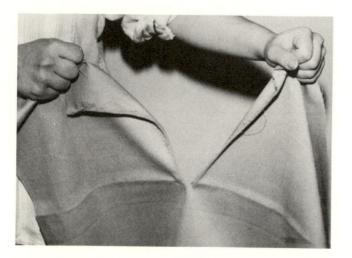

Tear Strength

Tear strength refers to the force required to break fabric or yarn in a torque or rotational pull, expressed in terms of pounds or grams per square inch.

The structure of a fabric relates to the tear strength of a fabric. Yarns grouped together share the stress and will result in greater tear strength. Structure which resists the ability of yarns to function together will decrease the tear strength of a fabric.

Finishes which coat fabrics or restrict yarn movement will tend to isolate yarns and decrease tear strength.

Peel-Bond Strength

Peel-bond strength is the force necessary to separate the plies of bonded or laminated fabric from each other, expressed in terms of ounces of pull per square inch.

Tests for peel-bond strength are made on fabrics in both wet and dry states.

Fabric width is the measurement of a piece of goods from the selvage across to the other selvage. Fabric width may be referred to as the:

- Breadth of the goods
- Crosswise measurement
- Horizontal measurement
- Filling direction measurement

Fabrics are produced in different widths with regard to:

- Structure and type of fabric
- Origin or location of manufacturing
- Processes and methods of manufacturing
- Availability of machinery or hand processes
- Cost of fabric
- Specific request

Depending on shrinkage and/or stretching control during finishing processes, fabric widths may be expressed in whole numbers within the range of the original width. Fabrics are usually produced in the following widths:

Inches	Centimeters
26–28	67.6– 71
32	81.3
36–39	91.4– 99.1
44–45	111.8–114.3
47–48	119.4–121.9
52–54	132.1–137.2
56–60	142.2–152.4
60–62	152.4–157.5
70–72	177.8–182.9
84	213.4
108	274.3

The Fabric Conversion Chart will be helpful in determining the amount of fabric needed when planning layout with different widths of fabric and for those using commercial patterns when fabric width does not correspond to width of fabric stipulated on pattern envelope.

Fabric Conversion Chart

Fabric Width (Inches)	32	35–36	39	41	44–45	50	52–54	58–60
Yardage	1⅞	1¾	1½	1½	1⅜	1¼	1⅛	1
	2¼	2	1¾	1¾	1⅝	1½	1⅜	1¼
	2½	2¼	2	2	1¾	1⅝	1½	1⅜
	2¾	2½	2¼	2¼	2⅛	1¾	1¾	1⅝
	3⅛	2⅞	2½	2½	2¼	2	1⅞	1¾
	3⅜	3⅛	2¾	2¾	2½	2¼	2	1⅞
	3¾	3⅜	3	2⅞	2¾	2⅜	2¼	2
	4	3¾	3¼	3⅛	2⅞	2⅝	2⅜	2¼
	4⅜	4¼	3½	3⅜	3⅛	2¾	2⅝	2⅜
	4⅝	4½	3¾	3⅝	3⅜	3	2¾	2⅝
	5	4¾	4	3⅞	3⅝	3¼	2⅞	2¾
	5¼	5	4¼	4⅛	3⅞	3⅜	3⅛	2⅞

Reprinted courtesy of Cooperative Extension Service, Rutgers University—The State University of New Jersey.

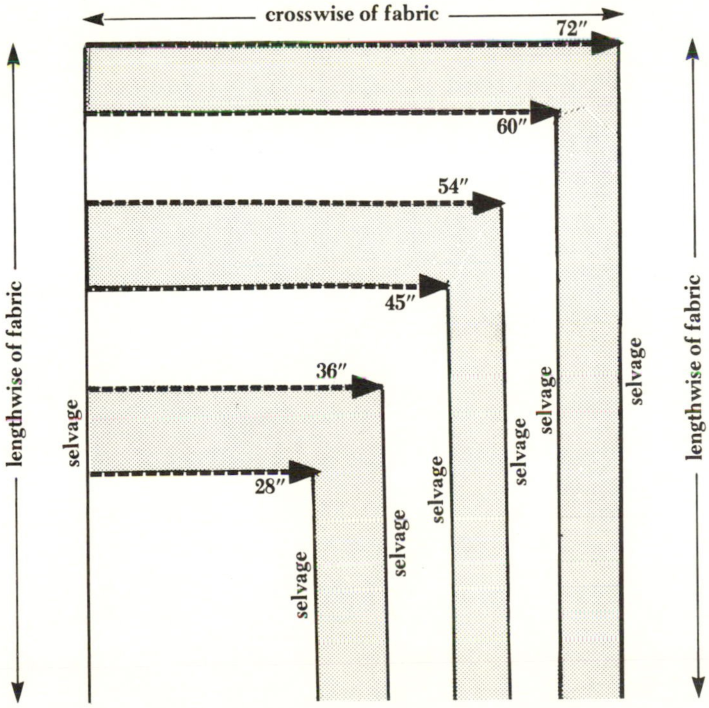

The weight of fabrics differs due to the difference in the number of yarns per inch as well as the size of yarns used in the various fabric structures. The variations of the fabric width in the making of cloth will also affect the weight of fabric, when calculations are based on the formula of the ounce per linear yard or number of yards to the pound.

The weight of fabric interrelates with the hand (the feel of fabric) and drapability qualities (the way the fabric will hang). Fabric weight becomes a determining factor in the selection of material and in the relationship to:

- End use for purpose of design
- Type and use of garment
- Climatic condition where garment will be used

Fabric weight can be estimated. The estimated weight should be based on the same area or size of fabric held, lofted or suspended and compared with fabrics of a known weight composed of the same fiber.

Specific Gravity of Natural & Man-made Fibers

The ratio of the weight of a given volume of fiber to an equal volume of water

Fibers	Percentage of Specific Gravity
Natural Fibers	
Asbestos	2.10–2.80
Cotton	1.54–1.56
Flax (Linen)	1.50
Jute	1.50
Silk	1.25–1.34
Wool	1.30–1.32
Man-made Fibers	
Acetate	1.32
Acrylic	1.14–1.19
Modacrylic	1.30–1.37
Nylon	1.14
Polyester	1.22 or 1.38 (Depending on the type of fiber.)
Rayon	1.50–1.53
Spandex	1.20–1.21
Triacetate	1.20–1.21

Data given in ranges may fluctuate according to introduction of fiber modifications and additions and deletions of fiber types.

Charts and tables listed are offered as guides. Variations in percentages and variables are due to information regarding fibers from different companies and the differences in the fiber type.

The following table is based on calculations of fabric weights estimated by the *ounces per square yard* formula.

Weight Characteristics	Fabric Weight
Delicate/Fine/Very lightweight	under 1 oz.
Lightweight	1.1–3 oz.
Medium-lightweight	3.1–5 oz.
Medium weight	5.1–7 oz.
Medium-heavyweight	7.1–9 oz.
Heavyweight	9.1–12 oz.
Very Heavyweight	over 12 oz.

Direct and accurate means of determining weight can be calculated using basic formulas. The methods of weighing fabrics are expressed in the following terms and calculated by basic formulas used in the industry.

Ounces per Square Yard The weight of a piece of fabric measuring 36″ by 36″. The same size area of comparative goods is weighed. By direct comparison the weight of each piece of goods can be determined. The formula for calculating ounces per square yard determines the weight with known square yardage:

$$OZ/YD^2 = \frac{OZ/YD}{1} \times \frac{36''}{\text{width of fabric}}$$

Ounces per Linear Yard The weight of a piece of fabric measuring 36″ in length and as wide as the fabric structure from selvage to selvage. The formula for calculating ounces per linear yard determines the weight with known linear yardage:

$$OZ/YD = \frac{OZ/YD^2}{1} \times \frac{\text{width of fabric}}{36''}$$

Linear Yards per Pound The weight of a piece of fabric based on equal fabric widths. The formula for calculating linear or running yards per pound determines how many pounds of fabric is in the yardage of goods:

$$YDS/LF = 16 \ OZ/YDS \text{ or } OZ/YD^2$$

"Yield" of Knitted Fabric How many yards of fabric can be knitted using a pound of yarn.

The following terms relate to fabric weight and to the *weight of the fiber.*

Density The ratio (relationship) of a mass (quantity) of substance (textile fiber) to a unit of volume (cubic centimeters), expressed in grams per cubic centimeters or pounds per cubic foot.
  A lightweight fiber produces a fabric that is warm without being heavyweight. A fabric can be thick and lofty and still be relatively lightweight.
  A lightweight fabric results from fibers of low density, while heavyweight fabrics result from fibers of high density. The lower the density the greater the covering power.

Specific Gravity The density of the fiber in relationship to the density of an equal volume of water at a temperature of 4-degree centimeters.

Density and specific gravity contribute to the properties of fabric by adding warmth without weight; producing a fabric that is lofty, full and light; adding buoyancy to the fabric.
  The weight of the fiber, yarn and fabric relate to comfort.

fine/lightweight

thick/heavyweight

Fabric Weight Conversion Table*
for Widths 36"–70"

Width	36"	38"	40"	42"	44"	46"	48"	50"	52"	54"	56"	58"	60"	62"	64"	66"	68"	70"
2.00	1.89	1.80	1.71	1.64	1.57	1.50	1.44	1.38	1.33	1.29	1.24	1.20	1.16	1.13	1.09	1.06	1.03
2.25	2.13	2.03	1.93	1.84	1.76	1.69	1.62	1.56	1.50	1.45	1.40	1.35	1.31	1.27	1.23	1.19	1.16
2.50	2.37	2.25	2.14	2.05	1.96	1.88	1.80	1.73	1.67	1.61	1.55	1.50	1.45	1.41	1.36	1.32	1.21
2.75	2.61	2.48	2.36	2.25	2.15	2.06	1.98	1.90	1.83	1.77	1.71	1.65	1.60	1.55	1.50	1.46	1.41
3.00	2.84	2.70	2.57	2.45	2.35	2.25	2.16	2.08	2.00	1.93	1.86	1.80	1.74	1.69	1.64	1.59	1.54
3.25	3.08	2.93	2.79	2.66	2.54	2.44	2.34	2.25	2.17	2.09	2.02	1.95	1.89	1.83	1.77	1.72	1.67
3.50	3.32	3.15	3.00	2.86	2.74	2.63	2.52	2.42	2.33	2.25	2.17	2.10	2.03	1.97	1.91	1.85	1.80
3.75	3.55	3.38	3.21	3.07	2.93	2.81	2.70	2.60	2.50	2.41	2.33	2.25	2.18	2.11	2.05	1.99	1.93
4.00	3.79	3.60	3.43	3.27	3.13	3.00	2.88	2.77	2.67	2.57	2.48	2.40	2.32	2.25	2.18	2.12	2.06
4.25	4.03	3.83	3.64	3.48	3.33	3.19	3.06	2.94	2.83	2.73	2.64	2.55	2.47	2.39	2.32	2.25	2.19
4.50	4.26	4.05	3.86	3.68	3.52	3.38	3.24	3.12	3.00	2.89	2.79	2.70	2.61	2.53	2.45	2.38	2.31
4.75	4.50	4.28	4.07	3.89	3.72	3.56	3.42	3.29	3.17	3.05	2.95	2.85	2.76	2.67	2.59	2.51	2.44
5.00	4.74	4.50	4.29	4.09	3.91	3.75	3.60	3.46	3.33	3.21	3.10	3.00	2.90	2.81	2.73	2.65	2.57
5.25	4.97	4.72	4.50	4.29	4.10	3.94	3.78	3.63	3.50	3.37	3.25	3.15	3.04	2.95	2.86	2.78	2.70
5.50	5.21	4.95	4.71	4.50	4.30	4.13	3.96	3.80	3.66	3.53	3.41	3.30	3.19	3.09	3.00	2.91	2.83
5.75	5.44	5.18	4.93	4.70	4.50	4.31	4.14	3.98	3.83	3.69	3.56	3.45	3.33	3.23	3.14	3.04	2.96
6.00	5.68	5.40	5.14	4.91	4.70	4.50	4.32	4.15	4.00	3.85	3.72	3.60	3.48	3.37	3.27	3.18	3.09
6.25	5.92	5.63	5.36	5.11	4.89	4.69	4.50	4.33	4.16	4.01	3.87	3.75	3.62	3.51	3.41	3.31	3.21
6.50	6.15	5.85	5.57	5.32	5.09	4.88	4.68	4.50	4.33	4.17	4.03	3.90	3.77	3.65	3.55	3.44	3.34
6.75	6.39	6.08	5.79	5.52	5.28	5.06	4.86	4.67	4.50	4.33	4.19	4.05	3.91	3.79	3.68	3.57	3.47
7.00	6.63	6.30	6.00	5.73	5.48	5.25	5.04	4.84	4.66	4.50	4.34	4.20	4.06	3.93	3.82	3.71	3.60
7.25	6.87	6.53	6.21	5.93	5.67	5.44	5.22	5.01	4.83	4.66	4.50	4.35	4.20	4.07	3.95	3.84	3.73
7.50	7.11	6.75	6.43	6.14	5.87	5.63	5.40	5.19	5.00	4.82	4.65	4.50	4.35	4.21	4.09	3.97	3.86
7.75	7.34	6.98	6.64	6.34	6.07	5.81	5.58	5.36	5.16	4.98	4.81	4.65	4.50	4.35	4.23	4.10	3.99
8.00	7.58	7.20	6.86	6.55	6.26	6.00	5.76	5.53	5.33	5.14	4.96	4.80	4.64	4.50	4.36	4.24	4.11

(Row labels under "Linear Yards per Pound")

*Reprinted courtesy of Allied Chemical Fibers.

Fabric Weight Conversion Table*
for Widths 72"–108"

Width	72"	74"	76"	78"	80"	82"	84"	86"	88"	90"	92"	94"	96"	98"	100"	102"	104"	106"	108"
	1.00	0.97	0.95	0.92	0.90	0.88	0.86	0.84	0.82	0.80	0.78	0.77	0.75	0.73	0.72	0.71	0.69	0.68	0.67
	1.13	1.09	1.07	1.04	1.01	0.99	0.96	0.94	0.92	0.90	0.88	0.86	0.84	0.83	0.81	0.79	0.78	0.76	0.75
	1.25	1.22	1.18	1.15	1.13	1.10	1.07	1.05	1.02	1.00	0.98	0.96	0.94	0.92	0.90	0.88	0.87	0.85	0.83
Linear	1.38	1.34	1.30	1.27	1.24	1.21	1.18	1.15	1.13	1.10	1.08	1.05	1.03	1.01	0.99	0.97	0.95	0.94	0.92
yards	1.50	1.46	1.42	1.38	1.35	1.32	1.29	1.26	1.23	1.20	1.17	1.15	1.13	1.10	1.08	1.06	1.04	1.02	1.00
per	1.63	1.58	1.54	1.50	1.46	1.43	1.39	1.36	1.33	1.30	1.27	1.24	1.22	1.19	1.17	1.15	1.13	1.10	1.08
pound	1.75	1.70	1.66	1.62	1.58	1.54	1.50	1.47	1.43	1.40	1.37	1.34	1.31	1.29	1.26	1.24	1.21	1.19	1.17
	1.88	1.82	1.78	1.73	1.69	1.65	1.61	1.57	1.54	1.50	1.47	1.44	1.41	1.39	1.35	1.32	1.30	1.27	1.25
	2.00	1.95	1.89	1.85	1.80	1.76	1.71	1.67	1.64	1.60	1.57	1.53	1.50	1.45	1.44	1.41	1.38	1.36	1.33
	2.13	2.07	2.01	1.96	1.91	1.87	1.82	1.77	1.74	1.70	1.66	1.63	1.59	1.56	1.53	1.50	1.47	1.44	1.42
	2.25	2.19	2.13	2.08	2.03	1.98	1.93	1.88	1.84	1.80	1.76	1.72	1.69	1.65	1.62	1.59	1.55	1.53	1.50
	2.38	2.31	2.25	2.19	2.14	2.09	2.04	1.99	1.94	1.90	1.86	1.82	1.78	1.74	1.71	1.68	1.64	1.61	1.58
	2.50	2.43	2.37	2.31	2.25	2.19	2.14	2.09	2.04	2.00	1.96	1.91	1.88	1.84	1.80	1.76	1.73	1.70	1.67
	2.62	2.55	2.49	2.42	2.36	2.30	2.25	2.20	2.14	2.10	2.05	2.01	1.97	1.93	1.89	1.85	1.82	1.78	1.75
	2.75	2.68	2.61	2.54	2.48	2.41	2.36	2.30	2.25	2.20	2.15	2.11	2.06	2.02	1.98	1.94	1.90	1.87	1.83
	2.88	2.80	2.72	2.65	2.59	2.52	2.46	2.41	2.35	2.30	2.25	2.20	2.16	2.11	2.07	2.03	1.99	1.95	1.92
	3.00	2.92	2.84	2.77	2.70	2.63	2.57	2.51	2.45	2.40	2.35	2.30	2.25	2.20	2.16	2.12	2.08	2.04	2.00
	3.13	3.04	2.96	2.88	2.81	2.74	2.68	2.62	2.56	2.50	2.45	2.39	2.34	2.30	2.25	2.21	2.16	2.12	2.08
	3.25	3.16	3.08	3.00	2.93	2.85	2.79	2.72	2.66	2.60	2.54	2.49	2.44	2.39	2.34	2.29	2.25	2.21	2.17
	3.38	3.28	3.20	3.12	3.04	2.96	2.89	2.83	2.76	2.70	2.64	2.59	2.53	2.48	2.43	2.38	2.34	2.29	2.25
	3.50	3.41	3.32	3.23	3.15	3.07	3.00	2.93	2.86	2.80	2.74	2.68	2.63	2.57	2.52	2.47	2.42	2.38	2.33
	3.63	3.53	3.43	3.35	3.26	3.18	3.11	3.03	2.97	2.90	2.84	2.78	2.72	2.66	2.61	2.56	2.51	2.46	2.42
	3.75	3.65	3.55	3.46	3.38	3.29	3.21	3.14	3.07	3.00	2.93	2.87	2.81	2.76	2.70	2.65	2.60	2.55	2.50
	3.88	3.77	3.67	3.58	3.49	3.40	3.32	3.24	3.17	3.10	3.03	2.97	2.91	2.85	2.79	2.74	2.68	2.63	2.58
	4.00	3.89	3.79	3.69	3.60	3.51	3.43	3.35	3.27	3.20	3.13	3.06	3.00	2.94	2.88	2.82	2.77	2.72	2.67

Reprinted courtesy of Allied Chemical Fibers.

Cotton/Cotton-type Fabrics

Fine/Delicate Weight	Lightweight	Medium-Lightweight	Medium Weight	Medium-Heavyweight	Heavyweight
Dotted Swiss	Batiste	Airplane Cloth/Byrd Cloth®	Boucle Yarn Cotton	Beach Cloth	Bark Cloth
Embroidery on Sheers	Broadcloth	Bedford Cord	Brocade	Bedford Cord (sueded finish)	Brocade Coating
Lawn	Cambric	Chambray	Chintz	Bengaline	Calcutta/ Bangladesh Cloth
Open Weaves	Challis	Chambray (corded)	Covert	Covert	Canvas
Organdy	Clokay	Iridescent Cloth	Damask	Crash	Chino
Swivel Weave	Embossed Cotton	Crepe	Drill Cloth	Cretonne	Cretonne
Voile	Embroidered Work	Damask	Duck	Damask	Damask
Crinkled Voile	Creponne	Dobby Weave	End & End (bottomweight)	Denim	Denim (smooth-faced)
	Damask	Flannelette	Eyelet	Flocked Swiss	Denim (brushed-faced)
	Dimity	Gauze Cord	Outing/Dommet Flannel	Drill Cloth	Double Weave Cloth
	Dimity with Cord	Gingham	Gauze Cloth	End & End (bottomweight)	Drill Cloth
	Dobby Weave	Hopsaking	Gingham	Gabardine	Duck
	End & End (topweight)	Jean Cloth	Homespun	Gauze Cloth	Gabardine
	Gauze Cloth	Madras	Hopsacking	Homespun	Jacquard Weave
	Gingham	Muslin	Jacquard Weave	Jacquard Weave	Khaki
	Jean Cloth	Oxford	Jean Cloth	Leno Weave	Leno Weave
	Lawn	Percale	Leno Weave	Osnaburg	Osnaburg
	Lawn (glazed-faced)	Plisse	Monk's Cloth	Pique	Pique
	Oxford	Polished Cotton	Muslin	Poplin	Poplin
	Percale	Printcloth	Pique	Ratine	Spot Weave
	Printcloth	Seersucker	Pongee	Sailcloth	Ticking
	Seersucker	Sheeting	Poplin	Sateen	
	Swivel Weave	Spot Weave	Sailcloth	Seersucker	
	Tattersall	Suede Cloth	Sateen	Spot Weave	
	Voile	White-on-White	Seersucker	Ticking	
	Crinkled Voile		Sheeting	Tricotine	
	White-on-White		Skip Denting	Twill	
			Open Effect	Whipcord	
			Corded Effect		
			Spot Weave		
			Suede Cloth		
			Whipcord		

Linen/Linen-type Fabrics

Fine/Delicate Weight	Lightweight	Medium-Lightweight	Medium Weight	Medium-Heavyweight	Heavyweight
—	Cambric Linen Handkerchief Linen Handkerchief Linen with Cord	Bisso Linen Dress Linen	Butcher Linen Crash Linen Dress Linen Dobby Weave Homespun Linen Suiting	Art Linen Butcher Linen Crash Linen Dobby Weave Homespun Jacquard Weave Novelty Effect Linen Suiting	Crash Linen Dobby Weave Jacquard Weave Novelty Effects Linen Suiting

Burlap/Burlap-type Fabrics

Fine/Delicate Weight	Lightweight	Medium-Lightweight
—	100% Jute Fiber Man-Made Fiber Simulated Burlap	100% Natural Fiber Man-Made Fiber Simulated Burlap

Silk/Silk-type Fabrics

Fine/Delicate Weight	Lightweight	Medium-Lightweight	Medium Weight	Medium-Heavyweight	Heavyweight
Chiffon China Silk Georgette Georgette (Double) Marquisette Mousseline de Soie Silk Gauze Ninon Organza Shantung Georgette	Barathea Broadcloth Tissue Faille Gazar Georgette Triple Open Weave Habutai Honan/Pongee Honan/Pongee (Dobby) Radium Silk Surah	Barathea Suiting Damask Faille Moiré Faille Poplin Shantung	Charvet Damask Mull Poplin Ottoman Shantung Faille	Bengaline Damask Hopsacking Matelassé Peau de Soie Rep Serge Sharkskin Silk Suiting Tussah/Wild Silk	Brocade Canvas Damask Homespun Ottoman Coating

Crepe/Crepe-Type Fabrics

Fine/Delicate Weight	Lightweight	Medium-Lightweight	Medium Weight	Medium-Heavyweight	Heavyweight
Albatross Chiffon Crepe Georgette Crepon/Crinkle Crepe	Crepe de Chine Crepe de Chine (Dobby) Lingerie Crepe/Crepe Set® Matelassé Crepe Meteor Crepe Satin-Faced Crepe	Flat Crepe Lingerie Crepe/Crepe Set®	Crepe-Backed Satin/Satin-Backed Crepe Crepe Faille Pebbly/Mossy Crepe	Bark Crepe Canton Crepe Crepe-Backed Satin/Satin-Backed Crepe	—

Satin/Satin-type Fabrics

Fine/Delicate Weight	Lightweight	Medium-Lightweight	Medium Weight	Medium-Heavyweight	Heavyweight
—	Brocade Charmeuse Charmeuse (Dobby Stripe) Ciré Satin Jacquard Satin Messaline	Brocade Ciré Satin Hammered Satin Jacquard Satin	Creped Satin Jacquard Satin	Antique Satin Bridal Satin Crepe Satin Duchesse Satin Thermal-Coated Satin/Milium®	Thermal-Coated/Napped-Back Satin

Taffeta/Taffeta-type Fabrics

Fine/Delicate Weight	Lightweight	Medium-Lightweight	Medium Weight	Medium-Heavyweight	Heavyweight
Paper Taffeta	Paper Taffeta Tissue Taffeta Yarn-dyed Taffeta Warp-Dyed/Printed Taffeta	Antique Taffeta Faille Taffeta Jacquard Taffeta Moiré Taffeta	Moiré Taffeta	—	—

Wool/Wool-type Fabrics

Fine/Delicate Weight	Lightweight	Medium-Lightweight	Medium Weight	Medium-Heavyweight	Heavyweight

Sheer Wools
Batiste
Challis
Wool Fancies
Wool Gauze
	Albatross
	Bedford Cord
	Double Cloth
	Étamine
	Gabardine (summerweight)
	Sheer Wools
	Voile
	Tweeds
	Herringbone
	Worsted
	Wool Fancies
	Waffle Cloth
	Wool Knits
	Jersey Knit
	Tropical Worsted
		Bedford Cord
		Bengaline
		Broadcloth
		Doeskin
		French-Back
		Double Cloth
		Eiderdown
		Étamine
		Wool Flannel
		Worsted Flannel
		Iridescent
		Sharkskin
		Wool Fancies
		Reverse Twill
		Unfinished Worsted
			Cassimere
			Covert Suiting
			Flannel
			Gabardine
			Homespun
			Iridescent
			Kasha Cloth
			Poplin
			Serge
			Suede Cloth
			Tartans
			  Clan Plaids
			  Glen Plaid
			  Hound's-tooth Check
			Tweeds
			  Bird's eye
			  Herringbone (Wool & Worsted)
			  Salt & Pepper
			Wool Knits
			Double Knit
				Baize
				Cheviot
				Double-faced Cloth
				Duvetyn
				Hopsacking
				Ratiné
				Tweeds
				  Donegal
				  Heather
				  Oatmeal
				Whipcord
					Astrakhan/Poodle Cloth
					Bolivia
					Cloque
					Double-faced Cloth
					Blanket/Cloth/ Plaid Back
					Fleece
					Gabardine Coating
					Homespun Coating
					Jersey
					Loden Cloth
					Mackinaw Cloth/ Buffalo Plaid
					Melton
					Ottoman Coating
					Polo Cloth
					Ratiné (plain & twill weave)
					Tricotine
					Tweeds (heavy-textured)

Specialty Hair/Specialty Hair Blended Fabrics

Fine/Delicate Weight	Lightweight	Medium-Lightweight	Medium Weight	Medium-Heavyweight	Heavyweight

—	Camel's Hair
	  100% Fiber
	  Blended Fiber
	Cashmere
	  100% Fiber
	  Blended Fiber
	Mohair
	  100% Fiber
	  Blended Fiber
	Gauze
	Rabbit Hair
	  Blended Fiber
		Alpaca Hair
		  100% Fiber
		  Blended Fiber
		Mohair
		  100% Fiber
		  Blended
		  Brushed-faced
		  Clear Finish
			Mohair
			  100% Fiber
			  Single-brushed Face
			  Double-brushed Face
				Rabbit Hair Cloth
				Blended Fiber
				  Coating
					Alpaca Cloth
					  Coating
					  Blended Fiber
					Cashmere Coating
					  100% Fiber
					  Blended Fiber
					Mohair
					  Blended Fiber
					Rabbit Hair Coating
					  Blended Fiber
					Zebaline®

Felt/Felt-type Fabrics

Fine/Delicate Weight	Lightweight	Medium-Lightweight	Medium Weight	Medium-Heavyweight	Heavyweight
—	Blended Fiber	100% Wool Fiber Blended Fiber	100% Wool Fiber Blended Fiber	100% Wool Fiber Blended Fiber	100% Wool Fiber

Knit/Knit-type Fabrics

Fine/Delicate Weight	Lightweight	Medium-Lightweight	Medium Weight	Medium-Heavyweight	Heavyweight

Jersey Knit
Sheer
Tricot Knit
Sheer
Sheer with Laid-in Yarn
	Interlock Knit
	Jersey Knit Variation
	Open Weave
	Raschel Knit
	  Lace Effect
	  Open Effect
	Rib Knit
	  1 x 1
	  Open Effect
	Tricot Knit
	  Lightweight
	  Patterned
	  Printed
	  Silk Finish
	  Stiff Finish
	  Transfer Stitch
	Tuck Stitch
	Intarsia
	Sweater Knit
	Laid-in Yarn
		Interlock Knit
		Jersey Knit Variation
		  LaCoste®
		  Tweed Effect
		Milanese Knit
		Raschel Knit
		  Lace Effect
		  Novelty Effect
		Rib Knit
		  1 x 1
		  2 x 2
		  Sweater
		Tricot Knit
		  Ciré Finish
		  Patterned
		  Polished
		  Silk Finish
		Tuck Stitch
		Intarsia
		Transfer Stitch
		Laid-in Yarn
			Double-faced Knit
			Double Knit
			Interlock Knit
			Jacquard Knit
			  Flat
			  Jersey
			  Rib
			  Smooth-faced/
			    Birdseye-backed
			  Nap-faced/birdseye backed
			Jersey Knit Variation
			  Pleated Effect
			Purl Knit
			Raschel Knit
			  Dishcloth Effect
			  Loop-Pile Fringe
			  Lace Effect
			  Novelty Effect
			Rib Knit
			  1 x 1
			  2 x 2
			  Variation
			Thermo Knit
			Tricot Knit
			Transfer Stitch
			Intarsia
			Sweater Knit
			Laid-in Yarn
				Interlock Knit
				Jacquard Knit
				  Blister
				  Jersey
				Purl Knit
				Raschel Knit
				  Crochet
				  Lace Effect
				  Tweed Effect
				Rib Knit
				  3 x 3
				  Piqué
				Tricot Knit
				Transfer Stitch
				Tuck Stitch/
				  Popcorn Effect
				Dropped/Missed Stitch
				Cable Stitch
				Intarsia
				Sweater Knit
				Laid-in Yarn
					Jersey Knit
					  Variation
					  Novelty Yarn
					Purl Knit
					Raschel Knit
					  Double Cloth Effect
					  Tweed Effect
					  Loop-Pile Fringe
					Rib Knit
					  4 x 4
					Intarsia
					Sweater Knit
					Laid-in Yarn
					Cable Stitch

Lace/Lace-type Fabrics

Fine/Delicate Weight	Lightweight	Medium-Lightweight	Medium Weight	Medium-Heavyweight	Heavyweight
Embroidered-type Pt d'Esprit Val-type	Binche-type Blonde-type Brussels-type Chantilly-type Filet-type Crochet Work Honiton-type Tatting	Duchesse-type Filet-type Darned Work Pt d'Esprit Rosepoint-type Large Motif Small Motif	Alencon-type Cut Work Eyelet-type Burnt-out Method Pt d'Angleterre Pt de Venice	Cluny-type Crochet-type Nottingham-type Pt Plat de Venice Shadow Lace	Chantilly-type Re-embroidered Macramé Venice-type/Gros Pt de Venice

Net/Netting/Net-type Fabrics

Fine/Delicate Weight	Lightweight	Medium-Lightweight	Medium Weight	Medium-Heavyweight	Heavyweight
Maline Net Net Pt d'Esprit Net Pt d'Esprit Tulle Tulle Tulle/Illusion Veiling	Fishnet Fine Hole	—	Cable/Laundry Net Fishnet Small Hole Medium Hole	Fishnet Large Hole	—

Pile Structured/Pile-type Fabrics

Fine/Delicate Weight	Lightweight	Medium-Lightweight	Medium Weight	Medium-Heavyweight	Heavyweight
—	Cut Velvet	Friezé Sculptured Terry Cloth Cut Velvet Transparent Velvet	Corduroy Feathercord Fine Wale Fleece Nap-faced Sweatshirt Terry Cloth Single-faced (knit ground) Double-faced (knit ground) Velour (knit ground) Velvet Crushed (knit & woven ground) Embossed Lyons Panne (woven ground)	Corduroy Mid Wale Thick-set Novelty Wale Fleece Baby Bunting Sweatshirt Plush Terry Cloth Single-faced (woven ground) Double-faced (woven ground) Chenille Stretch Jacquard Velvet Brocade Crushed (knit ground) Lyons Panne Velvet Cord Velour Velveteen	Corduroy Wide Wale Broad Wale Terry Cloth Double-faced (woven ground) Tufted Cloth Chenille Candlewick Chenille Velvet Chenille Yarn Velvet Cotton Flocked Velvet Cord Simulated Fur (high pile) Beaver Chinchilla Ermine Fox (red, silver, white, blue) Giraffe Astrakhan/ Persian Lamb Broadtail Lamb Sherpa/Sheared Lamb Leopard Lynx Mink Muskrat Ocelot Opossum Pony Rabbit Raccoon Seal Skunk Squirrel Teddy Bear Tiger Zebra

Metallic/Metallic-type Fabrics

Fine/Delicate Weight	Lightweight	Medium-Lightweight	Medium Weight	Medium-Heavyweight	Heavyweight
Embroidered Sheer Tricot Knit with Laid-in Metallic Yarn Metallic Lace Metallic Pt d'Esprit Lace Sparkle or Glitter Adhesive Bonded to Sheers	Jersey Knit with Weft-inserted Metallic Yarn Lamé Jersey	Lamé Gauze Woven Lamé Metallic Net Sparkle or Glitter Adhesive Bonded to Opaque Fabric Sparkle or Glitter Pigment Printed	Ciré Coated Jacquard Weave with Metallic Yarn Metallic Pile	—	—

Stretch/Stretch-type Fabrics

Fine/Delicate Weight	Lightweight	Medium-Lightweight	Medium Weight	Medium-Heavyweight	Heavyweight
—	Fiber Stretch Lycra® (180–220%) Yarn & Fabric Structure Stretch Stretch Lace	Fiber Stretch Lycra® (140–175%) Yarn Stretch Whipcord Yarn & Fabric Structure Stretch Double Knit	Fiber Stretch Lycra® (110–140%) Yarn Stretch Gabardine Yarn & Fabric Structure Stretch Double Knit Stretch Terry Stretch Finish Crimped Cloth	Yarn Stretch Canvas Chino Gabardine Satin Yarn & Fabric Structure Stretch Double Knit Stretch Terry	Yarn Stretch Denim Twill Yarn & Fabric Structure Stretch Double Knit Stretch Terry Stretch Lace Stretch Finish Crinkled Double Cloth

Multicomponent/Coated/Layered Fabrics

Fine/Delicate Weight	Lightweight	Medium-Lightweight	Medium Weight	Medium-Heavyweight	Heavyweight
—	Water-Repellent Resin-Coated Rip-Stop Nylon Taffeta	Film-Faced Bonded Simulated Leather Water-Repellent Resin-Coated Muslin Sheeting Vinyl Clear Film Quilted Gauze-backed Chemstitch®	Film-Faced Bonded Simulated Leather (textured) Flock-Faced Bonded Simulated Suede (patterned) (crushed) Water-Repellent Resin-Coated Duck Clear Vinyl Quilted Double-faced Knit-backed	Laminated Bonded Knit to Knit Film-Faced Bonded Simulated Leather Bonded Vinyl Film Water-Repellent Resin-Coated Gabardine Poplin	Adhesive Bonded Woven to Knit Flock-Faced Simulated Suede (double faced) Water-Repellent Solid Rubber Slicker Perforated Rubber Slicker

Hand is a subjective term that refers to the sensation of touch or feel of a fabric when the fabric is handled. Hand is also used to describe the body, texture and hang of the fabric. In order to react to the sense of touch and make a proper judgment, the fabric must be held in the hand and *felt*. The hand of fabrics provides a tactile sensation when the fabric is caressed, lofted, suspended, folded, bent, crushed, and released.

Fabric hand affects the flexibility, resiliency, and drapability qualities of a piece of fabric. There remains a subjective judgment on the feel of a piece of fabric and whether or not that fabric will work well in its intended purpose or use.

Factors affecting the hand of fabrics depend on:
- Content of fibers (natural or man-made)
- Type of fibers (staple or filament)
- Configuration of fibers (length, shape diameter, surface contours)
- Behavior of fibers (stiffness, bending qualities, flexibility, fineness)
- Arrangement of fibers in yarns or fabrics
- Size, ply, twist or texture of yarns
- Type of fabric structure
- Thread count and covering power in fabrics
- Type and method of finishing processes
- Type of color and surface-design applications

The hand of fabrics that refers to its flexibility, compressibility, resiliency, extensibility, surface contour and mass, surface friction, opacity, weight, and thermal-characteristics may be described as:
- Soft to crisp
- Limp to springy
- Pliable to firm
- Stretchy to inelastic
- Thin to bulky (thick)
- Loose to compact
- Delicate to coarse
- Smooth to rough (textured)
- Sheer to opaque
- Dull to lustrous
- Light- to heavyweight
- Cool to warm
- Dry to clammy

The following terms describe the touch, feel or hand of fabrics when being handled. These terms are arranged according to group/group-type sensations. The term *medium* can be applied to modify the areas between the extremes.

cottony/cotton-like	hard	fine	transparent thin
linen/linen-like	rigid	light	thick opaque
silky/silk-like	inelastic	heavy	bulky
woolly/wool-like	inflexible	thick	lofty
furry/fur-like	springy	gossamer	spongy
felt/felt-like	wiry	satiny smooth	open
leathery/leather-like	elastic	smooth	porous
rubbery/rubber-like	stretchy	coarse	loose
plastic/plastic-like	supple	sandy	firm
dull	pliable	harsh	compact
lustrous	clingy	scratchy	solid
limp	slippery	papery	cool
soft	flimsy	scroopy	dry
downy/velvety soft	sleazy	rough	warm
crisp	fragile	sheer	clammy
stiff	delicate	tissue thin	comfortable

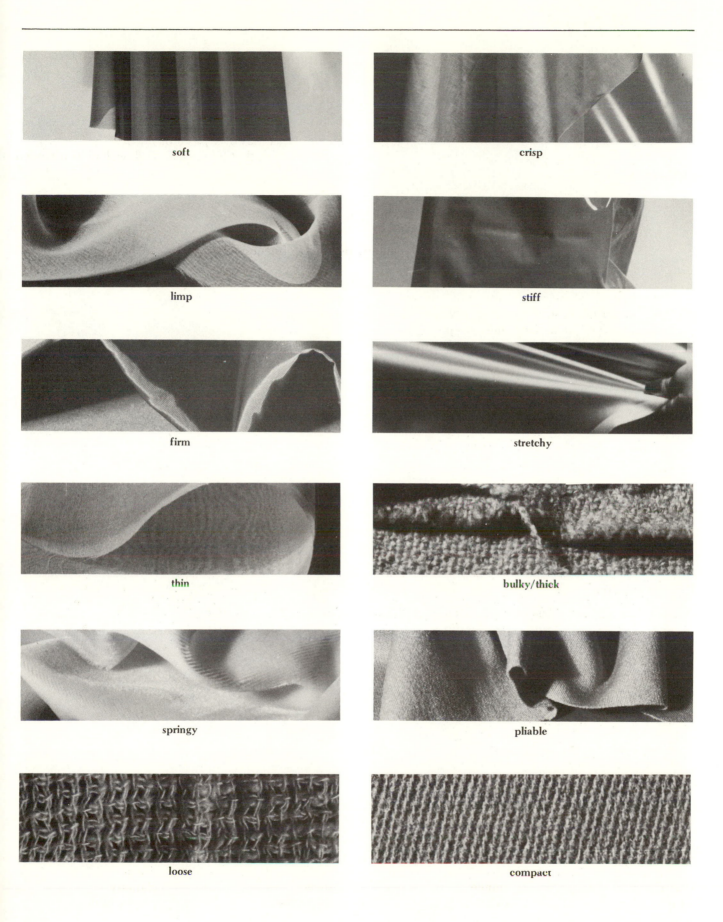

soft

crisp

limp

stiff

firm

stretchy

thin

bulky/thick

springy

pliable

loose

compact

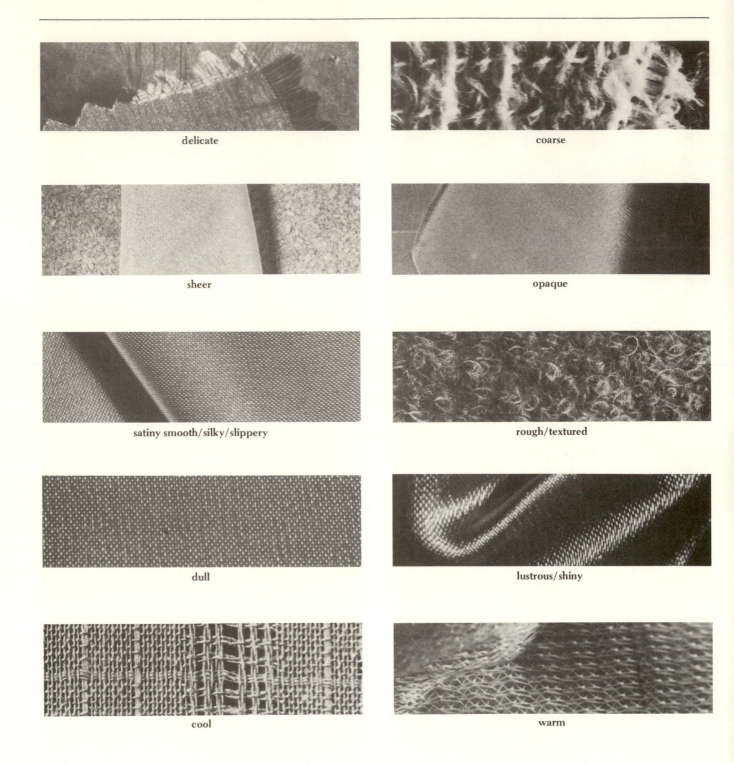

delicate

coarse

sheer

opaque

satiny smooth/silky/slippery

rough/textured

dull

lustrous/shiny

cool

warm

Cotton/Cotton-type Fabrics

Supple/Pliable	Soft/Medium Soft	Firm	Crisp/Hard/Harsh	Stiff/Rigid
Batiste	Batiste	Airplane/Byrd Cloth®	Beach Cloth	Bark Cloth
Challis	Bedford Cord	Bedford Cord	Bedford Cord	Canvas
Crepe	(sueded finish)	Bengaline	Bengaline	Chameleon/
Embroidered	Bouclé Yarn	Chambray	Brocade Coating	Iridescent
Fabrics	Broadcloth	Chambray Cord	Calcutta/Bangla-	Chino
Gauze	Cambric	Chino	desh Cloth	Organdy
Gauze Cloth Net	Challis	Dreponne	Chintz	
Hopsacking	Chambray	Damask	Covert	
Lawn	Chameleon/	Denim	Crash	
Leno Weave	Iridescent	Dobby Weave	Cretonne	
(lightweight)	Clokay/Embossed	Drill Cloth	Damask	
Monk's Cloth	Crepe	Double Cloth	Denim	
Swivel Weave	Creponne	Jacquard Weave	Dimity	
(lightweight)	Damask	Leno Weave	Dimity with Cord	
Voile	Dimity	(heavyweight)	Dotted Swiss	
Voile with Cord	Dimity with Cord	Muslin	Duck	
	Flocked Dotted	Percale	Embroidered Fabric	
	Swiss	Piqué	Eyelet	
	Novelty Cottons	Poplin	Gabardine	
	Dobby Weave	Printcloth	Gingham	
	Double Cloth	Sheeting	Jacquard Weave	
	Double Cloth	Spot/Clip Weave	Jean Cloth	
	Embroidered	(heavyweight)	Khaki	
	End & End	Twill Weave	Leno Weave	
	Topweight	Whipcord	(lightweight)	
	Bottomweight		Lawn	
	Eyelet		Glazed-faced	
	Flannel		Muslin	
	Dommet/Outing		Percale	
	Gauze Cloth Net		Piqué	
	Gingham		Plisse	
	Homespun		Poplin	
	Hopsacking		Printcloth	
	Jacquard Weave		Ratiné	
	Lawn		Sailcloth	
	Leno Weave		Skip Denting	
	Madras		Seersucker	
	Monk's Cloth		Sheeting	
	Muslin		Spot Weave	
	Osnaburg		Swivel Weave	
	Oxford		Ticking	
	Piqué		Tricotine	
	Percale		White-on-White	
	Polished Cotton			
	Pongee			
	Poplin			
	Printcloth			
	Sateen			
	Sheeting			
	Skip Denting			
	Spot Weave			
	Suede Cloth			
	Swivel Weave			
	Tattersall			
	Voile			
	Voile with Cord			
	Crinkled Voile			
	White-on-White			

Linen/Linen-type Fabrics

Supple/Pliable	Soft/Medium Soft	Firm	Crisp/Hard/Harsh	Stiff/Rigid

—	Butcher Linen
	Cambric Linen
	Crash Linen
	Dobby Linen
	Dress Linen
	Novelty Dress
	  Linen Weaves
	Handkerchief Linen
	Handkerchief Linen
	  with Cord
	Linen Suiting
	  (lightweight)
		Art Linen
		Butcher Linen
		Dobby Linen
		Jacquard Linen
		Linen Suiting
			Art Linen
			Bisso Linen
			Cambric Linen
			Crash Linen
			Dobby Linen
			Dress Linen
			Novelty Dress
			  Linen Weaves
			Handkerchief Linen
			Handkerchief Linen
			  with Cord
			Homespun Linen
			Jacquard Weave
			Linen Suiting
				—

Burlap/Burlap-type Fabrics

—	Man-Made Fiber	Man-Made Fiber Natural Fiber	Man-Made Fiber Natural Fiber	Natural Fiber

Silk/Silk-type Fabrics

Chiffon
China Silk
Faille Tissue
Georgette
  Double
  Triple
  Open Weave
  Shantung
	Barathea
	Bengaline
	Broadcloth
	Charvet
	Damask
	Habutai
	Honan/Pongee
	Silk Pongee Dobby
	Homespun
	Hopsacking
	Marquisette
	Mull
	Ottoman
	Radium Silk
	Serge
	Surah
	Tussah
		Barathea Suiting
		Brocade
		Moiré Faille
		Matelassé
		Ottoman
		Rep
		Surah Suiting
			Canvas
			Gazar
			Marquisette
			Mousseline de Soie/
			  Silk Gauze
			Ninon
			Organza
			Organza with
			  Embroidery
			Peau de Soie
			Shantung Faille
			Shantung (crisp
			  finish)
				Ottoman Suiting
				Poplin
				Rep
				Sharkskin
				Silk Suiting

Crepe/Crepe-type Fabrics

Chiffon
Crepe Georgette
	Canton Crepe
	Crepe-backed/
	  Satin-backed
	Crepe de Chine
	  Dobby
	Crepon/Crinkle
	  Crepe
	Lingerie Crepe/
	  Crepe Set®
	Matelassé Crepe
	Meteor Crepe/
	  Satin-faced Chiffon
		—	Albatross Crepe
			Bark Crepe
			Crepe Faille
			Pebbly/Mossy Crepe
				—

Satin/Satin-type Fabrics

Supple/Pliable	Soft/Medium Soft	Firm	Crisp/Hard/Harsh	Stiff/Rigid

Charmeuse
Charmeuse Dobby
	Bridal Satin
	Brocade
	Charmeuse
	Charmeuse Dobby
	Ciré Satin
	Creped Satin
	Hammered Satin
	Jacquard Satin
	Messaline Satin
	Thermo/Nap-backed
	  Satin
		Bridal Satin
		Crepe Satin/
		  Satin Crepe
			Antique Satin
			Thermo/Coated
			  Satin
				Bridal Satin
				Duchesse Satin

Taffeta/Taffeta-type Fabrics

—	Tissue Taffeta	—	Antique Taffeta Faille Taffeta Jacquard Taffeta Moiré Taffeta Warp-dyed/Warp- printed Taffeta	Paper Taffeta

Wool/Wool-type Fabrics

Supple/Pliable	Soft/Medium Soft	Firm	Crisp/Hard/Harsh	Lofty

Albatross Wool
Wool Crepe
Double Cloth
  Gauze-type
Sheers
  Batiste
  Challis
  Voile
Fancies
  Gauze
  Waffle Cloth
Wool Knit
  Jersey Wool
	Baize
	Broadcloth
	Doeskin
	Double Cloth
	Duvetyn
	Etamine
	Wool Flannel
	Kasha Cloth
	Suede Cloth
	Tweeds
	  Bird's Eye
	  Wool Herring-
	    bone
		Bedford Cord
		Bengaline
		Cassimere
		Cheviot
		Cloque
		Covert Suiting
		Wool Flannel
		Worsted Flannel
		Gabardine
		  (summerweight)
		Homespun Coating
		Iridescent
		  (plain weave)
		Mackinaw Cloth/
		  Buffalo Plaid
		Sheers
		  Challis
		Tartan Plaids
		  Clan Plaids
		  Glen Plaid
		  Hound's-tooth
		    Check
		Tricotine
		Tweeds
		  Birds's Eye
		  Donegal
		  Heather
		  Worsted Herring-
		    bone
		  Oatmeal
		  Salt & Pepper
		Fancies
		  Reverse Twill
		Tropical Worsted
		Unfinished Worsted
			French-Back
			Double Cloth
			Iridescent
			  (twill weave)
			Whipcord
			  Wool Knit
			  Double Knit
				Astrakhan/Poodle
				  Cloth
				Bolivia
				Covert Coating
				Double-faced
				  Cloth
				Blanket Cloth/
				  Plaid Back
				Eiderdown
				Fleece
				Gabardine Coating
				Homespun
				Homespun Coating
				Jersey
				Loden Cloth
				Melton
				Ottoman
				Polo Cloth
				Ratiné/Epongé
				Tweeds
				  Heavy-Textured

Specialty Hair/Specialty Hair Blended Fiber Fabrics

Mohair
  100% Fiber
  Blended Fiber
  Gauze
  Napped-Faced
Alpaca
  100% Fiber
  Lightweight
	Camel's Hair
	  100% Fiber
	  Blended Fiber
	Cashmere
	  100% Fiber
	  Blended Fiber
	Mohair
	  100% Fiber
	  Blended Fiber
	  Single-faced
	    Napped
	  Double-faced
	    Napped
	Rabbit Hair
	  Blended Fiber
	  Suiting
	  Coating
		Mohair
		  Blended Fiber
		  Clear Finish
			—	Alpaca
				  100% Fiber
				  Blended Fiber
				Alpaca Coating
				  100% Fiber
				  Blended Fiber
				Cashmere
				  100% Fiber
				Mohair
				  100% Fiber
				  Blended Fiber
				  Single-faced
				    Napped
				  Double-faced
				    Napped
				Mohair Coating/
				  Zebaline®

Felt/Felt-type Fabrics

Supple/Pliable	Soft/Medium Soft	Firm	Crisp/Hard/Harsh	Lofty

—	Medium Weight
	Medium-Light-
	  weight
		—	Heavyweight
			Medium-Heavy-
			  weight
				—

Knit/Knit-type Fabrics

Interlock Knit
  Fine Weight
Jersey Knit
  Fine Weight
  Lightweight
  Open Weave
    Effect
Tricot Knit
  Sheer
  Printed
	Double-faced
	  Knit
	Double Knit
	  Interlock
	Jacquard Knit
	  Flat
	  Jersey
	  Nap-faced,
	    Bird's Eye
	    Backed
	Jersey Knit
	  Striped
	  Tweed Effect
	  LaCoste®
	Milanese Knit
	Purl Knit
	Rib Knit
	  1 x 1
	  2 x 2
		Double Knit
		Tricot Knit
		  Heavyweight
		  Suiting
			Raschel Knit
			  Lace Effect
			Tricot Knit
			  Sheer
			  Heat-Set Resin
			  Stiff/Crisp
			    Finish
			  Lightweight
			  Patterned
			Transfer Stitch
			Intarsia
			Sweater Knit
			Laid-in Yarn
				Interlock Knit
				Jacquard Knit
				  Single-
				    Blistered
				  Jersey
				  Rib
				  Smooth-faced,
				    Bird's Eye
				    Backed
				Jersey Knit
				  Novelty Yarn
				    Effects
				  Pleated Effect
				Raschel Knit
				  Crochet Effect
				  Dishcloth
				    Effect
				  Loop Fringe
				  Double Cloth
				    Effect
				  Tweed Effect
				Rib Knit
				  2 x 2
				  4 x 4
				  Piqué Effect
				  Thermo Knit
				Tuck Stitch/
				  Popcorn Effect
				Cable Stitch
				Intarsia
				Laid-in Yarn
				Dropped Stitch
				Transfer Stitch
				Sweater Knit

Pile Surface/Pile-type Fabrics

Supple/Pliable	Soft/Medium Soft	Firm	Crisp/Hard/Harsh	Lofty/Bulky

Terry Cloth
  Velour
Velvet
  Cut
  Panne
Velour
	Corduroy
	  Feathercord
	  Fine Wale
	  Mid Wale
	  Thick-set
	Fleece
	  Nap-faced
	  Baby Bunting
	Friezé
	Plush
	Terry Cloth
	  Sculptured
	  Chenille
	  Single-faced
	Velvet
	  Cotton
	  Crushed (woven
	  ground)
	  Crushed (knit
	  ground)
	  Embossed
	  Transparent
	Simulated Fur
	  Astrakhan/
	    Persian Lamb
	  Rabbit
	  Shag
	  Sherpa/Sheared
	    Lamb
		Corduroy
		  Feathercord
		  Fine Wale
		  Mid Wale
		  Thick-set
		  Wide Wale
		  Broad Wale
		  Novelty Wale
		Velvet Cord
		Velveteen
			Terry Cloth
			  Single-faced
			  Double-faced
			Simulated Fur
			  Giraffe
			  Leopard
			  Ocelot
			  Pony
			  Sheared Seal
			Tiger
			Zebra
				Corduroy
				  Wide Wale
				  Broad Wale
				  Novelty Wale
				Terry Cloth
				  Double-faced
				  Stretch
				Tufted Cloth
				  Chenille
				    Candlewick
				  Chenille
				    Velvet/Velveteen
				  Chenille Yarn
				Simulated Fur
				  Beaver
				  Broadtail Lamb
				  Chinchilla
				  Ermine
				  Fox
				  Lynx
				  Mink
				  Muskrat
				  Opossum
				  Poodle Cloth
				  Raccoon
				  Sherpa
				  Skunk
				  Squirrel
				  Teddy Bear

Lace/Lace-type Fabrics

Embroidered-type				

Embroidered-type	Binche-type
	Blonde-type
	Brussels-type
	Cluny-type
	Crochet-type
	Embroidered-type
	Filet
	  Crochet-type
	Honiton-type
	Nottingham-type
	Pt de France-type
	Pt de Venice-type
	Rosepoint-type
	  Large Motif
	  Small Motif
	Shadow-type
	Val Lace/Val-type
		Chantilly-type
		  Re-embroidered
		Cluny-type
		Filet
		  Crochet-type
		  Darned-Work-
		    type
		Pt d'Esprit
		Pt Plat de
		  Venice-type
		Tatting/Tatted Work
		Val Lace/Val-type
			Chantilly-type
			Crochet Lace
			Cut Work
			Duchesse-type
			Embroidered-type
			Filet
			  Crochet-type
			  Darned-Work-type
			Pt d'Angleterre-type
			Tatting/Tatted Work
			Val/Val-type
				Macrame
				Pt de Venice/
				  Gros Pt de
				  Venice

Net/Net-type Fabrics

Supple/Pliable	Soft/Medium Soft	Firm	Crisp/Hard/Harsh	Lofty/Bulky

Cable/Laundry Net
Fishnet
    Fine Hole
    Small Hole
    Medium Hole
    Large Hole
	Cable/Laundry Net
	Fishnet
	    Fine Hole
	    Small Hole
	    Medium Hole
	    Large Hole
	    Tulle/Illusion
	    Veiling
		Cable/Laundry Net	Cable/Laundry Net
			Fishnet
			    Fine Hole
			    Small Hole
			    Medium Hole
			    Large Hole
			Maline Net
			Net/Netting
			Pt d'Esprit Net
			Pt d'Esprit Tulle
			Tulle
			Tulle/Illusion
			    Veiling
				Cable/Laundry Net
				Fishnet
				    Large Hole

Stretch/Stretch-type Fabrics

Supple/Pliable	Soft/Medium Soft	Crisp/Hard/Harsh	Lofty/Spongy

Fiber Stretch
    Lycra® (180–220%)
Yarn & Fabric
    Structure Stretch
    Double Knit
    Stretch Lace
	Fiber Stretch
	    Lycra® (140–175%)
	Yarn Stretch
	    Satin
	Yarn & Fabric Structure
	    Stretch Crimped Cloth
		Yarn Stretch
		    Canvas
		    Chino
		    Denim
		    Gabardine
		    Poplin
		    Twill
		    Whipcord
		Yarn & Fabric
		    Structure Stretch
		        Crinkled Double
		        Cloth
			Yarn & Fabric
			    Structure
			    Double knit
			        (medium weight)
			        (heavyweight)
			    Stretch Terry Cloth

Metallic/Metallic-type Fabrics

Supple/Pliable	Soft/Medium Soft	Firm	Crisp/Hard/Harsh	Lofty/Spongy

Jacquard Weave
  Metallic Yarn
Weft-Inserted
  Jersey Knit
  Metallic Yarn
Lamé Jersey
Lamé Gauze
Pile Metallic
Sparkle or Glitter Adhesive-Bonded to Crepe
	Ciré Coated
	Laid-in Tricot
	  Knit Metallic
	  Yarn
	Metallic Net
	Sparkle or
	  Glitter Printed
	  Design
		Metallic Net	Organza with
			  Metallic Embroidery
			Lace with Metallic
			  Yarn
			Pt d'Esprit Lace
			Metallic Net
			Sparkle or Glitter
			  Adhesive Bonded to
			  Organza
				—

Multicomponent/Coated/Layered Fabrics

Medium Soft	Firm	Crisp/Hard/Harsh	Lofty/Spongy

Film-Faced Bonded
  Simulated Leather
    (lightweight)
    (medium weight)
Flock-Faced Bonded
  Simulated Suede
    (nap-faced)
    (patterned face)
    (crushed face)
    (double-faced)
Water-Repellent Resin-Coated
  Muslin Sheeting
	Film-Faced Bonded
	  Simulated Leather
	    (lightweight)
	    (medium weight)
	    (textured)
	Flock-Faced
	  Simulated Suede
	    (nap-faced)
	    (crushed face)
	  Simulated Leather
	    (patterned face)
	    (double-faced)
	Water-Repellent
	  Resin Coated
	    Muslin Sheeting
	Quilted
	  Chemstitch®
		Water-Repellent Film-Faced
		  Solid Rubber Slicker
		  Perforated Rubber
		  Slicker
		Vinyl Fabric-Backed
		  Clear Vinyl
		Water-Repellent
		Resin-Coated
		  Duck
		  Gabardine
		  Poplin
		  Rip-Stop Nylon
		  Taffeta
			Adhesive Bonded
			  Woven to Knit
			Laminated Bonded
			  Knit to Knit
			Quilted
			  Double-faced
			  Gauze-backed
			  Knit-backed

10 ~ Texture

Texture is a term that refers to the surface differences of fabrics including tactile and visual qualities. Texture of fabric includes variations in feel from:

- Fine to coarse
- Smooth to raised
- Flat to sculptured
- Loose to compact
- Silky to grainy

Factors affecting the texture of fabrics depend on:

- Content of fibers (natural or man-made)
- Spinning processes
- Size, ply and count of yarns
- Type and construction of yarns
- Order of interlacing yarns
- Type and method of fabric structure
- Density of fabric structure
- Type and method of finishing processes
- Type of color and surface-design applications

Varying one or more of the components will change the texture of a fabric.

The following terms describe the texture of fabric when being handled. These terms are arranged according to group/group-type sensations. The term *medium* can be applied to modify the areas between the extremes. Some fabrics may fall into one or more categorized definitions used to define the texture of a fabric.

silky	frizzy
velvety	fuzzy
woolly	fluffy
furry	loopy
hairy	nubby
leathery	slubbed
piled	flecked
napped	seed
sueded	noil
felted	crinkly
tweedy	pebbly
crepey	firm
smooth	compact
satiny smooth	loose
slippery smooth	open
rough	flat
coarse	even
harsh	raised
scratchy	ridged/ridges
grainy	high and low
papery	corded
boardy	sculptured

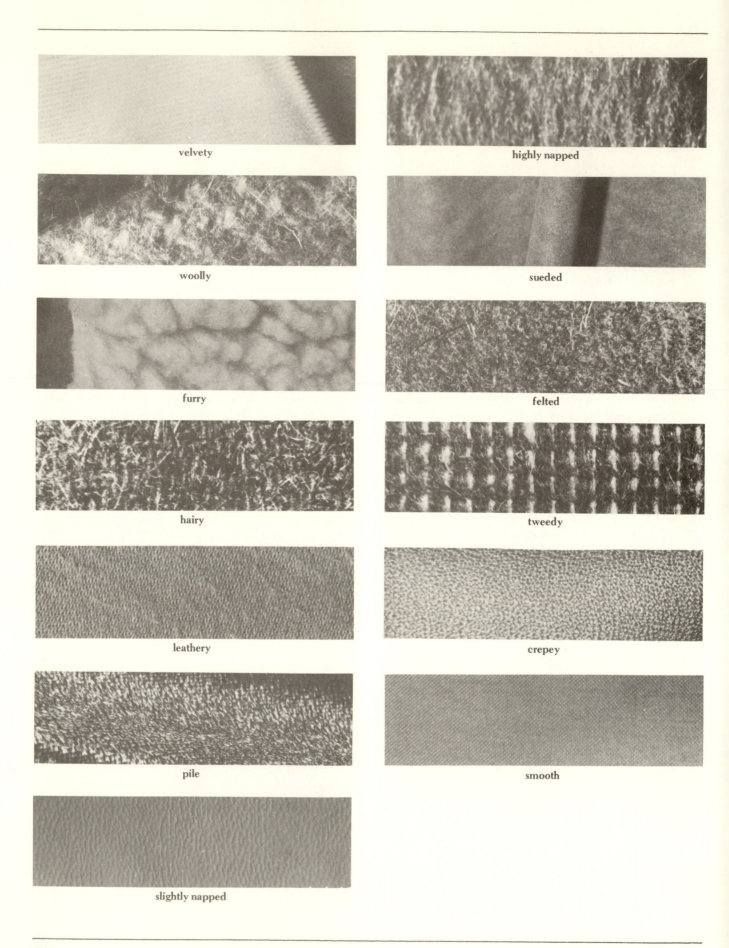

velvety

highly napped

woolly

sueded

furry

felted

hairy

tweedy

leathery

crepey

pile

smooth

slightly napped

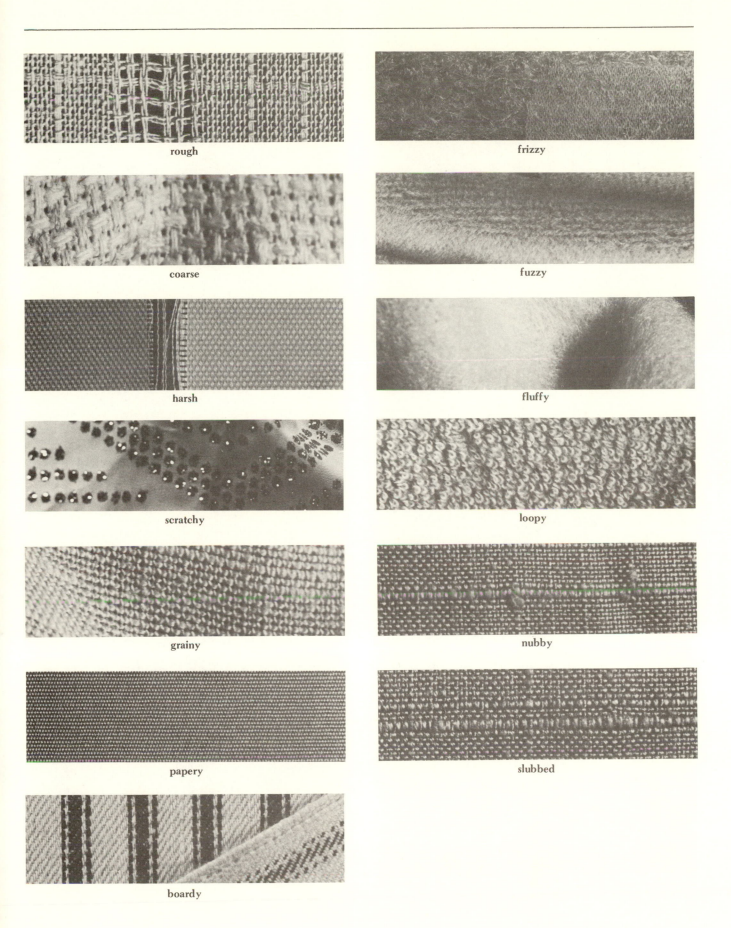

rough

frizzy

coarse

fuzzy

harsh

fluffy

scratchy

loopy

grainy

nubby

papery

slubbed

boardy

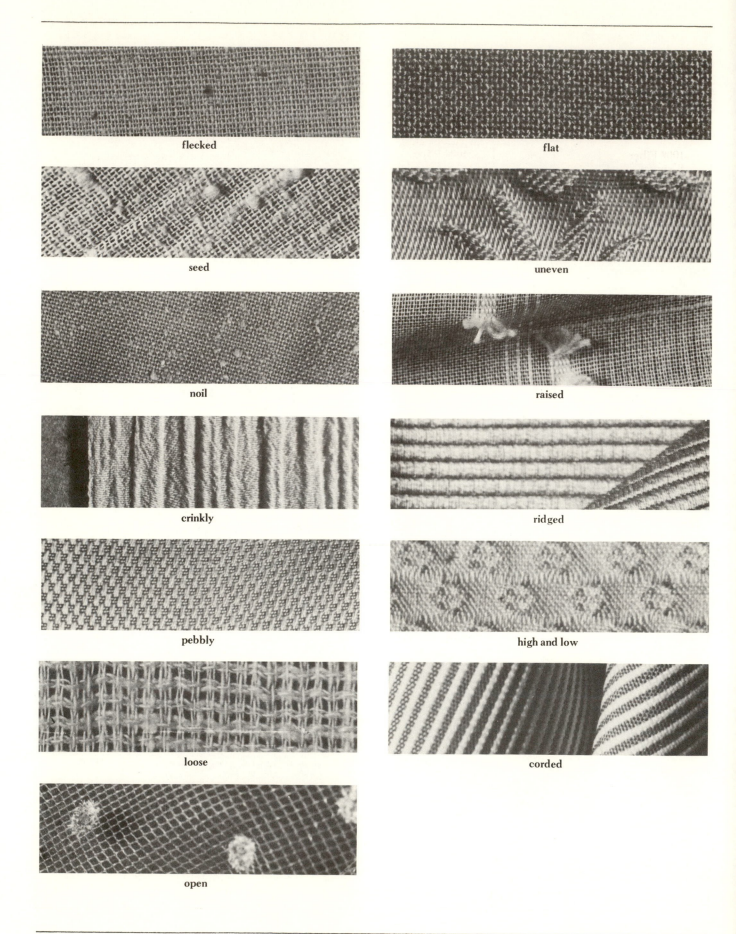

flecked

flat

seed

uneven

noil

raised

crinkly

ridged

pebbly

high and low

loose

corded

open

Specialty Hair/Specialty Hair Blended Fiber Fabrics

Flat	Napped/Sueded/Brushed	Relief/Raised/High & Low Sculptured Effects
Alpaca 100% Fiber Blended Fiber Mohair Clear Finish Blended Fiber	Alpaca Coating 100% Fiber Blended Fiber Camel's Hair 100% Fiber Blended Fiber Suiting Coating Cashmere 100% Fiber Blended Fiber Suiting Coating Mohair/Mohair Coating 100% Fiber Blended Fiber Single-faced Double-faced Rabbit Hair Blended Fiber Suiting Coating	Mohair Loop-faced

Felt/Felt-type Fabrics

	Napped/Sueded/Brushed	
—	100% Wool Fiber Blended Fiber Lightweight Medium-Lightweight Medium Weight Medium-Heavyweight Heavyweight	—

Metallic/Metallic-type Fabrics

Smooth/Flat	Coarse/Rough/Grainy	Relief/Raised/High & Low Sculptured Effects	Open Mesh

Ciré Metallic-Coated
Woven Lamé
	Jacquard Weave Metallic
	  Yarn
	Knit
	  Jersey with Weft-Inserted
	  Metallic Yarn
	Tricot with Metallic Laid-in
	  Yarn
	Lamé Gauze
	Lamé Jersey
		Organza with Metallic
		  Embroidery
		Sparkle or Glitter Adhesive
		  Bonded to Organza
		  or Crepe
		Sparkle or Glitter Metallic-
		  printed Design
			Lace
			  Metallic Chantilly Lace
			  Metallic Pt d'Esprit Lace
			Metallic Net

Net/Netting/Net-type Fabrics

Fine Open Mesh	Small Open Mesh	Medium Open Mesh	Large Open Mesh
Fishnet Maline Net Pt d'Esprit Net Pt d'Esprit Tulle	Fishnet Maline Net Net Pt d'Esprit Net Pt d'Esprit Tulle Tulle Tulle/Illusion Veiling	Cable/Laundry Net Fishnet Maline Net Net	Cable/Laundry Net Fishnet Maline Net

Simulated Fur Pile Fabrics

High Pile	Relief/Raised/High & Low Sculptured Effects	Cut Pile	Uncut Pile
Beaver Chinchilla Ermine Fox Lynx Mink Muskrat Opossum Rabbit Raccoon Shag Sherpa Skunk Squirrel Teddy Bear	Astrakhan/Poodle Cloth Broadtail Sherpa	Astrakhan Beaver Chinchilla Ermine Fox Giraffe Leopard Lynx Mink Muskrat Ocelot Opossum Pony Rabbit Raccoon Seal Shag Sherpa Skunk Squirrel Teddy Bear Tiger Zebra	Poodle Cloth

Multicomponent/Coated/Layered Fabrics

Smooth/Flat	Coarse/Rough/Grainy	Napped/Sueded	Relief/Raised/High & Low Sculptured Effects

Film-faced Bonded
  Simulated Leather
    (lightweight)
    (heavyweight)
Water-Repellent Film-
  Faced Bonded
  Solid Rubber Slicker
  Perforated Rubber
    Slicker
Water-Repellent Resin-
  Coated
  Muslin Sheeting
  Rip-Stop Nylon
  Taffeta
Vinyl Film to Clear Vinyl
  Backing
	Adhesive Bonded
	  Woven to Knit
	Laminated Bonded
	  Simulated Leather
	Film-Faced Bonded
	  Simulated Leather
	    (textured face)
	Water-Repellent Resin-
	  Coated
	  Duck
	  Gabardine
	  Poplin
		Simulated Suede Flock-
		  Faced
		  Patterned Face
		  Knit to Knit
		  Crushed Face
		Double-faced
			Water-Repellent Film-
			  Faced Bonded
			  Perforated Rubber Slicker
			Quilted
			  Double-faced
			  Gauze-backed
			  Knit-backed
			  Chemstitch®

Stretch/Stretch-type Fabrics

Slippery/Smooth	Flat	Coarse/Rough/Grainy	Relief/Raised/High & Low Sculptured Effects

Fiber Stretch
  Lycra® (180–220%)
  Lycra® (141–175%)
  Lycra® (110–140%)
Yarn Stretch
  Satin
	Yarn Stretch
	  Twill
	Yarn & Fabric Structure
	  Stretch
	  Lightweight Double Knit
	  Medium Weight
	    Double Knit
	  Heavyweight Double Knit
		Yarn Stretch
		  Canvas
		  Chino
		  Denim
		  Gabardine
		  Whipcord
		  Poplin
		  Whipcord
			Yarn & Fabric Structure
			  Stretch
			  Stretch Terry Cloth
			  Stretch Lace
			Stretch Finish
			  Crimped Cloth
			  Crinkled Double Cloth

Cotton/Cotton-type Fabrics

Smooth	Flat	Coarse/Rough/Grainy	Napped/Sueded	Relief/Raised/High & Low Sculptured Effects

Batiste
Broadcloth
Cambric
Challis
Chintz
Glazed-faced Lawn
Organdy
Percale
Polished Cotton
	Airplane/Byrd Cloth®
	Chambray
	Chameleon/
	  Iridescent
	End & End Cloth
	  Topweight
	  Bottomweight
	Gauze
	Gingham
	Lawn
	Madras
	Muslin
	Oxford
	Poplin (lightweight)
	Sailcloth
	Sateen
	Sheeting
	Tattersall
	Voile
		Bark Cloth
		Beach Cloth
		Bouclé Yarn Fabric
		Calcutta/Bangladesh
		  Cloth
		Canvas
		Chino
		Covert
		Crash
		Crepe
		Creponne
		Denim
		Drill Cloth
		Duck
		Gabardine
		Gauze
		Homespun
		Hopsacking
		Jean Cloth
		Khaki Cloth
		Leno Weave
		Monk's Cloth
		Osnaburg
		Pongee
		Poplin
		  Medium Weight
		  Heavyweight
		Ratiné
		Skip Denting/Open
		  Effect
		Ticking
		Tricotine
		Twill Weave
		Whipcord
		White-on-White
			Bedford Cord (sueded
			  finish)
			Denim (brushed-faced)
			Flannel/Flannelette
			Outing/Dommet
			  Flannel
			Suede Cloth
				Bedford Cord
				  (sueded finish)
				Bengaline
				Bouclé Yarn Fabric
				Brocade
				Corded Chambray
				Clokay/Embossed
				Creponne
				Damask
				Dimity
				Dimity Stripe
				Dobby Weave
				Dotted Swiss
				Dotted Swiss
				  (Flocked)
				Double Cloth Effect
				Embroidered
				  Fabrics
				Eyelet
				Jacquard Weave
				Leno Weave
				Monk's Cloth
				Plissé
				Skip Denting
				Seersucker
				Spot Weave/
				  Clip Spot Cut
				  Uncut
				Voile
				Crinkled Voile
				White-on-White

Linen/Linen-type Fabrics

Art Linen
Bisso Linen
Cambric Linen
Handkerchief Linen
	Cambric Linen	Butcher Linen
		Crash Linen
		Dress Linen
		Homespun
		Linen Suiting
			—	Dobby Linen
				Dress Linen
				  Novelty Effects
				  Open Effects
				Handkerchief Linen
				Handkerchief Linen
				  with Cord

Felt/Felt-Type Fabrics

Smooth	Flat	Coarse/Rough/Grainy	Napped/Sueded	Relief/Raised/High & Low Sculptured Effects
—	—	Natural Fiber Man-Made Fiber	—	—

Wool/Wool-type Fabrics

Smooth	Flat	Coarse/Rough/Grainy	Napped/Sueded/Brushed	Relief/Raised/High & Low Sculptured Effects

Tropical Worsted	Baize
	Broadcloth
	Cassimere
	Cheviot
	Double Cloth
	  Double-faced
	  French Back
	Étamine
	Gabardine (summer
	  weight)
	Iridescent
	Kasha Cloth
	Poplin
	Serge
	Sharkskin
	Sheers
	  Batiste
	  Challis
	  Voile
	Tartan Plaids
	  Clan Plaids
	  Glen Plaid
	  Hound's-tooth
	    Check
	Tweeds
	  Worsted
	    Herringbone
	Fancies
	  Reverse Twill
	    Weave
	Knits
	  Double
	  Jersey
	Unfinished Worsted
		Albatross Wool
		Crepe Wool
		Eiderdown
		Étamine
		Gabardine
		Homespun
		Homespun Suiting
		Iridescent
		Ratiné
		Tricotine/Cavalry
		  Twill
		Tweeds
		  Bird's Eye
		  Donegal-type
		  Heather
		  Heavy-textured
		  Oatmeal
		  Salt & Pepper
		Whipcord
		Fancies
		  Gauze
		  Reverse Twill
		    Weave
			Astrakhan/Poodle Cloth
			Bolivia
			Broadcloth
			Doeskin
			Double Cloth
			  Double-faced
			Duvetyn
			Flannel
			  Wool
			  Worsted
			  French
			Fleece
			Gabardine Coating
			Jersey
			Loden Cloth
			Mackinaw Cloth/
			  Buffalo Plaid
			Melton
			Polo Cloth
			Serge (napped-faced)
			Suede Cloth
			Tweed
			  Wool Herringbone
				Bedford Cord
				Bengaline
				Cloqué
				Covert Suiting
				Covert Coating
				Double Cloth
				  Double-faced
				  Blanket Cloth/
				    Plaid Back
				Ottoman
				Ratiné
				  Plain Weave
				  Twill Weave
				Tweeds
				  Heavy-textured
				Fancies
				  Waffle Cloth

Silk/Silk-type Fabrics

Smooth	Flat	Coarse/Rough/Grainy	Slubbed	Ribbed (Cross- or Lengthwise)	Relief/Raised/High & Low Sculptured Effects
Chiffon China Silk Triple Georgette Peau de Soie	Broadcloth Gazar Double Georgette Honan/Pongee Honan/Pongee Dobby Marquisette Mull Ninon Organza Radium Silk	Canvas Charvet Homespun Hopsacking Serge Sharkskin Silk Suiting	Habutai Honan/Pongee Shantung Shantung Faille Shantung Georgette Tussah/Wild Silk	Barathea Barathea Suiting Bengaline Faille Moiré Faille Tissue Faille Ottoman Ottoman Suiting Poplin Rep Surah Surah Suiting	Brocade Damask Open Weave Georgette Matelassé

Crepe/Crepe-type Fabrics

Smooth	Flat	Coarse/Rough/Grainy	Slubbed	Ribbed (Cross- or Lengthwise)	Relief/Raised/High & Low Sculptured Effects
Creped-backed Satin Crepe de Chine Dobby	Chiffon Crepe Flat Crepe Lingerie Crepe/Crepe Set® Meteor Crepe/Satin-faced Chiffon	Albatross Crepe Canton Crepe Crepe Georgette Pebbly/Mossy Crepe	—	Bark Crepe Crepe Faille Crepon/Crinkle Crepe	Matelassé

Taffeta/Taffeta-type Fabrics

Smooth	Flat	Coarse/Rough/Grainy	Slubbed	Ribbed (Cross- or Lengthwise)	Relief/Raised/High & Low Sculptured Effects
Paper Taffeta	Tissue Taffeta	—	Antique Taffeta	Faille Taffeta Moiré Tafetta Warp-dyed/Warp-printed Taffeta Yarn-dyed Taffeta	Jacquard Taffeta

Satin/Satin-type Fabrics

Smooth	Flat	Coarse/Rough/Grainy	Slubbed	Ribbed (Cross- or Lengthwise)	Relief/Raised/High & Low Sculptured Effects
Bridal Satin Crepe Satin/Satin Crepe Creped Satin Duchesse Satin Messaline Satin	Charmeuse Charmeuse Dobby Thermo-Coated Satin	—	Antique Satin	—	Brocade Hammered Satin Jacquard Satin Novelty Satin Fabrics Nap-backed Thermo Satin

Knit/Knit-type Fabrics

Smooth/Flat	Coarse/Rough/ Grainy	Napped/Sueded/ Brushed	Relief/Raised/High & Low Sculptured Effects	Open/Mesh Effect

Double Knit
Double-faced Knit
Interlock Knit
  Fine Weight
  Lightweight
  Medium Weight
  Heavyweight
Jacquard Knit
  Flat
Jersey Knit
  Sheer Weight
  Lightweight
  Striped
Milanese Knit
Tricot Knit
  Sheer Weight
  Lightweight
  Medium Weight
  Soft-Silk Finish
  Stiff Finish
  Polished
  Ciré
  Printed
Intarsia
Sweater Knit
	Jersey Knit
	  Tweed Effect
	  LaCoste®
	Purl Knit
	Raschel Knit
	  Tweed Effect
	Rib Knit Variation
	  Piqué
	Tricot Knit
	  Heavyweight
	Intarsia
	Sweater Knit
	Laid-in Seed Yarn
		Jacquard Knit
		  Nap-faced/
		  Bird'seye Back
		Bouclé Yarn
		Laid-in Yarn
			Jacquard Knit
			  Single Blistered
			  Jersey
			  Rib
			  Bird'seye Back
			Jersey Knit Variation
			  Pleated Effect
			Raschel Knit
			  Loop Fringe
			  Double Cloth
			Rib Knit
			  1 x 1
			  2 x 2
			  3 x 3
			  4 x 4
			Tricot Knit
			  Patterned
			Tuck Stitch
			  Tuck Stitch/Popcorn
			  Effect
			Cable Stitch
			Sweater Knit
			Laid-in Loop Yarn
				Jacquard Knit
				  Jersey
				Jersey Knit
				  Novelty Yarn
				  Open Effect
				Raschel Knit
				  Crochet Effect
				  Dishcloth Effect
				  Lace Effect
				  Tweed Effect
				Rib Knit Variation
				  Open Effect
				Tricot Knit
				  Sheer Weight
				  Patterned
				Dropped/Missed
				  Stitch
				Transfer Stitch
				Cable Stitch
				Intarsia
				Sweater Knit

Lace/Lace-type Fabrics

Flat Ground/ Flat Design	Flat Ground/ Raised Design	Flat Ground/ Raised Cut Work	Raised Fine-Cord Outlined Design	Sculptured/Relief Heavy-Cord Outlined Design

Binche-type
Blonde-type
Chantilly
Crochet
Filet
  Crochet-type
  Darned Work
Pt Plat de Venice
Rosepoint-type
  Small Motif
Val Lace/Val-type
	Brussels-type
	Cluny-type
	Crochet
	Duchesse-type
	Embroidered
	Honiton-type
	Nottingham-type
	Pt d'Angleterre-type
	Pt d'Esprit
	Pt de France-type
	Pt Plat de Venice
	Shadow Lace
	Val Lace/Val-type
		Cut Work
		  Eyelet
		  Eyelet-type
		  Burnt-out-type
		Needlepoint-type
		Pt Plat de Venice
			Alençon-type
			Crochet
			Rosepoint-type
			  Large Motif
				Chantilly
				  Re-embroidered
				Crochet
				Macramé
				Pt d'Esprit
				Pt de Venice
				Tatted Lace/Tatting
				Venice Lace/Gros Pt
				  de Venice

Pile Surface/Pile-type Fabrics

Napped/Sueded/Brushed	Flat Pile	High Pile	Relief/Raised/High & Low Sculptured Effects	Ribbed	Cut Pile	Uncut Pile
Fleece Nap-faced Baby Bunting Sweatshirt Tufted Cloth Chenille Velvet Flocked Velvet	Friezé Terry Velour Velvet Crushed Cut Panne Velour	Corduroy Thick-set Wide Wale Broad Wale Novelty Wale Tufted Cloth Chenille Candlewick Chenille Velvet Velvet Cotton Lyons Transparent Velveteen	Terry Cloth Sculptured Chenille Single-faced Double-faced Jacquard Tufted Cloth Chenille Yarn Velvet Brocade Crushed Cut Embossed	Corduroy Feathercord Fine Wale Mid Wale Thick-set Wide Wale Broad Wale Novelty Wale Tufted Cloth Chenille Candlewick Velvet Cord	Corduroy Feathercord Fine Wale Mid Wale Thick-set Wide Wale Broad Wale Novelty Wale Friezé Tufted Cloth Chenille Candlewick Velvet Brocade Cotton Crushed (woven ground) Crushed (knit ground) Cut Embossed Lyons Panne Transparent Velvet Cord Velveteen	Terry Cloth Sculptured Chenille Single-faced Double-faced Stretch Velour Jacquard Tufted Cloth Chenille Yarn

Luster is a term that refers to the light-reflecting qualities of a fabric which are produced by the reflection of light from a smooth surface. Luster also refers to the highlights and shadows on the surface of a fabric produced when light reflects a *relief*. Differences in the light-reflecting qualities result from the manner in which light diffuses from the surface of the fabric.

Luster of fabric includes variations in the light-reflecting qualities from:
- Dull to lustrous
- Matte to shiny
- Diffused to glowing
- Flat to textured
- Solid colored to pattern design

Factors affecting the luster or light-reflecting qualities of a fabric depend on:
- Content of fibers (natural or man-made)
- Shape and contour of fibers
- Spinning processes
- Size, ply and count of yarns
- Type and construction of yarns
- Covering power of yarns
- Order of interlacing yarns
- Type and method of fabric structure
- Density of fabric structure
- Type and method of finishing processes
- Type of color and surface-design applications

Varying one or more of the components will change the luster or light-reflecting qualities of a fabric.

The following terms describe the luster or light-reflecting qualities of fabrics. These terms are arranged according to group/group-type qualities. The term *medium* can be applied to modify the areas between the extremes. Some fabrics may fall into one or more categorized definitions used to define the luster of a fabric.

silky	matte	glittery
satiny	mellow	diffused
shiny	patina	shimmer
sheen	frosty	flicker
rich highlights	milky	moiréd
lustrous	muddy	texture
glossy	greyed	brocaded
brightness	natural	pile
brilliant	contrived	napped
gleaming	synthetic-looking	high and low
flashy	plastic	cords—ridges
lively	waxy	raised highlights
subdued	luminous	crushed effect
pleasingly dull	fluorescent	any combination of
dull	iridescent	dull and shiny
flat	sparkles	any combination of
dead-looking	flashy	light and dark
monotonous	glimmering	

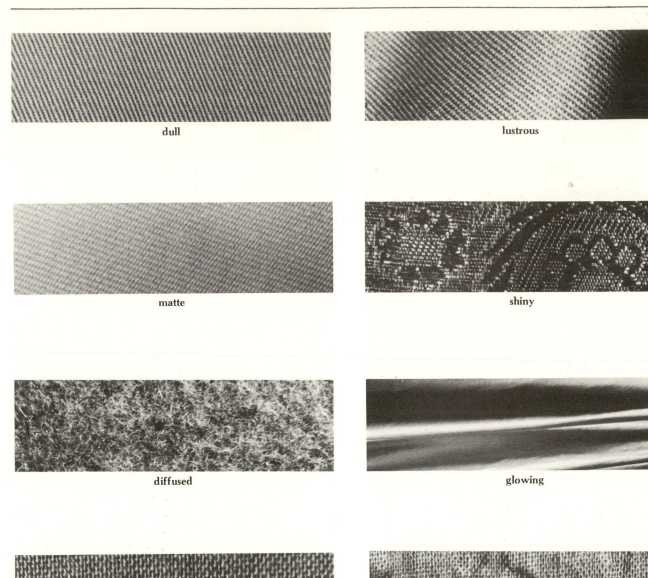

dull

lustrous

matte

shiny

diffused

glowing

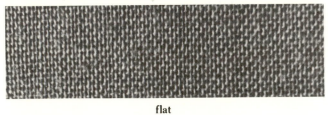

flat

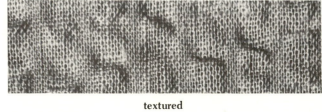

textured

solid colored

pattern design

Cotton/Cotton-type Fabrics

Dull/Flat	Matte/Subdued	Lustrous	Shiny
Bark Cloth	Airplane/Byrd Cloth®	Bedford Cord	Chintz
Beach Cloth	Bedford Cord (sueded finish)	Bengaline	Glazed-faced Lawn
Calcutta/Bangladesh Cloth	Broadcloth	Boucle Yarn Fabric	Polished Cotton
Canvas	Brocade	Brocade	
Crash	Challis	Cambric	
Cretone	Chambray	Challis	
Denim (brushed face)	Clokay/Embossed Cotton	Corded Chambray	
Drill Cloth	Crepe	Chameleon/Iridescent	
Eyelet	Creponne	Chino	
Flannel/Flannelette	Denim	Cretonne	
Dommet Flannel	Dotted Swiss	Damask	
Gauze Cloth	Flocked Dotted Swiss	Dimity	
Gauze Net	Double Weave Effect	Dimity Cord	
Homespun	Duck	Dobby Weave	
Hopsacking	End & End Cloth	Dobby Weave Effect	
Khaki	Topweight	Embroidered Fabric	
Monk's Cloth	Bottomweight	Gabardine	
Muslin	Embroidered Fabric	Jacquard Weave	
Osnaburg	Eyelet	Jean Cloth	
Printcloth	Gingham	Leno Weave	
Skip Denting/Open Effect	Jean Cloth	Organdy	
Sheeting	Lawn	Piqué	
Suede Cloth	Leno Cloth	Percale	
Ticking	Madras	Poplin	
	Oxford	Sateen	
	Pique	Skip Denting	
	Plisse	Spot Weave/Clip Spot	
	Pongee	Twill Weave	
	Poplin	Whipcord	
	Printcloth	White-on-White	
	Ratiné		
	Sailcloth		
	Seersucker		
	Skip Denting/Open Effect		
	Spot Weave/Clip Spot		
	Suede Cloth		
	Tattersall		
	Tricotine		
	Twill Weave		
	Voile		
	Crinkled Voile		

Linen/Linen-type Fabrics

Dull/Flat	Matte/Subdued	Lustrous	Shiny

Dobby Weave Linen	Butcher Linen
	Cambric Linen
	Crash Linen
	Dobby Weave Linen
	Dress Linen
	Novelty Dress Linen Weaves
	Handkerchief Linen
	Handkerchief Linen
	  with Cord
	Homespun Linen
	Jacquard Linen
	Linen Suiting
		Art Linen
		Butcher Linen
		Cambric Linen
		Crash Linen
		Dress Linen
		Novelty Dress Linen Weaves
		Handkerchief Linen
		Handkerchief Linen
		  with Cord
		Jacquard Linen
		Linen Suiting
			Bisso Linen

Burlap/Burlap-type Fabrics

Natural Fiber
Man-Made Fiber
	Natural & Man-Made
	  Fiber
		Natural & Man-Made
		  Fiber
			—

Silk/Silk-type Fabrics

Canvas
Charvet
Chiffon
Georgette
Double Georgette
Open Weave Georgette
Hopsacking
Mousseline de Soie/
  Silk Gauze
Mull
Rep
Serge
	Broadcloth
	Brocade
	Canvas
	Faille
	Gazar
	Triple Georgette
	Homespun
	Mousseline de Soie/
	  Silk Gauze
	Organza
	Poplin
	Radium Silk
	Shantung
	Shantung Georgette
	Silk Suiting
	Tussah/Wild Silk
		Barathea
		Barathea Suiting
		Bengaline
		Broadcloth
		China Silk
		Damask
		Faille
		Moiré Faille
		Tissue Faille
		Gazar
		Habutai
		Honan/Pongee
		Honan/Pongee Dobby
		Matelassé
		Ninon
		Organza
		Double Yarn Organza
		Ottoman
		Ottoman Suiting
		Peau de Soie
		Shantung
		Shantung Faille
		Sharkskin
		Surah
		Surah Suiting
			Damask
			Matelassé

Crepe/Crepe-type Fabrics

Dull/Flat	Matte/Subdued	Lustrous	Shiny

Albatross Crepe
Bark Crepe
	Canton Crepe
	Crepe Chiffon
	Crepon/Crinkle Crepe
	Crepe Georgette
	Flat Crepe
	Lingerie Crepe/Crepe Set®
	Pebbly/Mossy Crepe
		Crepe de Chine
		Crepe de Chine Dobby
		Crepe Faille
		Lingerie Crepe/Crepe Set®
		Meteor Crepe/Satin-
		   faced Chiffon
			Creped Satin
			Matelassé
			Meteor Crepe/Satin-
			   faced Chiffon

Satin/Satin-type Fabrics

Dull/Flat	Matte/Subdued	Lustrous	Shiny

Thermo Satin
  (napped back)
	Antique Satin
	Charmeuse
	Charmeuse Dobby
	Crepe-backed Satin/
	   Satin-backed Crepe
		Antique Satin
		Brocade Satin
		Ciré Satin
		Creped Satin
		Jacquard Satin
		Thermo Satin
		   Coated Back
		   Napped Back
			Bridal Satin
			Duchesse Satin
			Hammered Satin
			Jacquard Satin
			Messaline Satin

Taffeta/Taffeta-type Fabrics

Dull/Flat	Matte/Subdued	Lustrous	Shiny
—	Paper Taffeta Tissue Taffeta Warp-dyed/Warp-printed Yarn-dyed Taffeta	Antique Taffeta Faille Taffeta Jacquard Taffeta Moiré Taffeta	—

Wool/Wool-type Fabrics

Dull/Flat	Matte/Subdued	Lustrous	Shiny

Broadcloth
  Smooth Face
  Napped Face
Cheviot
Doeskin
Double Cloth
Etamine
Gabardine Coating
Homespun
Hopsacking
Jersey
Melton
Polo Cloth
Serge
Suede Cloth
Fancies
  Gauze
  Reverse Twill
  Waffle Cloth
	Albatross Wool
	Baize
	Bengaline
	Bolivia
	Cassimere
	Cloque
	Covert Coating
	Covert Suiting
	Crepe Wool
	Double-faced Wool
	Blanket Cloth/Plaid Back
	Duvetyn
	Eiderdown
	Wool Flannel
	Worsted Flannel
	French Flannel
	Gabardine
	Gabardine Coating
	Homespun Coating
	Kasha Cloth
	Loden Cloth
	Mackinaw Cloth/
	  Buffalo Plaid
	Ottoman
	Ratiné
	Sheers
	  Batiste
	  Challis
	  Voile
	Tartans
	  Clan Plaids
	  Glen Plaid
	  Hound's-tooth Check
	Tricotine
	Tweeds
	  Bird'seye
	  Donegal
	  Heather
	  Woolen Herringbone
	  Worsted Herringbone
	  Heavy Textured
	  Salt & Pepper
	Knits
	  Double Knit
	  Jersey Knit
	Unfinished Worsted
		Astrakhan/Poodle Cloth
		French Back Double Cloth
		Fleece
		Gabardine (summerweight)
		Iridescent Wool
		Ratiné
		Sharkskin
		Whipcord
		Tropical Worsted
			—

Specialty Hair/Specialty Hair Blended Fabrics

Dull/Flat	Matte/Subdued	Lustrous	Shiny

—	Alpaca Coating
	  100% Natural Fiber
	  Blended Fiber
	Alpaca Suiting
	  100% Natural Fiber
	  Blended Fiber
	Camel Hair
	  100% Natural Fiber
	  Blended Fiber
	  Coating
	  Suiting
	  Lightweight
	  Medium Weight
	  Heavyweight
	Cashmere
	  100% Natural Fiber
	  Blended Fiber
	  Lightweight
	  Medium Weight
	  Heavyweight
	Mohair
	  100% Natural Fiber
	  Blended Fiber
	  Napped Face
	Rabbit Hair
	  Blended Fiber
	  Coating
	  Suiting
		Alpaca
		  100% Natural Fiber
		  Lightweight
		Mohair
		  Blended Fiber
		  Looped-faced
		  Zebaline®
			—

Knit/Knit-type Fabrics

Dull/Flat	Matte/Subdued	Lustrous	Shiny

Double-faced Knit
Jacquard Knit (napped-face
  bird'seye back)
Raschel Knit
  Crochet Effect
  Dishcloth Effect
  Lace Effect
  Double Knit
Rib Knit
  1 x 1
  2 x 2
  4 x 4
  Open Effect
  Thermo Effect
Tricot Knit
  Printed
Dropped/Missed Stitch
Transfer Stitch
Intarsia
Sweater Knit
Laid-in Yarn
	Double-faced Knit
	Double Knit
	Interlock Knit
	  Cotton Fiber
	Jacquard Knit
	  Flat
	  Jersey
	  Rib
	  Napped-face
	    Birdseyeback
	Jersey Knit
	  Lightweight
	  Striped
	  Novelty Yarns
	  Tweed Effect
	  LaCoste®
	  Open Effect
	  Pleated Effect
	Purl Knit
	Raschel Knit
	  Lace Effect
	  Loop Fringe
	  Tweed Effect
	Rib Knit
	  1 x 1
	  2 x 2
	  3 x 3
	  Piqué
	Tricot Knit
	  Heavyweight
	  Patterned
	Transfer Stitch
	Tuck Stitch
	  Rib Effect
	  Popcorn Effect
	Cable Stitch
	Intarsia
	Sweater Knit
	Laid-in Seed Yarn
		Interlock Knit
		  Fine Weight
		  Lightweight
		  Medium Weight
		  Heavyweight
		Jacquard Knit
		  Single Blister
		  Jersey
		Jersey Knit
		  Sheer Weight
		Milanese Knit
		Purl Knit
		Rib Knit Variation
		  Piqué
		Tricot Knit
		  Fine Weight
		  Lightweight
		  Medium Weight
		  Soften Silk Finish
		  Stiff Finish
		  Patterned
		Transfer Stitch
		Intarsia
		Sweater Knit
		Laid-in Yarn
			Tricot Knit
			  Polished
			  Ciré

Lace/Lace-type Fabrics

Dull/Flat	Matte/Subdued	Lustrous	Combination: Shiny & Matte
Cluny-type	Blonde-type	Crochet	Alençon-type
Crochet	Brussels-type	Cut Work	Binche-type
Cut Work	Chantilly-type	Eyelet	Chantilly-type
Eyelet	Crochet	Eyelet-type	Re-embroidered Chantilly
Drawn Work	Cut Work	Drawn Work	Cut Work
Filet-type	Eyelet	Embroidered Lace	Eyelet
Crochet	Eyelet-type	Filet-type	Embroidered
Darned-type	Duchesse-type	Crochet	Burnt-out
Macrame	Embroidered Lace	Darned-type	Embroidered Lace
Pt de Venice	Filet-type	Macramé	Macramé
Pt Plat de Venice	Crochet	Nottingham-type	Nottingham-type
Shadow-type	Drawn Work	Pt de Esprit	Pt de Esprit
Tatted Lace	Honiton-type	Pt de Venice-type	Tatted Lace
Val Lace/Val-type	Macramé	Rosepoint-type	Val Lace/Val-type
Venice/Gros Pt de	Nottingham-type	Large Motif	Venice/Gros Pt de
Venice type	Pt de Angleterre	Tatted Lace	Venice-type
	Pt de Esprit	Val Lace/Val-type	
	Pt de France-type	Venice-type/Gros	
	Pt de Venice-type	Pt de Venice-type	
	Pt Plat de Venice-type		
	Rosepoint-type		
	Large Motif		
	Small Motif		
	Shadow-type		
	Tatted Lace		
	Val Lace/Val-type		
	Venice/Gros Pt de		
	Venice-type		

Net/Netting/Net-type Fabrics

Dull/Flat	Matte/Subdued	Lustrous	Shiny
Fishnet Pt d'Esprit Pt d'Esprit Tulle	Fishnet Maline Net Net Pt d'Esprit Net Pt d'Esprit Tulle Tulle Tulle/Illusion Veiling	Cable Net/Laundry Mesh Maline Net Fishnet Net Pt d'Esprit Net Pt d'Esprit Tulle Tulle Tulle/Illusion Veiling	Fishnet Pt d'Esprit Pt d'Esprit Tulle

Pile Surface/Pile-type Fabrics

Dull/Flat	Matte/Subdued	Lustrous	Combination: Shiny & Matte

Fleece
Sweatshirt Fleece
Baby Bunting Fleece
Terry Cloth
  Single-faced
  Double-faced
	Corduroy
	  Feathercord
	  Fine Wale
	  Mid Wale
	  Broad Wale
	  Novelty Wale
	Friezé
	Terry Cloth
	  Chenille
	  Double-faced
	  Jacquard
	  Stretch
	Flocked Velvet
	Velveteen
	Simulated Fur/High Pile
	  Sherpa
	  Teddy Bear
		Corduroy
		  Thick-Set
		  Wide Wale
		  Fleece (napped-face)
		Plush
		Terry Cloth Velour
		Velvet
		  Cotton
		  Crushed
		  Lyons
		  Panne
		  Transparent
		Simulated Fur/High Pile
		  Astrakhan/Persian Lamb
		  Poodle Cloth
		  Shag
			Terry Cloth
			  Chenille
			  Sculptured
			Tufted Cloth
			  Chenille Candlewick
			  Chenille Velvet/Velcle®
			  Chenille Yarn Cloth
			Velvet
			  Brocade
			  Crushed
			  Cut
			  Embossed
			  Velvet Cord
			Simulated Fur/High Pile
			  Astrakhan/Persian Lamb
			  Beaver
			  Broadtail
			  Chinchilla
			  Ermine
			  Red Fox
			  Silver Fox
			  White Fox
			  Blue Fox
			  Giraffe
			  Leopard
			  Lynx
			  Mink
			  Muskrat
			  Ocelot
			  Opossum
			  Poney
			  Rabbit
			  Raccoon
			  Seal
			  Sherpa/Sheared Lamb

Stretch/Stretch-type Fabrics

Dull/Flat	Matte/Subdued	Lustrous	Shiny

Yarn Stretch
  Canvas
  Denim
Stretch Finish
  Crimped Cloth
	Yarn Stretch
	  Chino
	  Gabardine
	  Poplin
	  Twill
	  Whipcord
	Yarn & Fabric Structure
	  Stretch
	    Double Knit (lightweight)
	    Double Knit (medium
	     weight)
	    Double Knit
	     (heavyweight)
	    Stretch Terry
	    Stretch Lace
		Fiber Stretch
		  Lycra® (140–175%)
		  Lycra® (110–140%)
		Yarn Stretch
		  Satin
		Stretch Finish
		  Crinkle Double Cloth
			Fiber Stretch
			  Lycra® (180–220%)

Multicomponent/Coated/Layered Fabrics

Adhesive Bonded
  Woven to Knit
Laminated Bonded
  Knit to Knit
Flock-faced
  Simulated Suede
  (patterned)
  (crushed)
  Simulated Double-faced
  Suede
Water-repellent Resin-coated
  Duck
  Poplin
Quilted
  Knit-backed
	Adhesive Bonded
	  Vinyl to Nonwoven
	  Woven to Knit
	Laminated Bonded
	  Knit to Knit
	  Vinyl to Nonwoven
	Film-faced
	  Simulated Leather
	  (lightweight)
	  (medium weight)
	  (heavyweight)
	  (patterned)
	Water-repellent Film Faced
	  Solid Rubber Slicker
	  Perforated Rubber Slicker
	Water-repellent Resin-coated
	  Muslin Sheeting
	Quilted
	  Double-faced
	  Chemstitch®
		Water-Repellent Film-Faced
		  Rubber Slicker
		  Vinyl Film to Backing
		  Vinyl/Clear Vinyl
		Water-repellent Resin-coated
		  Rip Stop Nylon
		  Taffeta
		Quilted
		  Double-faced
		  Gauze-backed
			—

12 ~ Opacity

Opacity is a term that refers to the light-admitting or light-obstructing qualities of a fabric. The term applies to the relative opacity or translucency of a fabric and the quality of opacity and translucency.

Opacity includes variations in light-admitting qualities from:
- Transparent to semi-transparent
- Light-admitting to light-obstructing
- Loose opaque to compact opaque
- Mesh openings to novelty weaves
- Thin to thick
- Light-colored to dark-colored

Factors affecting the opacity of a fabric depend on:
- Content of fibers (natural or man-made)
- Spinning processes
- Size, ply and count of yarns
- Type and construction of yarns
- Order of interlacing yarns
- Type and method of fabric structure
- Density of fabric structure
- Type and method of finishing processes
- Type of color and surface-design applications

Varying one or more of the components will change the opacity or translucency of a fabric.

The following terms describe the opacity—light-admitting or light-obstructing—qualities of fabrics. These terms are arranged according to group/group-type qualities. The term *medium* can be applied to modify the areas between the extremes. Some fabrics may fall into one or more categorized definitions used to define the opacity of a fabric.

sheer	thick
transparent	heavyweight
semi-transparent	light-obstructing
gauzey	solid
thin	shadowy
gossamer	light-colored
light-admitting	pale
lightweight	dark-colored
fineweight	combinations resulting from:
clear	embroidery
dim	novelty weaves
filmy	perforations
cloudy	cut-out work
loose opaque	applications
compact opaque	appliqués

sheer/transparent

semi-transparent

light-admitting

light-obstructing

loose opaque

compact opaque

open-mesh weave

novelty weaves

thin

thick

light-colored

dark-colored

Cotton/Cotton-type Fabrics

Transparent/Sheer	Semi-Transparent/ Semi-Sheer	Light Admitting	Loose Opaque	Compact Opaque

Dotted Swiss
Flocked Swiss
Embroidered (sheers)
Organdy
Spot/Clip Spot
  (sheers)
Swivel Weave (sheers)
	Batiste
	Bouclé Yarn (thin)
	Challis
	Creponne
	Dimity
	Dimity Stripe
	Embroidered (fine
	  weight)
	Eyelet
	Gauze
	Iridescent Cotton
	Lawn
	Leno Weave (fine
	  weight)
	Skip Denting/Open
	  Effect
	Spot/Clip Spot
	  (fine weight)
	Swivel Weave
	  (fine weight)
	Voile
	  Crinkled Voile
		Broadcloth
		Cambric
		Challis
		Chambray
		Corded Chambray
		Damask
		Dobby Weave
		  (lightweight)
		Embroidered
		  (lightweight)
		End & End
		  Topweight
		Gingham
		Iridescent Cotton
		Glazed-faced Lawn
		Madras
		Monk's Cloth
		Oxford
		Percale
		Plissé
		Polished Cotton
		Pongee
		Printcloth
		Skip Denting/Open
		  Effect
		Seersucker
		Sheeting
		Spot/Clip Spot
		  (lightweight)
		Swivel Weave
		  (lightweight)
		Tattersall
		White-on-White
			Beach Cloth
			Bouclé Yarn (light-
			  medium weight)
			Calcutta/Bangladesh
			Crash
			Cotton Crepe
			Cretonne
			Embroidered (medium
			  weight)
			Homespun
			Hopsacking
			Muslin
			Osnaburg
			Skip Denting/Open
			  Effect
			Spot/Clip Spot
			  (medium weight)
			Swivel Weave
			  (medium weight)
			Ratine
			White-on-White
			  (medium weight)
				Airplane/Byrd Cloth®
				Bark Cloth
				Bedford Cord
				  (sueded finish)
				Bengaline
				Brocade
				Canvas
				Double Cloth
				Embroidered
				  (heavyweight)
				Iridescent Cotton
				  (heavyweight)
				Chino
				Chintz
				Glazed Cotton
				Clokay/Embossed
				  Cotton
				Covert
				Damask
				Denim
				Denim
				  (brushed-face)
				Flocked Swiss
				  (heavyweight)
				Duck
				End & End
				  Bottomweight
				Flannel/Flannelette
				Dommet Flannel
				Gabardine
				Jacquard Cotton
				  (heavyweight)
				Jean Cloth
				Khaki
				Piqué
				Polished Cotton
				Poplin
				Sailcloth
				Spot/Clip Spot
				  (heavyweight)
				Suede Cloth
				Ticking
				Tricotine
				Twill Weave
				Whipcord

Linen/Linen-type Fabrics

Transparent/Sheer	Semi-Transparent/Semi-Sheer	Light Admitting	Loose Opaque	Compact Opaque

—	Handkerchief Linen	Bisso Linen
		Cambric Linen
		Handkerchief Linen
		Handkerchief Linen
		  with Cord
		Dress Linen
		Novelty Dress Linen
		  Weaves
			Dress Linen
			Novelty Dress Linen
			  Weaves
			Homespun Linen
			Linen Suiting
				Art Linen
				Butcher Linen
				Crash Linen
				Dobby Linen
				  (heavyweight)
				Jacquard Linen
				  (heavyweight)
				Linen Suiting

Burlap/Burlap-type Fabrics

Transparent/Sheer	Semi-Transparent/Semi-Sheer	Light Admitting	Loose Opaque	Compact Opaque
—	—	—	100% Natural Fiber Man-made Fiber	—

Silk/Silk-type Fabrics

Transparent/Sheer	Semi-Transparent/Semi-Sheer	Light Admitting	Loose Opaque	Compact Opaque

Chiffon
Embroidered Chiffon
Marquisette
Mousseline de Soie/
  Silk Gauze
	Gazar
	Georgette
	Double Georgette
	Triple Georgette
	Open Weave
	  Georgette
	Shantung Georgette
		Barathea
		Broadcloth
		China Silk
		Faille
		Tissue Faille
		Habutai
		Honan/Pongee
		Honan/Pongee
		  Dobby
		Mull
		Radium Silk
		Shantung
		Surah
			Canvas
			Charvet
			Homespun
			Hopsacking
			Serge
			Tussah/Wild Silk
				Barathea Suiting
				Bengaline
				Brocade
				Canvas
				Damask
				Faille
				Moiré Faille
				Matelassé
				Ottoman
				Ottoman Suiting
				Peau de Soie
				Poplin
				Rep
				Shantung Faille
				Sharkskin
				Silk Suiting
				Surah Suiting

Crepe/Crepe-type Fabrics

Transparent/Sheer	Semi-Transparent/Semi-Sheer	Light Admitting	Loose Opaque	Compact Opaque

—	Chiffon Crepe
	Crepe Georgette
	Creponne
	Crinkled Crepe
		Albatross Crepe
		Canton Crepe
		Crepe de Chine
		  Dobby
		Flat Crepe
		Lingerie Crepe/
		  Crepe Set®
			Bark Crepe
			Pebbly/Mossy Crepe
				Crepe Back Satin/
				  Satin-back Crepe
				Crepe Faille
				Matelassé Crepe
				Meteor Crepe/Satin-
				  faced Chiffon

Satin-Satin-type Fabrics

Transparent/Sheer	Semi-Transparent/Semi-Sheer	Light Admitting	Loose Opaque	Compact Opaque

—	—	Brocade Satin
		Charmeuse
		Charmeuse Dobby
		Creped Satin
		Messaline Satin
			—	Antique Satin
				Bridal Satin
				Brocade Satin
				Ciré Satin
				Crepe Satin/Satin
				  Crepe
				Duchesse Satin
				Hammered Satin
				Jacquard Satin
				Messaline Satin
				Thermo Satin
				  Napped-back
				  Coated-back

Taffeta/Taffeta-type Fabrics

Transparent/Sheer	Semi-Transparent/Semi-Sheer	Light Admitting	Loose Opaque	Compact Opaque

—	Paper Taffeta	Moiré Taffeta
		Tissue Taffeta
		Warp-dyed/
		  Warp-printed
		  Taffeta
		Yarn-dyed Taffeta
			—	Antique Taffeta
				Faille Taffeta
				Jacquard Taffeta

Wool/Wool-type Fabrics

Transparent/Sheer	Semi-Transparent/Semi-Sheer	Light Admitting	Loose Opaque	Compact Opaque

—	Sheers
	  Batiste
	  Challis
	  Voile
	Fancies
	  Gauze
		Albatross Wool
		Broadcloth
		  Smooth-faced
		  Napped-faced
		Crepe Wool
		Doeskin
		Double Cloth
		  (lightweight)
		Gabardine
		  (summerweight)
		Homespun
		Kasha Cloth
		Poplin
		Sheers
		  Challis
		Fancies
		  Reverse Twill
		  Waffle Cloth
		Wool Knit Jersey
		Tropical Worsted
		Unfinished Worsted
			Astrakhan/Poodle Cloth
			Double-faced Double
			  Cloth
			Eiderdown
			Étamine
			Homespun Coating
			Hopsacking
			Ratine
			Tweed
			  Heavy Textured
			  Oatmeal
				Baize
				Bedford Cord
				Bengaline
				Bolivia
				Cassimere
				Cheviot
				Cloqué
				Covert Coating
				Covert Suiting
				French Back
				  Double Cloth
				Blanket Cloth/
				  Plaid Back
				Double-faced Cloth
				Duvetyn
				Wool Flannel
				Worsted Flannel
				French Flannel
				Fleece
				Gabardine
				Gabardine Coating
				Iridescent Wool
				Jersey
				Loden Cloth
				Mackinaw Cloth/
				  Buffalo Plaid
				Melton
				Ottoman
				Polo Cloth
				Serge
				Suede Cloth
				Tartans
				  Clan Plaids
				  Glen Plaid
				  Hound's-tooth
				    Check
				Tricotine
				Tweed
				  Bird'seye
				  Donegal-type
				  Heather
				  Wool Herringbone
				  Worsted
				    Herringbone
				  Heavy Textured
				  Salt & Pepper
				  Oatmeal
				Whipcord
				Double Wool Knit

Specialty Hair/Specialty Hair Blended Fabrics

Transparent/Sheer	Semi-Transparent/ Semi-Sheer	Light Admitting	Loose Opaque	Compact Opaque

—	Mohair Gauze
	  100% Fiber
	  Blended Fiber
		Alpaca Hair
		Alpaca Hair Cloth
		Mohair
		  100% Fiber
		  Blended Fiber
		  Clear Finish
		  Brushed Face
		Rabbit Hair Cloth
		  Lightweight
			Mohair
			  100% Fiber
			  Blended Fiber
			  Single-faced
			  Double-faced
			  Looped Face
				Alpaca Coating
				  100% Fiber
				  Blended Fiber
				Camel Hair
				  100% Fiber
				  Blended Fiber
				  Lightweight
				  Medium Weight
				Cashmere
				  100% Fiber
				  Blended Fiber
				  Lightweight
				  Medium Weight
				  Heavyweight
				Mohair
				  Blended Fiber
				  Zebaline®
				Rabbit Hair
				  Blended Fiber
				  Medium Weight
				  Coating

Knit/Knit-type Fabrics

Open Stitch/ Mesh	Semi-Transparent/ Semi-Sheer	Light Admitting	Loose Opaque	Compact Opaque

Jersey Jacquard Knit
Jersey Knit
  Novelty Yarn
  Open Effect
Raschel Knit
  Crochet Effect
  Dishcloth Effect
  Lace Effect
  Tweed Effect
Rib Knit
  Open Effect
Tricot Knit
  Patterned
Dropped/Missed
  Stitch
Transfer Stitch
Intarsia
Sweater Knit
Laid-in Yarn
	Interlock Knit
	  Sheer Weight
	Tricot Knit
	  Sheer Weight
	  Lightweight
	  Laid-in Yarn
		Interlock Knit
		  Lightweight
		  Medium Weight
		  Cotton Fiber
		Jersey Knit
		  Lightweight
		  Striped
		  Tweed Effect
		  LaCoste®
		Milanese Knit
		Rib Knit
		  1 x 1
		  2 x 2
		Tricot Knit
		  Medium Weight
		  Soft Silk Finish
		  Stiff Finish
		  Polished Finish
		  Ciré Finish
		  Patterned
		  Printed
		Tuck Stitch
		  Rib Effect
		  Thermo Knit
		Intarsia
		Sweater Knit
		Laid-in Yarn
			Jersey Jacquard Knit
			Jersey Knit
			  Pleated Effect
			Purl Knit
			Rib Knit
			  1 x 1
			  2 x 2
			  Pique
			  Thermo
			Raschel Knit
			  Tweed Effect
			Tuck Stitch/Popcorn
			  Effect
			Cable Stitch
			Intarsia
			Sweater Knit
			Laid-in Yarn
				Double-faced Knit
				Double Knit
				Interlock Knit
				  Heavyweight
				Jacquard Knit
				  Flat
				  Single Blister
				  Rib
				  Smooth face,
				    Bird'seye back
				  Napped face
				Raschel Knit
				  Loop Effect
				Tricot Knit
				  Heavyweight
				Laid-in Yarn

Pile Structure/Pile-type Fabrics

Transparent/Sheer	Semi-Transparent/ Semi-Sheer	Light Admitting	Loose Opaque	Compact Opaque

—	Cut Velvet	Feathered Corduroy
		Friezé
		Velvet
		   Brocade
		   Panne
		   Transparent
			Terry Cloth
			   Chenille
			   Single-faced
			   Sculptured
			   Stretch
			Tufted Cloth
			   Chenille Yarn
				Corduroy
				   Fine Wale
				   Mid Wale
				   Thick-Set
				   Wide Wale
				   Broad Wale
				   Novelty Wale
				Fleece
				   Napped-faced
				   Sweatshirt
				Baby Bunting Fleece
				Plush
				Terry Cloth
				   Double-faced
				   Velour
				   Jacquard
				Chenille Candlewick
				Chenille Velvet/
				   Velcle®
				Velvet
				   Cotton
				   Crushed
				   Embossed
				   Flocked
				   Lyons
				   Velour
				   Velvet Cord
				Velveteen
				Simulated Fur
				   Astrakhan/Persian
				     Lamb
				   Beaver
				   Broadtail
				   Chinchilla
				   Ermine
				   Red Fox
				   Silver Fox
				   White Fox
				   Blue Fox
				   Giraffe
				   Leopard
				   Lynx
				   Mink
				   Muskrat
				   Ocelot
				   Opossum
				   Poney
				   Rabbit
				   Raccoon
				   Seal
				   Sherpa/Sheared
				     Lamb
				   Skunk
				   Squirrel
				   Teddy Bear
				   Tiger
				   Zebra

Metallic/Metallic-type Fabrics

Open Net or Mesh	Semi-Transparent/ Semi-Sheer	Light Admitting	Loose Opaque	Compact Opaque

Chantilly Lace
Pt d'Esprit Lace
Metallic Net
	Embroidered Sheer
	  Tricot Knit with
	  Metallic Laid-in
	  Yarn
	Sparkle or Glitter
	  Adhesive bonded to
	  Organza
		Jacquard Weave with
		  Metallic Yarn
		Jersey Knit with Weft-
		  inserted Metallic Yarn
		Lamé Jersey
		Sparkle or Glitter
		  Adhesive-bonded to
		  Crepe
			Lamé Gauze
			Metallic Pile
				Ciré Coated
				Lame Woven
				Sparkle or Glitter
				  Printed on Satin

Stretch/Stretch-type Fabrics

Transparent/ Semi-Transparent	Light Admitting	Loose Opaque	Compact Opaque

Fiber Stretch
  Lycra® (180–220%)
Yarn & Fabric Structure
  Stretch
    Stretch Lace
	Fiber Stretch
	  Lycra® (140–175%)
	  Lycra® (110–140%)
	Yarn & Fabric Structure
	  Stretch
	    Double Knit (lightweight)
		Yarn & Fabric Structure
		  Stretch
		    Stretch Terry Cloth
		  Stretch Finish
		    Crimped Cloth
			Yarn Stretch
			  Canvas
			  Chino
			  Denim
			  Gabardine
			  Poplin
			  Satin
			  Twill
			  Whipcord
			Yarn & Fabric Structure
			  Stretch
			    Double Knit
			    (medium weight)
			    (heavyweight)
			Stretch Finish
			  Crinkled Double Cloth

Multicomponent/Coated/Layered Fabrics

Transparent/Sheer	Semi-Transparent/ Semi-Sheer	Light Admitting	Loose Opaque	Compact Opaque

—	—	Water-repellent
		  Bonded
		    Vinyl/Clear Vinyl
		Water-repellent
		  Resin-coated
		    Rip-Stop Nylon
			Adhesive Bonded
			  Woven to Knit
			  Vinyl to Nonwoven
			Laminated Bonded
			  Knit to Knit
			  Vinyl to Nonwoven
			Film-Faced
			  Simulated Leather
			    (lightweight)
			    (medium weight)
			    (heavyweight)
			    (patterned face)
			Flock-Faced
			  Simulated Suede
			    (patterned)
			    (crushed)
			    (double-faced)
				Water-repellent
				  Solid Rubber Slicker
				  Perforated Rubber
				    Slicker
				  Vinyl Film to
				    Nonwoven
				Water-repellent Resin-
				  coated
				  Duck
				  Gabardine
				  Muslin Sheeting
				  Poplin
				  Taffeta
				Quilted
				  Double-faced
				  Gauze-backed
				  Knit-backed
				  Chemstitch®

Net/Netting/Net-type Fabrics

Widely Spaced (Less than 5 Points per Inch)	Moderately Spaced (5–10 Points per Inch)	Closely Spaced (15–25 Points per Inch)	Compactly Spaced (25 or more Points per Inch)

Fishnet
  Large Hole
Maline Net
  Large Hole
	Cable Net/Laundry Mesh
	Fishnet
	  Medium Hole
	Maline Net
	  Medium Hole
	Net
	Pt d'Esprit Net
		Fishnet
		  Small Hole
		Maline Net
		  Small Hole
		Net
		Pt d'Esprit Net
		Pt d'Esprit Tulle
			Fishnet
			  Fine Hole
			Maline Net
			  Fine Hole
			Pt d'Esprit Tulle
			Tulle/Illusion Veiling

Lace/Lace-type Fabrics

Mostly Net Ground/ Small Patterned Areas	Little Net Ground/ Mostly Patterned Areas	Light Admitting Ground/ Open Design Areas	Loosely Compacted Design

Blonde-type
Brussels-type
Embroidered-type
Filet-type
  Crochet
  Darned Work
Honiton-type
Pt d'Esprit
Pt de Venice-type
Rosepoint-type
  Large Motif
  Small Motif
Val Lace/Val-type
	Alençon-type
	Binche-type
	Chantilly-type
	Re-embroidered
	  Chantilly-type
	Cluny-type
	Crochet
	Duchesse-type
	Filet-type
	  Crochet
	  Darned Work
	Nottingham-type
	Pt d'Angleterre-type
	Pt de France-type
	Pt de Venice
	Pt Plat de Venice
	Shadow-type
	Tatted Lace
	Venice-type/Gros Pt
	  de Venice-type
		Cut Work
		Drawn Work
		Needlepoint-type
		Eyelet
		Burnt-out Method
			Crochet
			Filet-type
			  Crochet
			  Darned Work
			Macramé
			Nottingham-type
			Tatted Lace

13 ~ Drapability Qualities

The drape or drapability of a fabric refers to the manner in which the fabric falls, hangs, clings, shapes, molds, pleats, gathers, or flows on the model form or on the body. All fabrics drape. However, each fabric drapes or hangs differently.

Factors affecting the drapability qualities of a fabric depend on:
- Content and type of fibers
- Shape, length and configuration of fibers
- Size, ply and texture of yarns
- Thread count and covering power of yarns
- Type and method of fabric structure
- Weight, texture and hand
- Type and method of finishing processes applied to fibers, yarns or fabrics
- Type of color and surface-design applications

Drapability qualities may be objectively measured by the fabric's:
- Flexibility—pliable to stiff
- Compressibility—soft to hard
- Extensibility—stretchy to inelastic
- Resiliency—springy to limp
- Opacity—open to compact
- Weight—light to heavy
- Surface texture—smooth to rough

In this unit the result or analysis of a fabric's drapability *will not* be discussed as "poor drapability" or "good drapability." Also, "high drapability" will not be used as a descriptive term for a fabric that is soft or fluid. The result or analysis of a fabric's drapability or hand as good, poor or high should be determined by:
- The end use selected for the fabric
- The application of the fabric to the design of the garment
- The shape or silhouette desired for the garment

Drapability qualities of fabric can be tested, analyzed or determined by draping or suspending the fabric over the hand, model form or body. When draped or suspended ask yourself the following questions:
- Is the fabric lightweight and soft enough to be fluid?
- Does the fabric fall into soft, graceful folds or ripples?
- Does the fabric fall into many folds? Few folds? None at all?
- Does the fabric gather softly?
- Does the fabric fold softly and maintain soft pleats?
- Does the fabric fold crisply and maintain crisp pleats?
- Does the fabric tend to cling?
- Can the fabric be molded?
- Will the fabric be firm enough to retain the shape of a closely, fitted garment?
- Will the fabric sustain the fullness or bouffant shape of the silhouette?

Based on the preceding questions, the drapability qualities of a fabric may be described as the ability or tendency of the fabric to:
- Flow and be fluid
- Fall close to or cling to the shape and contour of the body
- Be shaped or molded by stretching
- Be shaped or molded by heat setting or by moisture and heat
- Fall into languid flares and ripples
- Fall into soft flares
- Fall into moderately, soft flares
- Fall into firm, crisp or stiff flares
- Fall into a wide cone
- Accommodate fullness by pleating
- Maintain a crisp fold, crease or pleat
- Maintain a soft fold or an unpressed pleat

- Accommodate fullness by gathering, elasticized shirring or smocking
- Allow fullness to retain a soft fall or soft, graceful fall
- Allow fullness to maintain a crisp effect
- Allow fullness to maintain a springy and/or lofty effect
- Allow fullness to maintain a bouffant effect
- Retain the shape of the garment
- Retain the silhouette of the garment
- Be better utilized if fitted by seaming and eliminating excess fabric

Evaluating Photographs

The following photographs illustrate the drapability qualities of fabrics in one of the following ways:
- After the fabric has been made into a garment
- The full width of the fabric draped on the model form:
  - On the straight grain with a gathered waistline
  - On the bias grain
  - Stretched to eliminate fullness and be molded to the body contours

The widths of the fabrics used for the straight (lengthwise) grain drapes range from 36–70 inches (9.14–177.8 cm).

Fabrics with border designs, finished edges, horizontal, and one-way motifs may be, and have been gathered on the crosswise grain. The amount of fabric take up and fullness handled for the crosswise drape is 45 inches (114.3 cm). Quality of fullness may be judged by how a fabric gathers with regard to the width.

From this comparison one may determine if more or less fullness is desired or required and plan accordingly when selecting or analyzing fabric for a design or particular silhouette.

Bias drape was done on the 45° angle of the fabric. Bias draping of less than 45° may be desired. Evaluating the size, amount and position of flares, cones and ripples will assist the designer in deciding whether a design is applicable for the particular fabric in a bias drape. Some fabrics cannot be used on the bias without consideration to edge finishes, weaves, patterns, nap or light-reflecting properties.

Stretch fabrics have been pulled to eliminate fullness and molded to body contours to show elongation factor and potential of the fabric. Fabric may be stretched more or less with regard to specific design, type and end use of fabric.

Viewing the completed garments allows the reader to analyze the potential use of the fabric and view how other designers have handled fullness by bias drape, pleating, gathering or other styling details.

For a complete analysis of the drapability qualities of specific fabrics refer to *Profiling Fabrics: Properties, Performance & Construction Techniques,* Book 3, in *The Language of Fashion Series.*

flow and be fluid/silk chiffon

flow and be fluid/chiffon

flow and be fluid/georgette

**fall close to or cling
to body/wool jersey**

**fall close to or cling
to body/crepe-backed satin**

**shaped or molded by stretching/
silk jersey knit**

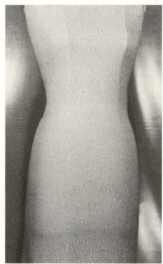

**shaped or molded by stretching/
cotton jersey knit**

**shaped or molded by heat
setting/thermoplastic polyester**

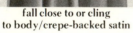

**shaped or molded by heat
setting/polyester serge**

**fall into languid flares and
ripples/silk chiffon**

**fall into languid flares and
ripples/silk georgette**

**fall into soft languid
flares/silk chiffon**

UNDERSTANDING FABRICS

fall into soft flares/
silk chiffon

fall into soft flares/
silk charmeuse

fall into moderately soft
flares/wool flannel

fall into moderately soft
flares/cotton broadcloth

fall into moderately soft
flares/wool broadcloth

fall into firm or crisp
flares/silk taffeta

fall into crisp cones or flares/
handkerchief linen (crisp finish)

fall into moderately crisp flares
and cones/silk crinkled organza

fall into firm flares/
corduroy (crisp finish)

fall into a stiff flare/
sisal cloth

fall into stiff, wide cones
and flares/coated fabric

fall into moderately wide
cones/rayon velvet

fall into a wide cone/
wool ottoman

fall into wide cones/
wide wale corduroy

accommodates fullness by
pleating/silk surah

accommodates fullness by
pleating/lightweight
alpaca cloth

maintains a crisp fold,
crease or pleat/linen

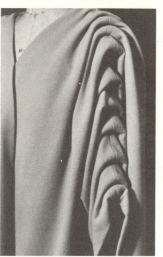

maintains a soft
fold/cashmere

maintains an unpressed
pleat/cashmere

maintains an unpressed/
pleat/wool melton

accommodates fullness by
gathering/dotted cotton Swiss

accommodates fullness by
gathering and elasticized
shirring/interlock knit

accommodates fullness by
elasticized shirring/
cotton sateen

accommodates fullness by
smocking/silk
interlock knit

allows fullness to retain soft
fall/dotted cotton Swiss

allows fullness to retain soft
graceful fall/jersey knit

allows fullness to retain soft
graceful fall/silk jacquard knit

allows fullness to retain soft
fall/wool jersey knit

allows fullness to maintain
crisp effect/poplin

allows fullness to maintain
crisp effect/silk organza
with crinoline petticoat

allows fullness to maintain
crisp effect/seersucker

allows fullness to maintain
springy effect/Lyons velvet

allows fullness to maintain
lofty effect/novelty wool weave

allows fullness to maintain
springy or lofty
effect/wool fleece

allows fullness to maintain
bouffant effect/tulle

allows fullness to maintain
bouffant effect/silk taffeta
with crinoline petticoat

DRAPABILITY QUALITIES

retains the shape of
the garment/poodle cloth

retains the shape of
the garment/double-faced wool

retains the shape of
the garment/silk gazar

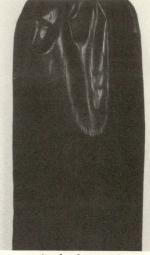

retains the shape of the
garment/moiré taffeta

retains the silhouette of
the garment/silk ottoman

retains the silhouette of the
garment/simulated leather

better utilized if fitted by
seaming and eliminating excess
fabric/wool gabardine

better utilized if fitted by
seaming and eliminating excess
fabric/double-faced wool

better utilized if fitted by
seaming and eliminating excess
fabric/double-faced quilted fabric

fabric draped on the
lengthwise (straight) grain/
striped jersey knit

fabric draped on the bias/
striped jersey knit

fabric draped on the
lengthwise (straight) grain/
lace with scalloped border design

Garment Care Labeling/
Specifications for Care Labels

The Federal Trade Commission's Rule on permanent care labeling for garments has been in effect since July 3, 1972. The Rule requires that most articles of wearing apparel bear permanent care labels. The care of fabrics begins with the fabric manufacturer or fabric mill who must supply requirements and limitations with regard to the care factors of fabrics. Statements must be made with respect to information regarding:

- The regular care of the garment
- Laundering, bleaching and dry cleaning
- Drying and safe drying temperature limits
- Ironing and safe ironing temperature limits
- Other procedures that may be considered as part of the regular care for the item
- A warning if an unusual care method appears to apply

All information must be in words, not in symbols, and must apply to all parts of the fabric or garment.

The care label may be printed or woven; sewn, fused or glued to the article. An overwrap on packaged garments or a securely affixed hangtag must be readily accessible to the consumer at the point-of-sale. An overwrap or hangtag can include more complete information on the care of the item, but the information should *not* conflict with the permanently affixed care label.

The following articles of wearing apparel are exempt from the Federal Trade Commission's Rule on permanent care labeling.

1. Articles of wearing apparel whose utility or appearance would be substantially impaired by the attachment of a permanent label. For example a very sheer blouse. If such an exemption is granted, the required care information must *accompany* the article, but need not be permanently affixed to it.
2. Articles of wearing apparel that sell at retail for $3 or less and that are completely washable under normal and foreseeable circumstances. For example, white cotton underpants.

The Rule requires retailers who sell fabrics over-the-counter for home sewing to supply care labels to the consumer with a code corresponding to the care information at the end of each bolt.

It is important when producing a garment to select linings, interfacings, trimmings, and findings with compatable care requirements to the fabric.

It is assumed by the consumer that all fabrics may be pressed or ironed under normal and safe ironing conditions and that all known washable fabrics may also be dry cleaned unless otherwise stated. Most fabrics that may be laundered or that wash well, however, may be affected by some types of fabric structure, types of finishing processes or intricate methods of garment construction and dry cleaning of the garment is advisable—unless otherwise stated.

The Federal Trade Commission has proposed a new rule to extend the care labeling requirements to manufacturers of carpets and rugs and knitting yarns. Care labels would be supplied to retailers for consumers who purchase these articles. This same proposed care labeling rule would require that care labels be attached permanently to the following items: suede and leather apparel, upholstered furniture, slipcovers, draperies, sheets and bedspreads, table cloths and towels.

A more complex reference and one adopted by the Federal Trade Commission in the proposed new rule is The American Society for Testing and Materials publication entitled, *Standard Definitions of Terms Relating to Care of Consumer Textile Products and Recommended Practice for Use of These Terms on Permanently Attached Labels* (ASTM D3136-72). This Standard can be found in the ASTM Annual Standards, Part 4 (Definitions of Terms) or Part 32 (Textiles, Yarns, Fabrics, General Methods), which are available in many libraries.

All parts of the garment must be dry cleaned, wet cleaned, and laundered in the same manner satisfactorily. If one part of the garment does not follow the same dry cleaning or laundering procedures as another, the garment is not serviceable. Compatible garment care relates to:

- Thread
- Interfacing
- Interlining
- Lining
- Fasteners
- Belts
- Shoulder pads
- Bindings
- Trimmings
- Findings
- Beads, beading, furs, etc.

The following care guides° were produced by the Consumer Affairs Committee of the American Apparel Manufacturer's Association, and are based on the Voluntary Guide of the Textile Industry Advisory Committee for Consumer Interests. They are made available here to help you understand the brief care instructions found on permanently affixed labels on garments. Be sure to read and to follow all care instructions on garments *completely*.

°Reproduced courtesy of Textile Distributors Association Inc. (T.D.A.)

Care Labels for
Machine Washable Garments

When label reads:	It means:
Machine Wash	Wash, bleach, dry and press by any customary method including commercial laundering and dry cleaning.
Home Launder Only	Same as above, but *do not* use commercial laundering.
No Chlorine Bleach	*Do not* use chlorine bleach. Oxygen bleach may be used.
No Bleach	*Do not* use any type of bleach.
Cold Wash/Cold Rinse	Use cold water from tap or cold water washing machine setting.
Warm Wash/Warm Rinse	Use warm water from tap or warm water washing machine setting.
Hot Wash	Use hot water from tap or hot water machine washing setting.
No Spin	Remove wash load *before* final machine spin cycle.
Delicate Cycle/Gentle Cycle	Use appropriate machine setting; otherwise wash by hand.
Durable Press Cycle/ Permanent Press Cycle	Use appropriate machine setting; otherwise use warm wash, cold rinse and short spin cycle.
Hand Wash Separately	Hand wash alone or with like colors.

Care Labels for
Non-Machine Washable Garments

When label reads:	It means:
Hand Wash	Launder only by hand in lukewarm (hand comfortable) water. May be dry cleaned.
Hand Wash Only	Same as above, but *do not* dry clean.
Hand Wash Separately	Hand wash alone or with like colors.
No Bleach	*Do not* use any type of bleach.
Damp Wipe	Surface clean with damp cloth or sponge.

Care Labels for Home-Drying Garments

When label reads:	It means:
Tumble Dry	Dry in tumble dryer at specified settings—high, medium, low, no heat
Tumble Dry/Remove Promptly	Same as above, but in absence of cool-down cycle *remove* garment *at once* when tumbling stops.
Drip Dry	Hang wet and allow to dry with hand shaping only.
Line Dry	Hang damp and allow to dry.
No Wring/No Twist	Hang dry, drip dry or dry flat only. Handle to prevent wrinkles and distortion.
Dry Flat	Lay garment on flat surface.
Block to Dry	Maintain original size and shape while drying.

Care Labels for Ironing or Pressing

When label reads:	It means:
Cool Iron	Set iron at lowest setting.
Warm Iron	Set iron at medium setting.
Hot Iron	Set iron at hot setting.
Do Not Iron	*Do not* iron or press with heat.
Steam Iron	Iron or press with steam.
Iron Damp	Dampen garment before ironing.

Care Labels for Dry Cleaning Garments

When label reads:	It means:
Dry Clean Only	Dry clean only, including self-service dry cleaning.
Professionally Dry Clean Only	Do not use self-service dry cleaning.
Do Not Dry Clean	Use recommended care instructions. *No* dry-cleaning materials should be used.

►

Care Labels for
Fabrics Sold by the Yard

When label reads:	It means:
Machine Washable	Machine wash warm.
Machine Washable—Dimensional Restorability Fabrics	Machine wash warm. Line dry.
Machine Washable—Permanent-Press & Drip-Dry Fabrics	Machine wash warm. Tumble dry; remove promptly.
Machine Washable—Delicate Fabrics	Machine wash warm, delicate cycle. Tumble dry, lowest cycle. Use cool iron.
Machine Washable—Pigmented Fabrics Pigment-Printed Fabrics	Machine wash warm. *Do not* dry clean.
All Hand Washable Fabrics	Hand wash separately. Use cool iron.
Dry Cleanable Fabrics	Dry clean only.
Pile Fabrics	Dry clean only
Vinyl Fabrics	Wipe with damp cloth only.

Care of Cotton-Fiber Fabrics

General care information regarding cotton fabrics made of cotton fibers. Check label of hangtag for specific information and care instructions.

1. Most 100 percent cottons can be washed by machine at the regular cycle with hot water. Use hot water for whites and color fastness.
2. Use chlorine bleach only on whites and colored fabrics which have been tested for color retention.
3. Wash cotton knits by hand to avoid excess shrinking or stretching.
4. Tumble dry at regular setting.
5. Use fabric softener to improve softness and comfort and to reduce wrinkling.
6. High temperature iron setting may be used.

Care of Silk-Fiber Fabrics

General care information regarding silk fabrics made of silk fibers. Check label or hangtag for specific information and care instructions.

1. Dry cleaning is best for silk.
2. Some silks can be hand washed—only if so labeled. Follow manufacturer's instructions. Prolonged soaking may damage colors.
3. If machine washable, use gentle cycle and warm water.
4. *Do not* use chlorine bleach on any silk fabric.
5. Avoid excessive rubbing.
6. Iron on the wrong side. Use a medium to low temperature setting. To avoid water spotting *do not* use steam.

Care of Flax-Fiber (Linen) Fabrics

General care information regarding linen fabrics made of flax fibers. Check label or hangtag for specific information and care instructions.

1. Machine wash in hot water.
2. Wash dark colors at lower water temperature to prevent fading.
3. Use chlorine bleach only on white linen. *Do not* bleach colored linen.
4. Tumble dry at regular setting.
5. Use hot iron. *Do not* press in sharp creases.
6. Dry cleaning is recommended to retain the shape and color of linen.

Care of Wool-Fiber Fabrics

General care information regarding wool fabrics made of wool fibers. Check label or hangtag for specific information and care instructions.

1. Woolens should be dry cleaned.
2. For those woolens labeled *washable* follow "care" or "how to launder" instructions on label.
3. *Do not* use chlorine bleach.
4. Steam or press with damp pressing cloth. Use a medium temperature iron setting.

Care of Acetate-Fiber Fabrics

General care information regarding fabrics made of acetate fibers. Check label or hangtag for specific information and care instructions.

1. Most acetate garments should be dry cleaned.
2. If laundering is indicated, use the following guide:
   A. Hand wash in warm water with mild suds.
   B. *Do not* wring or twist garment. Handle gently.
   C. Avoid soaking colored items (to avoid dye transfer).
   D. Machine wash in warm water and gentle cycle.
   E. Use fabric softener to reduce static buildup.
   F. Press while damp on the wrong side with cool iron. If finishing on the right side is required, use a pressing cloth.

NOTE: Acetate is adversely affected by acetone and other organic solvents such as nail polish remover and perfumes containing such solvents. Acetate fabric will dissolve.

Care of Acrylic-Fiber Fabrics

General care information regarding fabrics made of acrylic fibers. Check label or hangtag for specific information and care instructions.

1. Hand wash delicate items in warm water.
   A. Use fabric softener in every third or fourth washing to reduce static buildup.
   B. Gently squeeze out water. Smooth or shake out garment. Let dry on rustproof hanger.
2. Machine wash in warm water.
   A. Use a fabric softener during the final rinse cycle.
   B. Tumble dry at a low temperature setting.
   C. Remove garments as soon as tumbling cycle is completed.
3. If ironing is required, use a moderately warm iron.

Care of Anidex-Fiber Fabrics

General care information regarding fabrics made of anidex fibers. Check label or hangtag for specific information and care instructions.

1. Home launder or dry clean fabrics according to recommendations for companion fibers (or fibers or fiber yarns used with anidex fibers).
2. Chlorine bleach may be used in laundering.
3. Machine or drip dry, as desired.
4. Recommended safe ironing temperature is 320°F (161.3°C).

Care of Modacrylic-Fiber Fabrics

General care information regarding fabrics made of modacrylic fibers. Check label or hangtag for specific information and care instructions.

1. Dry cleaning or fur cleaning process is suggested for deep pile garments.
2. If laundering is indicated, use the following guide:
   A. Machine wash in warm water.
   B. Use a fabric softener during the final rinse cycle.
   C. Tumble dry at a low temperature setting.
   D. Remove articles as soon as tumbling cycle is completed.
   E. If ironing is required, use low temperature iron setting. *Never* use a hot iron.

Care of Nylon-Fiber Fabrics

General care information regarding fabrics made of nylon fibers. Check label or hangtag for specific information and care instructions.

1. Most items made from nylon can be machine washed using warm water.
2. Whites should be laundered only with other whites to retain freshness.
3. Use fabric softener in final rinse cycle.
4. Tumble dry at a low temperature setting.
5. Remove articles as soon as tumbling cycle is completed.
6. If ironing is required, use warm iron.

Care of Polyester-Fiber Fabrics

General care information regarding fabrics made of polyester fibers. Check label or hangtag for specific information and care instructions.

1. Pretreat any greasy stains before washing by rubbing in an undiluted liquid detergent or applying spray-type pretreatment product.
2. Most items made from polyester can be machine washed using warm water.
3. Use fabric softener in final rinse cycle.
4. Tumble dry at a low temperature setting.
5. Remove articles as soon as tumbling cycle is completed.
6. If ironing is desired, use a moderately warm iron.
7. Some items made from polyester can be dry cleaned. Pigment prints, commonly applied to polyester double knits, do not withstand dry cleaning well.

Care of Rayon-Fiber Fabrics

General care information regarding fabrics made of rayon fibers. Check label or hangtag for specific information and care instructions.

1. Most rayon fabrics machine wash well. Use gentle agitation.
2. Some types of rayon fabrics can be bleached, however, some finishes are sensitive to *chlorine bleach.*
3. Some types of rayon fabrics and garment construction make dry cleaning advisable to maintain shape and body.
4. If hand laundering is indicated, use the following guide:
   A. Hand wash in lukewarm water with mild suds. Gently squeeze suds through fabric. Rinse in lukewarm water. *Do not* wring or twist garment. Smooth or shake out garment. Let dry on a rustproof hanger.
   B. Press while damp on the wrong side with moderately warm iron. If finishing on the right side is required, use a pressing cloth.

Care of Triacetate-Fiber Fabrics

General care information regarding fabrics made of *triacetate fibers*. Check label or hangtag for specific information and care instructions.

1. Most garments containing 100 percent triacetate can be machine washed and machine dried.
2. If ironing is desired, use a high iron temperature setting.
3. Articles containing triacetate fibers require very little special care due mainly to the fiber's resistance to high temperature.
4. Pleated garments are best hand laundered.

NOTE: Triacetate is adversely affected by acetone and other organic solvents such as nail polish remover and perfumes containing such solvents. Triacetate fabric will dissolve.

Care of Spandex-Fiber Fabrics

General care information regarding fabrics made of *spandex fibers*. Check label or hangtag for specific information and care instructions.

1. Hand or machine wash in lukewarm water.
2. *Do not* use chlorine bleach on any fabric containing spandex.
3. Use oxygen or sodium perborate type bleach.
4. Rinse thoroughly.
5. Drip dry or machine dry.
6. If machine drying, use low temperature setting.
7. Ironing, if required, should be done rapidly and the iron should not be left in one position too long. Use a low iron temperature setting.

Care of Vinyl Fabrics

General care information regarding fabrics made of vinyl. Check label or hangtag for specific information and care instructions.

1. Garments cannot be dry cleaned.
2. Best cleaned by sponging with damp cloth and soap.
3. Articles made of vinyl require no pressing.

Laundering Conditions for Typical Washable Fabrics
(Machine or Hand Laundry)*

Types of Loads	Amount of Washing Action (Agitation)	Spinning or Wringing	Special Comments
Sturdy white and colorfast fabrics	Regular cycle or 10–18 minutes of regular agitation speed in the wash cycle and 2–6 minutes in the rinse cycle.	Regular cycle or regular spin speed and time. Normal pressure setting in wring cycle.	Provides best possible cleaning and water extraction for items that can withstand regular wash conditions.
Sturdy noncolorfast fabrics	Regular agitation speed. Reduce wash time to 6–8 minutes.	Regular spin speed and time. Normal wring cycle pressure.	Reduced wash time helps limit color loss. Handle quickly in hand washing from wash to rinse. Roll in a towel to absorb as much water as possible before drying.
Sturdy durable permanent press fabrics	Durable/permanent press cycle or 6–8 minutes of regular agitation speed in the wash cycle.	Durable/permanent press cycle or slow spin speed or 1–2 minutes of regular spin speed. Use light pressure in wring cycle.	Reduced wash time helps preserve finish. Slow spin, short spin time or light pressure helps minimize wrinkling.
Delicate fabrics including delicate synthetic or durable-press fabrics with delicate trim and knits	Gentle, durable/permanent press cycle, gentle cycle or knit cycle or 4–6 minutes slow agitation speed in the wash cycle and 2–3 minutes in the rinse cycle. If regular agitation speed is used, allow only 2–4 minutes in the wash cycle and 1–2 minutes in the rinse rinse cycle. Squeeze or rub gently by hand.	Gentle, durable/permanent press cycle, gentle cycle or knit cycle or 2–3 minutes of slow spin speed. Avoid wringing or use very light pressure.	Reduced agitation time and speed helps to protect delicate items, to preserve special finishes and to minimize shrinkage and snagging of knits. Reduced spin speed helps to minimize wrinkling.
Poorly constructed garments and fabrics that ravel or fray easily	Treat as delicate fabrics.	Bulky, absorbent items may benefit from regular spin or wring cycles.	Reduced wash time and speed will help minimize fraying and pulling apart at seams. Regular spin will not contribute to fraying.

Note: On some washers *regular speed* may be called *normal* or *fast* and *slow speed* may be called *gentle* or *delicate*.

*Reproduced courtesy of Procter & Gamble Education Services.

Laundering Conditions for Typical Washable Fabrics
(Machine or Hand Laundry) (continued)*

Types of Loads	Amount of Washing Action (Agitation)	Spinning or Wringing	Special Comments
Woolens— either woven or knit	Use slow agitation speed. Allow only 1–2 minutes in the wash cycle and 1–2 minutes in the rinse cycle. Squeeze gently when washing by hand.	Use regular spin speed. Use normal wringer pressure for blankets.	Agitation in both wash and rinse cycles must be reduced to an absolute minimum to minimize shrinkage and felting of woolens which have not been treated for shrinkage control. Treated woolens can be done in a knit cycle or delicate cycle. Regular spinning or wringing will not contribute to shrinkage and will speed drying.

Guide to Safe Water Temperature for Machine Laundering*

Temperature	Used For	Special Comments
Hot: 140° (approximately 60°C)	Sturdy Whites Colorfast Items Diapers Durable Press, if heavily soiled Wash and Wear, if heavily soiled	Gives quickest and best cleaning; sanitizes best. Not suitable for all fabrics.
Warm: 100°F ± 10°F (approximately 38°C ± 5°C)	Moderately soiled clothes Colored fabrics that are not colorfast Durable Press Wash and Wear Nylon, Acrylic, Polyester, Other Man-made Fiber Fabrics Silks Woolens	Reduces fading. Preserves finish of durable press. Tends to reduce wrinkling of fabrics containing nylon or polyester. Used most often for hand washing. Minimizes shrinkage of knits and woolens.
Cold: 80°F (approximately 27°C) or cooler	Extra sensitive colors Very lightly soiled items Rinsing—especially for durable press and other easy care fabrics	Cleaning is more difficult than in hot or even warm water. Minimizes wrinkling and fading of colors. Saves hot water supply.

*Reproduced courtesy of Procter & Gamble Education Services.

Types & Uses of Bleaching Products for Home Laundering

There are two basic types of bleaches commonly used in home laundering.
1. Chlorine-type bleach;
2. Oxygen-type bleach.

Many laundry problems are caused by a lack of understanding of the purpose and effects of household bleaches on fabrics. The chart is offered as a guide to use bleach properly.

Types of Bleaching Products & Their Use for Home Laundering*

Types of Bleach	Performance	Used on	Directions for Use
Liquid Chlorine-type Bleach°	Whitens Helps remove soil Removes stains Disinfects Deodorizes	White and bleachfast colored cotton, linen acrylic, modacrylic, nylon, polyester and durable press fabrics. *Do not* use on silk, wool mohair, some types of spandex fabrics.	Read and follow package directions. Measure recommended amount carefully. *Never* pour undiluted bleach directly onto colored fabrics.°°
Dry Chlorine-type Bleach°	Same as above	Same as above	Read and follow package directions. *Never* pour undiluted bleach directly onto colored fabrics.°°
Dry or Liquid Oxygen-type Bleach	Handles light-duty bleaching jobs	All washable fabrics and most washable colors	Read and follow package directions. Measure carefully and add to the washer after agitation has started or add with detergent as the machine fills and before clothes are added. *Never* pour undiluted bleach directly onto colored fabric.°°

°Reproduced courtesy of Procter & Gamble Education Services.

°°*Do not* use a chlorine-type bleach if iron is present in the water supply. *Do not* combine full-strength chlorine-type bleach and full-strength liquid detergent because noxious fumes can result. Be sure both products are diluted when using them together. Dilute bleach using one of the following methods:

1. Add bleach to at least 1 quart water before adding to load of laundry agitating in the washer.
2. Add bleach to wash water before adding laundry.

How to Test Colored Fabrics for Bleach-fastness

Regardless of the type of bleach used always test colored fabrics for bleach-fastness before using bleach on them.

Chlorine-type Bleach   Mix 1 tablespoon of bleach with ¼ cup of water. Apply one drop of this solution to an inconspicuous portion of the fabric. Be sure the solution penetrates the fabric. Let stand one minute. Then, blot dry with paper towel. If there is no color change, the item can be safely bleached.

Oxygen-type Bleach   Mix 1 tablespoon of bleach to ½ gallon of hot water. Dip an inconspicuous portion of the fabric up and down in the hot solution. If color does not bleed or if there is no color change, the bleach can be used as recommended for laundering or soaking.

   If the item is stained, it is best to bleach the entire item. Do not bleach just the stained area. In this way if there should be a slight lightening of color, the color change will be uniform over the whole item.

Tumble Drying Garments in an Automatic Dryer*

1. Read and follow the directions in the dryer's instruction book.
2. Clean the lint filter after each use.
3. Remove dryer-added fabric softener sheets after each use.
4. Avoid overloading the dryer. Large loads take longer to dry. If clothes do not tumble freely, they will be more likely to wrinkle.
5. *Do not* overdry fabrics. Overdrying can increase shrinkage, especially in knits. It may make fabrics feel limp and cause selvages to curl, making household linens harder to handle.
6. Remove durable-press items from the dryer as soon as it stops to reduce the likelihood of wrinkling. If this is not possible, let the dryer run a few more minutes to freshen the clothes. (Some dryers automatically provide intermittent tumbling after the drying period to help keep the clothes from wrinkling.)
7. *Do not* dry glass fiber fabrics automatically unless the hangtag or label states otherwise. Some glass fibers may break as a result of the tumbling action.
8. *Do not* dry foam-padded items such as bedroom slippers and bras.
9. Refer to the dryer instruction book for care of special items such as rubber or plastics.

Advantages	Disadvantages
Saves time and effort.	Initial cost of equipment.
Makes clothes soft, sometimes fluffy.	Cost of operation.
Smooths clothes. Removes wrinkles (particularly from man-made fiber and durable-press fabrics).	Uses more energy. Inadequate space for a dryer.
Is not dependent upon the weather.	

Line Drying Garments (Outdoors or Indoors)*

1. Be sure the clotheslines are clean before hanging clothes.
2. Secure the clothes carefully with clean clothespins.
3. Smooth items and straighten selvages, seams, collars, cuffs, etc., as much as possible while the item is wet. This will make pressing easier.
4. Dry colored items in the shade if possible to minimize fading.
5. If colored items must be hung in the sun, take them down as soon as they are dry.
6. Distribute the weight of a heavy item, such as a bedspread, over two or three lines rather than just one.

Advantages	Disadvantages
Line drying outdoors gives clothes fresh smell.	Dependent upon weather.
Enables large items (bedspreads, blankets) to dry thoroughly without agitation or tumbling action.	Clothes are stiffer than when tumble dried, because there is little air movement.
Little cost of equipment (clothespins, clothesline, etc.).	Clothes sometimes get dirty (as in an industrial community).
No energy required.	Sunlight can damage colors.
Not dependent upon weather.	Clothes take longer time to dry than when hung outdoors.
Convenient when only one or two small items are washed.	Inadequate space. Inconvenient.

Flat-Surface Drying*

1. Dry woolens and leather items away from direct heat.
2. Use a clean, absorbent surface (such as a towel) to speed drying. *Never* use newspaper because the ink can stain fabrics.
3. Some dryers provide a rack and a no-tumble setting for flat-surface drying.

Advantages	Disadvantages
Helps prevent shrinkage.	Inadequate space available.
Especially good for wool sweaters and some leather items.	Items dry slowly.

*Reproduced courtesy of Procter & Gamble Education Services.

Guide to Safe Ironing Temperature Limits for Fabrics

Fabrics	Safe Ironing Temperature Limits
Natural Fibers	
Cotton	400°–425°F (206.1°–220.1°C)
Flax (Linen)	450°F (234.1°C)
Silk	300°F (150.1°C)
Wool	300°F (150.1°C)
Specialty Hair	300°F (150.1°C)
Man-Made Fibers	
Acetate	250°–350°F (123.9°–178.1°C) (Press on wrong side)
Acrylic	300°F (150.1°C)
Anidex	*Do not* press.
Metallic	Cover with pressing cloth.
Modacrylic	225°F (108.1°C)
Nylon	300°–350°F (150.1°–178.1C°)
Polyester	325°F (164.1°C)
Rayon	350°–375°F (178.1°–192.1°C) (Press on wrong side)
Rubber/Synthetic Rubber	*Do not* press.
Spandex	300°F (150.1°C)
Triacetate	375°–400°F (192.1°–206.1°C) (Untreated)
Vinyl	*Do not* press.
Vinyon	200°F (94.1°C)
Blends/Blended Fibers	Lowest of the blended fiber types.
Mixed Fibers	Lowest of the mixed fiber types.

Spot & Stain Removal Products

Since prompt treatment helps in the removal of stains, it is wise to store the proper supplies. Here are some of the stain-removal materials you may want to keep on hand:

Bleaches Chlorine-type bleach; fabric color remover; oxygen-type bleach (nonchlorine, all fabric).

Detergents Enzyme pre-soak product; liquid laundry detergent; other laundry detergent; spray-type pretreatment products.

Soap Laundry soap; white bar soap.

Miscellaneous Stain Removers Ammonia; oxalic acid crystals°; rust-stain remover; white vinegar.

Solvents Dry cleaning solvent or spot remover°; nail polish remover; rubbing alcohol°; turpentine, steam distilled.

Other Supplies Clean white cloths and white paper towels.

Most of these products should be available at your grocery store or drugstore. Chemical and cleaning supplies to the trade carry a range of products.

°Products can be purchased at a drugstore.

Storing & Using Spot & Stain Removal Products Safely

Some stain-removal products are flammable; others are toxic. Treat them *all* with care.

1. Keep stain-removal products out of the reach of children and food products. Store in closed containers in a cool, dry place.
2. Read and heed all label warnings. Store stain-removal products in their original containers so you will have label directions to follow.
3. Empty and wash all containers immediately after using them. Glass or unchipped porcelain containers are best for stain-removal products. Plastic pans are fine, *except* when solvents are used. *Never* use a rusty container.
4. *Do not* get chemicals near your skin. Wash any spilled chemicals off your skin and the work surface immediately.
5. *Do not* breathe any more solvent vapors than necessary. Always use solvents in a well-ventilated room.
6. *Do not* use solvents near an open flame or an electrical outlet.
7. *Do not* add solvents directly into the washer or dryer. Launder or rinse out the solvent or be absolutely certain that all of the solvent has evaporated from the garment before putting it into a laundry appliance.
8. *Do not* mix stain-removal products together—especially ammonia and chlorine bleach or full-strength liquid detergent and full-strength chlorine bleach. Either of these mixtures can produce noxious fumes. If more than one stain remover is needed, use one, rinse it out thoroughly, and then use the other stain remover.

Spot & Stain Removal
Treatments for Fabrics

Many common stains can be removed by just washing the garment, especially if the stains are fresh. Some laundry products contain special ingredients such as enzymes or oxygen bleach to aid in removing stains. An enzyme pre-soak product will be particularly helpful in removing these common stains: body soil, blood, grass, gravy, milk, egg, cream soups, baby formula, baby foods, chocolate, puddings, ice cream, fruits, vegetables and other food stains.

If the stains have aged, it would be best to pre-soak the garments in warm water. This should be followed by a regular laundering. Often old, unknown stains can be removed and many yellowed fabrics can be restored by this method.

A laundry product containing oxygen bleach, such as Oxydol, will be helpful in removing highly colored stains such as tea, coffee, fruit juice, dye that has "bled" from another item, etc. An oxygen bleach is a mild bleach that can be used on fabrics that cannot withstand chlorine bleach. A product containing oxygen bleach will be most effective in removing stains when used in hot water. Use the hottest water the fabric can stand.

Even detergents with special stain-removing ingredients cannot remove all stains. At times it is necessary to use special products and/or treatments. Of course, there are some stains, too, that cannot be removed by even the most professional techniques.

The following information applies to all fabrics:
1. Know the fiber content of items in the wash. Read sewn-in labels or hangtags as you buy new articles. Mark each hangtag with a description of the article and keep these hangtags available for speedy reference.
2. Durable-press and polyester fabrics (such as Dacron, Fortrel, Kodel, Trevira) can firmly hold oily soils. Treat stains on these fabrics first with heavy-duty liquid laundry detergent, spray-type pretreatment products or dry-cleaning solvents and then launder. If stain remains, repeat the treatment. You may find some oily stains simply will not come out, especially if garments have gone through a dryer or have been ironed.
3. *Do not* use chlorine bleach on silk, wool or spandex.
4. *Do not* treat leather. Take it to your dry cleaner. If the dry cleaner does not handle leather, he can direct you to an expert in leather.

Although I cannot guarantee the success of the following methods in removing spots and stains, experience has shown that the methods are effective in most cases.

Acid Stains Rinse with water immediately. Then apply ammonia (to neutralize acid) and rinse again with water. If the fabric changes color, apply white vinegar and rinse with water.

Adhesive Tape Sponge with perchlorethylene in open air. Launder.

Alcoholic Beverage Sponge with cold water, then glycerine and water. Before laundering, rinse with vinegar water.

Antiperspirants See *Deodorants.*

Ballpoint Pen Ink Place blotter under fabric. Pour denatured alcohol through spot. Rub Vaseline into stain. Rub fireproof Energine into stain. Soak in detergent in solution and launder.

Blood Soak in cold water for about thirty minutes. If stain remains, soak in lukewarm ammonia water (3 tablespoons of household ammonia per gallon of water). Alternative: ordinary club soda. On thick fabrics, spread stain with paste of corn starch and water. Let dry and brush off.

Chewing Gum Put article in plastic bag and place in freezer. Gum may be removed from the surface with a dull knife. On washable fabrics, soften gum with egg white and launder.

Coffee Sponge with cool water or soak in cool water for at least thirty minutes. Work in soap or detergent and rinse thoroughly. Soak in warm water with enzyme containing product.

Cosmetics Dampen stain and rub with soap. Rinse and launder.

Crayons Loosen stain with kitchen shortening. Apply detergent and baking soda, working until outline of stain is removed. Launder, use chlorine bleach if safe, otherwise use oxygen bleach. On silk or wool, use fireproof Energine.

Deodorants and Antiperspirants A *light stain*—rub in an undiluted liquid detergent. Launder using hottest water safe for fabric. A *heavy stain*—place stain face down on paper towel and sponge back of stain with dry cleaning solvent. Let dry, rinse. Rub in an undiluted liquid detergent. Launder using hottest water safe for fabric.

Dye Transfer White fabrics that may have picked up dye from a colored fabric may be restored by using a fabric color remover. Launder. If color remains, launder again using chlorine bleach, if safe for fabric. For colored fabrics or non-bleachable whites, soak in an oxygen bleach then launder.

Eggs Sponge with cold water. If stain remains, work in a soap or detergent. If egg had dried, scrape off egg, then work in soap or detergent.

Eyebrow Pencil or Eye Shadow Rub in an undiluted detergent or soap and rinse well. Repeat if necessary.

Fabric Softeners For stains which may result from accidental spills; dampen the stain and rub with soap. Rinse. Repeat if necessary. Launder.

Fruit Stains (also berry) Stretch stained area over bowl and pour boiling water through it. If stain persists, sponge with lemon solution. Do not use soap and water on fresh fruit stains. Soak in enzyme containing product.

Gravy/Meat Juice (greasy stains) Sponge in lukewarm water. Launder in warm soapy water. On some fabrics, it may be necessary to rub soap or detergent thoroughly into stain and allow to stand for several hours before rinsing.

Grass Stains Work detergent into stains, then rinse. If safe for dye, sponge stain with alcohol solution (2 parts water, 1 part alcohol). Soak using an enzyme containing product.

Grease Place towel under stain, pour cleaning fluid through stained area. Launder in hot water.

Honey (syrup) Sponge with cool water or soak in cool water for thirty minutes. If trace of syrup remains, work in soap or detergent and rinse thoroughly.

Ice Cream Sponge in cold water. Apply either neutral detergent solution or vinegar water.

Ink Force water through stain. Then wash with soap or detergent several times. Then soak in warm suds containing 1 to 4 tablespoons of ammonia to a quart of water. Also try detergent and white vinegar. Also see *Ball Point Pen Ink.*

Iodine Treat with ammonia. Rinse with water.

Ketchup On washable articles, sponge with cool water and let set thirty minutes. Work in detergent and rinse.

Lipstick Loosen stain with cold cream or glycerine. Wash as usual in undiluted detergent. If necessary, rubbing alcohol may be used, if safe for fabric. Also try cleaning fluid, slowly poured through stained area.

Liquid Makeup Dampen stain. Apply undiluted liquid detergent. Work in and rinse well. Repeat if necessary.

Mildew Add ½ cup liquid Lysol to wash water in washing machine. On leather, sponge with 50% water and 50% rubbing alcohol.

Milk/Cream/Ice Cream Launder washable fabrics with plenty of soap. Repeat, if necessary. Also try enzyme detergent.

Mucus Soak with an enzyme detergent. Launder using chlorine bleach if safe for fabric. If not use an oxygen bleach with detergent.

Mud Allow to dry. Brush lightly. Launder.

Nail Polish If fabric is acetate, Arnel, Dynel or Verel, sponge stain with amyl acetate. On other fabrics use acetone.

Oil (fish, liver oil, linseed oil, machine oil, vegetable oil) Rub soap or detergent into stain and rinse with warm water. Or sponge with fireproof Energine.

Paint No one method will remove all stains. *Treat immediately.*

Latex, Acrylic, Water-base Paints. Treat stain while still wet. These cannot be removed after they have dried. Rinse in warm water to flush out paint, then launder.

Oil-base Paint, Varnish Apply the solvent recommended on the paint container. If container is not available, apply turpentine. Rinse. Rub with soap. Rinse and launder.

Perfume or Cologne Wash immediately in solution of detergent and hot water. Do not allow stain to age.

Perspiration Dampen stain and rub with soap (for silk fabrics, rub gently). Presoak with an enzyme detergent. Launder in hot water with chlorine bleach, if safe for fabrics. If perspiration has changed the color of the fabric, apply ammonia to fresh stains; vinegar to old stains. Rinse. Launder in hottest water safe for color and fabric.

Pet "Stains" Wash with solution of ¼ cup salt to 1 pint water. Then with ammonia solution—1 part ammonia to 20 parts water.

Rust Apply commercial rust remover solution and follow instructions on label. Do not use chlorine bleach. Rinse and launder.

Scorching If light scorching, wash with soap or detergent or wash with small amount of chlorine bleach added to wash water. For heavier scorching, cover stain with cloth dampened with hydrogen peroxide. Cover with dry cloth and press with iron. Rinse.

Shellac Sponge stain with alcohol, or soak in alcohol. Dilute alcohol with 2 parts water for use on acetate. If alcohol bleeds the dye, try turpentine.

Shoe Polish Apply undiluted liquid detergent. Rinse. If necessary, sponge with diluted rubbing alcohol (30% solution).

Soft Drinks Sponge immediately with cool water. If persistent, sponge with alcohol solution. Rub in glycerine and rinse after thirty minutes.

Soup Sponge with cool water. If stain remains, work in soap for detergent. Allow to dry. If greasy stain remains, sponge with Energine. If a colored stain remains after the fabric dries, use a chlorine or peroxygen bleach. Always test fabrics for color-fastness first.

Tar Scrape off as much as possible. Rub stain with petroleum jelly. Then sponge with cleaning fluid. Wash in warm, soapy water. Rinse.

Tobacco Dampen stain and rub with soap. Rinse. Soak in enzyme detergent or oxygen bleach. Launder. If stain remains, launder again using chlorine bleach, if safe for fabric.

Tomato Sponge with cold water. Work glycerine into stain and let stand for half hour. Sponge with soap and water.

Varnish Same as "paint."

▶

Vegetable Stains On washable articles, sponge with cool water and let set thirty minutes. Then work in detergent and rinse.

Urine Soak with an enzyme detergent. Launder using chlorine bleach if safe for fabric. If not use an oxygen bleach with detergent.

Vomit Sponge or soak in a solution of 2 quarts of cold water with ½ cup salt. Rinse in clear water and wash with warm soapsuds.

Walnut Stain Very difficult stain to remove. Boil washable articles in soap or detergent solution for fresh stains. If safe for fabric and stain remains, use chlorine or sodium perborate bleach treatment.

Water Stains Launder.

Wax (candle) Scrape off as much as possible. Place fabric between two paper towels and press with warm iron. Sponge final traces of oily stain with denatured alcohol and water (1 part alcohol, 2 parts water).

Wax (car, floor, furniture) Rub with soap or detergent and rinse with warm water. On some wash-and-wear fabrics, it may be necessary to let stand for several hours before rinsing. Launder as usual. Sometimes you may need to use grease solvent.

Wine Soak with enzyme detergent and hottest water safe for fabric. Launder. If stain remains, launder using chlorine bleach, if safe for fabric.

Spot & Stain Removal Treatments for Pure Wool Fabrics*

Alcoholic Beverages Place towel under stain. Use soda water. Fizz the soda and rub in gently towards center of stain.

Blood Blot with concentrated common starch paste. Rinse from *back* with mild soapy water.

Burning Cigarette Brush off.

Butter Sponge with perchlorethylene.

Chewing Gum Scrape off and sponge with perchlorethylene.

Chocolate Sponge with mild soapy water.

Coffee, Tea Sponge with glycerine. If glycerine is not available, use warm water.

Egg Scrape off and sponge with soapy water.

Food See *Alcoholic Beverage*.

Glue Sponge with alcohol.

Grease Sponge with perchlorethylene.

Ink Immerse in cold water.

Iodine Treat with cool water followed by alcohol.

Iron Rust Sponge with a weak solution of oxalic acid until stain disappears. Sponge carefully with household ammonia and rinse with water.

Lipstick May often be erased by rubbing white bread over area with a firm, gentle motion.

Mud Once dry brush and sponge from back with soapy water.

Tar, Road Oil Sponge with perchlorethylene.

Vaseline Sponge with perchlorethylene.

Wine (Red) Immerse in cold water.

*Reproduced courtesy of The Wool Bureau.

Fiber Resources

Allied Fibers and Plastics Company
Allied Chemical Corporation
1411 Broadway
New York, New York 10018

American Cyanamid Company
Wayne, New Jersey 07470

American Enka Company
Marketing Technical Department
Enka, North Carolina 28728

American Hoechst Corporation
Hoechst Fibers Division
1515 Broadway
New York, New York 10036

Amoco Fabrics Company
Fibers and Yarn Division
550 Interstate North Parkway
Atlanta, Georgia 30339

Avtex Fibers Inc.
1185 Avenue of the Americas
New York, New York 10036

Badische Company
Williamsburg, Virginia 23185

Belgian Linen Association
280 Madison Avenue
New York, New York 10016

Celanese Corporation
Celanese Fibers Marketing Company
1211 Avenue of the Americas
New York, New York 10036

Chevron Fibers, Inc.
Subsidiary of Chevron Chemical Company
7310 Ritchie Highway
Glen Burnie, Maryland 21061

Cotton Inc.
1370 Avenue of the Americas
New York, New York 10019

Courtaulds North America Inc.
104 West 40th Street
New York, New York 10018

Eastman Chemicals Products Inc.
Kingsport, Tennessee 37662

E.I. du Pont de Nemours & Company
Textile Fibers Department
Technical Service Section
Wilmington, Delaware 19898

Hercules Incorporated
Fibers Marketing Division
3169 Holcomb Bridge Road
Norcross, Georgia 30071

International Silk Association
c/o Rudolph Desco & Co.
580 Sylvan Avenue
Englewood Cliffs, New Jersey 07632

Mohair Council of America
183 Madison Avenue
New York, New York 10016

Monsanto Textiles Company
800 North Lindbergh Boulevard
St. Louis, Missouri 63167

Phillips Fibers Corporation
Subsidiary of Phillips Petroleum Company
P.O. Box 66
Greenville, South Carolina 29602

Wool Bureau, Inc.
360 Lexington Avenue
New York, New York 10017

Institute of Textile Technology
Charlottesville, Virginia 22902

International Fabricare Institute
P. O. Box 940, Joliet Illinois 60434
12251 Tech Road, Silver Spring, Maryland 20904

International Nonwovens & Disposables Association
10 East 40 Street
New York, New York 10017

International Silk Association
c/o Rudolph Desco & Co.
580 Sylvan Avenue
Englewood Cliffs, New Jersey 07632

Laundry & Cleaners Allied Trades Association
543 Valley Road
Upper Montclair, New Jersey 07043

Man-Made Fiber Producers Association, Inc.
1150 Seventeenth Street, N.W.
Washington, D.C. 20036

Mohair Council of America
183 Madison Avenue
New York, New York 10016

National Knitted Outerwear Association
51 Madison Avenue
New York, New York 10010

National Knitwear Manufacturers Association
350 Fifth Avenue
New York, New York 10001

National Retail Merchants Association
100 West 31 Street
New York, New York 10001

Neighborhood Cleaners Association
116 East 27 Street
New York, New York 10016

Textile Distributors Association
1040 Avenue of the Americas
New York, New York 10018

United States Department of Agriculture
Southern Regional Research Center
1100 Robert E. Lee Boulevard
New Orleans, Louisiana 70179

Wool Bureau, Inc.
360 Lexington Avenue
New York, New York 10017

Bibliography

Books

Advances in False-twist Texturing Processes. Manchester, England: Shirley Institute, 1974.

Alth, Max and Simon Alth. *The Stain Removal Handbook*. New York: Hawthorn Books, Inc., 1977.

American Association of Textile Chemists and Colorists. *AATCC Handbook on Bonded and Laminated Fabrics*. Research Triangle Park, N.C.: American Association of Textile Chemists and Colorists.

American Fabrics Encyclopedia of Textiles. 2nd ed. Englewood Cliffs, N.J.: Prentice-Hall, Inc., 1972.

American Home Economics Association. *Textile Handbook*. 4th ed. Washington, D.C.: American Home Economics Association, 1970.

Bath, Virginia Churchill. *Lace*. Indiana: Regnery/Gateway, Inc., 1974.

Beech, W.F. *Fiber-reactive Dyes*. New York: SAF International, 1970.

Bhatnagar, V.M., editor. *Advances in Fire Retardant Textiles*. Westport, Conn.: Technomic Publishing Co., Inc., 1975.

Birrell, V.L. *The Textile Arts: A Handbook of Fabric Structure & Design Processes*. New York: Harper & Row, 1959.

Blackmon, A.G. *Manual of Standard Fabric Defects in the Textile Industry*. Graniteville, S.C.: Graniteville Co., 1975.

Boyle, Michael. *Textile Dyes, Finishes, and Auxiliaries*. New York: Garland Publishing, Inc., 1977.

Carter, Mary E. *Essential Fiber Chemistry*. New York: Marcel Dekker, Inc., 1971.

Casper, M.S. *Nonwoven Textiles*. Park Ridge, N.J.: Noyes Data Corporation, 1975.

Celanese Fibers Marketing Co. *Fabric Performance Standards for Trademark Licensing*. Celanese Corp., 1972.

Chambers, Bernice G. *Color and Design*. Englewood Cliffs, N.J.: Prentice-Hall, Inc., 1951.

Clark, George L. *The Encyclopedia of Microscopy*. New York: Reinhold Book Co., 1961.

Clarke, W. *An Introduction to Textile Printing*. 4th ed. New York: Halsted Press, 1974.

Clifford, C.R. *Lace Dictionary*. New York: Clifford & Lawton Pub., 1913.

Cockett, S.R. and K.A. Hilton. *Dyeing of Cellulosic Fibres and Related Processes*. New York: Academic Press, Inc., 1961

Collier, A.M. *A Handbook of Textiles*. Elmsford, New York: Pergamon Press, Inc., 1971.

Cook, J.G. *Handbook of Polyolefin Fibres*. Watford, England: Merrow Publishing Company, 1967.

_____. *Handbook of Textile Fibres*, 2 Vol., 4th ed. Watford, England: Merrow Publishing Company, 1968.

Corbman, Dr. Bernard P. *Textiles: Fiber to Fabric*. New York: McGraw-Hill Inc., 1975.

Emery, Irene. *The Primary Structure of Fabrics*. Washington, D.C.: Textile Museum, 1966.

Feldman, Annette. *Handmade Lace & Pattern*. New York: Harper & Row, 1975.

Dictionary of Textile Terms, A. 12th ed. New York: Dan River Inc., 1976.

Fuhrmann, Brigita. *Bobbin Lace*. New York: Watson-Guptill Publications, 1976.

Goswami, B.B. *Textile Yarns*. New York: John Wiley & Sons Inc., 1977.

Greenwood, K. *Weaving: Control of Fabric Structure*. Watford, England: Merrow, 1975.

Hathorne, B.L. *Woven Stretch and Textured Fabrics*. New York: John Wiley & Sons Inc., 1975.

Hall, A.J. *The Standard Handbook of Textiles*. 8th ed. New York: John Wiley & Sons Inc., 1975.

_____. *Textile Finishing*. 3rd ed. New York: American Elsevier Press Inc., 1966.

Hearle, J.W.S. *Structural Mechanics of Fibers, Yarns and Fabrics*. New York: John Wiley & Sons Inc., 1969.

Henshaw, D.E. *Self-twist Yarn*. Plainfield, N.J.: Textile Book Service, 1971.

Hilado, Carlos J. *Handbook of Flammability Regulations*. Westport, Conn.: Technomic Publishing Co., Inc., 1975.

_____. *Flammability of Fabrics*. Westport, Conn.: Technomic Publishing Co., Inc., 1974.

Holker, J.R. *Bonded Fabrics*. Watford, England: Merrow, 1975.

Hollen, Norma and Jane Saddler. *Textiles*, 4th ed. New York: Macmillan Inc., 1973.

Huelson, T.L. *Lace & Bobbin: A History and Collectors Guide*. Cranbury, N.J.: A.S. Barnes & Co. Inc., 1973.

Identification of Textile Materials. 7th ed. Manchester, England: The Textile Institute, 1975.

International Nonwovens & Disposables Association. *Guide to Nonwoven Fabrics*. New York: International Nonwovens & Disposables Association, 1978.

Johanson, Sally. *Traditional Lace Making*. New York: Van Nostrand Reinhold Company, 1974.

Johnson, Thomas. *Tricot Fashion Design*. New York: McGraw-Hill Inc., 1946.

Jones, Mary Erwen. *Romance of Lace*. London, England: Spring Books.

Joseph, Marjory L. *Essentials of Textiles*. New York: Holt, Rinehart & Winston, 1976.

_____. *Introductory Textile Science*. New York: Holt, Rinehart & Winston, 1977.

Jourdain, M. *Old Lace: Handbook for Collectors*. B.T. Batsford, 1908.

Kleeburg, Irene Cummings, editor. *The Butterick Fabric Handbook*. New York: Butterick Publishing Co., 1975.

Koch, P.A. *Microscopic and Chemical Testing of Textiles*. Plainfield, N.J.: Textile Book Service, 1963.

Kushel, Lillian. *Fashion Textiles and Laboratory Workbook*. 2nd ed. New York: Taylor Career Programs, 1971.

Larsen, Jack Lenor and Jeanne Weeks. *Fabrics for Interiors*. Litton Education Publishing, Inc., 1975.

Linton, George E. *Applied Basic Textiles*. 2nd ed. (revised). Plainfield, N.J.: Textile Book Service, 1966.

_____. *The Modern Textile and Apparel Dictionary*. 4th ed. Plainfield, N.J.: Textile Book Service, 1973.

_____. *Natural and Man-made Textile Fibers*. 2nd ed. (revised). Plainfield, N.J.: Textile Book Service, 1973.

Lyle, Dorothy S. *Focus on Fabrics*. Silver Spring, Md.; International Fabricare Institute, 1964.

_____. *Modern Textiles*. New York: John Wiley & Sons Inc., 1976.

_____. *Performance of Textiles*. New York: John Wiley & Sons Inc., 1977.

Manchester Silk. H.T. Gaddum & Co. Limited, 1961.

Manly, Robert H. *Durable Press Treatments of Fabrics*. Park Ridge, N.J.: Noyes Data Corporation, 1976.

Marsh, J.T. *An Introduction to Textile Finishing*. 2nd ed. Plainfield, N.J.: Textile Book Service, 1966.

Moncrieff, R.W. *Man-made Fibers*. 6th ed. New York: John Wiley & Sons Inc., 1975.

Moon, Alma Chestnut. *How to Clean Everything*. New York: Simon & Schuster, 1968.

Moore, H. *Lace Book*. New York: Frederick A. Stokes Co., 1904.

Morton, W.E. and J.W.S. Hearle. *Physical Properties of Textile Fibers*. 2nd ed. New York: John Wiley & Sons Inc., 1975.

Moyer, Earl D. *Principles of Double Knitting*. Brooklyn, N.Y.: Montrose Supply & Equipment Co., 1972.

Paling, D.F. *Warp Knitting Technology*. Manchester, England: Columbine Press, 1972.

Pankowski, Edith and Dallas Pankowski. *Basic Textiles*. New York: Macmillan Inc., 1972.

Pfannschmidt, Ernst Erich. *Twentieth Century Lace*. New York: Charles Scribner's Sons, 1975.

Picken, Mary B., editor. *The Fashion Dictionary: Fabric, Sewing and Apparel as Expressed in the Language of Fashion*. New York: Funk and Wagnalls, Inc., 1972.

Piller, B. *Bulked Yarns*. Plainfield, N.J.: Textile Book Service, 1973.

Pizzuto, Joseph H. *Fabric Science*. 4th ed. revised by Arthur Price, Allen C. Cohen. New York: Fairchild Publications, 1980.

Pond, Gabrielle. *An Introduction to Lace*. New York: Charles Scribner's Sons, 1973.

Potter, M.D. and Dr. Bernard P. Corbman. *Textiles: Fiber to Fabric*. 4th ed. New York: McGraw-Hill Inc., 1967.

Powys, Marion. *Lace and Lace Making*. Boston, Mass.: Charles T. Branford Co., 1959.

Press, Jack J. *Man-made Textiles Encyclopedia*. New York: John Wiley & Sons Inc., 1959.

Reichman, Charles. *Advanced Knitting Principles*. New York: National Knitted Outerwear Association, 1964.

_____. *Double Knit Fabric Manual*. New York: National Knitted Outerwear Association, 1961.

_____. *Electronics in Knitting*. New York: National Knitted Outerwear Association, 1972.

_____. *Guide to Manufacturer of Sweaters, Knit Shirts and Swimwear*. New York: National Knitted Outerwear Association, 1963.

_____. *Knitted Fabric Primer*. New York: National Knitted Outerwear Association, 1967.

_____. *Knitted Fabric Technology*. New York: National Knitted Outerwear Association, 1974.

_____. *Knitting Encyclopedia*. New York: National Knitted Outerwear Association, 1972.

_____. *Principles of Knitting Outerwear Fabrics and Garments*. New York: National Knitted Outerwear Association, 1961.

Reisfeld, Aaron. *Control of Defects in Raschel Fabrics*. New York: National Knitted Outerwear Association, 1955.

_____. *Fundamentals of Raschel Knitting*. New York: National Knitted Outerwear Association, 1958.

_____. *Warp Knit Engineering*. New York: National Knitted Outerwear Association, 1966.

Rotenstein, Charles. *Lace Manufacture on Raschel Machines*. New York: National Knitted Outerwear Association, 1958.

Schneider, Coleman. *Embroidery: Schiffli and Multihead*. New Jersey: C. Schneider, 1978.

_____. *Machine-made Embroidery*. New Jersey: Schneider International Corporation, 1968.

Seydel, Paul V. and James R. Hunt. *Textile Warp Sizing*. Atlanta, Ga.; Long & Clopton, 1972.

Smirfitt, J.A. *An Introduction to Weft Knitting*. Watford, England: Merrow, 1975.

Storey, Joyce. *Van Nostrand Reinhold Manual of Textile Printing*. New York: Van Nostrand Reinhold Company, 1974.

Stout, Evelyn E. *Introduction to Textiles*. 3rd ed. New York: John Wiley & Sons Inc., 1976.

Textile Institute. *Identification of Textile Materials*. Manchester, England: Textile Institute, 1975.

_____. *Textile Terms and Definitions*. Manchester, England: Textile Institute, 1976.

Textile Research Institute. *Symposium on Transfer Printing*. Princeton, N.J.: Textile Research Institute, 1976.

Thomas, D.G.B. *An Introduction to Warp Knitting*. Watford, England: Merrow, 1971.

Von Henneberg, F.A. *Art & Craft of Old Lace*. 4 Weyhe, 794 Lexington Avenue, New York.

Waidle, Patricia. *Victorian Lace*. London, England: Herbert Jenkins, 1968.

Weber, Klaus Peter. *An Introduction to the Stitch Formations in Warp Knitting*. West Germany: Employees Association Karl Mayer E.V., 6053 Obertshausen.

Williams, Alex. *Flame Resistant Fabrics*. Park Ridge, New Jersey: Noyes Data Corporation, 1974.

Wingate, Dr. Isabel B. *Fairchild's Dictionary of Textiles*. 6th ed. New York: Fairchild Publications, 1979.

_____. *Textile Fabrics and Their Selection*. 7th ed. Englewood Cliffs, N.J.: Prentice-Hall, Inc., 1976.

Zielinski, S.A. *Encyclopedia of Hand Weaving*. New York: Funk & Wagnalls, Inc., 1959.

Znamerouwski, Nell. *Step by Step Weaving*. New York: Golden Press, 1967.

Pamphlets & Bulletins

Allied Chemical Corporation. *Caprolon Nylon*. A biography of Allied Chemical's nylon fiber, 1966.

_____. *The Performance Fibers*.

American Cyanamid Corp. *A Report on the Rocketing Sweater-Shirt Market*.

American Enka Co. *Encron Polyester Yarn*. General information and properties. Bulletin #PFP 1B. March 1971.

_____. *Rayon Yarn: Enka Rayon Filament Yarn*. General information and properties. 1972.

_____. *Enka Rayon Staple*. General information and properties. Bulletin #RSP 2A. March 1976.

American Fabrics. *American Fabrics*. 1954.

_____. *Rayon & Acetate*. 1969.

American Sheep Producers Council. *Glossary of Wool Fabric Terms*. Educational Pamphlet 6.

American Textile Manufacturing Institute. *All about Textiles*. January 1978.

_____. *How Textiles Are Made*.

_____. *101 Textile Terms*.

American Home Economics Association. Textile Handbook.

ASTM Standards, Part 24, Textile Materials. Philadelphia: American Society for Testing and Materials (published annually).

ASTM Standards, Part 25, Textile Materials. Philadelphia: American Society for Testing and Materials (published annually).

Avtex Fibers, Inc. *Vinyon HH Staple*. Technical Service Bulletin. S28R.

_____. *Vinyon Staple*. Technical Service Bulletin S28R-2.

_____. *Crimped Fiber & Rayon*. Technical Service Bulletin S53.

Badische Anilin & Soda Fabrik AG (Federal Republic of Germany). *Dyeing & Finishing of Polyester Fibers*.

_____. *Dyeing & Finishing of Acetate & Triacetate & Their Blends with Other Fibers*.

_____. *Dyeing & Finishing of Polamide Fibers & Their Blends with Other Fibers*.

Belgian Linen Association. *Belgian Linen*.

Burlington Industries, Inc. *Textile Fibers & Their Properties*. 1965.

Burlington Menswear. *Pyramid Cloth*.

Cooper Union Museum (The Greenleaf Collection), New York. *Textile Arts*. January 1964.

Courtaulds North America, Inc. *From Fiber to Fashion*.

Crestlan Cyanamid Corp. *Crestlan 67-A & 67-H*.

_____. *Crestlan Type 61-L*.

_____. *Important Difference between Sweatshirts*.

_____. *Laminated Sweat Jackets*.

Crompton-Richmond Co. *A Pile Fabric Primer*.

E.I. du Pont de Nemours & Company. *A Brief History of Dyes*.

_____. *Dupont Textile Products*.

_____. *Facts about Fabric*.

_____. *If You're Thinking Sweaters, Craft Yarns or Other Knits*.

_____. *Information about Nandel (Acrylic Yarn)*.

_____. *Modern Dyes & Their Properties*.

_____. *Modern Textile Dyeing & Printing*.

_____. *Qiana® Nylon*.

_____. *Technical Information Bulletins: Fibers, Processing, Dyeing, Finishing*.

Eastman Kodak Company. *Estron® Acetate Yarn: Specifications & Properties*. Textile Fibers Division. Publication #A-201B. June 1974.

_____. *Kodel® Polyester Filament Used as Filling in Spun Warp*. Textile Fibers Division. Publication #K-199A. January 1975.

_____. *Processing Kodel® Polyester Staple on the Cotton System*. Textile Fibers Division. Publication #K-103B-1. April 1976.

_____. _Processing Kodel® Polyester Staple on the Cotton System._ Textile Fibers Division. Publication #K-103C-1x. December 1976.

_____. _Properties of Verel Modacrylic Fibers._ Textile Fibers Division. Publication #V-355B. October 1975.

_____. _Textured Kodel® Polyester Yarns in Woven Fabrics._ Textile Fibers Division. Publication #K-212. October 1974.

FMC Corp. _Avril® Rayon: The Dependable Fiber._ 1968.

Hamilton Adams Imports Ltd. _Moygashel® Linens._

Herculon Inc. _Olefin Fiber: A New Look at Herculon._

Hoechst Fibers Inc. _Dyeing and Finishing of Hoechst Polyester._

_____. _Fashion and Special Dyeing Methods._

International Fabric Institute. _International Fair Claims Guide for Consumer Textile Products._ 1973.

Man-made Fiber Producers Association, Inc. _Man-made Fibers Fact Book._ 1978.

_____. _Facts on Man-made Fibers._ No. 3. Spring 1976.

_____. _Facts on Man-made Fibers._ No. 4. Summer 1977.

_____. _Guide to Man-made Fibers._ 1977.

J.B. Martin & Co., New York. _How to Sew and Care for Velvet._

Mayer, Christa C. _Three Centuries of Bobbin Lace._ New York: Cooper Union Museum, August 1966.

_____. _Two Centuries of Needle Lace._ New York: Cooper Union Museum, February 1965.

Mohair Council, New York. _Mohair: Production and Marketing in the United States._

Monsanto Company. _Draw-textured Yarn Technology._

_____. _Fashion Hang Up._

_____. _Predicting Garment Flammability._

_____. _Tech Talk._ August 1975.

_____. _Tech Talk._ 1979.

_____. _Technical Publications on Yarns and Fibers._

_____. _Yarns & Fibers Catalog._ 1977.

Dan River Inc. _Dan River: A Brief History._

_____. _Dan River Textile Process._

Wool Bureau Inc. _Knitwear._ (The Wool Library, Vol 4.)

_____. _Men's Wear._ (The Wool Library, Vol 3.)

_____. _Uniform & Career Apparel._ (The Wool Library, Vol. 5.)

_____. _Women's Fashion._ (The Wool Library, Vol. 2.)

_____. _Wool Fiber to Fabric._ (The Wool Library, Vol. 1.)

Textile Periodicals

American Drycleaner
American Trade Magazines, Inc.
500 North Dearborn Street
Chicago, Illinois, 60610
    Monthly. Covers all areas of interest to cleaners, including management and sales.

American Dyestuff Reporter
SAF International, Inc.
44 East 23 Street
New York, New York 10010
    Monthly. Covers wet-processing operations in textile mills, such as dyeing, printing and other chemistry-related areas.

American Fabrics Magazine
Doric Publishing Company, Inc.
24 East 38 Street
New York, New York 10016
    Quarterly. Reviews trends and new developments in fabrics. Special articles on special topics and problems. Includes numerous fabric swatches of the latest fabric designs.

America's Textiles—Knitter/Apparel Edition
Clark Publishing Company
106 East Stone Avenue
P. O. Box 88
Greenville, South Carolina 29602
    Monthly. For manufacturers of hosiery and knitted wear. Emphasis on new developments and financial conditions.

America's Textiles Reporter/Bulletin
Clark Publishing Company
106 East Stone Avenue
P. O. Box 88
Greenville, South Carolina 29602
    Monthly. For managers in the textile industry. Includes textile business/financial and manufacturing sections.

Clemson University Review of Industrial Management and Textile Science
Clemson University
College of Industrial Management and Textile Science
Clemson, South Carolina 29631
    Biannually. Lectures, papers, seminars and addresses in the fields of management and textile science.

Daily News Record
Fairchild Publications, Inc.
7 East 12 Street
New York, New York 10003
    Daily. Contains news about the textile industry, including much current information for textile manufacturers.

Industrial Fabric Products Review
Canvas Products Association International
600 Endicott Building
St. Paul, Minnesota 55101
    Thirteen times a year. Published for the industrial canvas fabric industry.

Journal of Home Economics
Official Organ of the American Home Economics Association
2010 Massachusetts Avenue, N.W.
Washington, D.C. 20036
    Monthly. Includes articles in the field of textiles and clothing which are primarily consumer oriented.

Knitting Times
Official Publication of the National Knitted
  Outerwear Association
51 Madison Avenue
New York, New York 10010
  Weekly. Covers business conditions, technical develop-
  ments, trends and forecasts in knitted fabrics and knitted
  apparel.

Modern Knitting Management
Rayon Publishing Corporation
303 Fifth Avenue
New York, New York 10016
  Monthly. Articles deal primarily with management aspects
  of the knitting industry.

Modern Textiles
Rayon Publishing Corporation
303 Fifth Avenue
New York, New York 10016
  Monthly. Covers marketing and technical activities in the
  man-made textile industry. Includes a special section on
  carpets.

Nonwovens Industry
Rodman Publications Inc.
P.O. Box 555
26 Lake Street
Ramsey, New Jersey 07446
  Monthly. Features articles on manufacturing processes,
  distribution and use applications of nonwoven textile
  products.

Textile Chemist and Colorist
Journal of the American Association of Textile
  Chemists and Colorists
P.O. Box 12215
Research Triangle Park, North Carolina 27709
  Monthly. Deals primarily with the chemistry of textiles
  and color. Very technically oriented.

Textile Industries
W.R.C. Smith Publishing Company
1760 Peachtree Road, N. W.
Atlanta, Georgia 30309
  Monthly. Aimed at management in the textile mill.

Textile Marketing Letter
Clemson University
Clemson, South Carolina 29631
  Monthly. Covers items of current interest to persons
  involved in sales and marketing of textiles.

Textile Organon
Textile Economics Bureau, Inc.
489 Fifth Avenue
New York, New York 10017
  Monthly. Market data for both the natural and man-made
  fiber industry.

Textile Technology Digest
Institute of Textile Technology
Charlottesville, Virginia 22902
  Monthly. Provides abstract coverage of current periodi-
  cals, books and patents in all areas of the textile industry.
  World-wide in scope, with abstracts of foreign language
  material translated into English.

Textile World
McGraw-Hill Publications
1175 Peachtree Street, N.E.
Atlanta, Georgia 30309
  Monthly. Covers technical developments in the textile
  industry.

Textracts
J. B. Goldberg
225 East 46 Street
New York, New York 10017
  Monthly. Provides brief abstracts (citing original sources)
  of articles dealing with the technical and business news of
  fibers, yarns, fabrics, dyes and finishes. Domestic and
  foreign coverage.

American Apparel Manufacturers Association
1611 North Kent Street
Arlington, Virginia 22209

American Association for Textile Technology
1040 Avenue of the Americas
New York, New York 10036

American Association of Textile Chemists and
  Colorists
Box 12215
Research Triangle Park, North Carolina 27709

American National Standards Institute
1430 Broadway
New York, New York 10018

American Sheep Producers Council
200 Clayton Street
Denver, Colorado 80206

American Society for Testing and Materials
1916 Race Street
Philadelphia, Pennsylvania 19103

American Textile Machinery Association
1730 M Street, N.W.
Washington, D.C. 20036

American Textile Manufacturers Institute, Inc.
1101 Connecticut Avenue, N.W.
Washington, D.C. 20036

American Yarn Spinners Association, Inc.
601 West Franklin Avenue
Gastonia, North Carolina 28052

Belgian Linen Association
280 Madison Avenue
New York, New York 10016

Carpet & Rug Institute
310 South Holliday Avenue
Dalton, Georgia 30720

Color Association of the United States, Inc.
200 Madison Avenue
New York, New York 10016

Cotton Inc:
1370 Avenue of the Americas
New York, New York 10019

Index

W

wale, 58
warp-faced satin weave, 114
warp-faced twill, 117
warp knit fabric structure,
    61–65
warp printing, 188
warp yarns, 98
wash-and-wear, 146–147
washing, 164
waterproofing finish, 137
water-repellent finish, 152–153
water-resistant finish, 152–153
weft-insertion warp knit, 65
weft knit fabric structure,
    61, 65–68
weft knit variations, 68
weight conversion table,
    232-233
weighted silk, 11
weight (fabric), 230-241
wet printing, 201
wet process, 87
wet spinning process, 4, 6
wet strength, 225
white discharge printing, 189
wicking, 204
widening, 60
width (fabric), 228–229
wild silk, 11
winch dyeing, 175

wool
    care, 296
    fiber characteristics, 12
    labeling act, 14
    performance expectations, 12
    stain removal treatments, 306
    spun yarns, 40
    terms, 14
    woolen, 13
    worsted, 13
woolen fabrics, 14
wool presensitizing, 161
Wool Products Labeling
    Act, The, 14
worsted fabrics, 14
woven fabric structure, 98–118
wrinkle recovery, 216
wrinkle-resistant finish, 153
w-pile structure, 89

Y

yarn direction, 49
yarns, 35–51
yarn shifting, 223
yarn slippage, 223
yarn twist
        degree, 50–51

Z

z-twist, 50

DATE DUE